Storytelling
Art and Technique

Storytelling™

Art and Technique

THIRD EDITION

Ellin Greene

Foreword by Augusta Baker

R. R. Bowker®
A Reed Reference Publishing Company
New Providence, New Jersey

Published by R. R. Bowker, a Reed Reference Publishing Company
Copyright © 1996 by Reed Elsevier Inc.
Library of Congress Cataloging-in-Publication Data
Greene, Ellin, 1927–
     Storytelling : art and technique / Ellin Greene. —3rd ed.
          p.   cm.
     Rev. ed. of Storytelling / Augusta Baker
     Includes bibliographical references and index.
     ISBN 0-8352-3458-4 (alk. paper)
     1. Storytelling—United States.   I. Baker, Augusta.
Storytelling.   II. Title.
LB1042.B34 1996
808.06'8543--dc20   96-11602
                                        CIP

ISBN 0 - 8352 - 3458 - 4

9 780835 234580

For Augusta Baker, my mentor and friend,
and for all who believe in the power of story

Contents

Foreword

I FIRST MET ELLIN GREENE when she was a student at the Rutgers Graduate School of Library Service. I had gone to the university to talk with the students about storytelling and to tell stories. From her attentive listening, I sensed Ellin's love of storytelling. Upon graduation from library school she was offered a position at the New York Public Library, but chose to stay at the Elizabeth (N.J.) Public Library where a new position as group work specialist had been created for her.

Ellin later took a course in storytelling that I was teaching at the New School for Social Research. She began telling stories from her English heritage background—tales collected by the folklorist Joseph Jacobs and the literary fairy tales of Eleanor Farjeon and Walter de la Mare. Eventually, she would go to England to do research for her doctorate on the relationship between Farjeon's imaginative play in childhood and her fairy tales for children.

Ellin became my assistant at the New York Public Library in September 1959. My work as supervisor of storytelling had been expanded and I needed an assistant. Sometime later, after I became coordinator of children's work and Ellin had worked as children's specialist in the Bronx Borough for a year, she became the assistant coordinator and storytelling and group work specialist. In that position she was responsible for the library's storytelling program in the boroughs of Manhattan, the Bronx, and Staten Island. She assisted experienced storytellers with program planning and shared story hours, trained new staff members in storytelling and picture-book reading, and from the new staff chose the tellers and planned the annual Storytelling Symposium held at the New York Public Library each May in honor of Marie Shedlock. During the summer months, she told stories at the Hans Christian Andersen statue in Central Park and at numerous other parks and playgrounds throughout the city.

In 1968 Ellin left the New York Public Library to teach at Rutgers, The State University of New Jersey and to earn a doctorate in creative arts education. She went on to join the faculty of the University of Chicago Graduate Library School where she taught courses in storytelling, library services to children, and early childhood materials and services. Her interest in picture-book art led to a grant from the National Endowment for the Humanities for "The Illustrator as Storyteller" project at Chicago and a traveling exhibition of Caldecott Medal and Honor Books in conjunction with the Kerlin Collection at the University of Minnesota. She chaired the Caldecott Committee in 1984 and was guest curator for the Roger Duvoisin retrospective exhibition at the Zimmerli Art Museum, Rutgers, in 1989.

Ellin returned to the New York Public Library in 1986 to serve as consultant and director of the library's Early Childhood Project, funded by a three-year grant from the Carnegie Corporation of New York. Out of this experience and her long interest in library service to young children, she wrote *Books, Babies, and Libraries: Serving Infants, Toddlers, Their Parents and Caregivers.*

In 1989 Ellin went to South Africa as an academic specialist for the United States Information Agency Bureau of Educational and Cultural Affairs. There she worked with READ, a nonprofit organization dedicated to the improvement of the quality of education in South Africa. She visited the black teacher-training colleges, conducted workshops on storytelling, and encouraged the students to rediscover their literary heritage. As this book goes to press, she is preparing to go to Japan where she has been invited to speak on storytelling and American children's picture books in connection with a year-long exhibition of the work of four Caldecott Medalists: Marcia Brown, Barbara Cooney, Robert McCloskey, and Marc Simont.

Ellin is a wonderful storyteller and an excellent teacher of storytelling. Her strength lies in her ability to recognize the potential in the neophyte storyteller and to help new tellers develop their own particular style of telling. The reader of this book will learn how to select a story, how to prepare and present a story, and what is even more important, the confidence to become a teller.

Storytelling: Art and Technique should, in my opinion, be required reading for all who are preparing to work with children in a public library or school library media center, as well as for those who are preparing to be library administrators, school principals, and curriculum specialists. I say this because I believe that people who work with children need to understand the importance of stories in the lives of children and the unique contribution that library storytelling can make in bringing children and books together, in helping children acquire language and literacy skills, and in giving children an appreciation of their literary and cultural heritage.

Storytelling in libraries in the United States is almost 100 years old. The program at the New York Public Library, with which I was associated for over 37 years, began its formal program of story hours in 1907 and continues today. Children needed to hear stories then and they still need to hear stories—perhaps even more so today. At a time when our nation is experiencing another great wave of immigrants and there is racial and ethnic tension throughout the world, folktales—the stuff of storytelling—remind people of the oneness of humanity. Children need to hear stories that give them a sense of their own culture as well as stories that introduce them to other ways of thinking and doing, and that *inherently* teach respect for other cultures.

New storytellers need to take time to learn a story well. This will eliminate the gimmicks such as those used as a crutch by tellers who lack confidence in the story or in their ability to tell it. It implies that administrators must give their staff time to find stories worth telling and time to prepare for the story hour. Library directors should recognize that the storytelling program is just as important as book selection and managing the children's room. Children will remember the library for the joy of story hour, not for the neat bookshelves in the children's room.

I am saddened that many young people coming out of library school today think that children do not want to listen to stories or that children will listen only if the stories are told in a highly dramatic manner. When I taught, I told students, "Let the story tell itself, and if it is a good story, and you have prepared it well, you do not need all the extras—the costumes, the gimmicks, the histrionics. Children of all ages want to hear stories. Select well, prepare well, and then go forth and just *tell*."

Augusta Baker

Preface

SINCE THE PUBLICATION OF the second edition of *Storytelling: Art and Technique*, storytelling organizations at the national, regional, state, and local levels have grown at a tremendous pace. The increased number of professional storytellers has brought storytelling to coffeehouses, theaters, concert halls, and festivals across the country, as well as to libraries and schools. Perhaps we have not yet seen "the renaissance of the troubadours and minstrels whose appeal will then rival that of the mob orator or itinerant politician" of which Marie Shedlock wrote in her introduction to *The Art of the Story-Teller* (Appleton, 1915), but storytellers have been featured on WABC-TV's *Good Morning America*, National Public Radio's *All Things Considered*, in airline magazines, and the *Wall Street Journal*.

Renewed interest in storytelling on the part of adults, and the research that demonstrated a positive relationship between hearing stories in early childhood and later emerging literacy, encouraged public librarians to reorder their story-hour priorities. Storytelling programs for infants and toddlers and their caregivers were added, while story hours for children in the middle age-group, that is, between the ages of 8 and 11, decreased in number. This trend became stronger as greater emphasis was placed on the children's librarian as manager or administrator of the children's room and less time was spent on story selection and preparation. The availability of professional storytellers, and the feelings of inadequacy that many librarians and teachers experienced as they compared their own storytelling with the polished performances of the professional tellers, also played a part in the decline of story hours for older children.

But storytelling has much to offer older children and young adults. In communities where other activities compete for the older child's attention and formal story hours do not attract listeners, librarians have discovered that these youngsters enjoy learning and practicing the art of storytelling themselves.

The whole language movement in the schools has made teachers more aware of the storytelling literature and how to use it in the classroom. The great wave of immigrants in recent years (in 1993, for example, more than 65,000 immigrant children from 188 countries entered the public school system in New York City) has impelled librarians and teachers to look for multicultural, multilingual materials. Folktales, probably more than any other literature, attest to the bond between peoples and the bond between people and the natural world.

Storytelling: Art and Technique is addressed to both beginning and experienced storytellers, especially those who work in a public library or school library media center, but parents and adults who work with children in Head Start, day-care centers, museums, and other recreational places where children gather, will find basic information about storytelling here.

The third edition has been written in response to the need to expand certain areas in the previous editions and to update the bibliographies. The same format—"a manual in the best possible sense"—was followed in order to make the information readily available. *Storytelling: Art and Technique* lends itself for use as a textbook in colleges and university courses or in-service workshops.

As in the first two editions, the emphasis is on storytelling as an *oral* art. Our visually oriented society has forgotten the power of the spoken word, reducing written language to everyday speech, but in storytelling, the full range of language is possible. Aidan Chambers, in his book *Introducing Books to Children* (Horn Book, 1983, p. 130) wrote:

> As children listen to stories, verse, prose of all kinds, they unconsciously become familiar with the rhythms and the structure, the cadences and conventions of the various forms of written language. They are learning how print "sounds," how to "hear" it in their inner ear. Only through listening to words in print being spoken does anyone discover their color, their life, their movement and drama.

Storytelling at its best is mutual creation. Children listen and, out of the words they hear, create their own mental images; this opening of the mind's eye develops the imagination. Many contemporary storytellers, in an effort to compete successfully with television and the visual arts, have turned away from the oral tradition, with the result that storytelling, particularly for younger children, is often limited to the sharing of picture books. As valuable as picture-book art is, I believe that listening can be a complete experience, even for young children.

Basically, *Storytelling: Art and Technique* is about the relationship between storytelling and the place of literature in a child's life. Through the stories themselves and through the interaction between teller and listener, traditional storytelling goes beyond the surface child to speak to the inner child. I am more concerned with touching this inner child, with nurturing the spirit-self, and with enriching and deepening a child's feelings, than with mere entertainment.

I have tried to bring together what I have gleaned about the art and technique of storytelling from personal experience, readings, and friendship with some of the finest storytellers practicing today. I have been privileged to have some of these storytellers—among them Carol Birch, Beth Horner, and Carole Walton—as students, and it has been a joy for me to watch them soar to such great heights. An equal source of joy are the many unsung former-student heroes and heroines who now tell stories on a *regular* basis in their classrooms, school library media centers, and public libraries. From colleagues Laura Simms and Susan Danoff, with whom I have conducted storytelling residencies, I have learned immeasurably. It would take too much space to name all the wonderful people I have met over the years through storytelling, but they all have had a part in this book and I dedicate it to them.

Chapter 1 is a brief overview of the history of storytelling, from its beginnings in preliterate society to its current renaissance. In Chapter 2 the focus is on storytelling to children in libraries. It includes biographical sketches of some of the early storytellers who gave impetus to the growth of storytelling in libraries and schools during the twentieth century. Well-known living storytellers have not been included. Much of the material in this chapter is based on unpublished manuscripts and papers from the files of the Office of Children's Services, the New York Public Library, with which Augusta Baker and I were closely associated for many years.

Chapter 3 restates the purpose and values of storytelling, and gives an update on current research. Storytelling is an art, and as such needs no justification. However, librarians and teachers often find themselves in the position of having to defend the inclusion of storytelling in their work to skeptical administrators and colleagues. Awareness of the educational values of storytelling will give new storytellers a sound basis for sharing stories with children.

Chapter 4 covers the principles of selection and the types of literature (both traditional and contemporary) that lend themselves to storytelling. Particular attention has been paid to selection because most librarians and teachers, unlike folklorists who gather their material directly from oral sources, are dependent on the printed word for their storytelling material. Knowing how to select the right story out of the vast body of literature today is one of the most important aspects of storytelling.

Chapter 5 is concerned with basic techniques of learning and telling a story and Chapter 6 with how to prepare an audience for listening and how to present stories.

In Chapter 7, "Storytelling to Children with Special Needs or in Special Settings," the section on "Storytelling to Deaf or Hearing-Impaired Children" was expanded by Joyce Gunn and includes a signed version of "The Little Red Hen" from *Beyond Words: Great Stories for Hand and Voice* by Valerie Marsh. Diane C. J. Matthias and Carole Walton contributed to the section on storytelling in museums.

The section on "Storytelling to Infants and Toddlers" in the second edition was expanded to form Chapter 8, "Storytelling to Young Children." My interest in storytelling to young children goes back to the very beginnings of my work as a children's librarian. Because of the research that demonstrated a connection between hearing stories read aloud or told during early childhood and becoming a reader and library user, and because librarians are being asked more frequently to present workshops on picture-book reading to Head Start and nursery school teachers and parents, I wanted to address this topic. Beautiful picture books roll off the presses daily, but all too often the stunning art work is accompanied by a weak text. The picture books cited within the text and in the bibliographies have been chosen as much for beauty of language as for visual delight.

Beth Horner expanded her tips on storytelling to young adults in the second edition to make Chapter 9, "Storytelling to Young Adults."

Succeeding chapters cover children and young adults as storytellers, program planning (with sample programs), and the administration of story-hour programs and in-service education.

Source materials for the storyteller are listed in the Appendix. During the past decade there has been an explosion of books on storytelling and the founding of publishing houses for storytelling materials, such as August House and Yellow Moon Press. I have read as many of the new books as time allowed and often called on storytelling colleagues for input. In the bibliographies I have listed those titles that I consider to be the most helpful for teacher- and librarian-storytellers. In some instances, the stories in a collection will need work to make them tellable. I have tried to indicate this in the annotation to forewarn the inexperienced storyteller. Some titles are listed primarily for the valuable background information they contain. I have also listed a sampling of storytelling recordings and videos that I consider valuable learning tools. The Parabola series, for example, offers an opportunity to hear Native American storytellers in a style that is different from the typical Western European style of telling.

My main reason for expanding the picture-book sections in the bibliographies was stated earlier. It is also a way to note the trend toward publishing picture books for *older children*. A third reason is that a well-designed picture book can help a new storyteller with the *pacing* of a story.

This book would not have been possible without the help and encouragement of many people. It was with much sadness that I undertook the work of revising and updating *Storytelling: Art and Technique* without my mentor and friend, Augusta Baker, so it gave me great joy when Larry Chilnick, Vice President, Editorial Development, and Managing Editor Catherine Barr allowed me to add a collection of stories in her honor.

Twelve storytellers were invited to select a story they learned in the early stages of becoming a storyteller and continue to tell—stories with lasting power—and to add a note about Augusta's influence on their growth as a storyteller. To make "A Baker's Dozen," I added one of the stories for which Augusta was best known, "Uncle Bouqui Rents a Horse," from *Uncle Bouqui of Haiti* by Harold Courlander (Morrow, 1942). Augusta's telling was unforgettable. Fortunately, for those who have never heard her in person, a recording of her telling is available on Folkways *Uncle Bouqui: Folktales from Haiti* (FP 107). My warmest thanks to the contributors, authors, and publishers who made this section of the book possible.

Thanks, too, to the publishers who so generously supplied review copies of materials listed in the bibliographies. It is my hope that publishers will consider bringing back in print those out-of-print titles listed.

Grateful acknowledgment is made to Robert Sink of the New York Public Library Archives for directing me to the photographs of children in the library taken by the noted photographer Lewis Hine for the Child Welfare Exhibit of 1911.

I am indebted to Carol Birch, Joyce Gunn, Beth Horner, Linda Marchisio, Valerie Marsh, Diane C. J. Matthias, and Carole Walton for their contributions to the text. Special gratitude is due Carole for reading the manuscript and for her invaluable suggestions. To the Storytelling Discussion Group of the American Library Association's Association for Library Service to Children, and to the many individual storytellers and students who suggested stories for the bibliographies, warm thanks.

Lastly a sincere thank-you to Nancy L. Bucenec, Managing Production Editor, for shepherding my book through the production stages with patience and grace.

Storytelling: A Historical Perspective

Stories have been told as long as speech has existed, and sans *stories the human race would have perished, as it would have perished* sans *water.*
    —*Isak Dinesen* [1]

STORYTELLING HAS BEEN CALLED the oldest and the newest of the arts. Though its purpose and conditions change from century to century, and from culture to culture, storytelling continues to fulfill the same basic social and individual needs. Human beings seem to have an innate impulse to communicate their feelings and experiences through storying. We tell stories in order to make sense of our world. We express our beliefs, desires, and hopes in stories, in an attempt to explain ourselves and to understand others. In *The Completed Gesture*, a book about the importance of story in our lives, John Rouse writes, "Stories are told as spells for binding the world together."[2]

According to Ruth Sawyer, "The first primitive efforts at conscious storytelling consisted of a simple chant, set to the rhythm of some tribal occupation such as grinding corn, paddling canoe or kayak, sharpening weapons for hunting or war, or ceremonial dancing. They were in the first person, impromptu, giving expression to pride or exultation over some act of bravery or accomplishment that set the individual for the moment apart from the tribe."[3] One of the illustrations Sawyer gives is this Innuit chant from Greenland:

I, Keokok, have slain a bear,
    Ayi–ayi–ayi—
A great bear, a fierce bear,
    Ayi–ayi–ayi—
With might have I slain him.
    Ayi–ayi–ayi—
Great are the muscles of my arm—
Strong for spear throwing—
Strong for kayak going—
I, Keokok, have slain a bear.
    Ayi–ayi–ayi—[4]

In this early period everyone was a storyteller just as every young child today is a storyteller. The three-year-old tells a story using gestures, mime, dance, sound, and language, as in an earlier age when the expressive arts were one. As human societies became more complex, art specialties— drama, dance, music—developed. Song separated from narration. Those persons who possessed charisma, a greater command of language, a good memory, and a fine sense of timing became the community's storytellers. Stories changed from first-person to third-person narratives. One theory is that deeds were so exaggerated that modesty required the teller to attribute them to a third party, and thus the hero tale was born. Storytellers became the genealogists, historians, and keepers of the culture, as well as its entertainers.

The first written record of an activity that appears to be storytelling is found in an Egyptian papyrus called the Westcar Papyrus (recorded sometime between 2000 and 1300 B.C.E.) in which the three sons of Cheops, the famous builder of pyramids, take turns entertaining their father with strange tales. The earliest known heroic epic, *Gilgamesh,* was first told by the Sumerians, the inventors of the written word, and was taken over by the Babylonians when the Sumerian civilization collapsed in 2000 B.C.E. There are evidences of *Gilgamesh* in Homer's *Iliad* and *Odyssey,* in the Greek mythologies, and in Hebrew scriptures. The tellers of the Greek myths created supernatural beings with the power to rule the terrifying forces of nature, and yet these gods had human frailties. Abraham and his descendants, the Israelites, preserved the stories within the Sumerian epic, changing them as storytellers do, and so, out of the story of the great flood came Noah and the ark. Scholars see a relationship between the bull painted by the cave artists, the Bull of Heaven in the *Gilgamesh* tale, Zeus transforming himself into a white bull to seduce Europa, the Greek myth of Theseus and Minos's minotaur (who was half man, half bull), and the buffalo dance of Native American tribes.

Storytelling was also looked upon as a way of teaching social and moral values. Both Plato and Aristotle mention storytelling to children in this connection, and the *Panchatantra* (c. 400 C.E.), compiled for the education of the royal children of India, teaches:

Whoever learns the work by heart,
Or through the storyteller's art
Becomes acquainted;
His life by sad defeat—although
The king of heaven be his foe—
Is never tainted.[5]

Among Native Americans, children were present during storytelling and were expected to listen. Among the Xhosa and Zulu peoples of Africa, storytelling was considered training in listening and telling; children were expected to learn the stories they heard from their elders.

The first professional storytellers were bards, or singer-performers. Bards were of two types: praise singers who sang of the great deeds of the forebears and leaders of the group, and chronicler-historians who recited genealogies and sang about historic events. In the *Odyssey,* Homer describes a banquet scene at which a blind bard sings of the quarrel between Odysseus and Achilles. As was the custom, the bard accompanied himself on a lyre, held with both hands. John Harrell, in his engaging narrative *Origins and Early Traditions of Storytelling,* notes that after about 200 years the demand for new forms and new styles of storytelling led to the demise of this Homeric tradition. The Homeridai who accompanied themselves on the kithara were replaced by rhapsodes who, instead of singing with a kithara, stood holding a staff called a rhabdos, which freed one of the storyteller's hands. This allowed the storyteller to move about and to gesture and to use his rhabdos as a prop. "The new dramatic style," Harrell remarks, "encouraged embellishments and strivings for effects. With this increasingly personalized performance of the epics, the rhapsode became more and more a celebrity in his own right. . . . The rhapsodes were very popular and always drew audiences, especially at festivals where they held contests . . . and outdid themselves to gain first prize."[6] The abuse of this new style eventually led to reform, but, as Harrell points out, "All subsequent styles are variants of these original, basic modes, and within them lie our roots."[7]

Two schools of storytelling came into existence during the time of the Roman Empire: the Gaelic school of *ollamhs* in Ireland and the Cymric school of bards in Wales. Aspiring storytellers attached themselves to a master storyteller, sometimes staying for several years and studying under different masters. Master storytellers were elevated to positions of great power. They owned certain stories and no apprentice could tell these without permission. In Ireland, an *ollamh,* or master storyteller, knew 350 stories, had a special chair, and could wear five colors, only one less than royalty, while more common folk were allowed to wear only one, two, three, or four colors, depending on their social standing. An *ollamh* was also entitled to wear a cloak made of many-colored bird feathers. The master Welsh bard was the *pinkerdd* and his apprentices were known as the *mabinogs* because every apprentice had to learn the group of tales called the *Mabinogion.* The *pinkerdd* told from the front of the great hall while the *mabinogs* told from the back. In Sawyer, we read that the *pinkerdd* was under the protection of the king. He was assigned the tenth chair from the king and his value was the handsome sum of 126 cattle. He received "a harp from the king, a ring from the queen, cloth and a horse from the king, linen from the queen; and from the court, a man's maintenance."[8]

Bards were known in Asia, Europe, Africa, the South Pacific, and among the Aztecs and the Mayans. Stories traveled from Asia to Europe and back, carried by traders and wandering minstrels. Anglo-Saxon gleemen and, later, Norman minstrels traveled all over England and continental Europe and passed along their tales in song, dance, and story. In Germany there were the minnesingers, members of the music and poetry guilds; in Russia there were the *skomorokhi* who performed a similar function. Women as well as men were bards. Colwell remarks, "How great a number of minstrels there were, we do not know, but we read that the king employed 426 minstrels at the wedding of Margaret of England in 1290, and that amongst the many minstrels on the payroll of Edward I there were two women with the intriguing names of Matill Makejoye and Pearl in the Egg."[9] In Africa, there was the "resident storyteller" and the "traveling storyteller." The former was part of a chief's household; his only responsibility was to keep alive the exploits of his leader. The "traveling storyteller," however, went from village to village with tales, anecdotes, and fables and became the collector of an oral, narrative tradition.

In western Europe storytellers reached the height of their power during the Middle Ages from the tenth to the fourteenth centuries. During the latter half of the Middle Ages, guilds of storytellers were organized. At the time of Charles IV a charter and coat of arms recognized the artistry of storytellers. Storytelling competitions were held. It is known that competitions took place in Wales as early as the late twelfth century; they continue today.

Scholars began to write down the stories and, with the invention of the printing press in 1450, the oral tradition began to wane, especially among the upper classes and the new middle class who were able to afford books. The storyteller's role as historian, genealogist, and newsbearer was usurped by the print media and the ascendance of science, which served to question literary wisdom. Storytelling gradually lost its spiritual force and became mere entertainment. In France Marie-Catherine d'Aulnoy's fairy tales and Charles Perrault's sophisticated retellings of the old folktales amused the French court, while the common folk continued to listen and to tell tales to ease the monotony of work and to bring laughter and wonder into their lives. Among the common folk, storytelling was so closely associated with spinning and weaving that "to spin a yarn" and "to weave enchantment" were synonymous with "to tell a tale."

Irish storyteller and poet Padraic Colum believed that the extension of the day's rhythm into night also contributed to the decline of storytelling.[10] Before daylight was extended by artificial means, day and night rhythms were very different, and long, dark nights lent themselves to storytelling. In time, storytelling was relegated to the nursery, where the tales were preserved for the folklorists to rediscover in the nineteenth century.

Jacob and Wilhelm Grimm revived an interest in the oral tradition when they collected stories from oral sources and published their collection *Kinder-und Hausmärchen* in 1812 and 1815. Their methodology has been criticized by modern folklorists but their work encouraged other nineteenth-century collectors, including Alexander Afanasyev (Russian), Joseph Jacobs (English), Peter Asbjørnsen and Jørgen Moe (Scandinavian), and Jeremiah Curtin (Irish). As scholars studied these collections they found striking similarities among the tales. Some folklorists attributed the similarities to universal emotions; the tales were fantasies that fulfilled human wishes and dreams. Others believed the tales were remnants of nature myths or ancient religious rituals. In the early 1900s Finnish folklorist Antti Aarne developed a classification system that assigned a type number to individual tales. American folklorist Stith Thompson carried this a step further and assigned a motif number to each significant element of a tale. His six-volume work, *Motif-Index of Folk-Literature*, was first published in 1932, with a revised edition published in 1955–1958. Both *The Types of the Folktale* by Aarne and Thompson's *Motif-Index of Folk-Literature* are essential tools for the storyteller. Margaret Read MacDonald followed Stith Thompson's classification in *The Storyteller's Sourcebook*, but she adapted it to meet the needs of teachers and librarians who work with children's collections.

As Anne Pellowski notes in her scholarly survey *The World of Storytelling*, "the Grimm tales must be considered as the single most important group of folk stories that affected storytelling for children. Their widespread appeal and their contemporaneous legitimacy helped European parents to believe it was important to continue telling stories to children, even though, in some cases, there was opposition from educational authorities."[11]

Fortunately, the great German educator Friedrich Froebel recognized the value of stories and made storytelling an important part of the kindergarten program that he founded in 1837. German emigrants to America took with them the idea of kindergartens, and in 1873 the first kindergarten was incorporated into a public school system in the United States. Instruction in storytelling was given in the kindergarten training schools, and in 1905 Sara Cone Bryant, a kindergarten teacher, wrote the first storytelling text to be published in America, *How to Tell Stories to Children*.

In 1903 a group of teachers attending summer school at the University of Tennessee, Knoxville, were inspired by their teacher, Richard T. Wyche, to organize the National Story Tellers' League. Wyche served as president of the league from 1903 to 1919, edited the league's journal, *The Storytellers' Magazine,* and wrote the second book of storytelling to be published in the United States, *Some Great Stories and How to Tell Them.* It is interesting to note that the two most vigorous storytelling organizations in the United States—the National Story Tellers' League and the National Storytelling Association (formerly, the National Association for the Preservation and Perpetuation of Storytelling)—began in Tennessee.

For most of the twentieth century, storytelling in the United States was generally associated with children. Librarians and teachers kept the art alive (see Chapter 2). In 1973 something happened that brought about the current interest in storytelling as entertainment for adults. Jimmy Neil Smith (then a high school teacher and later a restaurateur and mayor of Jonesborough, Tennessee) was riding in his car with some of his students when storyteller-comedian Jerry Clower came on the air. The students' enthusiastic response to Clower's monologue started Jimmy Neil thinking about organizing a storytelling festival. In October of that year, about 300 people gathered on the lawns and porches of the historic old houses in Jonesborough to swap stories. From that small gathering grew an annual storytelling festival that today draws thousands of storytelling enthusiasts from around the world.

In 1974 Smith founded the National Association for the Preservation and Perpetuation of Storytelling (NAPPS), later renamed the National Storytelling Association (NSA). The NSA has a membership of over 7,000 in the United States and Canada and several hundred members overseas. The association sponsors an annual storytelling festival the first weekend in October, and a summer conference, and administers "Tellabration! The Night of Storytelling" on the Saturday evening before Thanksgiving ("Tellabration" is sponsored locally by storytelling associations, libraries, theaters, and the like). NSA's publishing program includes *Storytelling Magazine, The National Directory of Storytelling,* books, and audiocassettes.

In 1995 NSA was awarded a $200,000 grant from the Tennessee General Assembly to create StoryNet, "an electronic information and communications network featuring stories, storytellers, and America's storytelling traditions."[12] Storytellers with access to the Internet will want to read "Storytelling in Cyberspace" by Mary C. Weaver in NSA's 1996 *National Storytelling Directory* and guidebook. Weaver cites STORY-TELL, maintained by Karen Morgan of Texas Woman's University, as the best list for storytellers. To subscribe, send an e-mail message to STORY-TELLREQUEST@TWU.EDU. Your message should be Subscribe Your Full Name. On the World-Wide Web, Weaver's favorite story spot is Sherri Johnson's site at Swarthmore College: http://www.cc.swarthmore.edu/~sjohnson/stories.

Adults have reclaimed storytelling for themselves. Perhaps storytelling fills the need for intimacy not easily found in our mobile society (and not offered by the electronic storyteller that invaded the family living room in the 1950s). Perhaps, as one storyteller commented, "It may be that as our world has metaphorically shrunk, we have had to confront the fact that we are part of a global community. As we seek to understand one another, what binds us together is beginning to seem more significant than what makes us different. Just as we have begun to recognize that the ecosystem of the earth is one inter-connected system, perhaps we are beginning to realize that the human experience is similarly connected."[13]

NOTES

1. Isak Dinesen, "The Cardinal's First Tale," in *Last Tales* (Random House, 1957), p. 23.
2. John Rouse, *The Completed Gesture* (Unicorn/Skyline Books, 1978).
3. Ruth Sawyer, *The Way of the Storyteller* (Viking, 1942, 1962), pp. 45–46.
4. Ibid., p. 46.
5. *The Panchatantra,* trans. by Arthur Ryder (University of Chicago Press, 1925), p. 16.
6. John Harrell, *Origins and Early Traditions of Storytelling* (York House, 1983), pp. 54–55.
7. Ibid., p. 61.
8. Sawyer, *The Way of the Storyteller,* p. 69.
9. Eileen Colwell, "Folk Literature: An Oral Tradition and an Oral Art," *Top of the News* 24 (January 1968): 177.
10. Padraic Colum, "Introduction," in *The Complete Grimm's Fairy Tales* (Pantheon, 1944), pp. vii–xiv.
11. Anne Pellowski, *The World of Storytelling,* expanded and revised (H.W. Wilson, 1990), p. 16.
12. *Inside Story,* NSA (August 1995), p. 1.
13. Tina-Jill Gordon, "Teachers Telling Stories: Seven-, Eight- and Nine-Year Old Children's Written Responses to Oral Narratives" (Ed. D. diss., Rutgers University, 1991), p. 2.

Storytelling to Children in Libraries

Daniel (age 5): "Why is the library the tallest building in town?"
EG (stumped): "I don't know. Why?"
Daniel (gleefully): "Because it has the most stories."

CHANGES IN ATTITUDE TOWARD children and several social movements that occurred in the United States during the second half of the nineteenth century and in the twentieth century encouraged organized storytelling, that is, formal presentations of stories, to groups of children. These movements included the development of playgrounds, settlement houses, and Sunday Schools; the founding of the YMCA in 1851 and the YWCA in 1866; and the founding of the Boy Scouts in 1910 and the Girl Scouts in 1912. In 1900 the American Library Association, formed in 1876, established a special division for librarians serving children.

Beginnings

The exact date of the first library story hour is uncertain, but it was about 1900. By 1896 Anne Carroll Moore had given storytelling a place in the children's room of the new Pratt Institute Free Library in Brooklyn, New York. Storytelling had been tried experimentally as early as 1899 in the Carnegie Library of Pittsburgh, just a year after the organization of the department for work with children. The program had such spectacular success that Frances Jenkins Olcott, who was the director of children's work, incorporated the story hour as a regular part of the program. In an article published in *Carnegie Magazine* in 1933, Elizabeth Botset of the Carnegie Library of Pittsburgh gave credit to another Pittsburgh librarian, Charlotte Keith Bissell, for the origin of library story hours. According to Botset,[1] Bissell noticed a group of younger children listlessly leafing through picture books in the library. She wondered what the result would be if a librarian told stories to such children and why the story hour, so successful in hospitals, had not been tried in libraries to introduce books. During this same period the Buffalo (N.Y.) Public Library experimented with storytelling on Sunday afternoons to stimulate interest in books and reading, and in 1899 started regular Saturday morning story hours. Similar experiments were carried out in other newly organized children's rooms. Librarians were seeking ways to bring together children and books and to interpret literature in an artistic rather than in a pedantic manner. They were already beginning to recognize the great potential of storytelling when, in 1900, Marie Shedlock came to the United States to lecture on Hans Christian Andersen and to tell his tales.

Marie Shedlock (1854–1935)

Marie Shedlock was born in France and grew up in England. She was a teacher of young children for many years before becoming a professional storyteller in 1890. Shedlock's lectures on storytelling formed the basis of a book that became a classic in storytelling, *The Art of the Story-Teller*.

It was on Shedlock's first visit to the United States that Mary Wright Plummer, director of the School of Library Science at Pratt Institute in Brooklyn, heard her tell stories in French and English at one of a series of matinees at Sherry's, a fashionable New York City restaurant. She told Hans Christian Andersen's "Tin Soldier," "The Swineherd," and "The Princess and the Pea," and the telling was unforgettable. Plummer invited Shedlock to tell stories to the trustees, directors, and faculty of Pratt.

When Anne Carroll Moore, head of the children's room at Pratt, heard Shedlock she decided that there must be a story hour for the children, too, and so, on a snowy Saturday morning in January 1903, Marie Shedlock returned to Pratt. When the program was over, a little girl asked Miss Moore, "Is she a fairy, or just a lady?" In later years Moore wrote, "There was never any doubt in my mind after that morning that a children's library should have a regular story hour."[2]

Shedlock did not use the affected speech that was in vogue at the time, nor was she didactic. It was her inspiration, as she traveled around the United States telling stories and lecturing on storytelling, that gave impetus to the idea of storytelling as a true art. Shedlock inspired others to become storytellers, among them Anna Cogswell Tyler, Moore's assistant at Pratt, and Ruth Sawyer, one of America's best-known storytellers. After Shedlock's visit to Boston in 1902, regular library story hours were established, and in 1911 the Boston Public Library hired Mary W. Cronan, a kindergarten teacher trained in the Froebel method and an experienced storyteller. She was soon joined by her husband, John, and her sister, Margaret Powers. The trio told the legends of heroes and saints to the children of immigrants in schools, playgrounds, and museums, as well as in the library.[3]

In Pittsburgh, too, storytelling assumed a new importance. Pittsburgh librarians began to hold weekly story hours in their branches and to take stories to the playgrounds. By 1909 Edna Whiteman was appointed supervisor of storytelling at the Carnegie Library of Pittsburgh. Whiteman selected the most suitable versions of stories for telling, arranged programs, and told stories in the children's rooms of the branch libraries. In 1916 she prepared the first edition of *Stories to Tell to Children: A Selected List*, now in its eighth revised edition.

In the Cleveland Public Library, Carolyn Burnite, who took over the organization of work with children in 1904, established storytelling as an important, regular part of that work. Usually two story hours a week were held in each branch library. Because storytelling was regarded as one of the children's librarians' responsibilities, time was allowed for the preparation of stories. As time went on, more and more children came to hear the stories; in 1909 the library reported a record attendance of 80,996.

At the same time, the Chicago Public Library was using the talent of an outstanding storyteller, Gudrun Thorne-Thomsen. Chief librarian Henry L. Legler was quoted in 1910: "We are now engaged in developing the branch library system of the city and no doubt storytelling will be made incidentally a feature of the work planned for the children's rooms. This work must be done by the children's librarians, the storytelling growing out of library work and merging into it in order that its most effective side be legitimately developed."[4]

Gudrun Thorne-Thomsen (1873–1956)

In 1944 a group of children's librarians at the New York Public Library listened to a small, quiet, unassuming woman tell "East of the Sun and West of the Moon." The story came alive as this master storyteller used only her lovely voice, perfect timing, and unobtrusive, spontaneous gestures to tell the tale. The storyteller was Gudrun Thorne-Thomsen.

Gudrun Thorne-Thomsen was born on April 8, 1873, in Trondheim, located on one of Norway's beautiful fjords. When she was four years old the family moved to Bergen, Norway's chief seaport, where she saw ships of many countries and listened to the sailors' tales from other lands. Her grandmother read to her and to the other children in the family and told them stories about the great Norse heroes and about trolls and nissen.

Gudrun's mother, Fredrikke Nielsen, was an actress, famous for her portrayal of the women in Henrik Ibsen's plays. The home Gudrun grew up in was an exciting place, frequented by musicians, poets, and writers, and alive with amateur theatricals, singing, and storytelling in which the entire family took part. It is little wonder that she grew up to love literature, to understand the strength and power of words, and to scorn careless speech.

When Gudrun was 15 years old, she came to Chicago to live with her mother's sister. There she trained to be a teacher at the Cook County

Normal School and came under the influence of Colonel Francis W. Parker, whom John Dewey called "the father of progressive education." In 1893, she married Georg Thorne-Thomsen and the young couple made their home in Chicago.

Gudrun joined the staff of Colonel Parker's new school. Parker's innovative ideas in education attracted the attention of William Rainey Harper, then president of the University of Chicago. Harper invited Parker to bring his school to the university as part of the newly formed School of Education and to become director of the Laboratory Elementary School. John Dewey, already at the university as head of the Elementary School of the Department of Pedagogy, was appointed head of the Laboratory High School. The laboratory schools were Froebel-inspired, and storytelling was prominent in the curriculum. Harper, active in the Chautauqua movement and a storyteller himself, strongly supported the 1901 appointment of Gudrun Thorne-Thomsen to the faculty of the university as teacher of third grade in the elementary school, critic teacher and instructor in the School of Education. She taught courses in oral reading, history, and literature for lower grades; reading in primary grades; children's literature; and storytelling.

During 1908–1909 Thorne-Thomsen was on leave from the University of Chicago to serve as a storyteller in branch libraries opened by the Chicago Public Library in park recreation buildings. These programs were jointly sponsored by the Chicago Public Library, the Chicago Association of Collegiate Alumnae, and the Chicago Woman's Club. The program was so successful that story hours became a regular part of the library's service to children. Thorne-Thomsen began retelling the old Norse folktales for children, and out of this came her first book, *East of the Sun and West of the Moon,* in 1912.

Her reputation as a gifted storyteller grew and Thorne-Thomsen was invited to lecture on storytelling throughout the Midwest, California, Oregon, and Hawaii. She annually lectured on storytelling and folklore at the Western Reserve Library School and the Carnegie Library School of Pittsburgh. In 1923 she and her husband joined the faculty of the Ojai Valley School near Santa Barbara, California, and she became the school's first principal.

Soon after her husband's death in 1936, Thorne-Thomsen retired as principal and launched a new career both as a visiting storyteller and as a recording artist for the Library of Congress and, later, for the Victor Company. Two books, *The Sky Bed* and *In Norway*, followed in the 1940s. In 1953 she was still training librarians in the art of storytelling in formal workshops and at informal gatherings.

"Perhaps the most wonderful thing of all," one of her students of that period reported, "was to make us feel that we could tell stories too; that it was not some difficult art to be mastered by only a few gifted individuals, but the rightful heritage of us all and a source of great joy."[5]

She died in 1956, but not before she knew—and took joy in the knowledge—that she would be honored with a day of storytelling at the storytelling festival to be held in Miami Beach during the 1956 American Library Association conference. "You librarians who work with children," she wrote in acknowledgment of the honor, "I congratulate you on keeping alive the art of storytelling."[6]

Anne Carroll Moore had not rushed to select her first storyteller even though she was convinced that a children's library should have a regular story hour. In later years she wrote:

> Finding a story-teller of the right sort was not easy. Poor story-telling is more disastrous than poor story-writing, which can be skipped or left entirely alone without affecting anyone else. I had been conscious from the first months of my personal work in a children's room of the need for investing reading with dramatic interest and pictorial tradition, if it were to have any real meaning in the daily lives of hundreds of children who were coming to the library.[7]

For a year after Shedlock's visit to Brooklyn, Moore conducted an experimental story hour, inviting different people to tell stories as she and the children listened. She described one memorable story hour in her book *My Roads to Childhood*:

> I learned a very great deal from listening. In the spring of that year Miss Shedlock came back again and told Hans Christian Andersen's "Nightingale." It woke the story-teller for whom I had been waiting so long, and on May Eve, a Robin Hood story from Howard Pyle and a true story out of her own childhood marked the first of Anna Cogswell Tyler's distinctive contributions to story-telling.[8]

Anna Cogswell Tyler (1859–1923)

Anna Cogswell Tyler, Moore's assistant at Pratt, had heard Marie Shedlock tell stories to the boys and girls of Brooklyn on that exciting Saturday morning. Tyler had dramatic training but, bowing to family pressures, she did not go on the stage; storytelling, however, was the answer to this dramatic urge. In 1907, a year after Moore was appointed the first supervisor of work with children at the New York Public Library, she brought Tyler to the library to develop a storytelling program. By 1909 a strong storytelling program was in progress and Tyler had been appointed the first supervisor of storytelling for the library. In a 1909 report she wrote:

We are striving to make a more direct application between the story told and the book itself. This we do by only telling stories that will interest the children in the special book from which the story is told. . . . The Assistant in Charge of Storytelling is giving more careful supervision to all those assistants telling stories in the libraries; helping in the choice of story, selecting the best versions to use, directing as far as possible their advance reading, and generally trying to so mould the work of the storyhour that it may assume a more definite, lasting and literary form, while trying in each case to fit the particular needs and interests of the children. Already the storyhour has assumed a more dignified and definite aspect both in the kinds of stories told and the manner in which the storyhour is being conducted. Each month the storyhour is fast losing its haphazard appearance and is entering upon its proper function in library economy— that of introducing children to the best kind of books, arousing a desire for a wider range in reading in boys and girls who, having fallen into the clutches of the series habit, seem unable to be interested in anything outside that rut until they listen to a well-told story of a great deed or a great romance, handle the book which contains it, learn to know where it may be found, and, the interest once aroused, the book is in constant demand.[9]

In 1909 the storytelling staff told stories to 28,325 children; in 1910, 1,008 story hours were held for 30,000 children in 36 branch libraries. Anna Tyler planned and held staff workshops, gave on-the-job training, and inspired the new storytellers with her own art. She knew the need for inspiration, and so she held the first Spring Storytelling Symposium in 1909, where fledgling storytellers could by the example of their own art inspire others to become storytellers. One of her innovative ideas was a weekly evening story hour for nonreading boys that was held in a branch library from November 1909 to May 1910. The boys' interest in books was stimulated, and the books used in the story hours began to circulate. (Figure 1).

Tyler's influence spread throughout the profession as she held workshops and chaired storytelling committees for the Playground Association of America, Clark University, New York City's Board of Education, and others. In 1921 she compiled her favorite stories in *Twenty-four Unusual Stories*. On her retirement in 1922 she was succeeded as supervisor of storytelling by her assistant, Mary Gould Davis.

Mary Gould Davis (1882–1956)

Mary Gould Davis was born in Bangor, Maine, on February 13, 1882, the seventh of eight children. Shortly thereafter, the family moved to the Cumberland Mountains of Kentucky, and though they finally settled in New York in 1896, Davis never lost her love for Kentucky and the mountain folk. Every night her mother read to the children, or their Irish nurse told them stories. It was a book-loving family, and half a century later

FIGURE 1. *Boys Reading Club, Yorkville branch, New York Public Library, 1910. Photograph by Lewis Hine. Courtesy of the New York Public Library.*

Davis still shared these stories and poems with boys and girls. According to Davis, she had a "haphazard education" under the guidance of a governess and in private schools, and then began her career in the Brooklyn Public Library. In 1910 she went to the New York Public Library, where she became an assistant to Anna Cogswell Tyler, whom she succeeded.

The new supervisor believed that only training and experience can make storytelling effective and that a controlled story hour encouraged the children to listen with a deep quietness, and so New York Public Library story hours, under her direction, were formal and dignified, with fresh flowers, a "wishing candle," and books on the table. The story-hour line, the well-planned program, careful selection of stories—all were part of Davis's philosophy. An adult who heard her tell stories during this period described her telling and the children's reactions to her:

> For them she changed these stories from being something with which you kept children quiet at the end of the day into something they must have, a part of their heritage of wonder and laughter, of understanding, of perception. The telling of a tale deserved the creative effort and discipline which a work of art demands. I have often wished I could draw adequately the faces of one of the audiences. Over all of them, young and old, passed each emotion evoked by the tale—awe, solemnity, suspense, and the quick flicker of humor. Her voice was gifted, her timing perfect, her gestures controlled. There was never anything histrionic, for a story was never a medium for her own virtuosity, but her consummate skill was the medium for her story. "That Foolish Mr. Bun," "The Timid Little Hare," "Molly Whuppie" have been passed on with as vivid and distinct personalities as those of people we know well.[10]

Beginning in 1923 Davis found time to travel abroad—to England, Italy, Spain, the Island of Skye in Scotland— to search out stories and to trace versions of those she already knew. *Truce of the Wolf* was her collection of tales from Tuscany and Umbria, and *Three Golden Oranges and Other Spanish Folk Tales*, with Ralph Boggs, was a collection of stories from Spain. In 1945 she collaborated with Ernest Kalibala in *Wakaima and the Clay Man*, a collection of East African folktales. She wrote a short biography of Randolph Caldecott, which was published on the occasion of the one hundredth anniversary of his birth, prepared new editions of the Andrew Lang "color" fairy-tale books, and contributed to many periodicals and encyclopedias. For several years she was editor of a department of the *Saturday Review of Literature,* "Books for Young People." From the classes she taught at the School of Library Service, Columbia University, storytellers carried her philosophy across the country and abroad. Davis retired from the New York Public Library in 1945 and died in April 1956.

The first day of the Miami Beach Storytelling Festival at the American Library Association conference, held in June 1956, was dedicated to Davis, and admiring librarians told stories there in her honor (Figure 2).

Another storyteller who was honored at the festival was Ruth Sawyer.

Ruth Sawyer (1880–1970)

Ruth Sawyer was born in Boston in 1880 but grew up in New York City where she was educated in private schools and in the Garland Kindergarten Training School. Her introduction to storytelling came from her Irish nurse, Johanna, who instilled in her a deep love of Irish folklore. Sawyer began telling stories and collecting folklore when she was sent to Cuba in 1900 to organize kindergartens. At Columbia University, where she had been awarded a scholarship, she studied folklore. She began to tell stories in schools, and then came the memorable experience of hearing Shedlock tell Andersen fairy tales. "It was Miss Shedlock who lighted the fuse that shot me into storytelling in earnest," she wrote.[11]

Sawyer's opportunity to delve seriously into the sources of folktales came first in 1905 and again in 1907 when the *New York Sun* sent her to Ireland to write a series of articles on Irish cottage industries, Irish folklore, and Gaelic festivals. During this trip, she heard what became perhaps her best-known story, "The Voyage of the Wee Red Cap." She told this story at her first library story hour at the Hudson Park branch of the New York Public Library in 1910, and thereafter it became a part of the library's Christmas tradition. Rarely did Sawyer miss the St. Nicholas Eve program, and rarely did she miss telling one of her Christmas stories. "Rich in feeling for Christmas, gifted with a beautiful singing voice, clear memory, keen sense of humor, faith in the unseen, and indomitable personal courage and capacity to share the interests of others, she has been able to give dramatic joy to thousands of as strangely assorted people as ever came together upon this earth."[12]

Sawyer told stories from one end of New York City to the other. She went to nearby states and later wrote:

> One of the best of my storytelling experiences was at the Boys' Club in Greenwich, Connecticut. There were about eighty boys in the club, confirmed crapshooters, pool-players and delinquents. I held them for the first three days by telling them stories of the Ringling Brothers Circus and the few days I had been traveling with it. From the circus we passed on to Kipling, Stockton, Mark Twain, and the boys started using the library.[13]

Later Sawyer went to Spain, and the stories she heard and retold were included in *Picture Tales from Spain*. Out of this experience, too, came *Tonio Antonio*. In Mexico she found material for *The Least One*. She collected

STORYTELLING FESTIVAL

Program Chairman, Mrs. Eulalie S. Ross, Public Library, Cincinnati, Ohio

Admission by ticket only (no charge). Tickets reserved in advance but not received and any tickets still available may be picked up at the Storytelling Festival ticket table in the lobby of the Fontainebleau Hotel Ballroom.

Tuesday, June 19, 10:00 a.m.
Fontainebleau Hotel—La Ronde Room

Stories told in memory of Mary Gould Davis

Mrs. Augusta Baker, New York Public Library: "The Goat Well" from *The Fire on the Mountain*, by Harold Courlander and Wolf Leslau.

Marjorie Dobson, Public Library, Indianapolis, Ind.: "The Peddler of Ballaghadereen" from *The Way of the Storyteller*, by Ruth Sawyer.

Shigeo Watanabe, New York Public Library: "The Old Man of the Flowers" from *The Dancing Kettle*, by Yoshiko Uchida. Mr. Watanabe will tell his story in Japanese.

Mary Strang, New York Public Library: *The Nightingale*, by Hans Christian Andersen from *The Art of the Storyteller*, by Marie L. Shedlock.

Wednesday, June 20, 10:00 a.m.
Fontainebleau Hotel—La Ronde Room

Storytelling Festival continued

Stories told in memory of Gudrun Thorne-Thomsen

Eileen H. Colwell, Public Library, Hendon, England: "Elsie Piddock Skips in Her Sleep" from *Martin Pippin in the Daisy Field*, by Eleanor Farjeon.

Stephanie Fraser, Enoch Pratt Free Library, Baltimore, Md.: "Miss Cow Falls a Victim to Mr. Rabbit" from *Uncle Remus, His Songs and His Sayings*, by Joel Chandler Harris.

Mrs. Rosemarie Höhne, Public Library, Cincinnati, Ohio: "The Wolf and the Seven Kids," by the Brothers Grimm. Mrs. Höhne will tell her story in German.

Marguerite A. Dodson, Public Library, Brooklyn, N.Y.: "The Great Bell of Peking" from *The Golden Bird*, by Katharine Gibson.

Thursday, June 21, 10:00 a.m.
Fontainebleau Hotel—La Ronde Room

Storytelling Festival continued

Stories told in honor of Ruth Sawyer Durand

Mrs. Frances Clarke Sayers, storyteller, author, and lecturer on children's literature, Los Angeles, Calif.: Hero Cycle from *The Wonder Smith and His Son*, by Ella Young; "Old Fire Dragaman" from *The Jack Tales*, by Richard Chase; "The Hare and the Hedgehog" from *Told Again*, by Walter de la Mare.

FIGURE 2. *Program for a storytelling festival presented by the Children's Library Association at the ALA Miami Beach Conference, June 19–21, 1956.*

Christmas stories from around the world and brought them together in *The Long Christmas. The Way of the Storyteller*, a book about storytelling as a creative art that continues to inspire both new and experienced storytellers, and *My Spain*, a "storyteller's year of collecting," followed.

Sawyer was awarded the Newbery Medal for *Roller Skates* in 1937, a story based on her childhood experiences in New York City, and the Regina Medal in 1965 for "a lifetime of distinguished contribution to children's literature." That same year she received the Laura Ingalls Wilder Award from the Children's Services Division (now the Association for Library Service to Children), of the American Library Association, for books that "over a period of years have made a substantial and lasting contribution to literature for children." Sawyer's acceptance of this award was a memorable occasion for the many storytellers who saw her stand before the large audience, a frail woman of 85 years, and with a deep and resonant voice begin, "Once upon a time . . ."

The beautiful voice was stilled forever when Sawyer died in 1970. Beryl Robinson, a Boston Public Library storyteller who had heard her often, wrote this remembrance of her:

> Ruth Sawyer's life brought rich gifts to children everywhere. Gifts of fun and laughter and wonder. Of thoughtfulness, deep absorption, and joy. Gifts that inspire courage and bring awareness of beauty. The stretching of the imagination, the opening of the heart, and the widening of the horizons that come whenever there is good storytelling, whether given richly by the master storyteller or read from a beautifully written page. But she was also a great teacher; and countless numbers of children in the future will share in her giving as their teachers and librarians follow the way of the storyteller she so brilliantly illumined for them.[14]

Characteristics of Library Storytelling

The close connection between storytelling and reading is characteristic of library storytelling. Thorne-Thomsen, who had a strong influence on the development of storytelling in libraries, believed that imaging exercises and listening to oral literature prepared children for reading. The imaging exercises that Thorne-Thomsen used in 1908 are similar to what psychologists today call "guided imagery." Children were asked to imagine the house they grew up in, the objects in the house, the faces they remembered. When children became stuck in decoding, Thorne-Thomsen advised their teachers to abandon any further effort at that task and, instead, to tell the children a story. As children listen to stories, they create images or pictures in their minds. We now know that even if a child can decode he may not be *reading*, that is, the words and sentences may have no *meaning* for him. To comprehend the meaning of printed material, the child must understand the oral language patterns and see the images that the printed words represent. This insight into the relationship of oral literature, imaging, and reading, shared by Gudrun Thorne-Thomsen, Francis Parker, and John Dewey, was lost for many years while schools emphasized the technical aspects of reading.

The early children's librarians thought of storytelling as a form of reading guidance. The purpose of the library story hour was to introduce children to the best kind of books and to broaden their reading interests. The Carnegie Library at Pittsburgh, for instance, became famous for its story-hour cycles on Greek myths, Norse mythology, and hero tales. At the New York Public Library, Anna Cogswell Tyler (quoted earlier) carefully selected stories from books on the library shelves on the assumption that story-hour listeners would want to read the stories for themselves. Circulation figures seem to bear this out. The children's librarian at the Cleveland Public Library noted in her annual report for 1909 that Hans Christian Andersen's *The Snow Queen* circulated 93 times at the two branch libraries where the story was told at story hour, compared with four circulations at the two branches where it had not been told. Such early reports show that the keeping of statistics to justify library programs is not new.

Storytelling in libraries was widely accepted though it was not without its critics. John Cotton Dana, then librarian of the Newark (N.J.) Public Library and past president of the American Library Association, thought that storytelling was the responsibility of the schools and considered it an ill use of the librarian's time and energy. Writing for *Public Libraries* in 1908, Dana labeled librarian-storytellers "altruistic, emotional, dramatic, irrepressible childlovers who do not find ordinary library work gives sufficient opportunities for altruistic indulgence," and advised any library that could spare such misguided souls "to set them at teaching the teachers the art of storytelling."[15] Fortunately, Dana's opinion reflected a minority point of view and storytelling continued to flourish in libraries. Librarians went out into the schools, playgrounds, and other recreational centers to tell stories, as reported in Moore's "Report of the Committee on Storytelling," published in *Playground* in 1910.[16]

Before leaving this early period it is worth noting, as Richard Alvey points out in his doctoral dissertation on organized storytelling to children in the United States, that approximately 1,000,000 immigrants entered the United States each year from 1900 to 1913.[17] Librarians looked on storytelling as a way of integrating many diverse heritages and of teaching English and the English language orally. Libraries in ports of entry, particularly New York and Boston, carried out extensive programs among immigrants. At the New York Public Library, story hours were occasionally told in a foreign language. These story hours were conducted by a library assistant of the nationality or by a foreign visitor.

FIGURE 3. *Getting tickets for story hour, Yorkville branch, New York Public Library, 1910. Photograph by Lewis Hine. Courtesy of the New York Public Library.*

FIGURE 4. *At the shelves after the story hour, Webster branch, New York Public Library, 1910. Photograph by Lewis Hine. Courtesy of the New York Public Library.*

FIGURE 5. *Italian boys listening to* Pinocchio *told in their native language by an Italian visitor at the New York Public Library, 1910. Photograph by Lewis Hine. Courtesy of the New York Public Library.*

FIGURE 6. *Story hour for Russian children at Rivington Street branch, New York Public Library, 1910. Photograph by Lewis Hine. Courtesy of the New York Public Library.*

Alvey also noted the conflict between storytelling as an art and story-telling as an educational device or as a way to increase book circulation. There were few librarians like Edna Lyman Scott who publicly stated that storytelling was "an art in itself, with the great underlying purpose of all art, to give joy to the world," and that "only as storytelling [was given] its real place in the world of art [could it attain] its full significance."[18] Nevertheless, librarians who had been influenced by the artistry of Marie Shedlock and Gudrun Thorne-Thomsen believed that storytelling demanded creative effort and discipline. Both Shedlock and Thorne-Thomsen emphasized simplicity, careful selection, and reliance on the human voice alone to convey the nuances of the story. Librarian-story-tellers considered themselves to be interpreters of literature for children; their goal was "to cultivate a capacity for literary appreciation in children." This attitude, which continues to the present day, was eloquently expressed by Alice M. Jordan, head of children's work at the Boston Public Library, in an article published in 1934 in the first Storytelling Issue of *The Horn Book Magazine*: "There is, as we know, a sensitiveness to the magic of words natural in some children, while in others it waits to be wakened. . . . Out of the repetition of melodious expressions as they reach the ear comes an appreciation of language not easily gained from the printed page."[19]

The first library story hours were planned for children age nine and older. By that age children were expected to have mastered the mechanics of reading, but librarians noticed that at about the same age children began to lose interest in reading. Picture-book hours for children ages five to seven started at the Carnegie Library of Pittsburgh as early as 1902 and other libraries soon followed.

Library story hours for children of school age reached a peak in the 1920s. In 1920 Jordan estimated that the Cronans were telling stories to 1,800 library listeners per week as well as to 4,000 classroom pupils in auditorium groups. Attendance at Carnegie Library story hours peaked in 1924 at nearly 150,000.

Shift in Emphasis from Oral Narration to the Printed Word

In 1919 Macmillan created the first juvenile department in a publishing house. Other publishers soon followed. *The Horn Book Magazine*, a literary journal, and *Elementary English Review* (now *Language Arts*) began publication in 1924. The influx of illustrators from Europe after World War I—artists influenced by the impressionists and expressionists, cubists, and other postimpressionists, who brought with them a rich tradition—and the development of better methods of reproducing art in books set the stage for the flowering of the American picture book.

In 1935 the Detroit Public Library began picture-book hours for preschoolers ages three to five. Library story hours for school-age children were scheduled less frequently as attendance declined. The proliferation of organized activities competed for the children's attention, and greater administrative demands made on children's librarians left less time for story-hour preparation.

This was the period, too, of the early-childhood movement. Lucy Sprague Mitchell spearheaded the "here and now" school of publishing—"here and now" meaning the familiar and immediate. Though perhaps still unaware of what was happening, the library profession—along with general society—was moving toward an emphasis on information. In 1939 Elizabeth Nesbitt, then associate professor of library science at Carnegie Library School, made an impassioned plea for the continuation of the library story hour and the importance of the storyteller as an interpreter of literature for the child. Nesbitt carefully distinguished between reading for information and reading for literary appreciation.[20]

The 1940s and 1950s saw an increase in the publication of informational books for children, accelerated in 1957 when the Russians launched Sputnik and interest in science skyrocketed. Library story hours for ages three to five flourished during the baby boom of the 1950s, but time needed for preparation for the story hour for older boys and girls was suspect in an increasingly technological society and a cost-effective economy. "Realists" questioned the value of imaginative stories in the child's development and spoke out against the violence in many of the folktales.

There were other changes taking place too. Beginning in the 1920s thousands of Puerto Ricans came to live in the United States. In an effort to serve the Spanish-speaking community better, the New York Public Library hired Pura Belpré, "the first public librarian who preserved and disseminated Puerto Rican folklore throughout the United States."[21] Belpré's work became increasingly important as the Puerto Rican population increased—from 69,967 in 1940 to 301,375 in 1950.

Pura Belpré (1903–1982)

Born on February 2, 1903, in Cidra, Puerto Rico, Pura Belpré was one of five children of Felipe Belpré Bernabe and Carlota Nogueras. Belpré recalled growing up "in a home of storytellers, listening to stories which had been handed down by word of mouth for generations. . . . As a child I enjoyed telling many of these tales that I heard. The characters became quite real to me. I remember during school recess that some of us would gather under the shade of the tamarind tree. There we would take turns telling stories."[22]

Her father was a building contractor whose search for work caused the family to move several times during Belpré's childhood. In spite of the many moves she was an excellent student and in 1919 she entered the University of Puerto Rico, intending to become a teacher. But a year later, on a trip to New York City to attend the wedding of her older sister Elisa, fate intervened.

Ernestine Rose, branch librarian of the 135th Street branch of the New York Public Library (later renamed the Countee Cullen branch), was looking for a bilingual assistant and offered the position to Elisa. When Elisa's husband refused to let his bride work, Elisa persuaded Pura to accept the position.

Initially, Belpré was assigned to work in both the adult and children's departments. She enrolled in the Library School of the New York Public Library and Columbia University where she studied Latin American literature, puppetry, and Portuguese. It was in the course in storytelling taught by Mary Gould Davis that she first told a folktale heard from her grandmother in Puerto Rico about the courtship of the pretty cockroach Martina and the gallant mouse Perez. Belpré yearned to tell the tales she remembered from childhood, but couldn't find them in any books in the library's collections. At that time it was standard library practice to tell stories only found in books, but Belpré's folkloric story made such a deep impression on Davis and on her fellow classmates that she was given special permission to tell her unpublished tales at the branch story hours.

In 1929 Belpré was assigned to the 115th Street branch in southwest Harlem, then a predominately Puerto Rican neighborhood. In her efforts to reach the Puerto Rican community she introduced bilingual story hours and obtained permission to allow the parents of the children to attend. The parents sat at the back of the story-hour room. Noting the children's enthusiastic response to a puppet show performed by Leonardo Cimino, brother of the children's librarian Maria Cimino, Belpré created her own juvenile puppet theater and began using puppets in her storytelling.

Belpré practiced outreach long before it became popular in the 1960s. She told stories and talked about library services at churches, community centers, neighborhood organizations, and schools. She initiated the library's celebration of *El Dia de Reyes* (the Feast of the Three Kings), which is observed on the sixth of January in Puerto Rico and throughout Hispanic America with Spanish *cuentos* (stories), *bailes* (dances), and *musica* (music). In 1932 Frederic Warne published *Perez and Martina: A Portorican Folk Tale*. It was Belpré's first book and the first Puerto Rican folktale published in the United States.

When the Puerto Rican population moved to the South Bronx and East Harlem, Belpré was transferred to the Aguilar branch on East 110th

FIGURE 7. *Pura Belpré telling to Hispanic children, New York Public Library, ca. 1938, 1939. Photograph courtesy of the New York Public Library.*

Street. There she continued her bilingual story hours, reading clubs, puppet theater, and outreach programs, and helped develop the library's Spanish-language collections.

In 1940 Belpré presented a paper, "Children: The Link Between the Spanish Adult and the Library," at the American Library Association conference in Cincinnati. During her visit to Cincinnati she met the conductor, concert violinist, and musicologist Clarence Cameron White. Belpré married White in December 1943, and took a leave of absence from the library to travel with her husband and to write. Her first collection, *The Tiger and the Rabbit and Other Tales*, was published in 1946.

After the death of her husband in 1960, Belpré returned to the New York Public Library to fill the newly created position of Spanish children's specialist. By then over 600,000 Puerto Ricans were reported to be living in New York City.

Belpré engaged her listeners with her quiet but animated manner of telling, her expressive eyes, and her warm smile. Puerto Rican folktales, such as "The Albahaca Plant," "The Earrings," "Juan Bobo," and "Perez and Martina," were favorites with her Hispanic listeners, but she could just as easily hold them spellbound with a Howard Pyle story.

Her writing continued and in the coming years she published *Juan Bobo and the Queen's Necklace: A Puerto Rican Tale*; a second edition of *The Tiger and the Rabbit and Other Tales*; a Spanish edition of *Perez y Martina*; Spanish and English editions of *Oté: A Puerto Rican Folk Tale*; *Santiago*, an original story; *Dance of the Animals: A Puerto Rican Folk Tale*; *Once in Puerto Rico*; and *The Rainbow Colored Horse*. In addition, she translated several English books into Spanish, made recordings, and compiled (with Mary K. Conwell) *Libros en Español: An Annotated List of Children's Books in Spanish*.

Belpré retired from the New York Public Library in March 1968, at the age of 65, but was persuaded by Augusta Baker to work two days a week in the South Bronx project. For the next decade she visited community centers and worked with neighborhood organizations. Once again, she incorporated puppetry into her storytelling. She designed "a collapsible puppet theater that was lightweight and easily transportable throughout the city" and "instructed the library staff in the arts of designing costumes, creating theatrical props, selecting appropriate story lines, preparing scripts, and acting with puppets."[23] The shows were tremendously popular with both staff and South Bronx residents.

Beginning in 1972 she began presenting puppet shows at El Museo del Barrio, assisted by the museum staff. Belpré designed the theater and made all of the puppets. A staff member described the puppet theater as

unique in that it was constructed like a kiosco, and in the future will be transformed into a bohio in keeping with Puerto Rican culture. Mrs.

White and her assistant are fully visible to the children watching the show. In this way the children are involved in the changes and different movements necessary in order to bring the puppets to life. This however, does not at all distract the children; in fact it seems to make it all the more interesting for them since they become involved with the little intricacies that make the puppets function.[24]

During this period Belpré was a frequent guest lecturer at colleges and universities throughout the United States. Wherever she went she told her Puerto Rican folktales and fostered a greater awareness of Puerto Rican culture.

On May 20, 1982, Pura Belpré was among the honorees at the sixth annual presentation of the Mayor's Awards of Honor for Arts and Culture, presided over by Edward I. Koch, then mayor of New York City. Belpré was honored for "her contribution to the Spanish-speaking community . . . and for enriching the lives of the city's Spanish-speaking children."[25] The following morning, when her brother went to wake her, he found that she had died in her sleep. Through her books and her storytelling art, Belpré left a legacy of rich Puerto Rican folklore that can be enjoyed by all children today.

As indicated earlier, during the political and social upheaval of the 1960s librarians reached out into the community with a fervor matched only by their pioneer counterparts at the turn of the century. They held stair-step story hours in urban ghettos and worked with Head Start teachers. Some of the children who attended these programs came from cultures rich in the oral tradition. A greater number were born into families that had neither an oral nor a print tradition. Librarians sought simpler storybooks to use with preschoolers who were not used to being read to at home. Music, especially the singing of folk songs, was added to the story-hour program. Story hours became less literary, less structured. Film programs and multimedia story hours became increasingly popular with children who were growing up with television.

Impact of Early-Childhood Research on Library Programming

Burton L. White's research while director of Harvard University's preschool project from 1965 to 1978 demonstrated the importance of interaction between children and their caregivers during the first three years of life, and that interaction's impact on language development, later cognitive functioning, personality, and social behavior. Other researchers, among them Howard Gardner and Brian Sutton-Smith, were exploring the young child's sense of story. Vivian Gussin Paley, a kindergarten teacher at the laboratory schools of the University of Chicago, was doing seminal work on the use of storytelling in the early-childhood classroom, for which she later received a MacArthur Foundation award.

Jean Piaget, the eminent Swiss psychologist who received recognition in Europe in the 1930s for his theories of cognitive development, was becoming more widely known to Americans through translations and interpretations of his writings. Piaget considered assimilation and accommodation to be the two most important processes for human functioning. The process of assimilation involves abstracting information from the outside world and putting the information into the organizing schemes that represent what the child already knows. Accommodation is the process by which the child modifies these schemes to fit his or her stage of developing knowledge. Betty Weeks, an early-childhood educator at the National College of Education in Evanston, Illinois, believes that listening to stories helps children with these processes. After listening to the story of Persephone, on a brisk March day with a tinge of spring in the air, a five-year-old remarked, "Mrs. Weeks, I don't think Persephone is with her mother quite yet."

Bruno Bettelheim's *The Uses of Enchantment: The Meaning and Importance of Fairy Tales*, published in 1976, also served to support storytelling to children. Though many adults could not accept Bettelheim's Freudian interpretations of familiar folk tales, his book persuaded them that fairy tales play an important role in a child's development.

In response to the growing evidence that young children were capable of responding to stories on a more sophisticated level than formerly thought, children's librarians began experimenting with toddler storytimes—storytelling programs designed for children from 18 months to 3 years of age, accompanied by a caregiver. At the same time, the noticeable lack of storybooks appropriate for toddlers led publishers to bring out attractive board books by talented authors and illustrators.

Effect of Professional Storytellers on Library Story Hours

After attending the National Storytelling Association's first storytelling festival in 1973, cousins Connie Regan and Barbara Freeman decided to leave their positions as librarians in Chattanooga to become traveling storytellers. Since 1975, thousands of librarians, teachers, and children have heard this popular duo, known as "The Folktellers." The Folktellers' success inspired others to leave their first profession to join the ranks of professional storytellers, that is, people who make their living solely or primarily through storytelling. Probably not since the Middle Ages have there been so many professional storytellers! They tell in coffeehouses, concert halls, theaters, churches, museums, parks, and playgrounds, as well as in schools and libraries. Their audiences include adults and children, and their performances are entertainment-oriented.

In an interview in *The Horn Book Magazine* Augusta Baker expressed her concern over the current trend toward the use of personal stories in storytelling, popularized by many professional storytellers, and the emphasis on performance.[26] Children enjoy hearing personal anecdotes from people important in their lives. Anne Carroll Moore, one of the earliest advocates of storytelling in the library, told personal anecdotes in her informal story hours at Pratt Library.[27] But children also need to know their literary heritage. Fewer opportunities (especially for older children) to hear traditional tales is cause for concern.

Even before the rise of a professional class of storytellers, librarians had changed their priorities from story hours for older boys and girls to storytimes for younger children. Almost all public libraries offer picture-book programs for preschoolers and children in the primary grades, and 93 percent of the librarians responding to Ann Carlson's survey in the early 1980s reported that they offer parent and child literature-sharing programs for children under the age of three.[28] The availability of beautiful picture books for young children and of traditional folk and fairy tales in picture-book format encourages this practice.

Only a small number of libraries offer story hours for children over eight years of age on a *regular* (weekly, semi-monthly, or monthly) basis. The tendency is to invite a professional storyteller to visit the school or public library on a special-occasion basis and to hold an occasional story hour in between visits or to read aloud to the children in between special events. While guest storytellers have always been an inspirational part of the library tradition—one has only to think of Marie Shedlock, Gudrun Thorne-Thomsen, and Ruth Sawyer—the library storytelling program was never dependent upon guest storytellers. Storytelling should not be limited to "special occasions" when the budget allows for a professional teller. Children need to hear stories each and every day.

Practically speaking, librarians cannot offer storytelling programs on a daily basis, but they can encourage parents to read aloud or to tell stories to their children for 15 minutes a day; they can encourage teachers to read aloud or to tell stories in their classrooms for 15 minutes a day; they can train teenagers to read aloud or to tell stories to younger children in the library; they can conduct storytelling workshops for day-care staff and other adults who work with children; they can use storytelling techniques in book talks and tell stories during class visits. The whole-language movement has made teachers more aware of children's literature and they are eager to learn effective ways of sharing literature with children. Through the work of Marie Shedlock and Gudrun Thorne-Thomsen, librarians and teachers realized the power of storytelling in passing on to children their literary heritage and this is still the primary purpose of storytelling to children in school and library settings. "True literacy comes from a deep-rooted love for stories . . . stories that enable children access to the magical worlds of written texts and the infinite possibilities to which these texts invite them."[29]

Pertaining to Baker's concern about the emphasis on performance, the shift in modern folklore scholarship from the study of the story itself to the study of the story within its context has served to reinforce the modern teller's focus on performance and the audience's reaction to it. Folklorists consider the physical and social environment in which the story is told essential for an understanding of its meaning, and the storyteller's voice, gestures, and interaction with the listeners are as important as the story itself.

In an article titled "There Are No Talent Scouts . . ." the author reflects on the professional storytellers' effect on librarian-storytellers.[30] The title of the article comes from Mary Gould Davis, who used to tell her students at Columbia University Library School, "There are no talent scouts in the audience of children," meaning that the story is more important than the teller. In this respect the librarian-storyteller's presentation is closer to that of the traditionalist than to that of the professional storyteller where the emphasis is as much, or even more so, on the performance as on the story. The traditionalist tells stories absorbed from a storytelling community while the librarian-storyteller usually tells from a background in storytelling literature, though he or she may combine elements of both traditions. It was said of Gudrun Thorne-Thomsen, "when she told a story, it was like watching a tree grow; you felt it coming from such roots!"[31]

Introducing children to literature through reading aloud and storytelling and encouraging them to participate in the creative act of story listening and telling require different skills from performing to large audiences.

> As with a traditional audience, children are not passive listeners, and they have a good ear for the spoken word since they still live in a predominately oral milieu. They do not demand a flamboyantly oral/visual performance (though many adults think it necessary). They do demand sincerity and openness, and they tend to suffer honest fools gladly. Like a traditional audience they do not stop to ask, "Was that profound and meaningful, or just amusing?" If a story is well told, they will absorb other levels of meaning that appeal to their levels of experience and understanding.[32]

Annual storytelling events—such as the New York Public Library's storytelling symposium held early in May in honor of Marie Shedlock's birthday; the Storytelling Institute (also held in May) at the C.W. Post

Center, Long Island University; and "A(ugusta) Baker's Dozen: A Celebration of Stories," sponsored by the Richland County Public Library, the College of Library and Information Science at the University of South Carolina, and the South Carolina State Library every April— offer inspiration to both novice and experienced storytellers. As the renowned librarian-storyteller Frances Clarke Sayers exclaimed, "It [storytelling] is a deathless art, lively and diverse, which like music, refreshes and revives those whom it touches even in its farthest reaches."[33]

NOTES

1. Elizabeth Keith Botset, "The Once-Upon-a-Time Hour," *Carnegie Magazine* 6 (February 1933): 266–269.
2. Anne Carroll Moore, *My Roads to Childhood: Views and Reviews of Children's Books* (Doubleday, 1939), p. 145.
3. Alice M. Jordan, "The Cronan Story Hours in Boston," *The Horn Book Magazine* 26 (November–December 1950): 460–464.
4. Anne Carroll Moore, "Report on Storytelling," *Library Journal* 35 (September 1910): 408.
5. Jasmine Britton, "Gudrun Thorne-Thomsen: Storyteller from Norway," *The Horn Book Magazine* 34 (February 1958): 27.
6. "Storytelling Festival at Miami Beach," *Top of the News* 13:1 (October 1956): 17.
7. Moore, *My Roads to Childhood*, p. 145.
8. Ibid.
9. Anna Cogswell Tyler, in a report dated 1909 in the files of the Office of Children's Services, New York Public Library.
10. Mary Rogers, in a letter in the files of the Office of Children's Services, New York Public Library.
11. Virginia Haviland, *Ruth Sawyer* (Walck, 1965), p. 22.
12. Anne Carroll Moore, "Ruth Sawyer, Story-Teller," *The Horn Book Magazine* 12 (January–February 1936): 34–38.
13. Ibid., p. 37.
14. Beryl Robinson, "Ruth Sawyer: 1880–1970," *The Horn Book Magazine* 46 (August 1970): 347.
15. John Cotton Dana, "Storytelling in Libraries," *Public Libraries* 13 (1908): 350.
16. Anne Carroll Moore, "Report of the Committee on Storytelling," *Playground* 4 (August 1910): 162ff. Reprinted in *Library Work with Children* by Alice I. Hazeltine (Wilson, 1917), pp. 297–315.
17. Richard Gerald Alvey, *The Historical Development of Organized Storytelling to Children* (University Microfilms Intl., 1981), p. 16.
18. Ibid., p. 35.

19. Alice M. Jordan, "Story-Telling in Boston," *The Horn Book Magazine* 10 (May 1934): 182.

20. Elizabeth Nesbitt, "Hold to That Which Is Good," *The Horn Book Magazine* 16 (January–February 1940): 7–15.

21. Julio L. Hernandez-Delgado, "Pura Teresa Belpré, Storyteller and Pioneer Puerto Rican Librarian," *The Library Quarterly* 62 (October 1992): 425–440. The section on Pura Belpré is based on material in this article and on the author's personal recollections.

22. Pura Belpré, "I wish to be like Johnny Appleseed." n.d., Pura Belpré Papers, Centro de Estudios Puertorriquenos, Hunter College Eveline Lopez Antonetty Puerto Rican Research Collection.

23. Lillian Lopez, Interview by Julio L. Harnandez-Delgado, May 31, 1989.

24. Mary Segarra Diaz, *Quimbamba: Bilingual Education Quarterly* (January 1973): 13.

25. Susan Heller Anderson, "Six Patrons of the Arts Receive Mayor's Awards of Honor," *New York Times,* May 21, 1982.

26. Henrietta M. Smith, "An Interview with Augusta Baker," *The Horn Book Magazine* 71 (May–June 1995): 292–296.

27. Frances Clarke Sayers, *Anne Carroll Moore: A Biography* (Atheneum, 1972), p. 77.

28. Ann D. Carlson, *Early Childhood Literature Sharing Programs in Libraries* (Library Professional Publications, 1985), p. 50.

29. Tina-Jill Gordon, "Teachers Telling Stories: Seven-, Eight- and Nine-Year Old Children's Written Responses to Oral Narratives" (Ed. D. diss., Rutgers University, 1991), p. 107.

30. Ellin Greene, "There Are No Talent Scouts. . . . " *School Library Journal* 29 (November 1982): 25–27.

31. Frances Clarke Sayers, "A Skimming of Memory," *The Horn Book Magazine* 52 (June 1976): 273.

32. Kay Stone, "'To Ease the Heart': Traditional Storytelling," *National Storytelling Journal* 1 (Winter 1984): 5.

33. Frances Clarke Sayers, "Storytelling," in *Anthology of Children's Literature,* by Edna Johnson, Evelyn R. Sickels, and Frances Clarke Sayers, 4th rev. ed. (Houghton, 1970), p. 1146.

3 Purpose and Values of Storytelling

. . . children who are not spoken to by live and responsive adults will not learn to speak properly. Children who are not answered will stop asking questions. They will become incurious. And children who are not told stories and who are not read to will have few reasons for wanting to learn to read.
—*Gail E. Haley*[1]

WHAT IS STORYTELLING? What is its purpose? What are its values? In an attempt to define storytelling, participants at a conference sponsored by the National Storytelling Association in 1989 spoke of "oral narration," "communication," "transmission of images," "revelation," "co-creation," "creating order out of chaos," and "worship." It seems easier to agree on what storytelling is *not*. Storytelling is not recitation, nor is it acting.

Lewis Carroll called stories "love gifts";[2] contemporary author Jean Little calls them "invitations to joy."[3] Both are apt descriptions, for telling a story is, indeed, giving a gift. Storytelling brings to the listeners heightened awareness—a sense of wonder, of mystery, of reverence for life. This nurturing of the spirit-self is the primary purpose of storytelling, and all other uses and effects are secondary.

Storytelling is a sharing experience. When we tell, we show our willingness to be vulnerable, to expose our deepest feelings, our values. That kind of nakedness that says we care about what we are relating invites children to listen with open minds and hearts. Enjoying a story together creates a sense of community. It establishes a happy relationship between teller and listener, drawing people closer to one another, adult to child, child to child. This rapport carries over into other areas as well, for children tend to have confidence in the person who tells stories well.

Library storytelling grew out of a desire to introduce children to the pleasures of literature, to excite children about books and reading. This viewpoint was eloquently expressed by Elizabeth Nesbitt:

> Story-telling provides the opportunity to interpret for the child life forces which are beyond his immediate experience, and so to prepare him for life itself. It gives the teller the chance to emphasize significance rather than incident. It enables her, through the magic quality of the spoken word, to

reveal to the child the charm and subtle connotations of word sounds, all the evanescent beauty emanating from combinations of words and from the cadence, the haunting ebb and flow, of rhythmical prose. It is through the medium of interpretation that all of us, adults and children, come to genuine appreciation. . . . Story-telling, rightly done, is such an art.[4]

By making the connection between storytelling and books—by telling a story and indicating the book from which it comes and pointing out that hundreds of other wonderful tales can be found in books—the storyteller is introducing reading as a source of enjoyment throughout life. With so many children's books in print, it is possible for a child to read a great number without reading even one worthwhile book. Through storytelling and reading aloud we can introduce books of quality that otherwise might be missed. Too, children are often ready for the literary experience a book offers before they are able to read it on their own. *Charlotte's Web* is the classic example of a book that can be enjoyed on several levels. Reluctant readers, who may never read fiction or fantasy, can also have a share in literature through the experience of hearing stories told or read aloud.

In our multicultural, multilingual classrooms and libraries, there will be children who are experiencing difficulty making the transition from oral to written narrative, as well as children from homes where books and reading are not valued. Storytelling can provide a transition, a bridge to reading. Storytelling allows these children to lose themselves in a story in the same way that fluent readers lose themselves in a book. And because the words go directly from the ear to the brain, story listening is an invaluable experience for beginning readers, reluctant readers, or children who have difficulty comprehending what they are reading.

From listening to stories, children develop a richer vocabulary. A kindergarten teacher who was telling "One-Eye, Two-Eyes, and Three-Eyes" to her class for the second time said the mother was very "angry." The children corrected her: "She was FURIOUS." The way the children emphasized "furious" made it clear that their first meeting with the word was in the story and it had make a strong impression on them.

The storyteller works with words. The sound of words, the way an author puts words together to form a rhythmic pattern, pleases the ear and evokes a physical response from the young child. Research indicates that there is a connection between the development of motor ability and language competence. That there is such a relationship comes as no surprise to anyone who has ever held an infant and shared aloud Mother Goose rhymes. The young child responds to the rollicking verses with rhythmic movements of the body.

To market, to market, to buy a fat pig,
Home again, home again, jiggety-jig;
To market, to market, to buy a fat hog,
Home again, home again, jiggety-jog.

The enjoyment of sound and rhythm is enhanced by the sensuous pleasure of close body contact.

But Mother Goose rhymes have more to offer than rhythm and repetition. A Mother Goose rhyme is a minidrama. Consider, for example, "The Old Woman and Her Pig." This simple tale has characters, conflict, and action that lead to a climax and satisfying resolution. The old woman must persuade her obstinate pig to go over the stile so that she can get home. She appeals to quite ordinary objects—a stick, fire, water, rope—and to common animals—a dog, ox, rat, cat—for help. These usually inanimate objects and dumb animals act with wills of their own, entering into the conflict. The conflict is resolved when the old woman fills the cat's request for a saucer of milk, thus starting a sequence of events that culminates in the pig's jumping over the stile.

Children find pleasure in the way an author uses words to create mood, to evoke response, to create images that please the inward eye, as in the following three excerpts:

Whenever fairies are sad they wear white. And this year, which was long ago, was the year men were tearing down all the old zigzag rail fences. Now those old zigzag fences were beautiful for the fairies because a hundred fairies could sit on one rail and thousands and thousands of them could sit on the zigzags and sing pla-sizzy pla-sizzy, softer than an eye wink, softer than a baby's thumb, all on a moonlight summer night. And they found out that year was going to be the last year of the zigzag rail fences. It made them sorry and sad, and when they are sorry and sad they wear white. So they picked the wonderful white morning glories running along the zigzag rail fences and made them into little wristlets and wore those wristlets the next year to show they were sorry and sad.

> From "How to Tell Corn Fairies When You
> See 'Em," in Carl Sandburg's *Rootabaga Stories*.[5]

Long, long ago the wind and the water were the closest of friends. Every day Mrs. Wind would visit Mrs. Water, and they would spend the day talking. Mostly they enjoyed talking about their children. Especially Mrs. Wind. "Just look at my children," Mrs. Wind would say. "I have big children and little children. They can go anywhere in the world. They can stroke the grass softly, and they can knock down a tree. They can go fast or they can go slowly. Nobody has children like mine."

> From "Why the Waves Have Whitecaps," in
> Julius Lester's *The Knee-High Man and Other
> Tales*.[6]

But that wasn't the end of Elsie Piddock; she has never stopped skipping on Caburn since, for Signed and Sealed is Signed and Sealed. Not many have seen her, because she knows all the tricks; but if you go to Caburn at the new moon, you may catch a glimpse of a tiny bent figure, no bigger than a child, skipping all by itself in its sleep, and hear a gay little voice, like the voice of a dancing yellow leaf, singing:

"Andy
Spandy
Sugardy
Candy
French
Almond
Rock!
Breadandbutterforyoursupper'sallyourmother'sGOT!'"

From "Elsie Piddock Skips in Her Sleep," in
Eleanor Farjeon's *Martin Pippin in the Daisy
Field*.[7]

Storytelling encourages the art of listening. Children experience the whole of a piece of literature, uninterrupted by questions or discussion. If the stories they hear are worth listening to, they are eager to learn the key that unlocks the symbols. Studies of children who read early indicate that hearing stories told or read aloud in early childhood is a common factor.

FIGURE 8. *When children are enjoying a story, their faces express interest, curiosity, and delight. Leslie Barban sharing a picture-book story at Richland County Public Library, Columbia, South Carolina. Photograph courtesy of the Richland County Public Library.*

Story listening may have an even greater significance in the young child's life. Howard Gardner writes in *The Arts and Human Development*:

> . . . story hearing and telling is a very special, almost religious experience for the young child, one which commands his absolute attention and seems crucial in his mastery of language and his comprehension of the world. The child identifies fully with the characters and episodes in the stories and integrates them with situations encountered in the remainder of his working day, even as he incorporates names, events, rhythms, melodies, sounds, even entire passages into his night-time monologues. The central role played by story hearing and storytelling in the lives of most young children leads me to speculate that the narrative impulse plays an important role in organizing the child's world; and the auditory and vocalizing systems may require a certain amount of stimulation which, though available from many sources, seems particularly well satisfied by literary experience.[8]

Hearing stories told gives children practice in visualization. As children listen they create the scenes, the action, the characters. The ability to visualize, to fantasize, is the basis of creative imagination. It also appears to have a positive effect on social and cognitive development. Children with a strong predisposition toward imaginative play seem to empathize with other children more readily. This is of special significance to educators who fear that cognitive skills may have been emphasized in the past at the expense of affective development. The noted Russian author and specialist in children's language and literature, Kornei Chukovsky, believed the goal of storytelling to be "fostering in the child, at whatever cost, compassion and humaneness—this miraculous ability of man to be disturbed by another being's misfortunes, to feel joy about another being's happiness, to experience another's fate as one's own."[9]

Literature gives children insight into the motives and patterns of human behavior. Bruno Bettelheim, in his book *The Uses of Enchantment: The Meaning and Importance of Fairy Tales*, discusses the role of fairy tales in helping children master the psychological problems of growing up:

> A child needs to understand what is going on within his conscious self so that he can also cope with that which goes on in his unconscious. He can achieve this understanding, and with it the ability to cope, not through rational comprehension of the nature and content of his unconscious, but by becoming familiar with it through spinning out daydreams—ruminating, rearranging, and fantasizing about suitable story elements in response to unconscious pressures. By doing this, the child fits unconscious content into conscious fantasies, which then enable him to deal with that content. It is here that fairy tales have unequaled value, because they offer new dimensions to the child's imagination which would be impossible for him to discover as truly on his own. Even more important, the form and struc-

ture of fairy tales suggest images to the child by which he can structure his daydreams and with them give better direction to his life.[10]

In stories, children meet all kinds of people. Although folktale characters tend to be one-dimensional (which makes it easier for young children to distinguish between good and evil and other opposites), what a variety of characters live in the tales—beauties and monsters, simpletons and wise folk, scoundrels and those without guile. What a wide range of human emotion—jealousy, love, hatred, contentment, greed, cunning, anger, compassion! When a young person asked P. L. Travers, "How can I learn to be a woman?," the creator of Mary Poppins replied, "Read Grimm's Fairy Tales! . . . For Grimm's—or any other collection of traditional tales or myths—is a mine of feminine lore. Every woman . . . can find there her prototype, a model for her role in life."[11] And every man, too.

Some parents worry about the violence in many folktales. In today's society even young children are exposed to violence on television or in real life. It may be of some comfort to know that psychologists believe the chants and rhythms in folktales contain the violence, enabling children to handle it. The words "Once upon a time . . . " also signal to the child that the story took place in a make-believe time and place, and that the child is safe within its confines.

Historically, storytelling has been used to educate as well as to entertain. Stories such as "Little Red Riding Hood" and "The Wolf and the Seven Little Kids" warned children to beware of strangers. "Little Eight John" and similar tales attempted to teach acceptable social behavior while other stories passed on the values of the culture. Meifang Zhang, a teacher of English at Shanxi University, Shanxi Province, China, and a former exchange scholar-researcher at the University of South Carolina in Columbia, observed that the ancient tales of her native land encouraged traditional Chinese values—respect for elders, obedience to parents, precedence of the group over the individual, and conformity to rules—whereas the new writers for children encourage individual initiative and performance.[12] As an example, Zhang cites "Who Will Be Our Future Monitor?" by Wang Anzi, in which an obedient girl is belittled and an aggressive boy is praised. The rationale for such stories is that modern China needs *bold* thinkers.

Storytelling is a way of keeping alive the cultural heritage of a people. It is akin to the folk dance and the folk song in preserving the traditions of a country for the foreign-born child and of building appreciation of another culture for the native-born child. Storytellers find that whenever they tell a story from the cultural background of their listeners, there is an immediate excitement.

In her book *Journey to the People*, Ann Nolan Clark wrote:

Children need to know children of other nationalities and races so that, inheriting an adult world, they find a free and joyous interchange of acceptance and respect among all peoples. . . . There is need for awareness that each group of people has its own special traditions and customs. There is need that respectful recognition be given these special traditions and customs. There is need for acceptance of these differences. There is tragic need for loving communion between children and children, children and adults, adults and adults—between group and group.[13]

Folklore is living proof of the kinship of human beings. Among various nations, similar stories are found, but they assume a variety of forms according to the culture in which they developed. Paul Bunyan is related to Ti-Jean. Over 300 years ago the French colonists brought the Ti-Jean stories to America; they soon became French-Canadian tales, and now they are part of the spoken tradition of the country. Glooscap was the hero-trickster of a great mythology shared by the Native Americans of Canada, Maine, and Massachusetts, and these stories show a likeness to both Norse and European folktales.

Research Update

There is much anecdotal information about the values of storytelling to children but scant "hard" research. A literature search of doctoral dissertations from January 1982 through March 1995 turned up 365 dissertations on storytelling, of which approximately 25 percent related to storytelling to children. Most of these came out of schools of education. Educational research has tended to focus on children's ability to recall and retell a story accurately. We need to back up our delightful anecdotal stories about children and storytelling with sound research, keeping in mind the principles set forth by Howard Rosen. Rosen calls much research on memory and comprehension of stories the "misguided work of 'scientific' ineptitudes" and proposes that researchers in this area follow four principles:

1. That it matters *which* stories we work with and that remembering and comprehending are especially related to the power of a story to engage with the world of feeling and thought in the listener;
2. That receiving a story is an exploration by the receiver(s), not a set of responses to someone else's questions in right/wrong format;
3. That we should ask *why* we should remember a story and not simply *what* we remember;
4. That the most constructive way of examining the hold a story has is for it to be presented in a propitious context and to be retold in an equally propitious one.[14]

During the past 20 years a great deal of research has been done on how children become literate and the relationship between listening and speaking, reading, and writing.[15] Research on the how and why of storybook reading development has focused on parent-child interactions or teacher-child interactions with storybook readings and the child's independent "readings." In a summary of her work with two- to five-year-olds, Elizabeth Sulzby writes, "The acquisition of literacy can be said to involve a transition from oral language to written language. First, early storybook reading by parents includes aspects of both oral and written language. Second, as children gain experience, storybook reading becomes more like conventional conceptualizations of written language. Third, children's earliest interactions with storybooks are mediated by an interactive adult and gradually become the performance of a text-as-monologue by the adult for the listening and observing child. Finally, storybook reading becomes a task which the child performs for another person or for himself/herself alone. As the child becomes a more independent 'reader' (long before s/he is reading conventionally from print), the language s/he produces for the storybook becomes more truly 'written language.'"[16]

Storybook readings introduce children to book language. Children learn the nature of the book and of print—what Don Holdaway calls "a literary set for learning to read."[17] They learn that in our culture a book is read from left to right and from top to bottom. They learn about "word-space-word" arrangement and punctuation. Most important, they learn that the squiggly marks on the page have meaning. At first, nonreading children "read" the pictures. Gradually, they learn that the words tell the story.

In an experimental study conducted in a kindergarten of the Haifa (Israel) School District, Arab children—who spoke in a local dialect (Ila'amiyah) that has no written form—were read to in literary Arabic during the last 15 to 20 minutes of each day over a period of five months while children in the control group were given a language development program on listening comprehension. Then the children in each group were individually tested on listening comprehension and a picture storytelling task. The children who had been read to performed better than those in the control group, not only in listening comprehension but in their knowledge of story structure (their stories were more cohesive, with a clear beginning, middle, and ending) and use of a richer vocabulary.[18] The results of this study have significance for teachers who work with children who are being introduced to literacy in a language they do not know, whether that language is of their own culture or of a different culture.

Research by McLean, Bryant, and Bradley suggests that sharing nursery rhymes with preschool children makes a difference in their learning to read by developing their sensitivity to the sounds of language, such as the alliteration in "Wee Willie Winkie" and "Goosey Goosey Gander."[19]

Past studies on the comparative effectiveness of storytelling presented in different media—the told story, the acted-out story, and the story presented on film—suggested that young children seem to remember the story best when some kind of interaction with the story takes place, such as in creative dramatics. When young children act out a story, they more easily identify with the characters in the story. Viewing a story on film seems least effective for recall of content. However, a more recent study by Laurene Brown found significant differences in *what* children took away with them from a story presented in two different media. Children ages 6, 7, 9, and 10 either watched *A Story, A Story* on a television monitor or heard it read aloud from the picture book. In retelling the story, the children who saw the television version used more active verbs. The book audience seemed more attentive to the sounds of language and retained more of the author's vocabulary in their retellings. For example, they called the characters by their book names, "Anansi" and "Osebo," whereas the viewers called them simply "man" and "the leopard." In interpreting the story, the book audience relied on the text and on personal knowledge and past experience.

Brown's study indicates that the oral medium helps develop language and the skills requisite to reading. The television medium, on the other hand, develops "visual literacy, skill at reading moving pictures, vividness of mental imagery and ability to remember picture information and to produce images themselves."[20] Many educators believe that television is destroying children's ability to imagine. Brown, an educational psychologist, disagrees, and takes a positive approach toward both media. Knowing the strengths and weaknesses of each medium in literacy development is valuable for librarians and teachers.

Giving Children Time to Read and to Reflect on Their Reading

In "Literacy and Literature," Charlotte S. Huck, author of *Children's Literature in the Elementary School* and a pioneer in bringing children's literature into the classroom, cites two studies of fifth graders. In the first study, the fifth graders were given 45 minutes to read each day and 15 minutes to share what they had read, in pairs or small groups of three or four. In the second study, another group of fifth graders averaged four minutes a day reading. Children in the first study read an average of 45 books each, with a range of 22 to 145 books. Huck does not say how many books the children in the second study read, but indicates the number was very low. She comments, "If we want children to become readers, we must give them real time to read, to become involved in books, and to have a chance to share books with their friends. If they are not reading outside school (and many are not), then we must reorder our priorities and give them time to read books of their own choosing inside school."[21]

Research suggests that children need opportunities to discuss the stories they have heard and to use what they have heard to construct their own meanings. Traditionally, librarians read a story straight through in order to maintain its literary integrity. Nursery school teachers, on the other hand, often interact with children during read-aloud sessions by asking questions and encouraging comments. When parents read aloud, they hold their children on their laps, focus attention on the book, and interrupt the reading to talk about what is happening. The parent's interruptions occur at places in the story where the child might not have the experience required to understand. The parent fills in, asks questions, or "scaffolds" the learning. The child's questions, quizzical looks, or misstatements show the adult what the child needs to know in order to understand the story. What we have learned from the research about the importance of interacting with the child has encouraged librarians to use more participation stories with younger children. Young children enjoy joining in the refrains, and it sharpens their listening and memory skills.

Children can be encouraged to use language by discussing stories, but there is a danger in the kind of questions asked. Chambers suggests open-ended questions, such as "Tell me about the parts you like most," "Tell me about the parts you didn't like," "Was there anything that puzzled you?" and "Did you notice anything in the story that made a pattern?"[22] During her school residences, storyteller Susan Danoff asks the children to describe the images ("pictures in your head") that they see as they listen to the story. Danoff also asks the children if they remember any special words, and how the story makes them feel. Such questions are much more appropriate than asking "Where was Cinderella when she lost her slipper?" and other questions of "fact." The ability to visualize, to make images, has been identified as an important strategy in reading comprehension. The child who can make mental images from the words on the page is better able to understand and remember what has been read. He is able to construct inferences and to make predictions. Olga Nelson found that after listening to a told story, fourth-grade students in three separate classrooms reported images that were "clear, vivid, varied, complex, multilayered, and interactive."[23] Nelson found that the images varied greatly from child to child. Visual images were reported most often, but the children also experienced auditory, olfactory, tactile, and gustatory images.

Activities That Extend the Storytelling Experience

The whole-language movement has made literature more central to the school curriculum, but one can still find an overuse of workbooks and nonrelated activities. An activity that deepens a child's appreciation of a story is appropriate, but too often activities are tacked on to provide a learning experience. To tell the story "The Blind Boy and the Loon" and then to have the children construct igloos of flour and salt or to talk about the coloration of the loon is not what the story is about. Having the children dramatize the story might be appropriate, however.

Many stories lend themselves to creative dramatics, and younger children especially enjoy this activity. You might have the children retell the story to a partner or in groups of three or four. Or you might invite the children to paint their favorite character or scene, or to express visually (that is, through art) how the story makes them feel. One of the most enthusiastic promoters of reading and storytelling is Caroline Feller Bauer. Her books (see Appendix) are a treasury of activities that help children make the story their own.

As a visiting storyteller, you may be asked by the teacher or staff person how to help the children build on the storytelling experience. Storyteller Doug Lipman suggests leaving a list of appropriate follow-up activities. For example, the teacher or staff person might tell or read aloud a variant of the tale, other stories from the same culture, or another story by the same author. Lipman recommends having older children and young adults analyze the story by focusing on one or more of the following elements: similarities, motifs, plots, themes. After this activity, the students might try to create a new story by keeping the plot but changing the setting and characters, or by keeping the theme and characters but changing the plot. Or the students might make up further adventures for one of the characters in the story.

Do not feel you must engage the children in some activity after a story. In their wonderful book *Stories in the Classroom*, Bob Barton and David Booth say, "Sometimes the children are making meaning from the collective hearing/reading of the story. They may call upon the experience later. There may be no need for external response at the moment. Reflective journals, putting the story into writing, remembering the story at a later date; all are modes of responding that help children build a story frame."[24]

Importance of Reading Aloud

According to *Becoming a Nation of Readers: The Report of the Commission on Reading*, one hour a day is devoted to reading instruction in the average classroom. Of that time, up to 70 percent is spent on worksheet-type activities that require only a perfunctory level of reading. The report concluded that the single most important activity for building the knowledge required for eventual success in reading is reading aloud to children.[25]

Children read to by a warm, caring adult associate reading with pleasure. In fact, parents and teachers have discovered that many children go through a stage in learning to read when they *refuse* to read themselves because they fear the reading aloud will stop!

Hearing stories read aloud gives children "a sense of story." If the stories are chosen from different genres (folktales, fiction, fantasy, biography, poetry, and nonfiction), children learn that each form of literature has its unique language, style, and structure. They learn patterns of language and develop an understanding of plot and characterization. This helps them with their own writing.

A former Rutgers student, Tina-Jill Gordon, explored the dynamic between teachers telling stories and the written narrative responses to these stories by children who are beginning writers. During the nine-week study, Gordon discovered that children "recall many details of the stories which they hear via storytelling" and that "telling oral literature stories to children inspires them to write about the stories, to imitate the stories, and to use the stories as a trigger for creating their own stories."[26] Well-known writers, such as Eudora Welty and Robert MacNeil, attest to the importance of hearing stories during their childhood. In her memoir, *One Writer's Beginnings,* Welty recalls: "Long before I wrote stories, I listened for stories. . . . Listening children know stories are there. . . . When their elders sit and begin, children are just waiting and hoping for one to come out, like a mouse from its hole."[27] MacNeil's mother read aloud to him often. Of *Winnie-the-Pooh* he wrote: "This was my first experience of being drawn into the spell cast by a storyteller whose words spin gossamer bonds that tie your heart and hopes to him. It was the discovery that words make another place, a place to escape to with your spirit alone. Every child entranced by reading stumbles on that blissful experience sooner or later."[28]

What Should Be Read Aloud?

Once you are hooked on *telling* stories, reading aloud may seem less satisfying, but reading aloud is a good way to introduce long stories that have complex sentence structure or more description than action, stories with wordplay that might slip past the children, literary fairy tales that must be word perfect (such as Sandburg's *Rootabaga Stories*), or that require more time to learn than you have time to give, or chapter stories. Read aloud from books that children might miss because the text is too difficult for them to read on their own at the time they are interested in the story. By reading a short selection or chapter, you may entice a few of the children into reading the entire book for themselves.

Choose a variety of story types. Younger children like stories about animals, humorous tales, and stories about children who are like themselves.

Older children like adventure stories, mysteries, and science fiction. Do not waste your time and the children's time by reading ordinary, dull, uninspiring, vocabulary-controlled stories. Read only what you enjoy, so that your enjoyment is transferred to the listeners.

The length of the material should be suitable to the maturity of the group. It is best to choose stories that can be read in one sitting if the children are young or if you find yourself with a different group of children each time you read, as often happens in a public library. Whole books can be read as serials, a chapter or two at a time. Myths, legends, hero tales, and tall tales lend themselves well to reading aloud. Poetry almost demands to be read aloud. Reading a poem aloud catches elements that may be missed when the poem is read silently.

A sampling of some favorite titles for reading aloud are listed in the Appendix. For further suggestions, see *Books Kids Will Sit Still For* and *More Books Kids Will Sit Still For* by Judy Freeman, *For Reading Out Loud! A Guide to Sharing Books with Children* by Margaret Mary Kimmel and Elizabeth Segel, and *The New Read-Aloud Handbook* and *Hey! Listen to This: Stories to Read Aloud* by Jim Trelease.

Is There an Art to Reading Aloud?

Reading aloud is an art and, like storytelling, requires careful selection and preparation. Read the material aloud by yourself to become aware of the rhythms and mood as well as the plot and characters. Know your material so well that you do not struggle over words and ideas and can look frequently at your listeners in order to involve them in the story.

Read in a natural voice but with expression and feeling. Vocal variety will keep your listeners interested. Strengthen your technical equipment—pleasant, flexible voice; clear enunciation; skillful pacing. The timing and the pause are as important in reading aloud as in storytelling. This is storytelling with the book. The reader appreciates, interprets, and calls attention to what the author has created with as much imaginative skill as possible. You might find it helpful to listen to authors reading from their own works (see "A Sampling of Storytelling Recordings" in the Appendix).

Is Storytelling More Important Than Reading Aloud?

Both storytelling and reading aloud are important to creating and sustaining children's interest in books and reading. Augusta Baker says that reading aloud does for a literate society what the telling of folktales does for a folk society. However, the teller, unhampered by the necessity of reading from a book, is able to communicate more fully with the listeners by using eye contact. And, as the great Irish *shanachie* Seumas MacManus wrote in the preface to his *Hibernian Nights*, "While the read story may possess the value of the story alone, the told story carries, superimposed on it, the golden worth of a good storyteller's captivating art and enhancing personality—trebling its wealth."[29] Reading aloud gives the potential storyteller a sense of security and confidence. Once you know you want to be a storyteller, close the book and begin! You will find the experience exhilarating!

NOTES

1. Gail E. Haley, Caldecott Award acceptance for *A Story, A Story* in *Newbery and Caldecott Medal Books: 1966–1975*, ed. Lee Kingman (Horn Book, 1975), p. 225.
2. Lewis Carroll, *Alice's Adventures in Wonderland & Through the Looking Glass.* Illus. by John Tenniel, 2 books, boxed set (Morrow, 1993).
3. Jean Little, "Invitations to Joy," a speech delivered at the Canadian Children's Book Centre, Annual Lecture #1, 1988.
4. Elizabeth Nesbitt, "Hold to That Which Is Good," *The Horn Book Magazine* 16 (January–February, 1940): 14.
5. Carl Sandburg, "How to Tell Corn Fairies When You See 'Em," in *Rootabaga Stories* (Harcourt, 1951), p. 210.
6. Julius Lester, "Why the Waves Have Whitecaps," in *The Knee-High Man and Other Tales* (Dial, 1972), p. 21.
7. Eleanor Farjeon, "Elsie Piddock Skips in Her Sleep," in *Martin Pippin in the Daisy Field* (Lippincott, 1937), p. 81.
8. Howard Gardner, *The Art and Human Development* (Wiley, 1973), p. 203.
9. Kornei Chukovsky, *From Two to Five*, trans. and ed. Miriam Morton (University of California Press, 1963), p. 138.
10. Bruno Bettelheim, *The Uses of Enchantment: The Meaning and Importance of Fairy Tales* (Knopf, 1976), p. 7.
11. P. L. Travers, "Grimm's Women," *New York Times Review*, November 16, 1975.
12. Meifang Zhang and W. Gale Breedlove, "The Changing Role of Imagination in Chinese Children's Books," *The Reading Teacher* 42 (February 1989): 406–412.
13. Ann Nolan Clark, *Journey to the People* (Viking, 1969), pp. 89, 27.
14. Howard Rosen, "The Importance of Story," *Language Arts* 63 (March 1986): 229.
15. Hillel Goelman, Antoinette Oberg, and Frank Smith, *Awakening to Literacy* (Heinemann, 1984); Don Holdaway, *The Foundations of Literacy* (Heinemann, 1979); Dorothy S. Strickland and Lesley Mandel Morrow, *Emerging Literacy: Young Children Learn to Read and Write* (International Reading Association, 1989); W. H. Teale and E. Sulzby, eds. *Emergent Literacy: Writing and Reading* (Ablex, 1986).

16. Elizabeth Sulzby, "Children's Emergent Reading of Favorite Storybooks: A Developmental Study," *Reading Research Quarterly* 20 (Summer 1985): 462.
17. Don Holdaway, *The Foundations of Literacy* (Heinemann, 1979).
18. Dorothy S. Strickland et al. "Storybook Reading: A Bridge to Literary Language," *The Reading Teacher* 44 (November 1990): 264–265.
19. M. MacLean, P. Bryant, and L. Bradley, "Rhymes, Nursery Rhymes, and Reading in Early Childhood," *Merrill-Palmer Quarterly* 33 (1987): 255–282.
20. Laurene Krasny Brown, "What Books Can Do That TV Can't and Vice Versa," *School Library Journal* (April 1986): 38–39.
21. Charlotte Huck, "Literacy and Literature," *Language Arts* 69 (November 1992): 523.
22. Aidan Chambers, *Booktalk* (The Bodley Head, 1985).
23. Olga Georgia Nelson, "Fourth-Grade Children's Responses to a Storytelling Event: Exploration of Children's Reported Images and Meaning Sources" (Kent State University, 1990).
24. Bob Barton and David Booth, *Stories in the Classroom: Storytelling, Reading Aloud and Roleplaying with Children* (Heinemann, 1990), p. 92.
25. R. C. Anderson, E. H. Hiebert, J. A. Scott, and I. A. G. Wilkinson, *Becoming a Nation of Readers: The Report of the Commission on Reading* (Center for the Study of Reading, 1985), pp. 74–75.
26. Tina-Jill Gordon, "Teachers Telling Stories: Seven-, Eight- and Nine-Year Old Children's Written Responses to Oral Narratives" (Ed.D. diss., Rutgers University, 1991).
27. Eudora Welty, *One Writer's Beginnings* (Harvard University Press, 1983), p. 4.
28. Robert MacNeil, *Wordstruck: A Memoir* (Viking, 1989), p. 17.
29. Seumas MacManus, "About Storytelling," in *Hibernian Nights* (Macmillan, 1963), p. vi.

Selection

Out of a rich reading background to select the story that exactly fits the day or the hour or the mood . . . that is to be a happy and successful storyteller. The ability to make the Story Hour a natural part of the life of a children's room, the experience that tells us how to group the children, how to protect them and ourselves from interruption, how to make the book that we tell the story from theirs as well as ours, how to recognize and direct the enthusiasm, the imagination and the faith that the story kindles—all these things become second nature after awhile. But the power to choose—that is very much harder to come by!
—Mary Gould Davis[1]

THE POWER TO CHOOSE involves knowledge of self, knowledge of storytelling literature, and knowledge of the group to whom one is telling.

Storytelling flows from a deep desire to share, the desire to be open about something that has touched one deeply. The choice of story and the manner in which it is told reveal one's inner self. Although the storyteller may be recreating a traditional tale, it is his or her experience of life that enters the telling and makes the story ring true. A soft-spoken, gentle young student chose to tell for her first story Grimm's "Fisherman and His Wife." Although she knew the plot perfectly, she was unable to hold the children's attention because she could not bring to her telling any understanding of the emotional makeup of the greedy wife. She made the wife's requests sound so reasonable that the dramatic conflict was lost and the children were bored. Some time later in the course, she told, successfully, Andersen's "Swineherd," a tale technically more difficult to learn and to tell. She was successful because her empathy with the emotions dealt with in the story gave color to her telling.

The storyteller must take the story from the printed page and blow the breath of life into it. This cannot be done unless the story has meaning for the one who is telling it, because children are quick to sense one's true feelings about a story. The storyteller, then, must enjoy the content, mood, or style and must have a desire to share this enjoyment. Frances Clarke Sayers, who recalled listening to the story "The Gingerbread Boy" as a child, remarked of the storyteller, "She told it as though she were relating a tale as great in magnitude as 'Hamlet,' as indeed it was for me, because it was for her. It was mystery, and tragedy, and delight."[2]

This knowing whether a story is right for you and your listeners is attained through trial and error—through the experience of telling and listening. But it also implies an enjoyment of storytelling literature and a wide knowledge of its background. A folktale is more likely to feel "right" if the storyteller has a thorough knowledge of the literature and the characteristics, customs, and ideals of the people or country from which the story has come. A literary fairy tale, on the other hand, requires that the storyteller empathize with the author. It is this genuine appreciation on the part of the storyteller that brings an intangible, personal quality to the telling of the story.

Finding stories one likes to tell may take more time than learning them. The storyteller reads constantly in search of new material. Rereading is important, too, because a story that may not appeal to the storyteller at first reading may appeal at another time.

There is a wide variety of literature to choose from: the great body of traditional literature (folktales, myths and legends, hero tales, fables, and drolls) and modern literature (such as the literary fairy tale, fantasy, fiction, and nonfiction, including biography). A long story can be broken down and told serially, or a single incident from a book may be selected for telling.

Poetry can be woven into the fabric of the story hour—offering fresh insights on the central theme, sharpening the senses—or it can stand on its own. It is made to be shared and not taught. The blending of poetry and folktales or fairy tales is a natural marriage, for both develop a child's imagination. Their combination in a single story hour can change the pace, create a mood, or add variety to the program. A poem can crystallize the meaning of a story or extend the story by reminding the listeners of a character or event in the tale. However, include a poem only if you truly like it, for false interest, dislike, and discomfort are all readily apparent to children.

Subject matter and concept must be considered in choosing poems, for these are the qualities that can place a poem beyond the comprehension and understanding of a child. On the other hand, many poems written for adults are appropriate to use in story hours for older boys and girls. As in the selection of stories, one must read widely in the area of poetry in order to make wise and appropriate selections.

There are poetry collections and poems for all ages, from Mother Goose to the Robin Hood ballads, from which to make a choice. Poems that have story content, strong rhythm, and descriptive language lend themselves well to the story hour. Quiet, gentle poems can set the mood for a special program. A nonsense poem sets the stage for a humorous story. Haiku is especially appropriate to the story hour, and its 17-syllable verse is often just right for a break between stories.

What Makes a Story Tellable?

A good story for telling is one that has something to say and that says it in the best possible way. It is a story that has vision as well as integrity and that gives a child something to hold. There should be sound values—compassion, humor, love of beauty, resourcefulness, kindliness, courage, kinship with nature, zest for living—but they should be implicit in the story, because a good story teaches without preaching.

Some of the characteristics of a good story are:

1. A single theme, clearly defined
2. A well-developed plot

   A brief opening introduces the main characters, sets the scene, arouses pleasurable anticipation, and then, almost immediately, the story plunges into action.

   Action unfolds through word pictures, maintains suspense, and quickly builds to a climax. Each incident must be related in such a way that it makes a vivid and clear-cut image in the listener's mind. One event must lead logically and without interruption to the next. There should be no explanations or descriptions except where they are necessary for clearness. Avoid stories with flashbacks, subplots, or long, descriptive passages that interfere with the flow of the story. The essential movement of the story must depend on events, not on attitudes.

   The ending resolves the conflict, releases the tension, and leaves the listener feeling satisfied.
3. Style

   Look for vivid word pictures, pleasing sounds, rhythm.
4. Characterization

   The characters are believable, or, in the case of traditional folktales, they represent qualities such as goodness, evil, beauty.
5. Faithfulness to source material

   Beware of the emaciated adaptation and the vocabulary-controlled tale.
6. Dramatic appeal

   Children need and enjoy a perfectly safe edge of fear and sadness. Marie Shedlock called storytelling "drama in miniature." She believed in satisfying the dramatic instincts of the child so that no child need say, as did one little girl, "It was no good; no one was killed. There were no lions, no tigers, no nothing at all."

7. Appropriateness for the listener
   A story's appeal depends on a child's age and interests. Restlessness often results from a poor choice. This criterion is developed at greater length in the pages that follow.

The youngest listeners, children from birth to age three, like Mother Goose rhymes, simple folk songs, lullabies, and lilting poetry. They enjoy stories with interesting sound patterns, such as *Goodnight Moon* by Margaret Wise Brown, and books that invite participation, such as *It Looked Like Spilt Milk* by Charles Shaw. Toy books and movable books fascinate toddlers. There are many titles to choose from today. In addition to familiar stories about the little dog Spot, try *Go Away, Big Green Monster!* by Ed Emberley, and *The Very Hungry Caterpillar* by Eric Carle. Children from three to five years old respond to rhythm and repetition; simple, direct plots in which familiarity is mixed with surprise; short dialogue; clear and simple images; action that quickly builds to a climax; and a satisfying ending. Young children blend fantasy with reality. In such a story as "The Three Bears," for instance, the chair and the bowl of porridge are familiar to children. Having them belong to the bears adds mystery and adventure to the story, but the situation is simple, and there are enough everyday events in it so that the children are not confused. They accept the unreal because it is close enough to the real world they know. The rhythm in stories for young children comes primarily from the repetition of words and phrases in a set pattern. Such phrases as "Not by the hair of my chinny-chin-chin," "Then I'll huff and I'll puff and I'll blow your house in," and similar repetition in "The Three Billy Goats Gruff," "The Gingerbread Man," and "The Old Woman and Her Pig" elicit a delighted response. Young children also enjoy stories like "The Bed," in which the sounds of animals are introduced. They like stories in which children like themselves have adventures, such as *Alfie Gets in First*, by Shirley Hughes, and *The Snowy Day*, by Ezra Jack Keats.

The six-, seven-, and eight-year-olds have a peak interest in traditional folktales and fairy tales, such as "One-Eye, Two-Eyes and Three-Eyes," "Cinderella," and "Mother Holle." F. André Favat found a close correspondence between the child's psychological characteristics at this stage in development and the characteristics of the folktale (i.e., egocentrism, and a belief in magic, animism, and retributive justice).[3] Through the story content children work through their inner fantasies and come to terms with the "real" world. Listening to these tales, they *are* Jack the Giant Killer or Molly Whuppie. The art form of the folktale also is very satisfying. In his introduction to *The Complete Grimm's Fairy Tales*, Padraic Colum discusses the patterns and rhymes in the folktales that make them so memorable. In "Rapunzel," for example, "the maiden has long hair and the witch confines her in a tower, and we do not know whether the tower makes it proper she should have long hair, or whether her long hair makes the tower part of the story." Good storytellers make the patterns evident. Mediocre storytellers "confuse the pattern by putting incidents in the wrong place, by using unfitting metaphors, by making a hurried beginning or a hurried end, by being unable to use the chiming words that made special, or, as we would say now, that featured some passage: 'puddle' with 'path,' 'tooth' with 'lose,' for example."[4]

The 9- to 11-year-olds enjoy the more sophisticated folktales, such as "Clever Manka" and "Wicked John and the Devil." They like trickster tales, and such tales appear all over the world. The stories about Anansi the spider and Waikama the rabbit from West Africa are the forerunners of the West Indian Anansi tales and the American Brer Rabbit stories. Raven and Coyote are Native American tricksters. In his introduction to *More Tales of Uncle Remus*, Julius Lester wrote, "Trickster's function is to keep Order from taking itself too seriously."[5] Perhaps that explains the special appeal of these stories for this age-group.

Children in the middle grades also seem to have an affinity for scary ghost stories—the grosser the better! This interest continues right into the teen years. "Mr. Fox," "Mary Culhane and the Dead Man," and any of the tales in Alvin Schwartz's Scary Stories series are sure to hold your listeners spellbound.

Children over nine are looking for something that will appeal to their developing powers of reason and judgment and to their concern about competency. George Shannon's popular Stories to Solve books, Nina Jaffe and Steve Zeitlin's *While Standing on One Foot: Puzzle Stories and Wisdom Tales from the Jewish Tradition*, and many of the African tales, such as "The Fire on the Mountain," present a challenge. Many of the African tales are of interest at this age because they all do not end "And they lived happily ever after"; these tales correspond more closely to the older child's growing understanding of the consequences of one's actions.

Take, for example, a tale from the Congo, perhaps best known in its picture-book edition, *The Magic Tree*, illustrated by Gerald McDermott. Storyteller Laura Simms recorded it under the title "Magoolie" for Weston Woods on *Stories: Old as the World, Fresh as the Rain*. It is the story of twin brothers. Their mother loves the strong, handsome twin and rejects the scrawny, weak twin. When the rejected son reaches manhood, he leaves home and, unwittingly, frees a people imprisoned in a magic tree. The people's queen, after making Magoolie handsome and rich, takes him for her husband. Magoolie (Mavungu in the picture-book edition) is happy for awhile, but after some time he desires to visit his mother and brother. Unable to dissuade him, his wife warns him not to reveal the source of his beauty and wealth. On the first visit, Magoolie heeds his wife's words, but on his second visit his tongue is loosened by too much beer and he reveals the secret. As he speaks, his fine clothes turn to rags and his face becomes ugly. Though he searches, he cannot find his wife and people. The storyteller asks, "Why did he betray those who loved him? Why did he trust those who did not care?" In the typical western European tale, at the moment of Magoolie's greatest despair, a helper would have appeared in the guise of an old crone or an animal and shown Magoolie how to find his way back to his wife and happiness. The African tale, however, leaves the young person with much to ponder.

Older children also enjoy the hero tales, myths, and legends. This is the time to introduce the retellings of the *Odyssey* by Padraic Colum and the legends of Robin Hood and King Arthur, as retold by Howard Pyle. The exaggerated humor of the tall tale is appreciated. Stories about Davy Crockett, Paul Bunyan, Pecos Bill, and John Henry should be told as if they were the "gospel truth."

Slightly older children, the 11- to 13- year-olds, are experiencing sexual awakening and are involved in a search for personal identity. The romantic stories of Eleanor Farjeon, the bittersweet fairy tales of Laurence Housman, the more elaborate tales from the *Arabian Nights*, the modern fairy tales of Jane Yolen, and the sly humor of Natalie Babbitt's stories about the Devil are enjoyed by these young people, who are ready to appreciate the plot, the beauty of language, and the deeper meanings that lie behind the words. The subtlety of African tales such as "The Woodcutter of Gura" is lost on children in the younger age groups, but they are fine choices for young-adult and adult audiences. *A Treasury of African Folklore* by Harold Courlander is an excellent sourcebook. Its subtitle describes the range of material that is included in this book: "the oral literature—myths, legends, epics, tales, recollections, wisdom, sayings, and humor of Africa." It is a must for the storyteller's shelf.

Stories of coming-of-age, such as those found in Joseph Bruchac's *Flying with the Eagle, Racing the Great Bear* and *The Girl Who Married the Moon*, by Joseph Bruchac and Gayle Ross, speak to young people about courage and responsibility.

What Kinds of Stories Are Needed in a Storyteller's Repertoire?

A storyteller must be flexible, as it is often necessary to change a program at the last minute. The makeup of the group may not be what the storyteller expected, or the time allotted for the program may have to be shortened or expanded. In building a repertoire, new tellers will want to include story types: action stories, romances, hero tales, "why" or *pourquoi* stories, humorous stories, short "encore" stories, and stories that appeal to a wide age-range.

Though storytellers will need to have different types of stories in their repertoires for different occasions, they often find that they feel more comfortable with certain kinds of stories than with others. Stories from one's own ethnic or cultural background are usually a happy choice for the beginning storyteller.

The novice would do well to turn to folktales, stories that have been passed down through word of mouth and polished over centuries of telling. These traditional tales have the essentials of a good short story: terseness, simplicity, and vigor. They begin simply, come to the point, and end swiftly and conclusively. They are full of action, and the action is carried forward by the main characters. There are no unnecessary words, but only the right ones, to convey the beauty, the mood, the atmosphere of the tale.

These stories come from the folk—workers, peasants, just plain people. They are as old as the human race. Though they were told primarily to amuse, they also contain the key to the ideas, customs, and beliefs of earlier peoples, for life then was told in a tale, not explained in a philosophy. Thus the folktale is enhanced by simplicity and directness—and this is the way it should be.

The qualities and atmosphere of the country in which folktales originate and the differences that natural environment and racial character make in the development of imaginative literature can be seen in a comparison of two excerpts from folktales:

> Across the wide sea-ocean, on the further side of high mountains, beyond thick forests, in a village that faced the sky, there once lived an old peasant who had three sons.
>
> From "The Little Humpbacked Horse," in
> Post Wheeler's *Russian Wonder Tales.*[6]

At once we are in Russia, that land of vast distances. What a different mood this scene evokes:

> Ol-Ambu followed a path that led to the grassland. Where the forest ended and the plains spread out before him, he stopped. He looked over the sea of brown grass with acacia trees and thornbushes scattered over it. And his eyes fell upon the largest giraffe he had ever seen.
>
> From "Ol-Ambu and He-of-the-Long-
> Sleeping-Place," in Verna Aardema's *Tales for
> the Third Ear: From Equatorial Africa.*[7]

Likewise, the storyteller can convey to children the kinship of peoples by telling variants of well-loved tales, such as "Cinderella" ("Yeh-Shen," "Vasilisa the Beautiful," "The Rough-Face Girl") and "Rumpelstiltskin" ("Tom Tit Tot," "Whuppety Stourie," "The White Hen").

The storyteller of some experience, or the beginning storyteller who has an affinity for certain authors, will also tell literary fairy tales. The literary fairy tale is a consciously created work of art by a known author. It bears the stamp of individuality that immediately sets it apart from others. Hans Christian Andersen, Eleanor Farjeon, Laurence Housman, Carl Sandburg, Oscar Wilde, and contemporary writers Natalie Babbitt, Isaac Bashevis Singer, Barbara Picard, and Jane Yolen are among those who have distinguished themselves in this genre.

The modern fairy tale does not invariably end happily; often it leaves one thoughtful and sad. Told sensitively, reflecting the writer's own attitudes, many of the literary stories are vivid, accurate commentaries on society and the individuals who struggle within it. Characters in these modern imaginative stories are individuals with distinct personalities, as opposed to the stock characters we meet in the folktale.

Literary fairy tales tend to be longer and more descriptive than folktales. The words are filled with the beauty of sound, for the writer of the literary fairy tale is a word stylist. If the order of the words is altered, the beauty may be lost.

Some literary fairy tales are almost like folktales. Their writers base their styles on folklore and do it so successfully that their stories may have as universal appeal as the folktales themselves. Howard Pyle was a writer who used the manner of the folktale. His collection *The Wonder Clock* is built on what folklorists call the framing story. His preface begins, "I put on my dream-cap one day and stepped into Wonderland." The whole of this preface, with its power to set the stage and to convey atmosphere, should be told before each of the stories. Then let the old clock strike and tell the story that you have selected.

Howard Pyle used the rhythm of folklore and its repetition. For example, in "The Swan Maiden," the king's son mounts the wild swan and then:

On flew the swan, and on and on, until, by and by, she said: "What do you see, king's son?"

"I see the grey sky above me and the dark earth below me, but nothing else," said he.

After that they flew on and on again, until, at last, the Swan Maiden said, "What do you see now, king's son?"

"I see the grey sky above me and the dark earth below me, but nothing else," said he.

So once more they flew on until the Swan Maiden said, for the third time, "And what do you see by now, king's son?"

But this time the prince said, "I see the grey sky above me and the dark earth below me, and over yonder is a glass hill, and on the hill is a house that shines like fire."

"That is where the witch with the three eyes lives," said the Swan Maiden.

From "The Swan Maiden," in Howard Pyle's
The Wonder Clock.[8]

In *Tales Told Again*, Walter de la Mare has taken 19 familiar folktales and touched them subtly with his genius. An English countryside seems the perfect setting for his humorous elaboration of the old fable in which the hedgehog beats the quick-footed but slow-witted hare; the hedgehog has his wife (who looks exactly like him) wait at one end of the field while he remains at the other. Every time the hare arrives at either end of the field, he sees the hedgehog, or so he thinks, and hears his laughing taunt, "Ahah! So here you are again! At last!" Errol Le Cain's handsome picture-book edition of de la Mare's retelling of "Molly Whuppie" is a fine introduction to this writer for younger listeners.

What Kinds of Stories Appeal to Groups in Which There Is a Wide Age Range?

Stories that can be enjoyed on different levels are good choices for the story-hour group composed of mixed ages. Younger children enjoy the plot and action, whereas older children enjoy the subtleties of humor and the interplay among characters. Younger children, hearing the story "Two of Everything" from *The Treasure of Li-Po,* by Alice Ritchie, marvel at the pot that can make two of anything the old couple puts into it, whereas older children—and adults—are amused by the couple's plight when another wife steps out of the pot! In Harold Courlander's "Uncle Bouqui Rents a Horse," young children find the mental image of two large families and livestock loaded on the horse great fun. Older children appreciate the outwitting of Uncle Bouqui. In presenting these stories, the storyteller should emphasize the aspects of the story that will appeal most to a particular group of listeners.

Where Can a Storyteller Find Stories That Have Known Appeal to Children?

There are many lists of stories. Two of the most helpful to the neophyte are *Stories: A List of Stories to Tell and to Read Aloud*, published by the New York Public Library, and *Stories to Tell to Children: A Selected List*, published by the Carnegie Library of Pittsburgh.

Stories is an annotated list, arranged alphabetically by story title. The annotations evoke the flavor of the stories. The list also includes bibliographies of background reading for the storyteller, poetry and stories for reading aloud, and recordings of stories. It is indexed by types of stories, such as "Clever and Heroic Women," "Action and Participation Stories," "Christmas," and others.

Stories to Tell to Children is arranged by age level and by types of stories. Suitability of material for radio and television is noted. Variants of the tales are given for many of the entries. No annotations are given.

Each of these lists is based on a program of regular story hours held over a period of more than 85 years. They represent the children's choices. Storytellers will want to have copies of both lists on their personal bookshelves.

Collections compiled by storytellers with extensive experience are also an excellent source for beginning storytellers (see Appendix).

Storytellers are very much aware of the differences between written and spoken language. Some recently published collections, such as those by Margaret Read MacDonald (see Appendix) and *Ready-To-Tell Tales*, edited by David Holt and Bill Mooney, offer stories in a form closer to oral speech. These collections are helpful to the beginning storyteller, but there is a danger, too. It is the danger of oversimplification. Every storyteller must make a story his or her own. Each person has a distinct pattern of speaking, a distinct rhythm, and each person will interpret characters and events in a story differently. If you slavishly "copy" the reteller's version, the story will not be *yours*. Use these retellings as models, but, whenever possible, go to the sources given in the text, and analyze what the reteller has done. This is part of becoming a storyteller.

How Does a Storyteller Develop Critical Ability?

The storyteller is someone who appreciates literature as a whole and knows good language, form, and substance. Critical ability is developed by reading widely and by constantly comparing recommended versions included on storytelling lists with newly published material. Careful attention should be given to the notes in collections by reputable compilers, such as Joseph Jacobs, Harold Courlander, and Richard Chase, and by reputable translators, such as Erik Haugaard and Elizabeth Shub.

Critical listening is developed by reading aloud various versions of the same story and selecting the one that sounds best. Listening to recordings made by fine storytellers (see Appendix) gives one a sense of good pacing and the importance of word tone.

How Does a Storyteller Recognize the Best Version or Translation of a Story?

Every year dozens of new translations or new retellings of the old tales come into our hands. We need to test them first in the light of our own personal knowledge of storytelling literature, based on continual study and reading, and then consider their vitality and their holding power with children.

The folktales we share with children are polished retellings of "raw" folklore. They are not only less violent, they are more homogenized. However, the versions we choose must catch the flavor of the people from which the tales come and must give a feeling for what those people value. The language should flow in the cadence of the original tongue.

The West Indian tales are a mixture of Carib and Arawak Indian, African, and European cultures. These stories are lively, dramatic, witty, and humorous. Philip Sherlock, author–editor of three collections of these tales, has modified the local pattern of speech without losing the rhythm and color of the islands. The Brer Rabbit stories, as told by Joel Chandler Harris, suffer from author-created dialect, while those from Julius Lester's *The Knee-High Man and Other Tales* and *The Tales of Uncle Remus* series, William J. Faulkner's *The Days When the Animals Talked*, and *The People Could Fly*, by Virginia Hamilton, are good examples of tellable tales from the rich tradition of American black folk literature. *Bo Rabbit Smart for True* is retold by Priscilla Jaquith in the poetic, lilting language of Gullah.

Look for collections in which the compiler gives the sources of the stories and adds explanatory notes about the background of the tales. Look too, whenever possible, for collections that explain the context of storytelling in the culture from which the stories come, such as *The Magic Orange Tree and Other Haitian Folktales*, by Diane Wolkstein. Since the publications of the second edition of *Storytelling: Art and Technique*, Libraries Unlimited has begun publication of its World Folklore Series. This series includes background information, photos of the people and the country, and notes about the stories and the tellers. Such information adds a subtle richness to the telling.

In selecting epics or hero tales, storytellers must be thoroughly familiar with different versions. Often they will have to make their own arrangement of the material, weaving together episodes from the various stories told about the hero, whether Robin Hood, King Arthur, or Cuchulain, that have come down by way of tradition.

Myths should reflect the people from which they originated. Compare Penelope Proddow's translation of *Demeter and Persephone* with Nathaniel Hawthorne's version in his *Tanglewood Tales*. Hawthorne embroiders the tale and diminishes the gods. Proddow retains the story's classic beauty.

Language should be beautiful, colorful, and descriptive. Compare the following excerpts from two versions of "The Golden Goose":

> There was once a man who had three sons, the youngest of whom was called the Simpleton. He was laughed at and despised and neglected on all occasions. Now it happened one day that the eldest son wanted to go into the forest, to hew wood, and his Mother gave him a beautiful cake and a bottle of wine to take with him, so that he might not suffer from hunger or thirst. When he came to the wood he met a little old grey man, who, bidding him good-day, said: "Give me a small piece of the cake in your wallet, and let me drink a mouthful of your wine; I am so hungry and thirsty." But the clever son answered: "If I were to give you my cake and my wine, I

should have none for myself, so be off with you," and he left the little man standing there and walked away. Hardly had he begun to cut down a tree, when his axe slipped and cut his arm, so that he had to go home at once and have the wound bound up. This was the work of the little grey man.

From L. Leslie Brooke's The Golden Goose Book.[9]

There was once a man who had three sons, the youngest of whom was called Dummling.

One day, the eldest son decided to go into the forest to cut some wood. Before he started his mother packed a lunch for him so that he might not suffer from hunger or thirst.

In the wood at midday, he stopped work and sat down to eat. Just then, a little old man appeared before him and said, "May I have a crust of bread and some milk? I am so hungry and thirsty."

But the young man said, "If I do, I shan't have enough for myself. Be off with you!"

He left the little man standing there and went on his way. But he had not been long at work, chopping down a tree, before he cut himself and had to go home to have it bandaged.

Now this was no accident. It was brought about by the little man, who had magic powers, and had decided that anyone as selfish as this fellow should be punished.

From "The Golden Goose," in Favorite Fairy Tales to Read Aloud.[10]

The second version has had a stamp of approval put upon it by a "distinguished panel" of experts that includes two educators and one librarian. But how much of the color and beauty of style will be lost to the child who hears this version rather than the other!

Another pitfall to avoid is the vocabulary-controlled book. Consider Hans Christian Andersen's "Ugly Duckling":

It was so beautiful out in the country. It was summer. The oats were still green, but the wheat was turning yellow. Down in the meadow the grass had been cut and made into haystacks; and there the storks walked on their long red legs talking Egyptian, because that was the language they had been taught by their mothers. The fields were enclosed by woods, and hidden among them were little lakes and pools. Yes, it certainly was lovely out there in the country!

The old castle, with its deep moat surrounding it, lay bathed in sunshine. Between the heavy walls and the edge of the moat there was a narrow strip of land covered by a whole forest of burdock plants. Their leaves were large and some of the stalks were so tall that a child could stand upright under them and imagine that he was in the middle of the wild and lonesome woods. Here a duck had built her nest. While she sat waiting for the eggs to hatch, she felt a little sorry for herself because it was taking so long and hardly anybody came to visit her. The other ducks preferred swimming in the moat to sitting under a dock leaf and gossiping.

Finally the eggs began to crack. "Peep . . . Peep," they said one after another. The egg yolks had become alive and were sticking out their heads.

"Quack . . . Quack . . . " said their mother. "Look around you." And the ducklings did; they glanced at the green world about them, and that was what their mother wanted them to do, for green was good for their eyes.

From "The Ugly Duckling," in *Hans Christian Andersen: The Complete Fairy Tales & Stories*, trans. by Eric Christian Haugaard.[11]

Now read the same part of the story from a Read-It-Myself book:

Once upon a time there was a mother duck. The mother duck had some eggs. "Quack, quack," said Mother Duck. "I must sit on my eggs. I must sit on my eggs a long time. One day the eggs will crack. Then little ducklings will jump out of the eggs."

So Mother Duck sat and sat. She sat on the eggs a long time. Then one egg began to crack. "Crack, crack" went the egg. "Crack, crack, crack." A little duckling jumped out.

"Jump, jump," went the duckling.

Mother Duck was so happy. "Quack, quack," said Mother Duck. "Quack, quack, quack." "Peep, peep," said the duckling. Soon another egg began to crack.

From Hans Christian Andersen's *The Ugly Duckling*, adapted by Frances K. Pavel.[12]

The story continues in this vein until all the eggs are hatched.

Yes, the child can easily read the second version, but as Clifton Fadiman has said, "What the child-mind measurers call a feeling of mastery is often only a feeling of boredom."[13] A simple but graceful retelling of Andersen's story for children to read on their own is *The Ugly Duckling*, retold by Lilian Moore.

The storyteller rejects the versions with undistinguished language and uses the ones with smooth, rhythmic style and language that add to the musical flow of the story.

What Is Fractured Storytelling?

Fractured stories are modernized renditions of traditional tales. They are often witty or bizarre. The tale may be told from the viewpoint of another character in the story; for instance, *The True Story of the Three Little Pigs by A. Wolf, as Told to Jon Scieszka*. The story may be reversed as in *The Three Little Wolves and the Big Bad Pig* by Eugene Trivizas, or the tale may be placed in a modern setting with characters speaking contemporary slang. Fractured tellings, such as those found in *The Stinky Cheese Man and*

Other Fairly Stupid Tales by Jon Scieszka and *Roald Dahl's Revolting Rhymes*, are fun to share with older listeners who are familiar with the traditional versions. Younger listeners need to hear the traditional versions. They are part of every child's literary heritage.

What Should I Do When Parents or Teachers Object to My Telling Stories with Witches, Ghosts, and Devils in Them?

The adults' objections usually come from a misunderstanding of the nature of folktales. Most folktale characters are symbols. The princess is usually a symbol of beauty, the witch a symbol of evil, but the meaning of the symbol varies from culture to culture. For example, in western European folktales, the dragon is a dangerous creature who devours human beings and must be slain, while to the Chinese the dragon is a symbol of good fortune. Try to "educate" the adults gently and calmly; be considerate of their feelings and beliefs.

Keep your listeners in mind when you choose your stories. If you choose your stories from a variety of cultures, your older listeners will begin to understand (subconsciously, at least) that folktale characters are symbols. This won't take away the magic, but it can get them thinking about cultural differences.

Is It All Right for a Storyteller from One Ethnic or Racial Group to Tell a Tale from Another Group?

This question is asked in almost every workshop. The best answer I've ever heard is the one given by Julius Lester in his foreword to *The Tales of Uncle Remus: The Adventures of Brer Rabbit*:

The most important element in telling these tales, or any folktale, is, do you love the tale? After all, what is a tale except a means of expressing love for this experience we call being human. If you love the tale, and tell it with love, the tale will communicate. If the language you speak is different from the language I speak, tell the tale in your language. Tell the tale as you would, not I, and believe in the tale. It will communicate its riches and its wonders, regardless of who you are. Trust the tale. Trust your love for the tale. That is all any good storyteller can do.[14]

NOTES

1. Mary Gould Davis, "The Art of Storytelling," paper delivered at a meeting of the American Library Assn., Washington, D.C., 15 May 1929.
2. Frances Clarke Sayers, *Summoned by Books: Essays and Speeches* (Viking, 1965), p. 96.

3. F. André Favat, *Child and Tale: The Origins of Interest* (National Council of Teachers of English, 1977).

4. Padraic Colum, "Introduction," in *The Complete Grimm's Fairy Tales* (Pantheon, 1944), p. ix.

5. Julius Lester, "Introduction," in *More Tales of Uncle Remus* (Dial, 1988), p. xiii.

6. Post Wheeler, "The Little Humpbacked Horse," in Wheeler, *Russian Wonder Tales* (Beechhurst, 1946), p. 67.

7. Verna Aardema, "Ol-Ambu and He-of-the-Long-Sleeping Place," in Aardema, *Tales for the Third Ear: From Equatorial Africa* (Dutton, 1969), pp. 59–60.

8. Howard Pyle, "The Swan Maiden," in Pyle, *The Wonder Clock* (Harper, 1887, 1915), pp. 232–233.

9. L. Leslie Brooke, *The Golden Goose Book* (Warne, 1905), unpaged.

10. "The Golden Goose," in *Favorite Fairy Tales to Read Aloud* (Grosset, 1958), pp. 5–6.

11. Hans Christian Andersen, *Hans Christian Andersen: The Complete Fairy Tales & Stories*, trans. by Eric Christian Haugaard, foreword by Virginia Haviland (Doubleday, 1974), p. 216.

12. Hans Christian Andersen, *The Ugly Duckling*, adapted by Frances K. Pavel (Holt, 1961), pp. 1–4.

13. Clifton Fadiman, "Holiday Handbook of Children's Reading," *Holiday* 30 (November 1961): 148.

14. Julius Lester, "Foreword," in *The Tales of Uncle Remus* (Dial, 1987), p. xxi.

Preparation

I think stories must be acquired by long contemplation, by bringing the imagination to work, constantly, intelligently upon them.
  —Ruth Sawyer[1]

STORYTELLING IS AN ART and, like all arts, it requires training and experience. However, anyone who is willing to take the time to find the right story and learn it well, and who has a sincere desire to share enjoyment of the story, can be a successful storyteller. A good part of our daily conversation is composed of stories, incidents, and anecdotes, for we are all storytellers a few steps removed from professional storytellers. Our language is somewhat less formalized, but we are still sharing our experiences and emotions.

Basic Approaches to Learning a Story

Storytelling is an individual art and each storyteller must discover his or her own best method of learning a story. However, there seem to be two basic approaches: the visual and the auditory. In the visual approach, the storyteller sees the story in a series of pictures, much like the frames of a filmstrip. In learning the story of "The Woman Who Flummoxed the Fairies," for example, the storyteller might see the following pictures:

1. the woman baking cakes and pastries for a wedding or a christening
2. the fairies longing for a bit of her cake and plotting to steal her away to be their baker
3. the woman baking cakes in the castle kitchen for the great wedding
4. the fairies hiding in flower cups and under leaves along the woman's path home
5. the fairies flying out at the woman and letting fern seeds drift into her eyes to make her sleepy
6. the woman asleep on the fairy mound
7. the woman waking up in fairyland and pretending to be happy and willing to bake a cake for the fairies

8. the woman asking the fairies to fetch things from her kitchen so that she can bake a cake for them
9. the fairies fetching the eggs, sugar, flour, butter, bowl, wooden spoons, and egg whisk, till they are tired out
10. the woman asking first for her cat, then for her dog, her babe, and finally her husband
11. the woman beating the cake batter, the baby screaming, the cat purring, the dog snoring, and the husband looking bewildered
12. complete bedlam—the woman giving the baby the spoon to bang with, the husband pinching the dog and treading on the tail of the cat
13. the fairies exhausted by the noise
14. the woman asking for an oven
15. the fairies letting her and her family go home after she promises to leave the cake by the fairy mound for the fairies
16. the woman and her family at home and content
17. the woman leaving the cake behind the fairy mound and finding the little brown bag of gold pieces the fairies left for her
18. the woman baking a cake every week for the fairies and receiving a bag of gold pieces in return
19. everyone living happily ever after[2]

The visual approach works well in learning a folktale because language is subordinate to action in this type of story. In the auditory approach, the storyteller is conscious of the sound of words and their arrangement. A break in the rhythm is a warning that the telling is off track. Those who use this approach often tape-record the story before learning it. Playing back the tape in relaxed moments or while doing undemanding chores facilitates the learning process. A word of caution may be in order for the neophyte. Be sure that you want to be a storyteller *before* you tape; the tape will bring out every imperfection of your voice and timing. Do not be discouraged. If the story you have chosen to learn has been recorded by a professional storyteller, you may prefer to listen to that recording until you have gained confidence in yourself. There are many outstanding recordings of stories available (See Appendix). However, some new storytellers find it distracting, in the early stages of learning, to listen to someone else telling a story because the beginner has a tendency to copy the recorded teller's pacing and inflections.

The beginning storyteller who has a great deal of self-confidence may wish to videotape the story. The videotape captures facial mannerisms and gestures as well as imperfections of voice and timing. It is a harsh learning tool but a very helpful one, provided you do not let it rob you of the pleasure of sharing the story. Videotaping is probably more helpful to the experienced storyteller who wants to perfect style and technique.

This is an appropriate place to mention mechanical devices, other than tape recorders, that storytellers may find helpful. Some storytellers claim that typing a story makes a "carbon copy" of it on the mind. Others find that outlining the story impresses it on the mind and the outline serves as a quick memory refresher when the story is told at a later date.

Cue cards may be used. As you read, whenever you come across a story you enjoy and want to learn, fill out a 4-by-6-inch index card with the following information: title, author, source, running time, characters, scenes, synopsis, and any rhymes or characteristic phrases you wish to memorize (Figure 9).

Choreographing, that is, marking the story to indicate voice inflections, pace, and timing, is another technique. Storyteller Carol Birch com-

Title:	"The Frog Prince"
Author:	Brothers Grimm
Source:	*Tales from Grimm*, trans. and illus. by Wanda Gág (Coward, 1936)
Running time:	8 minutes (determined by reading the story aloud)
Characters:	Princess, Frog Prince, King
Scenes:	Well under the linden tree Dinner table at the palace—repeated Bedroom of the Princess—repeated
Synopsis:	When the Princess loses her golden ball in the well, the frog rescues it on condition that the Princess will allow him to eat from her golden plate and sleep in her own little bed. The Princess is forced to keep her promise. On the third morning the spell is broken, and the frog changes into a handsome young Prince. When the Princess and the Prince grow up, they marry and live happily ever after.
Rhymes:	"Youngest Daughter of the King Open the door for me Mind your words at the old well spring Open the door for me."
Audience: 6–8-year-olds	

FIGURE 9. *Sample cue card.*

mented in the second edition of *Storytelling: Art and Technique,* "When first learning a story, I am very formal about modulation. I search for the best way to create the effect I want. In this way I shape a story from the beginning, noting places to pause, lines that come quickly, words that need emphasis, places to raise or lower my voice. This is like a musician working with phrasing and tempos, for a story changes with each telling, as music changes with each performance." (See example from Laurence Housman's "The Wooing of the Maze,"[3] Figure 10.)

Birch no longer feels the need to work on stories in this way, but her intent was to make the narrative sections more compelling. She writes, "Although storytellers generally color what characters say, they often speak narrative sections in a colorless way in an attempt to keep from distorting the author's voice or the omniscient narrator's voice. But it is the storyteller's voice that makes the telling 'distinctive.'"[4] Birch discusses the storyteller's voice in her essay "Who Says?" in *Across the Great Divide of Orality to Print in the Continuum of Storytelling.*

That same day/the Princess, sitting upon her throne and having crown and scepter in her hands, caused the gardener to be called into her presence. The courtiers thought it was very strange *(GRAND)* that the Princess should have a thing of such importance to make known to a *haughty* gardener *(like sucking on a lemon)* that it was necessary for her to receive him with crown and throne and scepter, as if it were an affair of state. *(gossipy, quick)*

To the gardener, when he stood before her, she said, "Gardener, it is my wish that there should be fashioned *(sly)* for me a very great maze, so intricate and deceitful that no man who has not the secret of it shall be able to penetrate therein. *(soften)* Inmost is to be/a little tower/and foun-) *(wistful, see each detail)* tains/and borders of *sweet*-smelling flowers and herbs. But the man who fashions this maze and has its secret *(unsure, halting)* must remain in it forever lest he should betray his knowledge to others. So it is my will that (you) should devise *(breathless)* such a maze for my delight and be yourself the prisoner *(hopeful)* of your own craft when it is accomplished.") *intense, she is prisoner to her heart – he has the key*

FIGURE 10. *Choreographed portion of "The Wooing of the Maze," in* The Rat-Catcher's Daughter: A Collection of Stories by Laurence Housman, *selected by Ellin Greene. Choreographed by Carol Birch.*

Basic Steps in Learning a Story

Allow time each day over a period of at least two to three weeks to make a new story your own. Live with your story until the characters and the setting become as real to you as people and places you know. Know it so well that it can be told as if it were a personal reminiscence.

Read the story from beginning to end several times. Read it for pleasure first. Then read it over with concentration. Analyze the story to determine where the appeal lies, what the art form is, what word pictures you want your listeners to see, what mood you wish to create. Before learning a story, Gudrun Thorne-Thomsen would ask herself, "What is it about the story that I want to share with children? Is it the humor? The rhythmic language? The sense of wonder? Beauty? What is its essential quality?" Whatever the particular quality and appeal of the story, the storyteller must respond to it, sense it, feel it intimately before giving it out again.

Read the story aloud and time it. Time it again when you begin to tell it. Some variation in time of reading and telling is to be expected, but if the telling takes much less time than the reading, it may indicate that parts were omitted or that you are speaking too quickly. If it takes much longer, you may have added to the tale or you may be speaking too slowly.

Learn the story as a whole rather than in fragments. Master the structure of the story. Perceive the story line. The story line consists of the beginning, which sets the stage and introduces the characters and conflict; the body, in which the conflict builds up to the climax; and the resolution of the conflict. Do not alter the essential story line. Note how the action starts, how it accelerates, how and where the transitions occur. Note sequences of names and events. Know absolutely what the successive steps are in the course of action. Test yourself by closing the book and making a list of these steps in proper order.

Master the style of the story. To retain the original flavor and vigor, memorize rhymes or characteristic phrases that recur throughout the story, such as these two:

Be bold, be bold, but not too bold,
Lest that your heart's blood should run cold.

> From "Mr. Fox," in Joseph Jacobs's *English Fairy Tales*.[5]

Now with cold grows faint her breath,
Fire will conquer frosted death.

> From "The Magic Ball," in Charles J. Finger's *Tales from Silver Lands*.[6]

Observe the sentence structure, phrases, and unusual words and expressions. The beginning and ending are important. You may want to memorize them. "Crick crack," says the storyteller on the Caribbean island of Martinique, and the children reply, "Break my back." "Once there was and twice there wasn't, when genies played polo in the old Turkish bath, when the camel was a salesman and the flea a barber . . ." is one traditional way of beginning a Turkish tale. "He was then married to the king's daughter, and the wedding lasted nine days, nine hours, nine minutes, nine half minutes and nine quarter minutes, and they lived happy and well from that day to this" is a characteristic Irish ending.

Make the story your own. Become familiar with the characters and the scenes. Build in your imagination the setting of your story. What are the main characters like—are they clever, kind, greedy, timid, mischievous? How are they dressed? How do they speak—in vernacular, short sentences, pompously? Visualize the happenings. Reproduce these happenings as though you were seeing and experiencing them. Imagine sounds, tastes, scents, colors. Only when you see the story vividly yourself can you make your audience see it. Eulalie Steinmetz Ross advised:

> Bring to the telling of the story any experience, any memory, any knowledge from life that will give breadth and depth to its interpretation. Hear the Sleeping Beauty Waltz as the French fairy tale weaves its spell of enchantment. See the Chicago skyline as the background for Carl Sandburg's "Two Skyscrapers Who Decided to Have a Child." Remember the lines of Robert Frost's poem, "Stopping by Woods . . ." as you tell Mary Wilkins' "The Silver Hen." Train yourself to see, and you unconsciously give your audience time to see also. The pace of the story will come to fit the action and the scene. You must give the story depth and conviction, setting and atmosphere, before you can make it live for your audience.[7]

Miming the actions, characters, and emotions develops a kinesthetic sense of the story that enhances the telling. Exaggerate your gestures and movements. When you tell to an audience you will not exaggerate, but through the process of exaggeration you will have freed your body.

Timing is the dramatic part of storytelling. Each story has its own pace; for example, "Sleeping Beauty" is slow and stately, "The Gingerbread Man" is sprightly, "Robin Hood" is strong and firm. Good timing makes the difference between the neophyte and the accomplished storyteller. Herein lies the value of listening to recordings by notable storytellers.

The following are few suggestions about timing:

1. Pause before any change of idea, before any significant word.
2. Emphasize words that carry meaning.
3. In general, take poetic and imaginative passages slowly; take rapidly the parts narrating action.

4. Build toward the climax. Change pace as you near it so that your listeners may know the pleasure of anticipation. Some climaxes are made more impressive by a gradual slowing down, others are highlighted by speeding up the rate of telling. Knowing whether to slow down or speed up comes with experience and sensitivity.

5. Conversation should be taken at a speed that is appropriate for the character speaking. Beginning storytellers often are afraid of using pauses, but when they are handled well, pauses can add drama and meaning, and they do not suggest nervousness or hesitancy.

6. Remember that the pause and a dropped voice can be more effective than the shout.

Practice telling the story aloud—to yourself, your pet, your family and friends, to anyone who will listen! Any hesitation reveals weak areas in your knowledge of the story. Practice wherever and whenever you can—while waiting in the doctor's or dentist's office, while traveling on public transportation, while doing undemanding chores. Ignore the stares of strangers, friends, family! Practice, practice, practice. As a final aid, just before going to sleep at night, read the story as printed in the book, slowly and aloud.

Practice in front of a mirror to catch distracting mannerisms. Gestures should be natural to the story and to the storyteller. The art of storytelling should not be confused with the art of acting. The storyteller interprets and expresses the ideas, moods, and emotions of the story, but never identifies with any character. The storyteller is not an actor but the medium through which the story is passed. There should be no studied gestures, no gimmicks, no tricks of changing voices to suit each character in the story. These only tend to detract from the story. Storytelling is a folk art and does not lend itself to the grand gestures of the stage.

Tone of voice should relate to what is going on in the story. The storyteller develops a sensitivity to words. Feel the appropriate emotion when you sound words, so that the word "dull," for example, has a dullness about it. Train your ear to hear rhythmic phrases. Chant the skipping-rope rhyme in "Elsie Piddock Skips in Her Sleep" as if in time to a jump rope.

Breathing and Relaxation Exercises

How you use your breath is important. Place your voice somewhere near the middle of the chest rather than in the head or upper chest. Breathing from the upper chest or head will give you a lighter, weaker tone; breathing from the abdomen will give you rich, full tones, connoting strength and vigor. Instead of assuming different voices for different characters, suggest characters by the amount of breath used. For example, instead of using a high-pitched, squeaky voice for the wee little bear in "The Story of the Three Bears," use a lighter breath. However, once you have differentiated the characters in any way you must be consistent throughout the story.

"Life is in the breath; therefore he who only half breathes, half lives" is a yogic proverb storytellers should heed. The person who breathes deeply has more life, is more "alive." Yogic breathing exercises relax the body and bring vitality. Here are directions for the "Complete Breath":

1. Sit in a cross-legged posture. Slowly exhale through the nose. Simultaneously contract the abdomen as far as possible to help empty all air from the lungs.
2. Slowly inhale through the nose. Simultaneously attempt to push out the abdominal area. This movement permits air being inhaled to enter the lower area of the lungs.
3. Continue the slow, quiet inhalation. Simultaneously contract the abdomen slightly and attempt to expand the chest as far as possible.
4. Continue the slow, quiet inhalation. Simultaneously raise the shoulders slowly as high as possible. This permits air to enter the high area of the lungs.
5. Hold breath with shoulders raised for a count of five.
6. Slowly and quietly exhale deeply, relaxing shoulders and chest as you exhale and contract abdomen.
7. When exhalation is completed, repeat.

There are many exercises besides yoga to relax the body (see Figure 11). Choose one that relaxes you. For example, rotate head on shoulders; relax throat by yawning; swing arms, then legs; rotate ankles. Here are two longer exercises that students find very relaxing:

1. Stand tall; raise your arms over your head; stretch high; tense every muscle. Think of yourself as a puppet on a taut string. Then, one by one, let your hands flop, bend your elbows, bring bent arms to your sides, bend forward from your waist, and hang limp with relaxed knees. Let your arms and hands dangle. Slowly come to an upright position. Repeat.
2. Lie on your back. Close your eyes and breathe slowly. Think of yourself as a rag doll filled with sawdust. Imagine that the sawdust is slowly seeping out of you, from toes to head. Let your whole body go limp. Remain in this position for five to ten minutes.

Speech Exercises

To overcome lazy habits of articulation, it is necessary to exercise the speech organs in much the same way that we exercise for muscular coordination in athletics or instrumental music. Regina Brown, an actress and

Movement Warm-Ups for Storytellers

Whether you need to calm down, loosen-up or energize before a performance, a few movement warmups can do the trick. Gentle yet invigorating exercise can release pre-performance tension, get you breathing properly (which is important for voice support), loosen your muscles so your body language will match naturally with your verbal portrayal of the story, and give you a nice refreshed positive attitude. Sounds great? Sounds impossible? It is great! It's not impossible! You can do it without dance training in five minutes time.

Here are a few gentle, natural exercises suited to a storyteller's pre-performance needs. These exercises are designed to be done standing without messing up your clothing. All the exercises are meant to make you feel good. If anything hurts, don't do it! With the stretching exercises don't bounce. Throughout all the exercises, breath in through your nose and out through your mouth. Once you know the sequence, it will only take you five minutes.

1. YAWN STRETCH
Standing up, yawn and stretch with as many parts of your body as you can (your back, neck, legs, arms, etc.) Open your mouth wide as you yawn. Think of stretching luxuriously on a lazy morning in bed. Do this several times.

2. ALIGNMENT
Stand with your feet parallel to one another, your weight balanced between your toes and heels, your feet directly under your pelvis; not wider, not narrower than your own body width. Gently tuck your buttocks under and draw you abdomen up and in. Imagine an eye hook in the top of your head that is attached to a cord that extends to the ceiling. Let the cord lengthen your whole spine, but keep your shoulders down and relaxed and your feet grounded on the floor. Try to feel long, yet relaxed. This position leaves plenty of room for your lungs and diaphragm, which support your voice. It also presents a positive self-image.

3. BREATH
Still standing aligned, take at least two full breaths in through your nose and out through your mouth. Close your eyes. Relax on each exhale. Breathe from your diaphragm. This means that the breath movement takes place in the abdomen, not the chest.

4. NECK
a) Chin Down: On your next exhale, let your chin come down toward your chest, but still keep the rest of your body upright and aligned. Stay in this position for two exhales. B) Neck swings: Leaving chin close to chest, move in gentle neck swings from right to left. Exhale each time you swing right. Do six repeats. c) Over Shoulder: Slowly lift head back to upright and look over your right shoulder. Stay for two exhales. Look over your left shoulder. Stay for two exhales. d) Side to Side: In a smooth slow manner, switch from looking over your left shoulder to looking over your right shoulder. Exhale as you look to right. Inhale as you return to the left. Repeat six times.

5. BACK STRETCH
a) Clasp hands behind your back and raise your arms as high as you can. Your should blades will push close together. Hold this position for two exhales. Unclasp hands. B) Clasp hands over your head. With straight arms, bring them as far behind your head as you can. They won't go very far. Hold for two exhales. Unclasp hands.

6. SIDE STRETCH
Reach right arm over your head toward the left. This stretches your right side. Hold for two exhales. Now, stretch your left arm over your head toward the right side. Hold for two exhales. This stretches the left side. Remember not to bounce.

7. SHAKE-OUT
Start by shaking your arms in a loose and jiggly manner. Then add other body parts. Add the shaking of your shoulders, add the shaking of your back and buttocks, add the shaking of your legs by shifting your weight from side to side.

Keep shaking loosely until you are shaking your whole body. Shake until your muscles feel slightly warm. Stop and stand aligned. Relax.

8. TOE PRESS WALK
Standing aligned, roll onto the ball of your right foot, bending your right knee slightly. Switch and roll onto the ball of your left foot. Keep switching right, left, right, left, similar to walking in place but always keeping your toes on the floor. Pick up the rhythm of your natural walking speed. Let your arms swing freely as if you were outside enjoying a country walk. Smile and think a positive thought about yourself.

9. ALIGNMENT
Align yourself as described in exercise #2. Close your eyes and relax on each exhale. Exhale twice. Open your eyes and really look around and see your space fully. Exhale and nod your head in affirmation that you are ready.

You can do voice warm-ups either before or after the movement warm-ups. It's up to your preference. I prefer to do my voice warm-ups after the movement exercises, then I go back and do exercise #8, the shake-out, one more time just before I go before my audience.

Try experimenting with the exercises. Adapt them in ways that suit your body best. Always remember to breathe when you exercise. Take time to make sure your body is in alignment.

You might like to try doing movement warm-ups everyday, even if you are not going to be performing. They are a great way to start the day. Or end it, if you want to wash away the tensions of a bad day.

Remember that your posture and body movement are physically connected to your breath and voice. Your body posture and movements affect people's interpretation of what you are saying. Body posture and movement affect your own self image and your mental attitude. Body, mind and spirit tell the story. Prepare your whole self for storytelling.

FIGURE 11. *Movement warm-ups for storytellers. Permission to copy given by Linda Marchisio.*

former staff member of the New York Public Library, worked for many summers as a storyteller in the parks and playgrounds. She suggests these exercises:

Tongue Exercises
1. Stick out tongue toward nose and try to touch nose; point tongue.
2. Stick out tongue toward chin and touch chin; point tongue.
3. Stick out tongue from right side of mouth; point tongue.
4. Stick out tongue from left side of mouth; point tongue.
5. Rotate tongue—encircle lips first to right, then to left.
6. Trill tongue.
7. Repeat "Around the rugged rock the ragged rascal ran" three times.

Lip Exercises
1. Pout, relax; pout, relax
2. Spread lips and say $\bar{e}$.
3. Round lips and say $\overline{oo}$.

Jaw Exercises
1. Move jaw from side to side.
2. Move jaw up and down.
3. Rotate jaw first to left, then to right, then open and close mouth slowly.

Take time to learn your stories. Marie Shedlock advised her students to learn no more than seven stories a year. She herself learned only three stories a year, but they were learned to perfection. Even if you only learn three stories a year, in ten years you'll know 30 stories. A repertoire of 30 stories of different types will serve you well. Don't be afraid to repeat your stories. Children enjoy hearing them again and again. Tell them at library story hours, to school classes, and during visits to youth organizations.

Learning a Folktale

1. Learn the folktale as a whole, using the visual approach (described earlier in this chapter). Do not memorize word for word.
2. Follow the steps described in the section "Basic Steps in Learning a Story" (earlier in this chapter).

The art of telling a folktale was, perhaps, best expressed by Mary Gould Davis in these words:

It needs no technique to tell a folk story. What it really needs is a knowl-edge of literature, a thorough enjoyment of the tale, and a picture in either the mental or the physical eye of the country that the tale comes from. The greatest enemy to the successful telling of a folktale is self-consciousness. There is no self behind a folk story—there is only a slow, natural, almost inevitable growth. If we put self into it we take away from its simplicity, its frankness, its almost ruthless reality. It should be our first care to select the editor or translator who has had the courage and the wisdom to let the story reflect not his own scholarship or his power as a writer, but the country from which it comes. Every bit of knowledge that we, as storytellers, have about that country helps us.[8]

Learning a Literary Fairy Tale

The literary fairy tales are more difficult to tell, and take longer to prepare because their beauty and vitality lie in their wording, which must be retained as nearly as possible. The storyteller is interpreting a piece of creative writing. Each word and its placement in the sentence have special value and importance in relation to the story as a whole. These stories must be memorized, but the storyteller must know them so well that the artificiality and mechanization of the memorization process are overcome. The storyteller reads and rereads the story until the memorization of it becomes an unconscious one and not one of rote learning.

Reading other stories by the same author will help the storyteller discover the rhythm of the author and will reinforce perception of his or her style. Authors have a very personal way of speaking. When we hear "O Best Beloved" we immediately think of Rudyard Kipling. We recognize Laurence Housman's voice in such passages as:

> Now anyone can see that a man who practiced so cunning a roguery was greedy beyond the intentions of Providence. . . . The gnome laughed to himself to see how the trapper was being trapped in his own avarice. . . . And now the rat-catcher was the richest man in the world: all his traps were made of gold, and when he went rat-hunting he rode in a gilded coach drawn by twelve hundred of the finest rats. This was for an advertisement of the business. He now caught rats for the fun of it and the show of it, but also to get money by it; for, though he was so rich, ratting and money-grubbing had become a second nature to him; unless he were at one or the other, he could not be happy.
>
> From "The Rat-Catcher's Daughter," in *The Rat-Catcher's Daughter: A Collection of Stories by Laurence Housman* selected by Ellin Greene.[9]

About the literary fairy tale, Mary Gould Davis wrote:

This type of story has always seemed to me very much dependent upon personality. If it does not kindle in us a responsive spark, if we do not feel that between the writer and us there is a peculiar understanding, then—no matter how carefully we learn it, how faithfully we tell it—it remains a dead thing. But when that spark is kindled, as instinctively, as unconsciously as the musician strikes the right note, we reproduce the style, the "power with words" of the author. We know, for instance, that it is a kind of betrayal to begin the story of "The Elephant's Child" with "Once Upon a Time." We may interest and please the children with the adventures of the young elephant and the crocodile; but, if we use that old traditional folk beginning, we know that we have struck the wrong key—we have left something out. And if we search ourselves thoroughly enough, we will find that the thing we have left out is no more and no less than Mr. Kipling! There is only one way in which to begin the story of "The Elephant's Child" and that is the way Kipling begins it—"In the High and Far Off Times, O Best Beloved. . . ." The quality in us that makes it possible for us to tell a stylist story successfully is closely akin to the quality that lets us read poetry successfully. A sense of rhythm and a sense of words—they go hand in hand. They are sister to the art of music and the art of dancing. They are the necessary part, I think, to the art of storytelling.[10]

Knowing and enjoying other stories by the same author bring an intangible quality to the telling. Give yourself time to get to know your author. Know in October that you want to tell an Andersen story in April. Steep yourself in Andersen as you learn your story.

Memorize the literary fairy tale, then forget it has been learned word for word and tell it naturally rather than in a recitative manner. It is far better to read such stories aloud than to spoil them with inept telling.

Should a Storyteller Who Does Not Like a Story or Who Is Offended by Parts of a Story Adapt It?

The best thing to do, if you dislike a story or find parts of it offensive, is to choose another story. It will be easier to learn as well as to tell. An adaptation by an inexperienced teller often changes or distorts the meaning of the story. This is unfair to the story and to the listeners. Should we let a little bird warn the Gingerbread Boy so he can run home to safety, or should we have the Fox eat him? We know the version the children prefer.

A young librarian was constantly asked by the neighborhood children in a branch of the New York Public Library to read Wanda Gág's *Millions of Cats*. One day she was ill and another librarian took her place in the reading-aloud area. The children asked her to read their favorite. When the librarian reached the part in the story where the cats fight and scratch so that only one poor little cat is left, the children all shouted, "No! That isn't the way the story goes." Questioning revealed that the first storyteller had permitted the cats to argue a bit and then run away and hide under bushes, leaving the forlorn little cat alone. When questioned, she stated that she changed that part of the story because she did not approve of violence in a children's book. The librarian was advised to select stories thereafter of which she approved, for storytellers must believe in and enjoy the stories they select for telling.

In his book *Once Upon a Time: On the Nature of Fairy Tales*, Max Lüthi discusses the internal consistency in the folktale and the importance of keeping that consistency. For example, the cruel punishment of the step-sisters in the Grimm version of "Cinderella" (pigeons peck out their eyes) is consistent with their self-inflicted wounds (cutting off part of their heel or toe in order that their foot will fit the slipper), whereas the haughty but less cruel step-sisters in Perrault's version are not only forgiven, but are married off to rich lords and invited to live at the palace. When story-tellers retell a tale, they need to be aware of this need for balance.

How Does a Storyteller Cut a Story?

Occasionally a storyteller may wish to shorten a story because it is too long for the time allowed, or the form is not best for dramatic effect, or the action is slowed down by long descriptive passages. Cutting a story requires knowledge of storytelling literature and knowledge of children's reactions to hearing stories. Such knowledge comes with experience. The experienced storyteller knows what to leave out. The beginning story-teller has a tendency to cut out all description and atmosphere and to reduce the story to a mere outline. An experienced storyteller cautions, "Don't have the characters acting on an empty stage." Select a good version of a story and stick with it. Such versions can be found in recommended lists or in collections compiled by storytellers. The storyteller who has gained a sense of security will know when a small alteration in some phrase would make for smoothness, a descriptive passage might be shortened, a section might be summarized, or superfluous details and unnecessary complications of plot (two or more threads of narrative) deleted.

How Does a Storyteller Amplify a Short Story?

The storyteller needs to flesh out the scenes and characters of a "bare-bones" story, using imagination to create vivid word pictures. In retelling the Haitian folktale "Uncle Bouqui Rents a Horse," Harold Courlander made the telling more interesting to the children by enumerating the people on the horse rather than simply stating, "And they were all on the horse."

The experienced storyteller is able to combine different versions of a story successfully. In doing so, it is wise to write out the story and learn the rewritten version. As in cutting a story, the storyteller must keep the story whole, presenting a single point of view and developing the events in logical sequence.

A good example is Ashley Bryan's *The Cat's Purr,* based on an old West Indian folktale, "Why Cats Eat Rats." Bryan deemphasized why cats eat rats and created a plausible origin of the cat's purr. The original folktale and its source are printed at the end of Bryan's book.

Should a Storyteller Use His or Her Own Words or the Author's Words?

Use the author's words if they are better than yours. Increase your own vocabulary. How many synonyms can you find for "beautiful," for "brave"? In telling stories in our own words, we often reuse the same words, especially adjectives. Be careful not to intersperse the story with "uh," "and now," and other speech mannerisms we can catch if we listen to ourselves. Respect the spare quality of such stories as those found in Joseph Jacobs's *English Fairy Tales,* and do not embellish them with your own additional words. Avoid slang when telling a traditional tale.

Are our colloquialisms appropriate to the story? The storyteller's own words should never change the meaning, the rhythm, or the cadence of a story. In telling Sandburg's "The Huckabuck Family and How They Raised Pop Corn in Nebraska and Quit and Came Back," a new storyteller changed "squash" to "pumpkin" because she thought that the children might not know "squash" pie, but that "everyone knows pumpkin pie." This showed her insensitivity to the sound of words. She didn't realize that Sandburg, the poet, had achieved a rhythm with "squash." This is made obvious by reading the following passage out loud, as written, and then reading it substituting the word "pumpkin" for "squash."

> And this was the year Pony Pony was going to bake her first squash pie all by herself. In one corner of the corn crib, all covered over with pop corn, she had a secret, a big round squash, a fat yellow squash, a rich squash all spotted with spots of gold.
>
> From "The Huckabuck Family and How They Raised Pop Corn in Nebraska and Quit and Came Back," in Carl Sandburg's *Rootabaga Stories.*[11]

"Squash" and "pumpkin" have an entirely different feeling—this is a sensual thing. Children do not grow linguistically or intellectually if we constantly revise downward.

What Should a Storyteller Do About Foreign Words?

For correct pronunciation refer to a dictionary or to a resource person, such as the language specialist, on your staff.

Should a Storyteller Use Dialects?

The *Random House Dictionary of the English Language* (2nd ed., unabridged, 1987) defines dialect as: "1. a variety of a language that is distinguished from other varieties of the same language by features of phonology, grammar, and vocabulary, and by its use by a group of speakers who are set off from others geographically or socially. 2. a provincial, rural, or socially distinct variety of a language that differs from the standard language, esp. when considered as substandard." Vernacular is a speech pattern that is the native language of a place or the plain variety of speech in everyday use by ordinary people. Regional vernacular is acceptable, while dialect used to indicate social or racial inferiority is offensive and misleading.

Syncopation of speech, with its rhythmical stress, is part of a storyteller's interpretation. In *God's Trombones*, James Weldon Johnson said, "He [the black poet] needs to find a form that will express the racial spirit by symbols from within rather than by symbols from without—such as the mere mutilation of English spelling and pronunciation."[12] Today such writers as Lucille Clifton, Virginia Hamilton, Julius Lester, and John Steptoe have achieved a form that is larger than dialect, that flows freely, and expresses the imagery, the idioms, the humor and pathos, the unique turns of thought often found in the black person's speech. This pattern is called black English, which speech specialists claim has different rules from standard English. The difference is in the phonology or sound systems. The rules of pronunciation vary. "Going" is standard English; "gonna" is the soft slur often found in black English; "gwine" is the offensive, author-created dialect.

The heavy Irish dialect in the out-of-print editions of Seumas MacManus was translated by MacManus himself when he wrote *Hibernian Nights*. He retained the flavor of the original tales by the use of imagery, musical narrative, humor, and colloquialisms in dialogue.

Few storytellers are able to use dialect to good advantage. Ruth Sawyer told Irish stories superbly because she had been imbued with the richness of the Irish tongue from early childhood by an Irish nurse. But even this great storyteller did not sound natural when she assumed a German dialect to tell a German folktale. Much practice is required to capture dialect and to use it in a relaxed and comfortable manner. It is better in most cases, therefore, to avoid dialect and, instead, retain the rich expressions, the cadence, the flavor, and the inflection of the particular speech patterns.

Regional vernacular is not only acceptable but often necessary in storytelling. For example, in telling the story "Wicked John and the Devil," from Richard Chase's *Grandfather Tales*, the storyteller must refer to "sweet milk" rather than "milk," because the former places the story geographically. As a matter of fact, the author of this story once pointed out to his audience that in Appalachia the person asking for milk rather than "sweet milk" might be served buttermilk!

After Working on a Story for Some Time, How Does a Storyteller Overcome Boredom?

There seems to be a point in the learning process when a plateau is reached and all effort is drudgery. Accept this and let the story go for a few days or a week, then return to it. Recall the emotions the story originally aroused in you. When you tell the story to children and you see the wonder in their faces or the laughter in their eyes you will feel that all the time spent on learning it was worthwhile.

What Are the Qualities of a Good Storyteller?

The early storytellers had qualities that are just as important today. One must have a keen enjoyment of one's material and a burning desire to share one's enthusiasm with others. Elizabeth Nesbitt, a storyteller long associated with the Carnegie Library of Pittsburgh, said:

> Storytelling, like anything else, cannot achieve its rightful best unless it is done with understanding, integrity, and acceptance of the fact that it requires thought, care, time, and knowledge in selection and preparation, and recognition of the necessity for a special kind of artistry in the telling. The art of storytelling is a spontaneous, unsophisticated art. [13]

It holds, therefore, that storytelling is an individual art, and that each storyteller will bring a special kind of appreciation, imagination, and interpretation to the telling. Extensive reading and building of background are necessary, for the storyteller must think of the story as a part of the whole literature to which it belongs, and of the storyteller as the medium through which the story comes to life.

All creative artists share the same qualities—enthusiasm, spontaneity, imagination, perception, insight. A good storyteller is also a vital human being who finds joy in living, and who can reach the heart and mind of a child. Taste and appreciation grow as the storyteller is exposed to art, to music, and to dance; the entire range of feelings, intellect, and spirit comes alive. Good storytellers, like good wine, age well. The words of the story may not change, but what the storyteller brings to the story changes with the experience of living. The author will never forget standing at the back of the auditorium of Donnell Library Center, New York Public Library (there were no seats left for staff in the standing-room-only crowd) the evening that Ruth Sawyer, age 78, put aside the microphone and held her audience spellbound with her deep, rich voice and consummate telling.

Children demand the best, and they walk away from anything less. Good storytelling presupposes a willingness to work hard. In "Storytelling—A Folk Art," a chapter in *The Way of the Storyteller*, Ruth Sawyer says that she has no basic recipe for good storytelling. The most important requirement for her is the right approach and the recognition that storytelling is a folk art. She does, however, list certain invariables—experience, building of background, creative imagination, and a gift for selection.

Marie Shedlock had these qualities, as have other great storytellers. Ruth Sawyer was inspired by Shedlock and remembers:

The qualities that Miss Shedlock brought to her art, and of which she gave so abundantly to all who listened, have remained for us the high mark of perfect storytelling. Voice and the spoken word were the medium for the art, and she used them with that same care and appreciation with which a painter uses line, color, and perspective. She had a wonderful voice, perfectly pitched, flexible. She never droned. Her sense of timing was always right: she knew the value of a pause. Her power to build expectation as the story grew combined both the traditional art and that of the conscious and trained artist. She belonged to those stories she told as the traditional storyteller belonged to those which had been handed down to him, an enduring legacy. Everyone who remembers her telling of the fairy tales of Hans Christian Andersen knows how deeply rooted was this kinship. [14]

NOTES

1. Ruth Sawyer, *The Way of the Storyteller* (Viking, 1942), p. 142.
2. Sorche Nic Leodhas, "The Woman Who Flummoxed the Fairies," in Leodhas, *Heather and Broom: Tales of the Scottish Highlands* (Holt, 1960), pp. 35–43.
3. Laurence Housman, "The Wooing of the Maze," in *The Rat-Catcher's Daughter: A Collection of Stories by Laurence Housman,* selected by Ellin Greene (Atheneum, 1974), p. 59.
4. Carol Birch, personal correspondence with the author.
5. Joseph Jacobs, "Mr. Fox," in Jacobs, *English Fairy Tales* (Dover, 1898), p. 154.
6. Charles J. Finger, "The Magic Ball," in Finger, *Tales from Silver Lands* (Doubleday, 1924), p. 45.
7. Eulalie Steinmetz Ross, in a manuscript in the files of the Office of Children's Services, New York Public Library. Appears in slightly altered

form in *The Lost Half-Hour: A Collection of Stories,* ed. Eulalie Steinmetz Ross (Harcourt, 1963).

8. Mary Gould Davis, "The Art of Storytelling," paper delivered at a meeting of the American Library Assn., Washington, D.C., 15 May 1929.

9. Laurence Housman, "The Rat-Catcher's Daughter," in *The Rat-Catcher's Daughter: A Collection of Stories by Laurence Housman,* pp. 3, 5, 6–7.

10. Davis, "The Art of Storytelling."

11. Carl Sandburg, "The Huckabuck Family and How They Raised Pop Corn in Nebraska and Quit and Came Back," in Sandburg, *Rootabaga Stories* (Harcourt, 1951), pp. 170, 173.

12. James Weldon Johnson, *God's Trombones* (Viking, 1927), p. 8.

13. Elizabeth Nesbitt, "The Art of Storytelling," *Catholic Library World* 34 (November 1962): 143–145.

14. Ruth Sawyer, "Storytelling: Fifty Years a-Growing," in *Reading Without Boundaries,* ed. Frances Lander Spain (New York Public Library, 1956), p. 61.

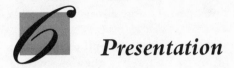

Presentation

*Let the story tell itself, and if it is a good story and you have prepared it well,
you do not need all the extras—the costumes, the histrionics, the high drama.
Children of all ages do want to hear stories. Select well, prepare well, and then
go forth, stand tall, and just tell.*
—*Augusta Baker* [1]

A SMALL BOY SAT between two adults at the village soda fountain. He had
just been collected from his first library story hour, and a celebration was
in order. The storyteller sat three stools away, unrecognizable in winter
scarf and hood. The curious adults were trying in vain to pry some statement of reaction to the story hour from the boy, a most reluctant
informer, until at last one of them complained with some asperity, "You
could at least tell us how the teacher told the stories? Did she read them
from a book? Did she tell them from memory?" "Oh, mother," he
explained with a long sigh, "she just told them from herself." [2]

No storyteller ever received higher praise, for the ultimate goal is to tell
a story so simply and directly that it appears to be told "from yourself." All
the emphasis should be placed upon the story rather than upon the storyteller, who is, for the time being, simply a vehicle through which the
beauty and wisdom and humor of the story come to the listener.

Telling the Story

Before beginning, call up the essential emotions of the story as you first
felt them. When you tell from the part of you that was touched by the
story, the story becomes yours.

Breathe deeply and begin. No matter what the opening words of the
story are, the tone should be intimate.

Look directly at your listeners. As you tell, let your gaze move from
one to another so that each child feels involved in the telling of the story.
Break direct eye contact only to look at an imaginary scene or object you
want your listeners to see, or when you engage in dialogue between two
or more characters during the telling.

Speak in a pleasant, low-pitched voice with enough volume to be heard easily by listeners in the last row. Speak clearly, distinctly, smoothly, and at a pace suitable for the story.

Gestures, if used at all, should be natural to the teller and to the action of the story. If gestures draw attention to themselves they are wrong. Exaggerated gestures usually indicate a futile attempt to draw attention away from inadequate preparation. Do not stand motionless as if you were a stick of wood, but do not dramatize the action of the story, for example, "marching up and down the road," "bowing," and so forth. The children may be fascinated with your movement, but they will not remember your story.

Avoid nervous mannerisms, such as biting your lips or pulling at a strand of hair. Stand with your two feet firmly on the floor. Do not rock.

Use your hands naturally. Don't jam them in your pockets. Don't stand with arms crossed in a hostile posture. If you do not know what to do with your hands, hold them behind your back. "Keep your listeners in the *what* of the story, not in the how of the telling," advises an experienced storyteller.

The storyteller establishes the mood of the story hour. Physical appearance, a pleasant expression, a smile, personal warmth, pleasure in the story, all give a sense of enjoyment (Figure 12).

Sometimes new storytellers wonder what to wear. Dress comfortably and simply. Children appreciate a bright scarf or attractive jewelry, but nothing should distract from the story. In a large hall, wearing something colorful will focus attention on the storyteller. However, there is no need to wear a "costume." Beware of jangly bracelets, long beads, and other potential distractions. One well-known storyteller wore long strands of beads. She always asked that she be reminded to remove them before the story hour. Otherwise she would begin to handle them during her telling, and the children would be as interested in whether the beads would break as they would be in the story.

A story hour can be held anywhere. Lack of a separate room is no excuse for not having a storytelling program. What is needed is a setting that is informal and an atmosphere that is relaxed and intimate. In the classroom, children may remain in their regular, assigned seats, but an informal seating arrangement is preferred. A semicircle of listeners facing the storyteller seems to be the most effective arrangement. The storyteller can be heard and seen easily by all the children. Do not let the semicircle be too wide, or the storyteller's head will have to turn from side to side like a spectator's at a tennis match. If there are 28 children in the group, it is better to have 4 rows of 7 chairs than 2 rows of 14 chairs. Seat the children on chairs or on the floor so that no child is directly behind another. The children should face away from the sunlight or any windows where

FIGURE 12. *Patrick Ryan telling stories at the University of Chicago laboratory school. (Photograph © Jeremiah Schatt.)*

traffic or other distractions may divert their interest. The storyteller will sit or stand, depending on the size of the group and visibility. It may be more comfortable to sit when telling to a small group or to younger children, but standing gives better eye span and, therefore, better control. It also gives the storyteller freedom of movement. The exception is when you are telling to very young children, or when you are sharing picture books with young children. In such a situation it is best for the storyteller to sit on a low stool or chair so that the storyteller and the pictures are at the children's eye level (see Chapter 8). If the storyteller is comfortable and confident, the children will be too. The arrangement of storyteller and listeners in Figure 13 will permit everyone to see and hear the storyteller easily.

Ask the children to put aside anything they are carrying (books, marbles, purses, dolls, and so on) on a separate table or under their chairs. If they have books in hand, they will surely peek into them during the storytelling. They really are not disinterested in your telling, but some children can focus on two things at once. This can deflate you as a storyteller, and it may distract other listeners.

If there is a separate story-hour room, check the heat and ventilation before the program begins. A room that is too warm and without sufficient air will make children drowsy.

If there is no separate story-hour room, use a screen to give a sense of privacy. Locate the storytelling area away from room traffic, circulation desk, and telephone.

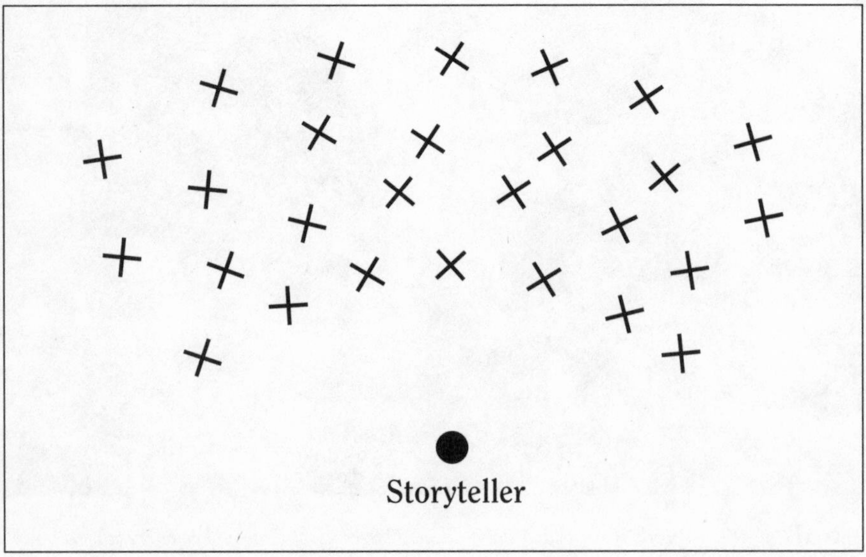

FIGURE 13. *Seating arrangement for a story hour.*

Place on the "story-hour table" the books from which you are telling, some fresh or dried flowers or leaves, and, if you like, the "wishing candle" and realia related to the stories.

Introduce the book from which the story is taken. This can be done naturally by picking up the book, either before or after the story, and saying, "This story is from . . . ." All children, whether or not they are readers, like to hear a good story told well. After they have heard it, book-loving children want to read it again for themselves. Even girls and boys who are not natural readers will turn to a book once it has been "opened" for them by the warmth and intimacy of a storyteller's voice and personality.

No explanations of the story are necessary. Occasionally the storyteller may wish to give a short introduction. Some books, such as Eleanor Farjeon's *The Little Bookroom*, Howard Pyle's *The Wonder Clock*, and Harold Courlander's *Uncle Bouqui of Haiti*, have natural introductions. Introductions should be interesting and simple; you are not giving a lesson. You can develop your own short introduction (for example, "In Haiti there are two very important men. One is named Bouqui and he is a fat, good-natured fellow. The other is his best friend, Ti-Malice, a skinny little fellow who always tricks Bouqui. One time, Bouqui . . .) and then go straight into the story. The ages of your listeners will determine the type and extent of your introduction. If you are telling a long story serially, prepare a short summary to refresh the children's memory and to introduce the story to newcomers. If you tell one incident from a long book, briefly introduce the characters and the situation in which they find themselves.

No definitions of "strange" words are necessary. Frequently, inexperienced storytellers feel that they must define all unfamiliar words in order for children to understand the story. They forget that the context of the story and the child's imagination are enough to supply definitions. If children do not understand a word, they will ask, or if they look puzzled and the word is essential for meaning, the storyteller can substitute a synonym the next time the word is used in the story. For example, if the storyteller is telling "The Squire's Bride" and realizes that the children do not know what a bay mare is, the storyteller can substitute the word "horse" in the following sentence: "Some pulled at the head and the forelegs of the mare (horse) and others pushed from behind, and at last they got her up the stairs and into the room."

Then there are words that give atmosphere, and it really doesn't matter what they mean. In her delightful article "The Pleasant Land of Counterpane," Claudia Lewis recalls her childhood encounter with Robert Louis Stevenson's poem "The Land of Counterpane."

[The poem was] magical simply because of that bewildering word counterpane. Yes, of course, my mother explained to me what it meant, and in some rational part of my mind I know very clearly what it meant. Yet it was not a word current in the everyday speech of the people around me; and it suggested a baffling combination of windowpane and kitchen counter. At the same time, what a splendid-sounding word it was! I must have closed off that rational corner of mine and let my thoughts go romping off with whatever textural images and associations the word called up, and fortunately for me, my mother did not drill in the meaning. I was left to enjoy the poem, and enjoy it I did, in my own way. It would be difficult for me to describe just what "the pleasant land of counterpane" was to me (and still is). This is a case of the quality of a particular word spilling over and giving color to a whole poem, or rather, to the poem one reconstructs inwardly in heightened imaginative dimensions.[3]

If a storyteller becomes bogged down in a vocabulary lesson, the pleasure is diminished for the children, who should be allowed to relax and enjoy the story.

In planning a satisfying story hour, the storyteller must be concerned with a variety of practical problems as well as with the content. Some of these concerns are reflected in the following questions.

Should the Story-Hour Group Be Large or Small?

When no visuals are used there is no need to restrict group size. However, a group of 20 to 30 children is a comfortable size, especially for the beginning storyteller. The ability to project to large groups comes with experience. If you anticipate frequent story hours to large groups or storytelling out of doors, you will need to learn how to project your voice without distorting its quality.

Occasionally, the storyteller is asked to tell stories at a school assembly. Although this can be done effectively, it is difficult to create an intimate "from me to you" feeling in an assembly setting. If you have such a request, you might ask to tell to several smaller groups of children rather than to a large assembly. Telling to several groups on the same day may be physically more demanding of the storyteller, but it makes for more satisfying story hours.

How Is a Listening Mood Created?

The mood is created by attractive surroundings—a well-ventilated room, comfortable seating, and the story-hour table with appropriate, authentic realia, clean books, some fresh flowers or leaves, and the wishing candle, if it is to be used. The rituals of the story-hour line and the wishing candle also help to establish a listening mood. However, it is the storyteller who is most important in setting the mood. The storyteller's manner should be dignified but friendly. It should say, "Listen deeply, for I have something special to share with you."

What Is the Story-Hour Line and What Are Its Advantages?

The story-hour line can be used wherever there is a separate story-telling area. Have the children assemble in a line away from the story-hour area. This gives the children a chance to quiet down before the story hour. It gives the storyteller a chance to assess the group. This is the time to ask the children to put away personal items and to collect story-hour tickets, if used.

Children like the formality and it creates a mood of wonder, as described in this excerpt from the psychoanalysis of a 24-year-old woman, who recalled going to story hour when she was about seven years old:

> This just reminded me of my greatest happiness and excitement as a child. And that was going every Friday afternoon after school to storytelling in the Public Library. It was not just ordinary storytelling. First, all of the children lined up and waited. . . . Then they led us down into a room in the cellar with chairs all arranged in rows. The room had the most immense and useless windows you ever saw. Not only were they completely out of reach, but the shades were always drawn tight so that the room was dark except for the glow of two immense candles on a desk at the front. And behind the desk, illuminated by the candlelight, was the prettiest face imaginable. I am quite sure there was a body attached to the face. But I do not remember it. She must have been the librarian . . . but then I never thought of her as being a mere librarian any more than a child can conceive of its mother as a little baby. She was a real fairy that came to tell us stories. I loved the first story best always because there were two more to come. I hated, hated, hated, having to go upstairs when all the stories were done.[4]

How Is the Wishing Candle Used?

The lighting of the wishing candle indicates the start of the program (Figure 14). Before lighting the candle, the storyteller may say, "Once the candle is lit, no one speaks but the storyteller." Wishes are made silently at the end of the story hour, and the seated children blow out the candle, which is held by the storyteller, or one child—perhaps a birthday child—may be chosen to blow out the candle while everyone makes silent wishes. Be sure to use a dripless candle to avoid being sprayed with wax when the candle is blown out!

How Should I Introduce My Story?

"Once upon a time," or words to that effect, invite the children into the story world. The words and your manner of speaking let the children know that they are about to enter a different realm where extraordinary things happen but where they are perfectly safe. With younger children, storyteller Maggie Kimmel draws a magic circle around the group where all within are safe. With older children, you might open your story hour with Shel Silverstein's poem "Invitation" from *Where the Sidewalk Ends.*

Sometimes you will want to give some background about the country or people from which the story comes. Knowledge gained through background reading, authors' notes, travel, and personal experiences enriches the telling when shared with the children. If you are telling a literary fairy tale, tell the children something about the author's life, perhaps an incident from the author's childhood.

Ask yourself, what is the purpose of my introduction? To get the attention of the listeners? To set the stage? To let the audience adjust to my voice and manner of speaking? Then act accordingly, but keep your introduction short, just enough to whet the children's appetite for the story they are about to hear.

How Can a Storyteller Avoid Having a Dry Mouth?

1. Swallow to get the saliva glands working.
2. Whenever possible, before telling a story, get off by yourself. Do some yoga or other relaxation exercises (see Chapter 5). If privacy is not possible, take a few deep breaths and yawn discreetly before you begin your story.

What Is the Place of Musical and Nonmusical Recordings in the Story Hour?

Music can set the mood for the story. For example, you might play a recording of the "Sleeping Beauty Waltz" before telling the fairy tale. Opening the story hour with a song also sets the mood. Songs can introduce or reinforce the story, or serve as a link between stories.

You might play an activity record, such as *Bean Bag Activities,* or one of Ella Jenkins's rhythmic band records, for a break in the preschool story hour.

With older children, a recording can be used to introduce an author. Several poets, among them Carl Sandburg, Jack Prelutsky, and Shel Silverstein, have recorded their poems for children. Children would enjoy hearing Virginia Hamilton reading a tale from her collection *The People Could Fly.*

To give non–Native American children the flavor of traditional Native American storytelling, play one of the tapes in the Parabola Storytime series. A favorite is Gayle Ross telling her Cherokee animal stories.

Music and stories are natural partners. To quote librarian Jane Marino,

FIGURE 14. *Augusta Baker lights the wishing candle at a storytelling hour at the Chatham Square branch of the New York Public Library. Photograph courtesy of the New York Public Library.*

"When you sing a song you are telling a story that is set to music." For additional suggestions, see Marino's *Sing Us a Song: Using Music in Preschool and Family Storytimes* and William Painter's *Musical Story Hours: Using Music with Storytelling and Puppetry.*

Do I Need Permission to Tell a Story?

If you are telling stories in a public library or school as part of your work as a librarian, teacher, or school library media specialist, you do not need permission to tell. However, always acknowledge your sources and credit the reteller or compiler of the collection from which the story is taken. If you are a professional storyteller, and especially if the audience is charged an admission fee, you may need to get permission from the person who owns the copyright. Whether you are a paid storyteller or not, if you tell a story on radio or television and the story is protected under copyright, you will need written permission from the author and/or publisher.

To acquire permission, write a letter to the author in care of the publisher or call the publisher direct. Ask for the person in charge of copyright permission. In your letter or telephone call, give complete bibliographic information for the story: title, author, reteller, or editor's name, name of collection in which the story appears, publisher, and date of publication. Most permission departments require a copy of the entire story along with the title and copyright page of the collection. Indicate how you wish to use the material: the occasion, event site, number of performances, etc. Enclose a stamped, self-addressed envelope with your request. You might want to enclose a draft permission agreement. A request to use a story should be sent to the publisher well in advance of the scheduled date of the program as the permission process can take several weeks.

Does the Presentation of a Story Differ When It Is Told to Different Age Groups?

In telling to different age groups, the storyteller's facial expressions, attitude, or approach to the story may be different. The listeners play an important role. Children will be responding to the story line, adults and older children to the subtle humor or poignancy of a tale. The subtle interplay between husband and wife in "Two of Everything" is lost on children but not on adults. In telling "Uncle Bouqui Rents a Horse" to adults, the last sentence, "'It's *certainly a day* to remember,' Madame Boqui said," is spoken with a sarcastic inflection. Of course there are many stories that can be told successfully to different age groups without changing the presentation. "Mr. Sampson Cat" is one of them.

How Can a Storyteller Tell If the Children Are Enjoying the Story?

When children are enjoying a story their faces express interest, curiosity, delight. Sometimes they express their pleasure by listening quietly with little or no expression on their faces. A deep sigh and a faraway look seen on a face at the end of the story usually mean that you have reached that child. Some children do not seem to be paying attention at all; yet these same children will ask you for the story several weeks after you have told it. The new storyteller must remember that a story that is a roaring success with one group can leave another cold. Do not be discouraged. Continue to work on any story you really like. Accept failure along with your successes.

What Does a Storyteller Do If the Children Seem Disinterested?

An element of flexibility is needed. Restlessness often occurs when the story chosen is inappropriate for the group or when the storyteller has failed to capture the imagination of the children at the beginning. Sometimes the storyteller can recapture the children's interest by telling with greater conviction. However, if this fails, it is best to summarize the remaining part of the story and bring the story hour to a close or, if possible, to tell a different type of story. The story hour should be remembered with joy.

If you know beforehand that you will be telling to children who have little or no experience in listening to stories, you might want to use Leslie Morrow's approach. Morrow, a professor in the Graduate School of Education, Rutgers—The State University of New Jersey, who is well known for her work in emergent literacy, says that when she first starts storytelling to such children she uses 70 percent manipulatives and 30 percent pure telling. Manipulatives include flannel board figures, puppets, stick figures, dolls, and other realia. Gradually she changes the percentages, so that by the end of the school year the percentages are reversed, and the children are actively listening.

What Is the Best Way to Handle Disruptions?

The storyteller must be aware of the audience. Because the storyteller respects both story and listeners, no one should be allowed to disrupt what promises to be an enjoyable listening experience. Do not permit two little girls who are giggling and whispering to each other to sit together. They will surely whisper in the middle of the story even though they are following it closely.

Weave discipline into your telling. For example, in coping with restless listeners, you might insert as part of your story, "You two boys in the back could never guess. . . ." One storyteller, who was telling a story about a beautiful princess, used this ploy with "success" beyond her expectations. As she told her story she looked directly at a little girl who was chewing bubble gum and interjected, "And the princess did not chew gum." The girl was so surprised she swallowed her gum!

The following example may be helpful in handling a difficult situation: As you start to tell the story, you are aware that one boy is surreptitiously punching another. For a few seconds you tell the story directly to them. Your tone of voice is firm. You look away in order to give the boys a chance to behave, but they continue to punch each other. Now they are challenging you. As you continue the story, you take a few steps toward them. Your tone of voice and body language are clearly understood by the boys. You move away again and continue the story. The third time they misbehave, you stop the story and tell them they will have to leave if they continue to disrupt the story hour. You apologize to the other children that this has happened, then go on with the story. If the two boys do not settle down, you ask them to leave. The storyteller has a responsibility to the group and cannot let a few children spoil the story hour.

What Should Storytellers Do If They Forget the Story?

Because the book from which you are telling your story will be close by on the story-hour table, place a small marker in the first page of your story. If you forget your story, pick up the book and open it to the marker, which will guide you to your story. (Without a marker you might search nervously through the book and lose your poise.) Many times a glance at the place in the story where you forgot will set you free again, and you can put the book back on the table. If not, *read* the rest of the story. More often than not, if you know the story well and you have a moment of forgetfulness, you can improvise until the story comes back to you. If you forget an essential part of the story say, "Did I tell you that . . . ?" Most times, if you don't indicate you have forgotten your story, your audience won't know. Nervous laughter or "I forgot to tell you that . . . " give you away.

How Does a Storyteller Conclude the Story Hour?

End with the ending of the story. When the story is over, its spirit remains. Honor the story with a minute or two of silence (Marie Shedlock recommended five minutes of complete silence after a story). Do not ask questions about the story or try to elicit comments. Let the children leave the story hour with their own private thoughts. Do not invade their privacy. After the few minutes of silence, a simple "Thank you for coming"—not a corny "We have been down the road to fairyland"—is a good conclusion to the story hour held in the public library or recreation center. Now is the time to announce the next story hour. Direct the children to books. Let the children go two or three at a time to avoid disrupting other areas of the library. Be available after the story hour to discuss stories with those children who take the initiative, who *want* to talk.

What Is the Difference Between a Performer-Storyteller and a Librarian- or Teacher-Storyteller?

In the current renaissance of storytelling the subtle line between performance and telling is becoming increasingly hard to define. Constance A. Mellon, Associate Professor at East Carolina University, suggests that the difference lies in the relationship between the teller and the listener. "And the focus of that relationship is the story."[5]

Performer-storytellers have a dramatic style. Usually they have had some theatrical and voice training, have stage presence, and enjoy being "on stage" and telling to a large audience. Mary Gould Davis called the librarian- or teacher-storyteller who enjoys telling stories to children but who does not like to give a performance "the children's storyteller." She wrote, regarding the two types of storytellers:

> Almost anyone who knows and loves a good tale . . . can tell it effectively to a small, intimate group. To make a story effective to a large group in a more or less formal atmosphere requires what Marie Shedlock calls "the art of the storyteller": an interpretive art as subtle and as challenging as that of the musician or the painter. To broaden and to perfect this art one can give years of study and comparison, of travel to the countries from which the stories come. One can study the latent possibilities of the human voice, inflection, emphasis, the use of the pause. But, because in the minds of the children the important thing is not the storyteller but the *story*, one can, with no training nor experience whatsoever, take the book, tell the *right* tale and hold the boys and girls in a "listening silence."[6]

More recently, Kay Stone wrote in the same vein:

> As with a traditional audience, children are not passive listeners, and they still live in a predominantly oral milieu. They do not demand a flamboyantly oral/visual performance (though many adults think it necessary). They do demand sincerity and openness, and they tend to suffer honest fools gladly. Like a traditional audience they do not stop to ask, "Was that profound and meaningful, or just amusing?" If a story is well told, they will absorb other levels of meaning that appeal to their levels of experience and understanding.[7]

Stories may be interpreted in many ways. All that matters is that the style fit the teller. Two students told "Tom Tit Tot." One imbued the story with mystery and all kinds of psychological implications. The other told the tale as if she were the "gatless" young girl herself. Both tellings were successful because they were appropriate for the story and for the teller.

I Feel Intimidated by Professional Storytellers. How Can I Gain Confidence As a Storyteller?

There are different levels of proficiency in storytelling, just as there are in any art. As an amateur pianist is not in competition with the concert pianist, the librarian- or teacher-storyteller is not in competition with the professional storyteller. You are sharing your love of stories and giving children a pleasurable listening experience. All that is asked of you is that you tell the best you can and that you continue to stretch and grow as a teller.

To become an accomplished storyteller you need to experiment with different methods of learning and with different styles of telling. There is no one *right* way to tell a story. Listen to a recording of the same story told by two different tellers. For example, if you listen to "The Steadfast Tin Soldier" as told by Frances Clarke Sayers and then as told by Mary Strang, you will become aware of how two master storytellers bring differences to the telling—in tone of voice, pacing, characterization, and emphasis. It is similar to hearing the same piece of music played by different orchestras and conductors.

A story is not really yours until you have told it to at least three different audiences. Children respond differently from adults, and children respond differently according to their moods. You may be startled when the children laugh at something that you, the adult, did not think funny. By telling the story to different groups you discover more about the story and you learn how best to pace it. Professional storytellers have the advantage of telling the same story many times and to many different audiences.

What Is the Difference Between Telling a Story to an Individual Child at Home and Telling a Story to a Group of Children?

The adult telling a story to an individual child at home is very much aware of that child's interests, fears, likes, and dislikes. This knowledge makes it easier to choose a story that will appeal. The telling is informal and interruptions are permitted since there is no time schedule to keep. Telling to a group of children is more formal—the larger the group, the more formal the presentation, usually, but there are exceptions, such as storytelling around a campfire. The storyteller does not expect all the children in the group to have the same listening experience or to like the tale equally well.

It would not be appropriate to tell a story to one or two children in exactly the same manner that it would be told to a group of children. The experience might be too intense, too emotionally demanding of the child. In a group, a child is freer to let his or her mind engage in imaginative play.

Is There a Place for Spontaneous Storytelling?

Storytelling should not be limited to the scheduled story hour. If you are prepared and an opportunity presents itself, such as a quiet day in the public library, at school when a story would relate naturally to the classroom discussion, or at the end of an activity when the children need a change of pace, tell a story or read aloud.

NOTES

1. Henrietta M. Smith, "An Interview with Augusta Baker," *The Horn Book Magazine* 71 (May–June 1995): 296.
2. Eulalie Steinmetz Ross, Manuscript in the files of the Office of Children's Services, New York Public Library.
3. Claudia Lewis, "The Pleasant Land of Counterpane," *The Horn Book Magazine* 42 (October 1966): 543.
4. From the personal files of Augusta Baker.
5. Constance A. Mellon, "Storyteller or Performer? You Can't Tell the Difference Without a Scorecard," *School Library Journal* 33:2 (October 1986): 122. Excerpted from *By Word of Mouth* (Winter 1986).
6. Mary Gould Davis, "The Art of Storytelling," paper presented at a meeting of the American Library Assn., Washington, D.C., 15 May 1929.
7. Kay Stone, "'To Ease the Heart': Traditional Storytelling," *National Storytelling Journal* 1 (Winter 1984): 5.

Storytelling to Children with Special Needs or in Special Settings

Before Cushla was born, I would have laid claim to a deep faith in the power of books to enrich children's lives. By comparison with my present conviction, this faith was a shallow thing. I know now what print and picture have to offer a child who is cut off from the world, for whatever reason. But I know also that there must be another human being, prepared to intercede, before anything can happen.

—Dorothy Butler [1]

MAINSTREAMING OVER THE PAST decade has brought many more children with special needs—the mentally disabled, the blind and partially sighted, the deaf and hearing-impaired, the physically handicapped, the chronically ill, the emotionally disturbed—into the story-hour group. But the skills needed for effective storytelling to these children are rarely covered in the library-school curriculum or in the storytelling literature.

The storyteller who tells to children with special needs must have the qualities of a good storyteller—only more so. Extra warmth and extra sensitivity to the group's needs are necessary in order to sustain good listening. Each child must be seen not as handicapped, but as a child with a handicap, that is, the emphasis must be on the *whole* child (Figure 15).

The recently passed Americans with Disabilities Act (ADA), which mandates accessibility for persons with disabilities to all public facilities and activities, has increased the awareness of librarians as they plan story hours and other programs for children with special needs. This awareness often focuses on physical facilities and costs. For example, it is necessary to run an induction loop around the program room if hearing-impaired children use the library regularly. This loop, when used with an amplifier, sets up a magnetic field that enables sound to be picked up by a device attached to a child's hearing aid. To inform librarians of the implications of the ADA for staff training and program planning, as well as facilities and costs, the ALA/ALSC Library Service to Children with Special Needs committee updated its program support publication, "Programming for Serving Children with Special Needs." Additional information can be found in *Meeting the Needs of People with Disabilities: A Guide for Librarians, Educators, and Other Service Professionals* by Ruth A. Velleman. For inspira-

FIGURE 15. *Whatever their physical or mental limitations, children and young people enjoy a tale. Spencer Shaw telling stories at the Special Human Resources School, Albertson, Long Island, New York. (Photograph © George E. Ernst.)*

tion, read *Cushla and Her Books* by Dorothy Butler, a loving account of the remarkable role stories played in the life of Butler's multiple-disabled grandchild.

"Storytelling to children with special needs is a joy and a challenge," writes Louise M. Pulley, Forsyth County (N.C.) Public Library System. She continues:

> The storyteller will find that there is a greater need to use facial and vocal expression, body language and animation to get and hold the attention of the children. Use visuals, such as flannelboard stories, finger puppets, story dolls, and other realia. Flannelboard stories are very successful due to the simplicity of the patterns, ease of movement and clarity of story. Be sure the pictures are large enough to be seen by the entire group and sturdy enough for repeated handling. Make the pieces move by "walking" them across the board, moving them to match the action of the story, and removing them as soon as they are not needed. Use the fewest pieces possible for the story line to avoid confusion of multiple changes. Know the story well, have all pieces in the order they are to be used. Children love the sequential stories, one character building on the others as in "Henny Penny," "Gingerbread Boy," etc. Get the children to name the character with you, join in the repetitive phrases, repeat the sing-song storyline![2]

Storytelling to children with special needs is indeed a joy—and a challenge. Following are additional suggestions, arranged by types of disabilities.

Storytelling to Blind or Partially Sighted Children

Storytelling to blind or partially sighted children is done much as it is for children with sight. However, because facial expressions and body movement are lost on the listeners, the storyteller's voice quality and choice of words are extremely important. A pleasing, musical voice is a great asset to all storytellers, but it is vital for the storyteller who tells to blind children. For blind children, beauty of language comes through the sound.

Storytelling is important to blind children for language development. Choose stories with vivid mental images. Craig Werner, a blind child and now a teacher of children's literature, writes that the stories he enjoyed most as a child were those with long descriptive passages, such as the fairy tales of Hans Christian Andersen. He concludes that *imagination* is the most important faculty involved in understanding and appreciating a good story.[3]

Fine filmstrips, such as those produced by Weston Woods, can be used successfully with partially sighted children. They also enjoy sing-alongs and playing with simple musical instruments.

Storytelling to Mentally Disabled Children

Mentally disabled children function intellectually below the average. They tend to be even more literal-minded than most children and have difficulty understanding abstract concepts. They enjoy simple stories about animals and familiar things. Look for strong plot, obvious humor, simple vocabulary, and concrete language rather than abstractions. Be prepared to substitute synonyms for unfamiliar words. Use pictures and realia to illustrate unfamiliar words.

Choose picture-book stories in which the pictures tell the story. Bruno Munari's story *The Birthday Present* has surefire appeal. Mark, the truck driver, is taking a birthday present to his little boy, John. When his truck breaks down, he must find other means of transportation. The unusual format of the book, the simple story line, the various and familiar means of transportation, and the adult male main character give this book special appeal to older mentally disabled children.

The tight structure of the folktale, with its definite beginning, middle, and ending, is particularly satisfying to these children, and cumulative folktales (see Appendix) are enjoyed as much for their repetition and rhythm as for their plot. Participation stories are also popular, especially those in which the children are invited to respond to animal sounds. Having the children retell the story in another form, for example, through creative drama or dance, reinforces the story.

Storytelling to Learning-Disabled Children

Learning-disabled children often exhibit disorders in listening, speaking, and thinking processes. Other characteristics include disorientation, distractibility, disorganization, a limited attention span, and lack of eye-hand coordination. Attention deficit disorder falls into this category.

Brevity and concreteness in the selection of stories for this group have been advised in the past. However, Jed Luchow, a teacher of young learning-disabled children, found that unity "expressed in oneness of mood, plot, character, harmony between picture and story, or harmony between picture and detail" is more relevant.[4] Luchow cites *Mike Mulligan and His Steam Shovel* by Virginia Lee Burton, *Whistle for Willie* by Ezra Jack Keats, and *Where the Wild Things Are* by Maurice Sendak as examples.

Multisensory story hours are enjoyed by learning-disabled children. For example, after telling "The Crab and the Jaguar," play a recording of sea sounds and let the children look at and touch a variety of seashells, coral, and other "treasures of the sea" that the crab might have seen.

Storytelling to Emotionally Disturbed Children

Emotionally disturbed children tend toward hyperactivity, impulsiveness, and anxiety. It is hard for them to adjust to new situations or activities. They usually have a very short attention span and need immediate rewards.

Tell stories that have quiet humor. Tell more slowly. Involve the children in the telling. *Listen and Help Tell the Story* by Bernice Wells Carlson contains stories and activities that can be used effectively. The ALA/ALSC Library Service to Children with Special Needs committee suggests following the reading or storytelling with "an art activity in which the children illustrate an aspect of the story. The illustrations are then displayed to provide recognition of the children's efforts. Simple, clearly defined, yet creative, art and craft activities, such as sponge painting and easy cardboard construction, may also reinforce positive behavior."[5]

Storytelling to Deaf or Hearing-Impaired Children

Telling stories to children with impaired hearing requires very special techniques. Visual presentation provides the meaning. Sit or stand with the light on your face and draw drapes to keep out bright sunshine and minimize glare. Make use of facial expressions and body movement. Speak more slowly and in a moderate tone of voice, but do not mouth each word, as this distorts normal rhythm. A lip-reader is looking for the thought, not single words. Male storytellers should remember that lips can be read more easily if there is no mustache or beard.

In terms of language understanding, hearing-impaired children are often two to three years behind children whose hearing is not impaired. For example, folktales and fairy tales for the hearing child of age 7 or 8 may not be appropriate for the hearing-impaired child until age 9 or 10. It is sometimes necessary to adapt the story drastically, something not recommended when telling to hearing children. To make the thought clear, repeat, paraphrase, and rephrase what is being said. Beauty of language to children whose hearing is impaired is a matter of understanding the *meaning* of words.

Children with impaired hearing cannot use their eyes and ears simultaneously. They cannot look at pictures and read lips or signing at the same time. If you are using a picture book, close the book (instead of holding it open with the pages turned toward the children) as you tell. Then open the book to show the picture, or show the pictures after each section of the story as appropriate. Picture-book stories with action, repetition, and humor, such as *Mr. Gumpy's Outing* by John Burningham, *The Very Hungry Caterpillar* by Eric Carle, and *Rosie's Walk* by Pat Hutchins, work well.

Children with hearing problems usually tire more quickly when they are required to pay close attention to looking or listening. Extra concentration is called for; therefore, one story—or two short stories—may be sufficient for the storytelling period. After telling the story, let the children "act it out" through pantomime or dance.

More and more librarians are learning to sign stories. With one million deaf or hearing-impaired children in the United States, it is highly likely that at some time you will encounter hearing-impaired children in your story hour. If you have never seen anyone sign stories, watch Connie Regan-Blake tell "I Know an Old Lady" on the video *Pennies, Pets and Peanut Butter: Stories for Children* (see Appendix). Many community colleges offer courses in signing. Your public library will have dictionaries in American Sign Language and in Signed English.

Look at the children's book series produced by Mary Beth Miller in collaboration with Remy Charlip and George Ancona, beginning with *Handtalk: An ABC of Finger Spelling & Sign Language*. Laura Rankin's *The Handmade Alphabet* shows human hands forming the sign for each letter with an alphabetically keyed object on the same page. *Simple Signs* by Cindy Wheeler introduces 28 signs for words used by young children, such as "cookie," "more," and "love."

Key signs for ten nursery tales and ten original stories can be found in *Beyond Words: Great Stories for Hand and Voice* by Valerie Marsh. (See Figure 16 for an example.) Gallaudet College Press publishes nursery rhymes and favorite nursery tales in Signed English. Use these books for learning the signs, but show children the beautiful picture-book editions of these stories after they have "heard" them. Hearing-impaired children have as much need for beautiful picture-book art as hearing children. Putnam set a model when it published a sign language edition of Eric Hill's *Where's Spot?* with text and illustrations identical to the original.

Joyce Gunn, branch librarian of the San Ramon Public Library, has been signing stories for 22 years. Gunn offers the following basics of signing a story:

> Any story you choose to sign should meet the basic criteria of a good story [as discussed in Chapter 4]. It must, however, meet some additional criteria in order to be a good story for signing. A story with unfamiliar or very long names, such as the German folktale "Rumpelstiltskin" or Gail Haley's *A Story, A Story,* is difficult to sign. Each name needs to be finger-spelled or abbreviated; thus much of the flavor of the story is lost. In *A Story, A Story* there is an additional problem: the words that describe sounds, such as "sora, sora, sora," are difficult for hearing-impaired listeners to understand.
>
> A story that has a long or complicated rhyme, especially one using nonsense words, is also difficult to sign. The repetition becomes tedious to both the signer and the audience. If, however, the repetition is very short, like

The Little Red Hen

Far ago, there was a Little Red Hen. She was friends with a duck, a cat, and a dog. The Little Red Hen worked hard all day long. But the duck, the cat, and the dog did not! They did not like to help.

One fine spring day, Little Red Hen found some grains of wheat. She took them home. She asked, "Who will help me plant these grains of wheat?".

"Not I," said Duck.
"Not I," said Cat.
"Not I," said Dog.
"Very well then, I'll plant the seeds myself," said Little Red Hen. And she did.

One fine summer day, Little Red Hen went out to the garden. She saw that the wheat was growing. She asked, "Who will help me water the wheat and pull the weeds?"

"Not I," said Duck.
"Not I," said Cat.
"Not I," said Dog.
"Very well then, I'll water the wheat and pull the weeds myself," said Little Red Hen. And she did.

One fine fall day, Little Red Hen went out to the garden. She saw that the wheat was very tall and golden. She asked, "Who will help me cut down the wheat?"

"Not I," said Duck.
"Not I," said Cat.
"Not I," said Dog.
"Very well then, I'll cut the wheat myself," said Little Red Hen. And she did. Little Red Hen scooped the wheat into her wagon and asked, "Who will help me take this wheat to the mill. It must be ground into flour."

"Not I," said Duck.
"Not I," said Cat.
"Not I," said Dog.
"Very well then, I'll take it myself." said Little Red Hen. And she did.

One fine winter day, Little Red Hen walked into her kitchen. She saw the wheat flour. She said "This day is a good day to bake. I will bake a loaf of bread* with the wheat flour. Who will help me bake the bread?"

"Not I," said Duck.
"Not I," said Cat.
"Not I," said Dog.
"Very well then, I'll bake it myself," said Little Red Hen. And she did.

Soon Duck smelled the baking bread. Soon Cat smelled the baking bread. Soon Dog smelled the baking bread.

When the bread was all done, Little Red Hen said, "Who will help me eat the bread?"

"I will!" said Duck.
"I will!" said Cat.
"I will!" said Dog.
"But who planted the wheat? Who watered the wheat and pulled the weeds? Who cut the wheat? Who took the wheat to the mill to be ground into flour? Who baked the bread?" asked Little Red Hen.

"Not I," said Duck.
"Not I," said Cat.
"Not I," said Dog.
"Very well then, I'll eat the bread myself. And she did.

FIGURE 16. *Signing "The Little Red Hen," from* Beyond Words: Great Stories for Hand and Voice *by Valerie Marsh (Alleyside Press, 1995). Reprinted by courtesy of Valerie Marsh.*

little

"L"-shape hands, index tips out, then move close together.

Red

Brush lower lip twice with RH "R" sign.

Hen

"Three"-shape RH. Tap thumb on chin.

Duck

Snap thumb, index and middle fingers together at mouth.

Cat

Place thumb and index of RH "9" at side of upper lip. Pull away twice.

Dog

Pat right thigh twice, then snap fingers twice.

Not

RH knuckle left, "A"-shape. Place extended thumb under chin, then move out.

Did

Move open hands, palms down, from side to side. Then swing RH open "B," tips forward, twice.

Help

Place LH "A," thumb up, in RH palm. Raise both hands.

Wheat

LH, palm up, "5" shape, fingers cupped. Brush fourth finger of RH "W" up against LH fingers. Repeat.

Palm left, "I"-shape RH, then place thumb side on chest.

the rhyme in Wanda Gág's *Millions of Cats*, your audience can join in with the signing of the rhyme.

Consider the following suggestions when signing to a group:

1. speak and enunciate normally
2. keep your hands fairly close to your lips without covering your mouth
3. use facial expressions and body language
4. wear clothes that will make your hands easily visible
5. make clarity, not speed, your goal
6. be aware of the abilities of your audience, adjusting your speed and content accordingly

Hearing and non-hearing children can enjoy stories together with the assistance of a signer. The storyteller tells the story slowly and watches the person signing to make sure they are together. The children with impaired hearing should be seated where the signer is clearly visible to them.

During story time for an audience that includes both hearing and hearing-impaired young children, teach the finger plays in sign language to everyone. This creates a sharing environment in which the hearing-impaired children can help the other children with the signs. Almost any finger play works well for signing because of the simple vocabulary.

With a mixed group of children third grade and above you can use string stories. These stories tend to have very simple story lines and the audience can participate with their own strings after the first telling. This works best if you have an interpreter sign the story while you tell and manipulate your string. (Be certain to give the audience time to focus on your moves with the string.) If you do not have an interpreter, ask a member of the audience to manipulate the string with your guidance. Children who are used to signing are very adept with their hands and seem to enjoy these stories very much. It is best to give each child a loop of string after you tell the story and then teach them the moves. Always encourage them to take the string home and learn new moves.

Simple songs, such as "The Alphabet Song," are excellent to use with mixed audiences using sign language. If the songs are repeated often enough, soon all those attending will be "singing" them with their hands.

Explore your community for counselors or teachers of deaf or hearing-impaired children, for community college classes in sign language, or for local or state advocacy groups for the deaf. You will find guidance and discover new ideas and materials. The rewards you receive from sharing stories with these children will be many.

Storytelling to Children in Hospitals

Time passes slowly for the hospitalized or chronically ill child. Chronically ill children may spend short or extended periods of time in hospitals or they may need to be cared for at home. This group includes children with asthma, rheumatoid arthritis, heart disease, cancer, and other long-term illnesses. The storyteller, equipped with all types of stories—picture books, simple folktales, a short literary tale to read aloud—and perhaps a puppet or two, can help ease the child's concerns and bring the gift of shared pleasure.

The storyteller visiting a hospital should be prepared to read to an individual child or to a group of children. Most likely the group will include a wide age-range. A beginning storyteller once went to a hospital to share picture books with young children. Her audience turned out to be a group of fifth- and sixth-grade boys. Fortunately, she knew a story that pleased them. Then she confessed her predicament and invited them to share her own delight in picture-book art. Because she had not talked down to them, the boys thoroughly enjoyed their introduction to the picture-book world.

There is a special need for reading aloud and storytelling in the clinic waiting room. Often parents must sit with their children a long time, waiting to be called by the doctor. The children become restless; they run and romp, and very often are overexcited by the time the doctor is ready to examine them. Experience has shown that the medical staff usually welcomes a "quiet time" before the examination. And librarians have discovered that the clinic is a wonderful place to introduce parents and other caregivers to the library and its services!

Storytelling Outdoors

In many communities storytellers from the public library visit parks and playgrounds on a regular schedule of story hours, especially during the summer months. The summer storytelling program, which brings librarians into contact with readers and nonreaders, is often a child's introduction to the public library and to books. Storytellers on the staff of recreational centers and camps use the outdoors as the setting for the story hour. Informal storytelling is carried on while the children are resting after games or are just sitting around talking. However, during the scheduled period set aside for storytelling, the story is the primary activity. Many playgrounds have special story hours scheduled during the mornings when activity is slow. This keeps the group fairly small and easier to control.

Summer story hours in parks present a real challenge to storytellers. Often the groups are very large and have a wide age-span—from toddlers to grandparents. Mothers bring their children, a recreation leader sees the story-hour group and brings a group to join it (sometimes in the middle of the story), teenagers stop to listen, dogs bark and romp around the periphery. Every possible distraction can be present. Such situations

FIGURE 17. *"Listening to Life Stories: African-American Voices That Teach Us All," the Children's Museum of Indianapolis. Photograph courtesy of the Children's Museum of Indianapolis.*

demand poise, a strong voice, and a careful selection of stories. The story-teller must be flexible and unflappable.

Find a quiet, shady, secluded area, away from swimming and wading pools and noisy play areas. Invite the children to sit on the ground in a semicircle with the smaller children in front. Give the children plenty of legroom. The storyteller usually stands so that the children can hear the story and see the storyteller more easily.

Plan the program for about 25 to 30 minutes. Bring along a few pic-ture books with large, colorful pictures in case you need to begin your program with stories for the youngest. Tell two or three short, surefire sto-ries, full of dramatic action and a good helping of humor. Folktales are a wise choice. Keep the program relaxed and informal.

Storytelling is used extensively in camp programs. There is no set time to tell stories, but storytelling around a campfire at night has a magic of its own. Use the locale, whether woods, seashore, or mountains. A starry night is the perfect time to tell legends of the stars and sky beings. Ghost stories are a favorite, but these are best reserved for older boys and girls; younger children enjoy scary stories in more familiar surroundings. On a rainy evening the leader might suggest that the youngsters take turns telling stories indoors. These round-robins encourage children to become storytellers.

Storytelling in Museums

Many museums carry out a regular storytelling program for children. This practice can be traced back to 1911 in the Boston Museum of Fine Arts and to 1918 in the Metropolitan Museum of Art (one of the places where Marie Shedlock lectured on storytelling). The purpose of these early story hours was to stimulate children's interest in art in general and in particular in works of art in the galleries. No matter how vivid the printed descriptions identifying art objects are in the galleries, the art does not speak without some context. Young people, especially, can develop a personal involvement with art if they feel an emotional connection with a character in a painting, or know why or how a certain object was used in the past. Today, when art museums are shifting the emphasis of their mis-sion from collecting to educating, storytelling has become a powerful means of connection between the language of words and the language of images.

In April 1995 the Children's Museum of Indianapolis opened a perma-nent interactive educational exhibit called "Life Stories: African-American Voices That Teach Us All." The exhibit was intended to:

help families of all backgrounds understand and appreciate the role of sto-rytelling and oral tradition, both in the African-American community as

well as their own. . . . The exhibit is designed as a composite neighborhood
street made up of several settings. Each stage or setting provides a different
context in which a group of stories are told. As visitors amble down the
"street," they may visit a family and "eavesdrop" on the Sunday dinner conversation or hear a bedtime story. They might stop by the barber shop to
hear the latest "stories" or watch TV and shoot the breeze. Maybe they'll
get lucky and arrive at "the stoop" just as the three neighborhood storytellers get ready to spin a couple of good yarns. They might climb in the
car and become an active participant in the story that "Aunt Janice" has to
tell as she taxis kids all over the neighborhood. Or perhaps they will go
into the storefront church to hear the story of why the oral tradition is so
important to the African-American community. Before they leave, each
visitor will have an opportunity to visit the story bank to deposit a story
from their own family or to withdraw a good story to take home.[6]

The exhibition was developed with large participation from the local
African-American community. The stories were gathered from oral history interviews as well as traditional folklore. A sample tape sent included
a Brer Rabbit story and an Anansi tale, some family stories, and a personal
recollection about slavery, all beautifully interpreted by African-American
professional storytellers.

Diana C. J. Matthias, Curator of Academic Programs, and Carole
Walton, storyteller at the University of Notre Dame's Snite Museum of
Art, describe innovative connections between museums and storytellers:

Museums have devised imaginative ways to incorporate stories into their
calendar of events. In 1993 the Toledo Museum of Art held a story-writing
contest that focused on "the family dinner in African-American culture."
High school students were encouraged to submit entries that referred to
their own or imagined experiences, and to view the museum's newly
acquired collage, *The Family Dinner* by African-American artist Romare
Bearden. Prize winners read and performed their entries at a special event
celebrating the acquisition of this work of art. The Snite Museum held a
similar event in 1995 when it hosted a storytelling session performed
entirely by children between the ages of 8 and 13. The children read their
own stories, which had won prizes in a competition judged by the staff of
the local public library.

At the Elvehjem Museum of Art, University of Wisconsin, Anne
Lambert, Curator of Education, blends art and literature from a non-
Western culture by focusing on the Hindu epic story *The Ramayana*. The
program was originally developed in partnership with the University of
Wisconsin Theatre for Children and Young People, which produced a companion play called "Tales of South Asia." This play, together with a packet of
slides of Hindu objects from the museum collection, and a script were
made available to teachers so that works of art and literature from Hindu
culture and belief could be presented to students in a comprehensive way.

Some museums focus a day of storytelling on the subject of a work in
their collection. An example is the day of medieval stories about knights

and princesses planned by Susan Kuliak of the Art Institute of Chicago and held on April 23, St. George's Day, to remind visitors of the museum's painting *St. George Killing the Dragon* by Bernardo Martorell.

Whenever feasible, the storytelling takes place in the galleries where the audience is close to objects that draw on the same cultural traditions as the stories being told. A sixteenth-century Madonna and Child by Jacopo Sansovino, for example, makes present the object of the juggler's devotion in the tale called "The Clown of God." For the past ten years, Amy Jared of the Philadelphia Museum of Art (and a storyteller herself) has arranged a monthly gallery program called "Tales and Treasures" for children from ages 6 to 12, and other storytelling and reading events for children ages 3 to 5. At the University of Notre Dame's Snite Museum of Art, storytelling takes place in the galleries on selected Saturday mornings, and the adults and children enjoy the way each story clearly matches the historical, geographical, mythical, or ethnic background of the art.

If the large number of visitors prevents gallery presentations, audiences can meet in atriums, auditoriums, or special rooms away from the art. At the Indiana University Art Museum, Edward Maxedon has arranged a monthly storytelling series called "Museum Muses." Professional storytellers work with Maxedon to form historical or thematic links between stories and images. The stories are told in the atrium, followed by a gallery discussion or a hands-on workshop. After listening to stories from Indonesia, for instance, children and adults visited the museum's Indonesian collection and then returned to the atrium to make shadow puppets.

Wherever the audience gathers, the tellers try to make vivid connections among the stories, the intentions and techniques of the artists, the purposes and meanings of the artifacts, and the cultures they represent.

Museums attract both professional and volunteer storytellers. At the Indianapolis Museum of Art, Bob Sander of Stories, Inc., holds the position of storyteller-in-residence. He performs regularly on the afternoon of every fourth Sunday. Storyteller Marcia Lane helped children at New York's Metropolitan Museum of Art see the connection between symbols of power on their T-shirts and powerful symbolic animals in a special exhibit. Searching for animal symbols intrigued the children and prompted them to look at all the artifacts carefully. Then Lane told stories in which those same animals (turtle, frog, and bear) had roles. With their polished performance skills and wide repertoire, professionals draw large groups of listeners and may attract a new audience, but smaller institutions may not be able to afford the professionals' fees more than once or twice a year.[7]

As a librarian and member of a community agency serving children, with expertise in storytelling, you may be asked to tell stories or to train the museum docents in storytelling. If you are asked to give a workshop for museum docents, you will need to familiarize yourself with the collections, whether a toy museum, a museum of natural history, an art museum, or other institution. You will need to spend time gathering story collections and selecting individual stories that complement artifacts in the museum. Only then will you be ready to meet with the docents. The emphasis of your workshop will be on selection and the technique of learning and presenting stories. Introduce the docents to a basic text, such as *Storytelling: Art and Technique,* and to resources such as D. L. Ashliman's *A Guide to Folktales in the English Language* and Margaret Read MacDonald's *The Storyteller's Sourcebook.* Give examples of matching a story with an artifact, like those cited here. Prepare a short annotated bibliography to get the docents started.

Because they contain works of art from all over the world, museums offer an ideal setting for telling stories from many lands. Storytellers match their tales either to the image in a work of art or to artifacts, such as a mask, a vase, or a dress from a historical period or geographical area. Hearing "Little Burnt Face," a Native American variant of "Cinderella," for example, while looking at a ceremonial dress made of deerskin and trimmed with beads (that might have been worn in the marriage ceremony at the end of the story) makes both the dress and the story memorable. This same artifact could be used when telling *Love Flute* by Paul Goble.

Many museums have in their African galleries a pair of Ibeji twins. Using Harold Courlander's *Treasury of African Folklore* as the basis for a retelling of "How Twins Came Among the Yoruba," the storyteller might tell the tale while standing near the artifact. As children listen to the story, they learn why the Yoruba so revere twins and how representations of a dead twin remain part of family events. Yoruba mothers carry the representation, or doll-like figure, with them. They "feed" it during mealtimes and pay special attention to it during festivals. The attention paid to a dead twin ensures that its spirit will not be angry and cause trouble in the family. The artifact helps to focus the children's attention; they remember the twins and the story because they care about the families who rejoiced and grieved.

Standing in front of a large painting of a peasant woman wearing the shawl, long skirt, apron, cap, and rough shoes that would remind people of the clothing worn by the poor in the story, Carole Walton tells "Vasilissa the Fair." Walton also brings with her a Russian doll that fits neatly inside the pocket of her apron. At appropriate moments in the story, she takes out the magical doll and speaks to it in character. The children are mesmerized.

At the Snite Museum where Walton tells, there are two paintings representing the well-known myth of Demeter and Persephone. Standing near the magnificent painting *The Rape of Proserpine* by Jean François de Troy, Walton's colleague Anne Pendl tells the version most people know. The painting depicts the story with a stunning contrast of light (Persephone's bare torso and uplifted arms) and darkness (cloaked Pluto and jet-black fire-breathing horses leading to a murky corner of the painting). Next, Walton tells the older pre-Hellenic myth of Demeter and Persephone (based on information found in *Lost Goddesses of Early Greece* by Charlene Spretnak) while standing near *Bacchus and Ceres* by Francesco de Mura. This painting gives her a chance to talk about the potentially confusing name changes from the Greek in her story to the Roman in the title. The painting features a large vertical figure of Ceres clad in a loose white garment and holding a spray a wheat. Before the story time Walton places a simple vase with three sheaves of wheat nearby; children notice and appreciate such attention to detail.

Museum staff have observed that visitors who are untrained in looking at art usually spend only a few seconds before a particular painting or sculpture, but when they listen to a story told in front of a carefully chosen object, they may spend as long as 20 minutes sitting in one place in the museum. During this time they are listening, imagining, concentrating. Art objects alone cannot represent the rich diversity and the creativity of our ancestors. Storytellers, too, help to keep alive the people of the past—their energy and sense of humor, their virtues and the physical attributes they admired, the dangers they faced, and the dreams they wished to pass on to those who follow.

Storytelling on Radio and Television

> To sustain a story on the air for twenty minutes or more with the use of only one instrument, the voice, although it may sound easy, is really a most demanding act. The storyteller's voice must have great range and flexibility. . . . He must convey the "feel" of each new character at once solely by the use of his voice.[8]

If you are invited to tell stories on radio and television, choose stories for their broad appeal, literary quality, action, and a minimum of detail. Folktales are excellent choices, though modern stories and literary fairy tales can be used. They should appeal to as wide an audience as possible. Select a story that requires no cutting or a minimum of cutting to fit the time allotted.

A 15-minute radio show is a good length; television producers usually want a 30-minute show. The latter must be planned with visuals, and so the story should be selected with this in mind. A story that requires 30 minutes to tell cannot be squeezed into a 15-minute time slot. Shortening a story by only 2 minutes requires substantial cutting, so try to find an appropriate story that is short enough to require very little change.

Nevertheless, it is important to learn how to cut a story, if necessary. Do not eliminate all description, because this kind of background information is necessary in order to create a mood and establish atmosphere and visualization. A word here and there, an unnecessary phrase, a digression, can all be eliminated. For example, cut "Once upon a time there was" to "Once there was." Eliminate adjectives where they seem superfluous. The result will be a tightened story, which becomes a script to be read word for word.

If the story you have chosen is not long enough for the allotted time, stretch the program with poetry or song or both. A lively theme song can be used as an introduction and as a fade-out to set the mood for the program.

Plan programs well in advance. Obtain the permission of the publisher to use any copyrighted materials that are needed for the program. Be sure to give credit to the author, illustrator, and publisher of any book used, whether or not it is protected by copyright.

During the broadcast it is very important for the storyteller to watch the director or floor manager for cues and to follow directions. Be prepared to improvise, especially during the last few minutes of the program. Do not speak too quickly, but do not drag out the story. Enunciate clearly, use a natural manner and voice, avoid overdramatization, but do not eliminate all the drama in your telling, especially on radio. Use the dramatic pause and perfect its timing. Have a glass of water handy for that unexpected tickle in the throat. (The glass of water and any notes you have can be hidden from the camera by placing them behind your books.) Look directly into the camera, not at the monitor, and remember that the microphone picks up the slightest noise—a cleared throat, a sigh, the rattle of papers. It is difficult for most storytellers to tell a story to a microphone or to a camera, so try to picture a group of listeners as you tell. Let the enjoyment of the story come through in your voice if the medium is radio, and through your voice and facial expression if the medium is television.

NOTES

1. Dorothy Butler, *Cushla and Her Books* (Horn Book, 1980), p. 107.
2. Louise M. Pulley, Correspondence with the author.
3. Craig Werner, "A Blind Child's View of Children's Literature," *Children's Literature* 12 (1984): 209–216.
4. Jed P. Luchow, "Selecting Picture Storybooks for Young Children with Learning Disabilities," in *The Special Child in the Library,* ed. Barbara Holland Baskin and Karen H. Harris (American Library Assn., 1976), p. 49. Reprinted in *Jump over the Moon,* ed. Pamela Petrick Barron and Jennifer Q. Burley (Holt, 1984), p. 406.
5. Evelyn Walker, ed., *Programming for Serving Children with Special Needs,* prepared by the Library Service to Children with Special Needs Committee, Association for Library Service to Children (American Library Assn., 1994), p. 10.
6. Rita C. Organ, Curator, Programmer of African-American Materials, The Children's Museum of Indianapolis. Correspondence with the author.

7. Diana C.J. Matthias and Carole Walton, "Storytelling in Art Museums," in *Advisory* (National Art Education Assn., Summer 1996). Sections of this *Advisory* are reprinted here with the permission of the authors.
8. Lilian Okun, *Let's Listen to a Story* (Wilson, 1959), pp. 11–12.

Storytelling to Young Children

. . . sharing books, rhymes, and pictures is one of the richest experiences we can offer young children, and one of the most rewarding experiences we can offer ourselves.
—Jan Ormerod[1]

THE FIRST LIBRARY STORY hours were designed for children eight years and older, the age when children were expected to know *how* to read (as noted in Chapter 2). Librarians wanted to encourage young readers, and considered storytelling a form of reading guidance. Picture-book hours for younger children soon followed, but it was not until the 1940s that picture-book programs for the three- to five-year-olds became a regular part of library service to children.

The parent and child literature-sharing programs for infants and toddlers and their caregivers began in 1935 with the "Mothers' Room" program started by Clarence Sumner, director of the Youngstown (Ohio) Public Library. Sumner was a visionary who saw the Mothers' Room as "the 'builder' and 'feeder' for the Children's Room, being the logical first unit in the program of the public library."[2] The Mothers' Room was designed to encourage literature-sharing activities between mothers and preschoolers, not with the purpose of teaching young children to read, but "to impress upon their minds the pleasures of literature."[3] The Mothers' Room collection included picture storybooks and books and magazines on parenting. Lectures were presented every other week on children's reading, child care, and family relations. The movement spread nationwide, but after World War II, for reasons still unclear, librarians focused their attention on the three- to five-year-olds. One reason was the influx of picture-book artists from Europe and the improved technology that made possible the making of beautiful picture books for young children.

Library story hours for the three- to five-year-olds began in the late 1930s, and by 1940 were firmly established as part of regular library work. When the federal government initiated Head Start in 1965, attention once more turned to the role of the parent or primary caregiver as the child's first teacher. The Harvard Preschool Project (1965-1978) clearly demonstrated the importance of the first three years of life in intellectual, emotional, social, and language development. Such programs substantiated the research and writings of Swiss psychologist Jean Piaget on early learning. This new information convinced librarians of the need to shift their orientation away from the librarian-child–centered preschool story hours toward infant and toddler parent-child–centered programs.

Parent and Child Literature-Sharing Programs

Today, most public libraries offer storytimes for toddlers. Many offer literature-sharing programs for infants as young as six months. Storytimes for children under age three are informational programs designed to introduce parents and other caregivers to library materials and services and to demonstrate effective ways of sharing literature with very young children. The goals of the parent and child literature-sharing program are:

1. To bring parents an awareness of quality books and nonprint materials developmentally appropriate for young children
2. To give parents participatory experiences in sharing literature with their children and an opportunity to observe effective storytelling
3. To introduce the public library as a resource center for parents
4. To provide a place for first-time parents to meet
5. To give infants and toddlers a joyous experience so that they will associate books and libraries with pleasure [4]

Encourage parents to make storybook reading a part of their children's everyday life. The research shows that children who are read to early on and who associate books with pleasure are likely to become lifelong readers. From listening to stories, children learn story structure, patterns of language, the connection between the squiggly lines on the page and words, and the connection between words and meaning. Even though infants and toddlers may not understand much of what is read to them, they are learning to connect the world of books to the world around them. This helps them later as they learn to read and write.

Before starting a parent and child literature-sharing program, carefully consider the practical issues. Is there a quiet, self-contained area, away from distractions, where the parents and infants and toddlers can listen to stories and enjoy other appropriate storytime activities together? Are there enough books and other materials to support the program? Is there enough staff? Librarians who have conducted many parent and child literature-sharing programs estimate that a 15- to 20- minute storytime may require two hours of preparation time. There are books to help you with program planning (see titles listed under "Resources for Planning Early

Childhood Services for the Storyteller," at the end of this chapter), and of course you can repeat a program during another series or on visits to early childhood centers.

Many librarians have found it is impossible to schedule the number of storytimes demanded by older, better-educated parents who want the best for their children. At the other extreme, there are communities where teenage parents—some still children themselves—are unaware of library services that could help them, and communities where people are totally unaware of what the library has to offer because they are newly arrived from countries in which library service is not well developed. Hard decisions have to be made. If you cannot offer as many storytimes within the library as you would like, consider offering a series or limiting attendance to one series only. You might schedule workshops for day-care and Head Start staff in selection and presentation of literature to young children, so they can conduct their own programs, or you might make a demonstration video to show to parents and child caregivers.

The earliest introduction to literature is through the ear—lullabies, nursery rhymes, and the like—but lap reads can begin as soon as the infant is able to support his or her own head, at about three months. In *Family Storybook Reading,* authors Denny Taylor and Dorothy Strickland say "Books are like lullabies: they caress a newborn baby, calm a fretful child, and help a nervous mother."[5] During the parent and infant literature-sharing program you can introduce parents to board books, story rhymes, play songs, and singing games that they can enjoy with their young children at home. Infants delight in looking at the photos of babies in *The Baby's Book of Babies* by Kathy Henderson and the soft watercolor paintings in *Time for Bed* by Mem Fox. They appreciate the sharp figure-ground contrast in Tana Hoban's *Black on White* and *White on Black.*

Children younger than 18 months of age are not ready for much story listening in a group, but enjoy interacting with the parents or caregivers in turn-taking games, such as "pat-a-cake" and "peek-a-boo"; chanting nursery rhymes; singing; and looking at clear, bright pictures. They relish the sounds of language. Use Mother Goose nursery rhymes, perhaps accompanied by flannel-board figures, and simple stories with familiar objects (such as *Goodnight Moon* by Margaret Wise Brown, and *"More More More," Said the Baby: 3 Love Stories* by Vera Williams).

Here is a sample "Finger Fun for Babies" program based on one offered at the Portland (Maine) Public Library and contributed by Phyllis Fuchs, children's librarian at the Curtis Memorial Library in Brunswick, Maine. Fuchs writes that the program requires energy to maintain a brisk pace throughout the 20-minute session and she recommends having two presenters who offer the rhymes alternately. Each rhyme is introduced with a cheerful descriptive phrase intended to get everyone ready; for

FIGURE 18.   *Infant story hour at Wolfsohn Library, King of Prussia, Pennsylvania.*
(Photograph © Barbara Kernaghan.)

example, "Here's a bouncing one" or "Get ready for a fall." Each rhyme is repeated twice and accompanied by appropriate actions.

1. Pat a cake, pat a cake, baker's man . . .
2. "Let's twinkle." Twinkle, twinkle little star . . . opening and shutting fingers for twinkles.
3. "A bouncing one"—Ride a cock horse to Banbury Cross . . .
4. This little piggy went to market . . .
5. "Get ready for a big jump!" Leg over leg the dog went to Dover . . .
6. "Get ready for a fall." Humpty Dumpty . . .
7. Hickory, dickory, dock . . .
8. "Get your rowing arms ready." Row, row, row your boat . . .
9. Five little ducks went swimming in the water . . . with a clap for each quack.
10. Diddle diddle dumpling, my son John. . . . This becomes a bouncing rhyme.
11. The eensie weensie spider . . .
12. Trot trot to Boston. . . . A lap rhyme with a drop between the adult's legs for the child.
13. Tommie Thumb is up and Tommie Thumb is down, Tommie Thumb is dancing all around the town. . . . This song and finger play continue using all the fingers in turn: Peter Pointer, Toby Tall, Ruby Ring, and Baby Finger.
14. The wheels on the bus . . .
15. Depending on the time, the presenter might ask for a request or two.
16. At this point, the presenter might invite the babies to choose a book from a pile of books placed in the middle of the floor and take it to the adult so child and adult can look at a book together.
17. After a few minutes for sharing books, the presenter closes the program with a song, such as "If You're Happy and You Know It, Clap Your Hands."

You can find lots of other good program ideas in books listed under "Resources for Planning Early Childhood Services for the Storyteller," at the end of this chapter.

By age two or younger, children are able to follow a simple story plot. As Hannah Nuba observes in "Books and Babies,"

the age of two is ideal for introducing books to children in a library group setting. By age two, children have developed a strong command of language. They love picture books about familiar experiences, with lilting repetitions and colorful, recognizable illustrations.

Two-year-olds are very concrete in their thinking and not ready to deal with subtle plot lines, abstractions, or fine distinctions. Book experiences for the toddler have until now been mainly on the lap of a caring adult. In the library setting, children still need to see the book close up, page by page, with the librarian occasionally tracing a finger under the text (as parents should do at home) to show the letter-sound-meaning connection.

As the children take their cues from the sounds, the printed symbols on the page, the meaning and enjoyment of the story, the illustrations, and repeated listening experiences, a lifelong link between reading and pleasure will have been forged.[6]

Young children's approach to picture books is a literal one. They expect the pictures to tell them the story. They like to pore over details, such as the bear motif that L. Leslie Brooke incorporates in his pictures throughout the story of "The Three Bears" in *The Golden Goose Book*. Since they cannot read, children's pleasure comes through the senses, especially through their eyes and ears. They need pleasing word sounds and pictures. Stories with rhythm, repetition, and nonsensical words delight. This is the perfect time for Mother Goose.

Toddlers enjoy books that they can interact with—books with pictures that have a flap to lift and books that surprise children with pictures that pop up. *Go Away, Big Green Monster!* by Ed Emberley is an instant hit with the two- and three-year-olds who enjoy the empowerment the story gives them. Toddlers like stories that ask them to anticipate or guess, such as *The Very Hungry Caterpillar* by Eric Carle, and Eric Hill's popular series about the little dog Spot. They enjoy picture books with a simple story line involving commonplace objects and everyday events, like Ezra Jack Keats's stories about Peter. The world is still new to toddlers and they are fascinated by things that older children take for granted.

If you are a beginning storyteller and have not had much experience with very young children, the thought of trying to hold the attention of a group of two- and three-year-olds may be daunting. The trick is to remember to have fun. Little children differ in the ways they like to listen to stories. Some will listen quietly, some will want to join in, while others may get up and wander about. The "wanderers" are the reason it is important to enclose the children within a safe space. A circle works best, with each child sitting in front of the parent or other caregiver.

A typical toddler storytime might include the following components:

theme song or music to settle the group (use same each week in a storytime series)
attention-getter, such as the use of a puppet
name song, where everyone is greeted by name by the librarian or puppet

hand or finger play
story
activity song, rhyme song, circle song
second story
ending song
book sharing, where children and parents or other caregivers look at
  books together

It isn't necessary to center your program around a theme, but many educators believe that a theme helps young children to focus and refocus their attention, thus reinforcing learning. Toddlers like themes about feelings (happy, sad, surprised, mad), simple concepts (colors, opposites), noises/sounds, things that move, achieving independence, and family. Whether or not you use a theme, be sure your program has variety and rhythm. Here are two sample toddler storytime programs. (For further ideas, see "Resources for Planning Early Childhood Services for the Storyteller," at the end of this chapter.)

Toddler Storytime Program
SUBJECT: Rabbits
SONG: "Hello, everybody, hello" (If you have a rabbit puppet have the puppet greet each of the children by name during the song.)
STORY: *The Runaway Bunny* by Margaret Wise Brown
FINGER PLAY: "Little Rabbit"

I saw a little rabbit go hop, hop, hop
  (hop in place)
I saw his long ears go flop, flop, flop
  (hands above head, "flop" wrists over and back)
I saw his eyes go blink, blink, blink
  (blink eyes)
I saw his little nose go twink, twink, twink
  (wiggle nose)
I said, "Little Rabbit, won't you stay?"
  (make a beckoning motion)
He looked at me and hopped away!
  (hop quickly)

STORY: *Mr. Rabbit and the Lovely Present* by Charlotte Zolotow
ACTIVITY SONG: "Shake Your Sillies Out"
STORY: *Rabbit's Morning* by Nancy Tafuri (Engage the children in conversation about the pictures.)
SONG: "If You're Happy and You Know It, Clap Your Hands"

FIGURE 19. *Librarian Curtis Kiefer and toddlers "shake their sillies out" at storytime, Free Library of Philadelphia. Courtesy of the Free Library of Philadelphia.*

Toddler Storytime Program

SUBJECT: Mother Goose

Play selections from Maurice Ravel's *Mother Goose Suite* as the children enter the story-hour room through the maze in *Johnny Crow's Garden*. (The idea of a maze comes from Susan Pine, Materials Specialist, Office of Children's Services at the New York Public Library. Pine duplicated the maze in *Johnny Crow's Garden* and decorated it with Mother Goose characters for a program for young children at the Bloomingdale branch.)

Sing a song from *Jane Yolen's Mother Goose Songbook*.

STORY: *Johnny Crow's Garden* by L. Leslie Brooke

Meet Mother Goose characters. Recite several Mother Goose rhymes as you introduce "Little Miss Muffit," "Humpty Dumpty," "Old King Cole," et al., using flannel-board figures. Say the rhyme twice. Have the children act it out the second time around.

STORY: *The Owl and the Pussycat* by Jan Brett

Close with a song or two from *Jane Yolen's Mother Goose Songbook*.

The Preschool Story Hour

The preschool story hour is designed for children ages three to five. Usually the children attend alone while the parents and caregivers use the time to browse in the parenting collection or in the adult department. In *Booksharing: 101 Programs to Use with Preschoolers,* Margaret Read MacDonald makes "a plea for the inclusion of parents as participants in preschool programs,"[7] but, traditionally, the preschool story hour was considered to be the child's introduction to literature and art in a group setting *on the child's own.* Whether to open up the preschool hour to adults will depend on your community's needs and your own feelings about this. Preschoolers behave differently when their parents are in the story-hour room. One thing you want to avoid is having the parents and caregivers congregate adjacent to the listening area, distracting the children (and the storyteller!) with noisy conversation. If possible, at the first preschool story hour in a series, have another librarian meet with the parents and caregivers to explain the purpose and goals of the preschool story hour and to introduce them to outstanding picture books for young children and some techniques in reading aloud. If no staff member is available, a video, produced by the library staff and covering the same points, can be shown. A third alternative is to encourage the parents and caregivers to browse in the parenting and adult sections of the library. Emphasize to the parent or caregiver the importance of remaining in the library building, as little children sometimes become upset or frightened and it is only a familiar, beloved face (and arms) that will comfort them.

The preschool story hour should provide the following: [8]

1. First lessons in group experiences on their own
2. The ability to sit quietly, to listen to words with open ears, to look at pictures with seeing eyes
3. An introduction to the best in children's literature
4. Opportunities to select books for home reading

Hold the program in a separate room or a quiet corner of the children's room and make it as attractive as possible. Display the picture books you will use in the program with some fresh flowers on a low table. The storyteller usually sits on a stool or low chair, with the children seated on a rug or cushions in a semicircle around the teller. With this arrangement, the children can see the pictures as the storyteller reads the story with the pages of the book turned outward. This means that the storyteller must be thoroughly familiar with the story, but the storyteller does not memorize the text. In preparation, read the book aloud at least twice—first for the story line, and second for the placement of the words in relation to the pictures. Hold the book as you would for a group of children, pictures at their eye level, and practice until you feel comfortable. Most people are comfortable reading the text from the side, with the book cradled in one arm; others have mastered the art of reading the text upside down as they hold the book at the top of its spine and turn the pages. If the group is large (12 to 15 is the ideal size but larger groups can be handled with help), move the book in a sweeping motion so that all of the children in the group can see the pictures. If you practice holding the book in front of a mirror you will quickly learn how to hold it without tilting the pictures. Turn the pages slowly, to give the children time to enjoy the pictures.

Read the story naturally and unhurriedly. A gentle, quiet voice will encourage the children to listen attentively. Read with feeling and expression.

Young children enjoy hearing the same stories over and over. You can add a new dimension to familiar stories by presenting a flannel-board version of a book read previously, or by *telling* the story without using the pictures. This will encourage the child's growing power to imagine. The nursery tales that come from the oral tradition are meant to be *told*. Modern imaginative stories in which the pictures are an integral part of the story (such as *Where the Wild Things Are* by Maurice Sendak) should by read word for word. The pictures and words are so closely interwoven that they should be presented as a unity.

The preschooler is irresistibly attracted to poetry. Kornei Chukovsky, author of *From Two to Five* and a poet himself, writes, "There is hardly a child who does not go through a stage in his preschool years when he is not an avid creator of word rhythms and rhymes."[9] Keep a fine anthology on the storyteller's shelf, such as *Talking Like the Rain: A First Book of Poems* by X. J. Kennedy and Dorothy M. Kennedy.

Be flexible and willing to accommodate the children's attention span and mood. If the children become restless, change the pace with a song, a finger play, or a stretch. Little children are fascinated by handkerchief stories and stories told with objects, such as nesting dolls or paper cutting. See *The Family Storytelling Handbook,* by Anne Pellowski, for instructions.

Be prepared for interruptions. Acknowledge the child with a smile or nod, then go on with the story. Be gentle but firm. Anyone who has seen the film *The Pleasure Is Mutual* will recall the scene where the preschoolers are about to take over the storytime with their exuberance. The storyteller interrupts their enthusiastic comments with a firm "But when you do go . . . " and jumps right into the story.

The preschool story hour usually lasts about 25 to 30 minutes. You may want to extend the program with a *related* activity, such as dramatic play or creative movement based on the story, or by having the children retell the story using flannel-board figures. And, of course, you will want to encourage the parents and caregivers to help the children select books to borrow from the library.

Some libraries offer preschool story hours throughout the year, but most librarians find it more feasible to offer a six- to eight-week series three or four times a year. If there are many preschoolers in your community, you may have to limit a child's attendance to one series. The program is usually held mid-morning or early evening so as not to interfere with afternoon nap time. Occasionally, libraries hold "pajama parties" for preschoolers and older toddlers and their parents in the early evening.

A typical preschool story hour will include three or four stories, with a finger play, poem, or song in between the stories. There are many finger-play collections, but *Ring a Ring O'Roses: Finger Plays for Pre-School Children,* published by the Flint (Mich.) Public Library (one of the first libraries to hold preschool story hours), is an outstanding resource.

The program can be arranged around a theme or not, as you feel comfortable. If you like to work with themes, browse in Margaret MacDonald's *Booksharing: 101 Programs to Use with Preschoolers* and *A to Zoo: Subject Access to Children's Picture Books,* 4th edition, by Carolyn W. Lima and John A. Lima.

Here are two sample preschool story hours:

Preschool Story Hour Program
SUBJECT: Elephants
MUSIC: Selections from Camille Saint-Saëns's *Carnival of the Animals.*
STORY: *Seven Blind Mice* by Ed Young.

FINGER PLAY:

> An elephant goes like this and that
> (rocking sideways, hands stiff out to sides)
> He's terribly big and he's terribly fat
> (continue rocking motion, taking stiff steps)
> He has no fingers (wiggle fingers)
> He has no toes (wiggle toes)
> But OH MY GOODNESS WHAT A NOSE![10]

Make trunk with arms clasped and walk around swinging it.
STORY: *Little Elephant* by Tana Hoban and Miela Ford
STORY: *The Elephant and the Bad Baby* by Elfrida Vipont
ACTION SONG:[11] "One Elephant"

> One elephant went out to play
> On a spider's web one day.
> He had such enormous fun,
> He asked another elephant to come.[11]

Form a circle. One child goes to the middle and chooses another to join after song. Each then chooses another until only parents are left as the circle.
STORY: *Tabu and the Dancing Elephants* retold by Rene Deetlefs

Preschool Story Hour Program
SUBJECT: Gardening
SONG: "Everything Grows" by Raffi
STORY: *Wild Wild Sunflower Child Anna* by Nancy White Carlstrom
FINGER PLAY: Repeat these words from *Wild Wild Sunflower Child Anna* as you do appropriate actions:

> Digging in the garden
> Kneeling on her knees
> Leaning on elbows
> Whispering to the seeds
> Anna sifts the soil lightly through her fingers
> Anna talking, Anna walking
> Sunshine
> Grow, grow
> Grow in the garden, Anna

STORY: *Growing Vegetable Soup* by Lois Ehlert
SONG: "Inch by Inch: The Garden Song" by David Mallett
STORY: *The Carrot Seed* by Ruth Krauss

The Picture-Book Hour

The picture-book hour for five-, six-, and seven-year-olds is probably the easiest storytelling program to plan and conduct. By this age, most children have participated in group activities and have developed some social skills. They have listened to stories and are familiar with story patterns. They are ready for picture books with more narrative than those used in the preschool hour. Interest in the folktale peaks during this period and many beautiful editions of the traditional tales are available. If the book has many pages of text that have no pictures, learn the tale and tell it without the pictures, just as you would to an older group. Share the pictures *after the telling.* The folktales were meant to be *told;* they can stand on their own without illustration. Modern imaginative stories in which the text and pictures are interwoven should be read with the pictures facing toward the children as the story unfolds. If the text is long, read the page with the book turned toward you, then show the illustration to the children after each page.

Children this age enjoy literary fairy tales, such as *Many Moons* by James Thurber and Rudyard Kipling's *Just So Stories.* Use poetry, action rhymes, or participation stories in between the longer stories. See *Juba This and Juba That* by Virginia A. Tashjian for suggestions. This change of pace offers a break from intensive listening. Here are three sample picture-book hours:

Picture-Book Hour Program
THEME: African animal tales
STORY: *How the Ostrich Got Its Neck* retold by Verna Aardema
STORY: *Anansi and the Moss-Covered Rock* retold by Eric A. Kimmel
ACTION STORY: "The Lion Hunt" in *Juba This and Juba That* selected by Virginia A. Tashjian
STORY: *Lazy Lion* by Mwenye Hadithi and Adrienne Kennaway

Picture-Book Hour Program
THEME: Native American tales
    Selections from *The Trees Stand Shining: Poetry of the North American Indians* by Hettie Jones
STORY: *The Legend of the Cranberry* retold by Ellin Greene
STORY: *The First Strawberries* retold by Joseph Bruchac

Musical Picture-Book Hour Program
STORY: *Peter and the Wolf* by Ian Beck

MUSIC: Play "Peter and the Wolf" by Sergei Prokofiev and have the children guess which instrument represents each character in the story.

STORY: *The Philharmonic Gets Dressed* by Karla Kuskin

Hold the picture-book hour in the story-hour room or in a quiet area of the children's room, away from traffic and noise. The program is usually held after school hours or on Saturday and lasts 30 to 45 minutes. Before the children arrive, arrange the picture books from which you will read on the story-hour table, with fresh flowers and the wishing candle. A group of 20 to 30 children is a comfortable number, and 30 to 40 minutes is a reasonable period of time for quiet listening. Tell the children that once the candle is lit, no one speaks but the storyteller. At the end of the story hour, let the children make a wish and blow out the candle. (For safety reasons, do not use the wishing candle with toddlers or preschoolers. Young children are fascinated by the flame and may reach out to touch it, not realizing the danger.) After the story hour, encourage the children to browse at the tables where you have placed the story-hour books and other picture books that they might like to borrow for reading at home. This is an opportunity to talk informally with the children and any parents who are present, to listen to the children's comments about books, and to suggest other titles that the children might enjoy.

The emphasis of this chapter has been picture-book storytelling, but listening can be a complete experience, even for young children. Occasionally, *tell* a short story in between the picture-book presentations. You can find lots of good tales to tell to young children in the folk and fairy tale collections listed under "150+ Titles to Share with Young Children" at the end of this chapter. Also, see the section "Stories to Tell" in the Appendix.

NOTES

1. Jan Ormerod, "Designing Books for Babies," in *Books, Babies, and Libraries: Serving Infants, Toddlers, Their Parents and Caregivers,* by Ellin Greene (American Library Assn., 1991), p. 172.

2. Clarence W. Sumner, *The Birthright of Babyhood* (Nelson, 1936), p. 41.

3. Ibid., p. 42.

4. Ellin Greene, *Books, Babies, and Libraries: Serving Infants, Toddlers, Their Parents and Caregivers* (American Library Assn., 1991). Sections of this chapter are taken from the author's book and are reprinted here with the permission of the author and the publisher.

5. Denny Taylor and Dorothy S. Strickland, *Family Storybook Reading* (Heinemann, 1986), p. 23.

6. Hannah Scheffler Nuba, "Books and Babies," in *Infancy: A Guide to Research and Resources* (Garland, 1986), p. 145.

7. Margaret Read MacDonald, *Booksharing: 101 Programs to Use with Preschoolers* (Library Professional Publns., 1988), pp. 3–4.

8. Augusta Baker, *Once Upon a Time . . .* (New York Library Assn., 1955), p. 3.

9. Kornei Chukovsky, *From Two to Five*, trans. and ed. Miriam Morton, foreword by Frances Clarke Sayers (University of California Press, 1963), p. 64.

10. MacDonald, *Booksharing*, p. 145.

11. Ibid.

Resources for Planning Early Childhood Services for the Storyteller

Books

Butler, Dorothy. *Babies Need Books*. 2nd ed. New York: Penguin, 1988, o.p.

Chukovsky, Kornei. *From Two to Five*. Rev. ed. Trans. and ed. by Miriam Morton. Foreword by Frances Clarke Sayers. University of California Press, 1988. ISBN 0-520-00237-7

DeSalvo, Nancy. *Beginning with Books: Library Programming for Infants, Toddlers, and Preschoolers*. Shoe String Press, 1992. ISBN 0-208-02318-6

Greene, Ellin. *Books, Babies, and Libraries: Serving Infants, Toddlers, Their Parents and Caregivers*. American Library Assn., 1991. ISBN 0-8389-0572-2

Jeffery, Debby. *Literate Beginnings: Programs for Babies and Toddlers*. American Library Assn., 1995. ISBN 0-8389-0640-0

MacDonald, Margaret Read. *Booksharing: 101 Programs to Use with Preschoolers*. Library Professional Publns., 1988. ISBN 0-208-02159-0

Marino, Jane. *Sing Us a Story: Using Music in Preschool and Family Storytimes*. H. W. Wilson, 1994. ISBN 0-8242-0847-1

Marino, Jane, and Dorothy Houlihan. *Mother Goose Time: Library Programs for Babies and Their Caregivers*. H. W. Wilson, 1992. ISBN 0-8242-0850-1

Nichols, Judy. *Storytimes for Two-Year-Olds*. American Library Assn., 1987. ISBN 0-8389-0451-3

Nuba, Hannah, Michael Searson, and Deborah Lovitky Sheiman, eds. *Resources for Early Childhood: A Handbook*. Garland, 1994. ISBN 0-8240-7395-9

Ring a Ring O'Roses: Finger Plays for Pre-School Children. 9th ed. Flint (Mich.) Public Library, 1988.

Tashjian, Virginia. *Juba This and Juba That: Favorite Children's Songs to Sing, Stories to Tell, Rhymes to Chant, Riddles to Guess, and More!* 2nd ed. Illus. By Nadine B. Westcott. Little, Brown, 1995. ISBN 0-316-832340

Taylor, Denny, and Dorothy S. Strickland. *Family Storybook Reading.* Foreword by Bernice E. Cullinan. Heinemann, 1986. ISBN 0-435-08249-3

Films, Videos

The First Three Years. Summary program featuring Burton L. White. Center for Parent Education, n.d. 55 min. 16mm film or video.

Libraries Are for Babies, Too! Smith Atwood Video Services, 1995. 20 min. video. Distibuted by ALA Video/Library Video Network.

Read to Me: Libraries, Books, and Your Baby. Greater Vancouver Library Federation, 1987. 15 min. video.

150+ Titles to Share with Young Children

Mother Goose, Nursery Rhymes, Finger Plays, Action Rhymes, Lullabies, Poetry and Song

Aliki. *Hush Little Baby: A Folk Lullaby.* Simon & Schuster, 1972. ISBN 0-671-66742-4

Chorao, Kay. *The Baby's Lap Book.* Dutton, 1991. ISBN 0-525-44604-4

Christelow, Eileen. *Five Little Monkeys Jumping on the Bed.* Clarion, 1989. ISBN 0-89919-769-8

Clark, Emma Chichester. *I Never Saw a Purple Cow and Other Nonsense Rhymes.* Little, Brown, 1990. ISBN 0-316-14500-9

Cole, Joanna, and Stephanie Calmenson. *Pat a Cake and Other Play Rhymes.* Illus. By Alan Tiegreen. Morrow, 1992. ISBN 0-688-11038-X

Cousins, Lucy. *The Little Dog Laughed and Other Nursery Rhymes.* Dutton, 1990. ISBN 0-525-44573-0

Dabcovich, Lydia. *Sleepy Bear.* Dutton, 1982. ISBN 0-525-39465-6

deAngeli, Marguerite. *Marguerite deAngeli's Book of Nursery and Mother Goose Rhymes.* Doubleday, 1954, o.p.

dePaola, Tomie. *Tomie dePaola's Mother Goose.* Putnam, 1985. ISBN 0-399-21258-2

Fox, Mem. *Time for Bed.* Illus. By Jane Dyer. Harcourt/Gulliver, 1993. ISBN 0-15-288183-2

Ginsburg, Mirra. *Asleep, Asleep.* Illus. by Nancy Tafuri. Greenwillow, 1992. ISBN 0-688-09153-9

Griego, Margot C., et al. *Tortillitas Para Mama: And Other Spanish Nursery Rhymes, Spanish and English.* Illus. by Barbara Cooney. Holt, 1981. ISBN 0-8050-0285-5

Hall, Nancy Abraham, and Jill Syverson-Stork. *Los pollitos dicen: Juegos, rimas y canciones infantiles de paises de hable hispana/The Baby Chicks Sing: Traditional Games, Nursery Rhymes, and Songs from Spanish-*

Speaking Countries. Illus. by Kay Chorao. Little, Brown, 1994. ISBN 0-316-34010-3

Hart, Jane, comp. *Singing Bee! A Collection of Favorite Children's Songs.* Illus. by Anita Lobel. Lothrop, 1982. ISBN 0-688-41975-5

Hughes, Shirley. *Rhymes for Annie Rose.* Lothrop, 1995. ISBN 0-688-14220-6

Jacques, Florence Page. *There Once was a Puffin.* Illus. By Laura McGee Kvasnosky. Dutton, 1995. ISBN 0-525-45291-5

Jaramillo, Nelly Palacio. *Grandmother's Nursery Rhymes: Las Nanas de Abuelita.* Illus. by Elivia. Holt, 1994. ISBN 0-8050-2555-3

Lamont, Priscilla. *Ring-a-Round-a-Rosy: Nursery Rhymes, Action Rhymes, and Lullabies.* Little, Brown/Joy Street, 1990. ISBN 0-316-51292-3

Kennedy, X. J., and Dorothy M. Kennedy. *Talking Like the Rain: A First Book of Poems.* Illus. by Jane Dyer. Little, Brown, 1992. ISBN 0-316-48889-5

Lear, Edward. *The Owl and the Pussycat.* Illus. by Jan Brett. Putnam, 1991. ISBN 0-399-21925-0

Marks, Alan. *Over the Hills and Far Away: A Book of Nursery Rhymes.* North-South, 1994. ISBN 1-55858-285-1

————. *Ring-a-Ring o' Roses and a Ding, Dong, Bell: A Book of Nursery Rhymes.* Picture Book Studio, 1992. ISBN 0-88708-187-8

Marzollo, Jean. *Pretend You're a Cat.* Illus. by Jerry Pinkney. Dial, 1990. ISBN 0-8037-0773-8

Moore, Lilian, comp. *Sunflakes: Poems for Children.* Illus. by Jan Ormerod. Clarion, 1992. ISBN 0-395-58833-2

Ormerod, Jan. *Jan Ormerod's To Baby with Love.* Lothrop, 1994. ISBN 0-688-12558-1

Prelutsky, Jack. *Read-Aloud Rhymes for the Very Young.* Illus. by Marc Brown. Introduction by Jim Trelease. Knopf, 1986. ISBN 0-394-87218-5

Ra, Carol F. *Trot, Trot to Boston.* Illus. by Catherine Stock. Lothrop, 1987. ISBN 0-688-06190-7

Raffi. *The Raffi Singable Songbook.* Illus. by Joyce Yamamoto. Crown, 1988. ISBN 0-517-56638-9

Sharon, Lois & Bram. *Sharon, Lois & Bram's Mother Goose: Songs, Finger Rhymes, Tickling Verses, Games and More.* Illus. by Maryann Kovalski. Little, Brown, 1986. ISBN 0-316-78281-5

Sweet, Melissa. *Fiddle-I-Fee: A Farmyard Song for the Very Young.* Little, Brown/Joy Street, 1992. ISBN 0-316-82516-6

Watson, Wendy. *Wendy Watson's Mother Goose.* Lothrop, 1989. ISBN 0-688-05708-X

Weiss, George David, and Bob Thiele. *What a Wonderful World.* Illus. by Ashley Bryan. Simon & Schuster/Atheneum, 1995. ISBN 0-689-80087-8

Weiss, Nicki. *If You're Happy and You Know It.* Greenwillow, 1987. ISBN 0-688-06444-2

———. *Where Does the Brown Bear Go?* Greenwillow, 1989. ISBN 0-688-07862-1

Westcott, Nadine Bernard. *Peanut Butter and Jelly: A Play Rhyme.* Dutton, 1987. ISBN 0-525-44317-7

Wyndham, Robert. *Chinese Mother Goose Rhymes.* Illus. by Ed Young. Putnam/Sandcastle, 1989. ISBN 0-399-21718-5

Yolen, Jane. *Jane Yolen's Mother Goose Songbook.* Musical arrangments by Adam Stemple. Illus. by Rosekrans Hoffman. Boyds Mills, 1992. ISBN 1-878093-52-5

———. *The Lap-Time Song and Play Book.* Musical arrangements by Adam Stemple. Illus. by Margot Tomas. Harcourt, 1989. ISBN 0-15-243588-3

———. *Sleep Rhymes Around the World.* Boyds Mills, 1994. Illustrated by 17 international artists. ISBN 1-56397-243-3

Zelinsky, Paul O. *The Wheels on the Bus.* Dutton, 1990. ISBN 0-525-44644-3

Board Books, Concept Books, Toy Books

Baer, Edith. *The Wonder of Hands.* Photos by Tana Hoban. Simon & Schuster, 1992. ISBN 0-02-708138-9

Bang, Molly. *Ten, Nine, Eight.* Greenwillow, 1983. ISBN 0-688-00906-9

Brown, Margaret Wise. *Goodnight Moon.* Illus. by Clement Hurd. HarperCollins, 1947. ISBN 0-06-020705-1

———. *The Quiet Noisy Book.* Illus. by Leonard Weisgard. HarperCollins, 1993. ISBN 0-06-020845-7

———. *Runaway Bunny Board Book.* Illus. by Clement Hurd. HarperCollins, 1991. ISBN 0-06-107429-2

———. *The Summer Noisy Book.* Illus. by Leonard Weisgard. HarperCollins, 1993. ISBN 0-06-020855-4

———. *The Winter Noisy Book.* Illus. by Leonard Weisgard. HarperCollins, 1986. ISBN 0-06-020865-1

Carle, Eric. *The Very Hungry Caterpillar.* Philomel, 1994. ISBN 0-399-20853-4

Crews, Donald. *Freight Train.* Greenwillow, 1978. ISBN 0-688-80165-X

Emberley, Ed. *Go Away, Big Green Monster!* Little, Brown, 1992. ISBN 0-316-23653-5

Grindley, Sally. *Shhh!* Illus. by Peter Utton. Little, Brown, 1991. ISBN 0-316-32899-5

Henderson, Kathy. *The Baby's Book of Babies.* Photos by Anthea Sieveking. Dial, 1988. ISBN 0-8037-0634-0

Hill, Eric. *Where's Spot?* Putnam, 1980. ISBN 0-399-20758-9

Hoban, Tana. *Black on White* and *White on Black.* Greenwillow, 1993. ISBN 0-688-11918-2; ISBN 0-688-11919-0 (board books)

———— *What Is That?* Greenwillow, 1994. ISBN 0-688-12920-X (board book)

Isadora, Rachael. *I Touch.* Greenwillow, 1985. ISBN 0-688-04255-4; ISBN 0-688-10524-6 (board book). *I Hear* and *I See* are companion books.

MacDonald, Suse. *Alphabatics.* Simon & Schuster/Bradbury, 1986. ISBN 0-02-761520-0

Martin, Bill, Jr. *Brown Bear, Brown Bear, What Do You See?* Illus. by Eric Carle. Holt, 1992. ISBN 0-8050-1744-5

Numberoff, Laura. *If You Give a Mouse a Cookie.* Illus. by Felicia Bond. HarperCollins, 1985. ISBN 0-06-024587-5

Porter-Gaylord, Laurel. *I Love My Daddy Because . . .* and *I Love My Mommy Because . . .* Illus. by Ashley Wolff. Dutton, 1991. ISBN 0-525-44624-9 (board book); ISBN 0-525-44625-7 (board book)

Shaw, Charles. *It Looked Like Spilt Milk.* HarperCollins, 1947. ISBN 0-06-025566-8

Tafuri, Nancy. *Have You Seen My Duckling?* Greenwillow, 1984. ISBN 0-688-02797-0

————. *Rabbit's Morning.* Greenwillow, 1985. ISBN 0-688-04063-2

Wellington, Monica. *All My Little Ducklings Board Book.* Dutton, 1995. ISBN 0-525-45360-1

Modern Stories (Imaginative and Realistic) to Share with Older Toddlers and Preschoolers

Arnosky, Jim. *Watching Foxes.* Lothrop, 1984. ISBN 0-688-04259-7

Bemelmans, Ludwig. *Madeline.* Viking, 1958. ISBN 0-670-44580-0

Bernstein, Ruth. *Little Gorilla.* Clarion, 1986. ISBN 0-395-28773-1

Buckley, Helen E. *Grandfather and I* and *Grandmother and I.* Illus. by Jan Ormerod. Lothrop, 1994. ISBN 0-688-12533-6; ISBN 0-688-12531-X

Burningham, John. *Mr. Gumpy's Motor Car.* HarperCollins, 1976. ISBN 0-690-00799-X

————. *Mr. Gumpy's Outing.* Holt, 1971. ISBN 0-8050-0708-3

Carlstrom, Nancy White. *Wild Wild Sunflower Child Anna.* Illus. by Jerry Pinkney. Macmillan, 1987. ISBN 0-02-717360-7

deBrunhoff, Jean. *The Story of Babar.* Random House, 1937. ISBN 0-394-80575-5

Dorros, Arthur. *Abuela.* Illus. by Elisa Kleven. Dutton, 1991. ISBN 0-525-44750-4

Ehlert, Lois. *Growing Vegetable Soup.* Harcourt, 1987. ISBN 0-15-232575-1

Ets, Marie Hall. *Play with Me.* Viking, 1955. ISBN 0-670-55977-6

Fleming, Denise. *In the Small, Small Pond.* Holt, 1993. ISBN 0-8050-2264-3

————. *In the Tall, Tall Grass.* Holt, 1991. ISBN 0-8050-1635-X

Ford, Miela. *Little Elephant.* Illus. by Tana Hoban. Greenwillow, 1994. ISBN 0-688-13140-9

————. *Sunflower.* Illus. by Sally Noll. Greenwillow, 1995. ISBN 0-688-13301-0

Ginsburg, Mirra. *Across the Stream.* Illus. by Nancy Tafuri. Greenwillow, 1982. ISBN 0-688-01204-3

Harper, Isabelle, and Barry Moser. *My Dog Rosie.* Scholastic, 1994. ISBN 0-590-47619-X

Henkes, Kevin. *The Biggest Boy.* Illus. by Nancy Tafuri. Greenwillow, 1995. ISBN 0-688-12829-7

Hoffman, Mary. *Amazing Grace.* Illus. by Carolina Binch. Dial, 1991. ISBN 0-8037-1040-2

Hughes, Shirley. *Alfie Gets in First.* Lothrop, 1982. ISBN 0-688-00848-8

Hutchins, Pat. *Little Pink Pig.* Greenwillow, 1994. ISBN 0-688-12014-8

————. *Rosie's Walk.* Simon & Schuster/Macmillan, 1968. ISBN 0-02-745850-4

Johnson, Tony. *Little Wild Parrot.* Illus. by Ora Eitan. Morrow/Tambourine, 1995. ISBN 0-688-13456-4

Keats, Ezra Jack. *The Snowy Day.* Viking, 1962. ISBN 0-670-65400-0

————. *Whistle for Willie.* Viking, 1964. ISBN 0-670-76240-7

Krauss, Ruth. *The Carrot Seed.* Illus. by Crockett Johnson. HarperCollins, 1945. ISBN 0-06-023351-6; *The Carrot Seed Board Book.* HarperCollins, 1993. ISBN 0-694-00492-8

Lobel, Arnold. *Frog and Toad.* HarperCollins, 1996. ISBN 0-06-44167-9 (boxed set, 4 books; also see other stories about Frog and Toad)

London, Jonathan. *Froggy Gets Dressed.* Illus. by Frank Remkiewicz. Viking, 1992. ISBN 0-670-84249-4

Marshall, James. *George and Martha.* Houghton, 1972. ISBN 0-395-16619-5 (also see other stories about George and Martha)

Minarik, Else H. *Little Bear's Visit.* Illus. By Maurice Sendak. HarperCollins, 1961. ISBN 0-06-024265-5 (also see other stories about Little Bear)

Oxenbury, Helen. *Tom and Pippo and the Bicycle.* Candlewick, 1994. ISBN 1-56402-321-4 (also see other stories about Tom and Pippo)

Potter, Beatrix. *The Tale of Peter Rabbit.* Warne, 1987 new ed. with new reproductions. ISBN 0-7232-3460-4 (also see other "Tale of . . . " classics by this famous author-illustrator)

Pryor, Ainslie. *The Baby Blue Cat Who Said No.* Viking, 1988. ISBN 0-670-81780-5

Rankin, Joan. *The Little Cat and the Greedy Old Woman.* Simon & Schuster/McElderry, 1995. ISBN 0-689-50611-2

Reiser, Lynn. *Night Thunder and the Queen of the Wild Horses.* Greenwillow, 1995. ISBN 0-688-11791-0

Ringold, Faith. *Tar Beach.* Crown, 1991. ISBN 0-517-58030-6

Sendak, Maurice. *Where the Wild Things Are.* Harper, 1963. ISBN 0-06-025492-0

Shannon, George. *April Showers.* Illus. by Jose Aruego and Adriane Dewey. Greenwillow, 1995. ISBN 0-688-13121-2

———. *The Surprise.* Illus. by Jose Aruego and Adriane Dewey. Greenwillow, 1983. ISBN 0-688-02313-4

Vipont, Elfrida. *The Elephant and the Bad Baby.* Illus. by Raymond Briggs. HarperCollins, 1986. ISBN 0-698-20039-X

Waddell, Martin. *Can't You Sleep, Little Bear?* Illus. by Barbara Firth. Candlewick, 1992. ISBN 1-56402-007-X

———. *Farmer Duck.* Illus. by Helen Oxenbury. Candlewick, 1992. ISBN 1-56402-009-6

Wahl, Jan. *Little Gray One.* Illus. by Frané Lessac. Morrow, 1993. ISBN 0-688-12037-7

Williams, Linda. *The Little Old Lady Who Was Not Afraid of Anything.* Illus. by Megan Lloyd. HarperCollins, 1986. ISBN 0-690-04586-7

Williams, Vera B. *A Chair for My Mother.* Greenwillow, 1982. ISBN 0-688-00914-X (also see other titles in this series)

———. *"More More More," said the Baby: 3 Love Stories.* Greenwillow, 1990. ISBN 0-688-09173-3

Yashima, Taro. *Umbrella.* Viking, 1958. ISBN 0-670-73858-1

Yolen, Jane. *Owl Moon.* Illus. by John Schoenherr. Philomel, 1987. ISBN 0-399-2145

Traditional Folk and Fairy Tales to Share with Older Toddlers and Preschoolers: Collections

Note: For traditional folk and fairy tales for children ages 5 and older see Appendix.

Baumgartner, Barbara, reteller. *Crocodile! Crocodile! Stories Told Around the World.* Illus. by Judith Moffatt. Dorling Kindersley, 1994. ISBN 1-56458-463-1

Brooke, L. Leslie, illus. *The Golden Goose Book.* Afterword by Neil Philip. Houghton Mifflin, 1992. ISBN 0-395-61303-5

Haviland, Virginia. *The Fairy Tale Treasury.* Illus. by Raymond Briggs. Dell, 1986. ISBN 0-440-42556-5

Lester, Julius. *The Knee-High Man and Other Tales.* Illus. By Ralph Pinto. Dial, 1972. ISBN 0-8037-4593-1

Lottridge, Celia Barker. *Ten Small Tales.* Illus. by Joanne Fitzgerald. Macmillan/McElderry, 1994. ISBN 0-689-50568-X

Oxenbury, Helen, reteller and illus. *The Helen Oxenbury Nursery Story Book.* Knopf, 1992. ISBN 0-394-87519-2

Rockwell, Anne, ed. *The Acorn Tree and Other Folktales.* Greenwillow, 1995. ISBN 0-688-10746-X

Windham, Sophie, reteller. *Read Me a Story: A Child's Book of Favorite Tales.* Scholastic, 1991. ISBN 0-590-44950-8

Single Titles

Aardema, Verna, reteller. *Borreguita and the Coyote.* Illus. by Petra Mathers. Knopf, 1991. ISBN 0-679-80921-X

———. *How the Ostrich Got Its Long Neck.* Illus. by Marcia Brown. Scholastic, 1995. ISBN 0-590-48367-6

Barton, Byron. *The Little Red Hen.* HarperCollins, 1993. ISBN 0-06-021676-X

———. *The Three Bears.* HarperCollins, 1991. ISBN 0-06-020423-0

Brett, Jan. *Goldilocks and the Three Bears.* Putnam, 1990. ISBN 0-399-22004-6

———. *The Mitten: A Ukrainian Folktale.* Putnam, 1990. ISBN 0-399-21920-X

Brown, Marcia. *Once a Mouse.* Simon & Schuster/Scribners, 1972. ISBN 0-684-18490-7

———. *Stone Soup.* Simon & Schuster/Scribners, 1979. ISBN 0-684-92296-7

Deetlefs, Rene. *Tabu and the Dancing Elephants.* Illus. by Lyn Gilbert. Dutton, 1995. ISBN 0-525-45226-5

deGerez, Tree. *When Bear Came Down from the Sky.* Illus. by Lisa Desimini.Viking, 1994. ISBN 0-670-85171-X

Grimm, Jacob, and Wilhelm Grimm. *The Bremen Town Musicians.* Trans. by Anthea Bell. Illus. by Bernadette Watts. North-South, 1992. ISBN 1-55858-140-5

———. *The Elves and the Shoemaker.* Retold and illus. by Bernadette Watts. North-South, 1986. ISBN 1-55858-035-2

———. *Little Red-Riding Hood.* Illus. by Trina Schart Hyman. Holiday, 1983. ISBN 0-8234-0470-6

Kimmel, Eric A. *Anansi and the Moss-Covered Rock.* Illus. By Janet Stevens. Holiday, 1990. ISBN 0-8234-0689-X

Percy, Graham, illus. *The Cock, the Mouse, and the Little Red Hen.* Candlewick, 1992. ISBN 1-56402-008-8

Rounds, Glen, reteller and illus. *Three Little Pigs and the Big Bad Wolf.* Holiday, 1992. ISBN 0-8234-0923-6

Sandburg, Carl. *The Wedding Procession of the Rag Doll and the Broom Handle and Who Was in It.* Illus. by Harriet Pincus. Harcourt, 1978. ISBN 0-15-695487-7

Slobodkina, Esphyr. *Caps for Sale.* HarperCollins, 1947. ISBN 0-201-09147-X

Thurber, James. *Many Moons.* Illus. by Marc Simont. Harcourt, 1990. ISBN 0-15-251872-X

Young, Ed, trans. and illus. *Lon Po Po: A Red-Riding Hood Story from China.* Putnam, 1989. ISBN 0-399-21619-7

———. *Seven Blind Mice.* Putnam, 1992. ISBN 0-399-22261-8

Musical Recordings: A Sampling

American Folk Songs for Children. Sung by Pete Seeger. Smithsonian/Folkways SF 45020

Babes, Beasts, and Birds. Sung by Pat Carfra. Lullaby Lady Productions/dist. by Alcazar JOL 3

Baby and Me: Playsongs and Lullabies to Share with Your Baby. Sung by Rachael Buchman. A Gentle Wind GW 1055

Baby Games: 6 Weeks to 1 Year. Created by Priscilla Hegner, with musical arrangements by Dennis Buck. Kimbo Educational KIM 9102/9102C

The Baby Record Featuring Bob McGrath and Katharine Smithrim. Kids Records KRLIKRC 1007

Baby's Bedtime. Lullabies from Kay Chorao's book, sung by Judy Collins. Lightyear Entertainment LIGHT 5105. (Other titles in this series include *Baby's Morningtime,* sung by Judy Collins, LIGHT 5104 and *Baby's Nursery Rhymes,* sung by Phylicia Rashad, LIGHT 5107.)

BabySong. Sung by Hap and Martha Palmer. Educational Activities AR 713/AC713

Bean Bag Activities. Kimbo Educational KIM 7055/7055C

Birds, Beasts, Bugs and Little Fishes. Sung by Pete Seeger. Smithsonian/Folkways SF 45021

Camels, Cats and Rainbows. Sung by Paul Strausman. A Gentle Wind GW 1009

Did You Feed My Cow? Fred Koch and a group of children present the songs of Ella Jenkins. Red Rover Records RRR–333

Early, Early Childhood Songs. Sung by Ella Jenkins. Smithsonian/Folkways SF 45015

Golden Slumbers: Lullabies from Far and Near. Harper Children's Audio 0-89845-104-3. Traditional lullabies performed by Pete Seeger and Oscar Brand.

Hello Everybody! Playsongs and Rhymes from a Toddler's World. Sung by Rachael Buchman. A Gentle Wind GW 1038

If You're Happy and You Know It Sing Along with Bob. Vols. 1 and 2. Sung by *Sesame Street*'s Bob McGrath. Kids' Records KRL/KRC 1009 and KRL/KRC 1014

It's Toddler Time. Sung by Norm Michaels and Lynn Roberts. Kimbo Educational. KIM 0815/0815C

Mainly Mother Goose: Songs and Rhymes for Merry Young Souls. Performed by Sharon, Lois & Bram. Elephant Records EF 301 (Listen to other titles by this popular trio from Canada.)

More Singable Songs. Performed by Raffi. KSR 8104/8104C

Singable Songs for the Very Young. Performed by Raffi. KRS 8102/8102C

Songs and Games for Toddlers. Kids Records KRL 1016/KRC 1016

Songs to Grow On for Mother and Child. Sung by Woody Guthrie. Smithsonian/Folkways SF 45035

Toddlers on Parade. Sung by Lynn Roberts. Kimbo Educational KIM 9002/9002C

You'll Sing a Song and I'll Sing a Song. Sung by Ella Jenkins. FC 7664C

Storytelling to Young Adults

At a time when the young person feels bombarded by inner changes and the world's expectations and constraints; at a time when the adult feels bombarded by the resulting changes, questions, and criticisms, the coming together of story-teller and listener is even sweeter, and the naturally occurring rapport developed between teller and listener even more powerful. Don't think that storytelling isn't important for this age group. It is even more important!
—Beth Horner [1]

YOUNG ADULTS OFTEN QUESTION the appropriateness of storytelling as an activity for them, but many of the values of storytelling discussed in Chapter 3 are pertinent to the needs of adolescents. For example, literary fairy tales, with their underlying meaning, humanistic philosophy, and bittersweet mood, are especially meaningful to young people who are becoming aware of their individuality and who find their values in conflict with society. These tales give the young adolescent courage to explore his or her inner space, dreams, images, and feelings, and through imagination, to construct a self.

In her article "To Tell or Not to Tell: Storytelling for Young Adults," Beth Horner recommends "a gradual exposure to storytelling by integrating it into successful existing programs or into situations in which the young adult is a captive audience, such as the school assembly or classroom."[2] A guest storyteller can ask to be introduced as one who has come to talk *about* storytelling rather than as a storyteller.

Classroom projects, such as collecting family stories, using stories as a springboard to creative writing, or learning to tell stories to young children (see Chapter 10), create an interest in storytelling for its own sake.

Many adults are intimidated at the prospect of telling stories to adolescents. However, this age group can also be the most satisfying and fun group with which to share stories. An excellent aid is *Storytelling for Young Adults: Techniques and Treasury* by Gail de Vos. This book is divided into two major sections. The first section presents the values of storytelling for young adults and basic storytelling techniques for this age-group, and suggests how to integrate storytelling and storytelling techniques into the classroom. The second section summarizes approximately 200 stories (with sources and timing) and gives the complete text of 21 stories "that have been tried and tested with young adult audiences."[3]

In this chapter, Beth Horner, a professional storyteller and former librarian, discusses the elements of a successful storytelling program for young adults: story selection, presentation (how to introduce and present the program), and program flow.

Story Selection

According to Jean Piaget's theory of intellectual development, adolescence marks the stage of "formal operations," the stage at which one can logically consider abstract ideas. Thus adolescents are able to consider ideas beyond their own experience and to look at issues from several different viewpoints. It is at this stage in life that one begins to challenge accepted ideas and beliefs, to draw away from the values and expectations of authority figures. Struggling to form an identity, but not yet ready to be completely independent, the young adult tends to rely on his or her peer group for beliefs and values. Facing adulthood with its responsibilities can be overwhelming. These factors and the added confusion caused by hormonal changes and physical growth can make for a challenging period of development.

This said, it is not surprising that teens like stories that provide a bit more intellectual challenge, that are more psychologically complicated, that contain characters who are not necessarily all good or all evil, that poke fun at accepted values or authority figures, that provide a look at some darker aspects of life and an opportunity to face fearful beings and situations, that include family conflict, that hint at the complications of emotional and physical love, and that speak to feelings of powerlessness.

Specific categories of stories that are particularly popular with young adults include ghost, horror, and suspense tales; urban-belief tales; humor, including fractured tellings of well-known tales; myths, hero tales, and legends; folktales; historical tales; tales of life's conflicts and issues; riddle tales; and science fiction.

Ghost, Horror, and Suspense Tales

The most popular type of story for young adults is the tale of suspense. These stories speak to many of the issues mentioned earlier. Suspense tales are good program openers because they immediately dispel any thought that storytelling is too babyish for young adult audiences. Surefire suspense stories include such folktales as "Sop Doll," "The Skull," "Mary Culhane and the Dead Man," "The Phantom Black Carriage," "Mr. Fox," and "The Weeping Lass at the Dancing Place," and longer literary tales—requiring editing to make them easily tellable—such as "The Monkey's Paw" and "Occurrence at Owl Creek Bridge."

Edgar Allan Poe, Judith Gorog, Maria Leach, Ruth Manning-Sanders, and Sorche Nic Leodhas all have collections containing tales with varying levels of suspensefulness. Recommended recordings include *The Tell-Tale Heart and Other Terrifying Tales, Chillers*, and *Tales from the Other Side.*

Some people object to stories with ghosts and witches. Yet the reason there are so many tales of ghosts and other frightening creatures is that these stories are psychologically important in our lives. According to psychologists, we vicariously experience whatever the main character in a story experiences. When the main character overcomes his or her own fears and defeats a frightening being or situation, we learn to face and defeat our own fears as well. This is an essential part of learning to live in a complicated world. Making a brief statement to this effect before or after telling one of these stories might help you and your listeners feel more relaxed. You might even remark that the reason there are so many headless creatures in stories is that the thing we fear more than anything in the world is losing our heads! This lighthearted approach usually puts listeners at ease so that they can listen and enjoy the story. At the same time, we need to respect the wishes of our listeners and sponsors. If, prior to the program, the sponsor requests stories without witches or ghosts, honor that request. There are many suspenseful tales that include neither.

Urban-Belief Tales

An offshoot of the suspense tale is the urban-belief tale or urban legend. These tales are popular with young adults because they often contain elements of suspense or eeriness. Young adults find them intriguing, too, because they are told as if they actually happened. Teens who have heard variations of these stories immediately become interested, and a rapport is established between teller and listener. Good sources include collections by Jan Brunvand, Daniel Cohen, and Alvin Schwartz.

Humor, Including Fractured Tellings of Well-Known Tales

Shared humor is a strong bonding tool. However, "what is funny" varies from age-group to age-group, and from culture to culture. Humor is usually best understood by one's peer group and, sometimes, best shared in one's peer group, so selecting a humorous story can be tricky. As mentioned earlier in this chapter, young adults find the irreverent, satirical tales funny because they poke fun at accepted standards. For example, our culture's emphasis on physical beauty as a requisite for happiness is turned on its head by Natalie Babbitt's sly wit in "The Very Pretty Lady."

Tales with a humorous, surprise ending, such as "Those Three Wishes" by Judith Gorog, are of interest to this age-group because this group enjoys the unexpected. Another successful humorous tale to tell to young adults is "The Mousedeer and the Buffalo Chip," an Indonesian story that can be heard on the recording *An Evening at Cedar Creek*. The humor revolves around the familiar theme of the weak outwitting the strong, this time with the help of a little manure! In "The Two Old Women's Bet," the women compete to see whose husband is the most foolish. Noodlehead stories, such as those found in *When Shlemiel Went to Warsaw,* allow young people to laugh at themselves and to feel superior at the same time.

Irreverence is particularly appreciated by young adults, but they are also fascinated by literary, poetic, and even cultural variations of well-known tales. All speak to that stage of seeing things from different points of view and branching away from the well-known or generally accepted. Consider *Fables for Our Time* by James Thurber, *Fables You Shouldn't Pay Any Attention To* by Florence P. Heide, and selections from *American Literature in Parody* edited by Robert P. Falk. Jane Yolen's *Sleeping Ugly,* Vivian Vande Velde's *Tales from the Brothers Grimm and the Sisters Weird,* and the collections by William J. Brooke are amusing take-offs on folk and fairy tales familiar from childhood. Poetic versions of well-known tales are found in *Disenchantments: An Anthology of Modern Fairy Tale Poetry* by Wolfgang Mieder, and *Transformations* by Anne Sexton. A few satirical pieces such as "And Although the Little Mermaid Sacrificed Everything to Win the Love of the Prince, the Prince, Alas, Decided to Wed Another" are included in Judith Viorst's poetry collection *If I Were in Charge of the World.*

Myths, Hero Tales, and Legends

Young adults enjoy the grand adventure story. They are fascinated by tales with multidimensional characters to whom they can relate. These tales include myths about the Greek and Norse gods and goddesses, Arthurian legends, and epics such as *Beowulf* and the *Odyssey.* It can be difficult to work these epic tales into easily learnable and tellable tales. Storyteller Ron Adams, a 23-year veteran of teaching Egyptian, Greek, and Norse mythologies through storytelling in his English classes at Collinsville (Ill.) High School, finds *Mythology* by Edith Hamilton to have the most easily tellable form of the myths, clearly edited with strong plot lines. Adams also recommends *Bulfinch's Mythology* and *The Golden Bough.* Barbara McBride-Smith, storyteller and librarian, combines mythology and satire in her retellings of myths on her recording *Medusa and Other Good Ol' Greeks.* An excellent example of condensing an epic is Syd Lieberman's 13-minute retelling of Beowulf's first adventure on his recording *The Tell-Tale Heart and Other Terrifying Tales.*

Folktales

Cultural variations of traditional tales are of interest because they provide a whole different take on what is considered an old story, but they are best told in the middle of the program rather than at the beginning. There are many ways to find these tales, including resource books such as

Margaret Read MacDonald's *The Storyteller's Sourcebook*.[4] Tales can be found simply by browsing in the picture-book section of the library. There one finds such gems as *Moss Gown, Lon Po Po: A Red Riding Hood Story from China*, and *Yeh Shen: A Cinderella Story from China*. One might not think of the picture-book collection (ordinarily considered appropriate for children) as a source, but the stories in these books are often of interest to young adults.

Historical Tales

The historical story is extremely powerful and, if well edited and well told, of particular interest to young adults. Look to history and historical figures for storytelling material, and be prepared to structure what you find. The historical story intrigues because it tells of events (often heroic and, just as interesting, often commonplace) that actually took place. These tales often portray real-life issues that teens deal with on a daily basis. There are numerous sources on the library shelf. Consider excerpts from *Selma, Lord, Selma: Girlhood Memories of the Civil Rights Days* by Sheyann Webb, Rachel West Nelson, and Frank Sikora. This firsthand account of two African-American teenagers' experiences during the turbulent Civil Rights uprisings and marches in Selma, Alabama, in the 1960s is vividly and clearly told. Another true and exciting story, "Where the Girl Rescues Her Brother," tells of a young Cheyenne woman who rescued her brother from Crow scouts during a battle near Rosebud Creek in present-day Montana. Joseph Bruchac and Gayle Ross tell us that the battle took place only a few days before the Lakota and Cheyenne victory against the forces of Lieutenant Colonel George Armstrong Custer at Little Bighorn.

Tales of Life's Conflicts and Issues

Love, depression, family conflict, war, acceptance by others, and similar issues are the subject of many folk and literary tales and are of particular importance to adolescents. Wait until the middle or later part of a program before telling these stories to young adult listeners; by that time, they will be more comfortable with the idea of storytelling and will be better able to listen and absorb these more sensitive tales. "Oliver Hyde's Dishcloth Concert" delves into the loss of a loved one, depression, and the importance of one's community when facing life's difficult times. "Like Meat Loves Salt" is a King Lear tale of family conflict, betrayal, and learning the meaning of true family love. "A Young Woman of Vietnam," a retelling of a Chinese folktale, is a poignant but slightly humorous story of cross-generational conflict and acceptance; "The Apple Tree" speaks to family acceptance of a wayward son. "Whitebear Whittington," "Owl," and "Count Alaric's Lady" address different aspects of romantic love.

Riddle Tales

Intrigued by an intellectual challenge, young adults enjoy riddle tales such as "Clever Manka," "The Smuggler," and those found in George Shannon's Stories to Solve series and *While Standing on One Foot: Puzzle Stories and Wisdom Tales from the Jewish Tradition* by Nina Jaffe and Steve Zeitlin. "Sir Gawain and the Loathly Lady," an Arthurian tale about obtaining power over one's own destiny, centers around the question "What is it that women most desire?"

Science Fiction

Young adults enjoy science fiction and fantasy; they are fascinated by worlds, beings, and societies totally different from the known. The stories of Ray Bradbury and Isaac Asimov are highly recommended; try Bradbury's "All Summer in a Day" and Asimov's "The Ugly Little Boy."

Presentation (How to Introduce and Present the Program)

A brief, simple introduction enhances a program if it anticipates anything that might block the listeners from enjoying the story and if it indicates to the listeners that the teller respects them, their experiences, and their opinions. If the young adult listeners are new to storytelling and scoff at the idea, it is helpful to dispel immediately any notion that storytelling is "just for little kids," so that they can relax and enjoy the program. Briefly discuss the function of storytelling in society. Explain that this ancient art was originally a form of entertainment for adults and that there is a current revival of storytelling for adults with many festivals, concerts, and recordings that are not for children (in particular, mention "Tellabration," celebrated throughout the United States on the Saturday evening before Thanksgiving). Present this material in an informative rather than a defensive manner. This kind of introduction will assure young adults that you do not consider them to be children, that you respect them, and that you will treat them as adults. If you plan to accompany any of your stories with an autoharp or other musical instrument, you might ask the group to observe this storytelling style with an analytical eye and decide whether the addition of music detracts from or enhances the story. After the story, ask for their opinions. Such follow-up again indicates your respect for their intelligence and viewpoint.

If a story has an odd name or strange phrase that you know will distract your listeners, mention it ahead of time, indicating the source of the phrase or name, and suggest that they simply "ride with it" when it shows up in the story. For example, before telling the story "Sop Doll," mention the term "job of work" and explain that different cultures use different words or phrases to describe the same thing and that "job of work" simply refers to what we call "a job." Explain that one of the characters makes a very odd sound and says something that might at first seem to be gibberish. Suggest that they listen closely and see if they can figure out the meaning. After the story, ask for their interpretations of the term "sop doll" and then explain that "doll" is a colloquialism for paw or hand and that "sopping" is similar to dunking.

Program Flow

Carefully planning the flow of the program is important. Consider beginning the program with a suspense tale told in a straightforward manner, avoiding exaggerated voice changes or an overly dramatic style, thus easing the listener into the storytelling experience. Young adults associate the suspenseful tale as appropriate for adults and immediately become engrossed and can relax and listen to the program instead of punching their buddies and rolling their eyes to indicate to their peers that they are not taken in by a children's activity. Some storytellers start with a "jump" story that startles the listeners and causes them to laugh at themselves and each other, and to relax even more. A good rapport is now established. You may choose to cement this rapport by next telling an urban-belief tale before moving on to other types of stories.

Once listeners realize that they are going to enjoy the program and have confidence in the teller, they will relax and be able to absorb and enjoy a wider variety of story content and styles; they will become interested in the stories and the storytelling process. The middle and later part of the program can include any number of the types of stories mentioned earlier, stories that might take more intellectual concentration to absorb or that ask for deeper emotional involvement. Include at least one quieter, subtler, more sensitive tale that speaks to some of the conflicts and issues with which teens grapple. These stories do not necessarily get an overt reaction, but often they are the ones best remembered and the ones that have the most impact.

Lastly, it works well to close the program with a humorous tale. By the end of the program, there is a better understanding of what both the teller and listeners "consider to be funny." Ending with a humorous story closes the program on an upbeat, satisfying note.

Notes

1. Beth Horner, Storytelling to Young Adults Workshop held at Mundelein College during Children's Reading Round Table Conference, October 1990. A major portion of Chapter 9 consists of material presented by Beth Horner in her workshops and reflects her extensive experience in storytelling to young adults.
2. Beth Horner, "To Tell or Not to Tell: Storytelling for Young Adults," *Illinois Libraries* 65 (September 1983): 458-464.

3. Gail deVos, *Storytelling for Young Adults: Techniques and Treasury.* Libraries Unlimited, 1991.

4. Margaret Read MacDonald, *The Storyteller's Sourcebook: A Subject, Title and Motif Index to Folklore Collections for Children. Neal-Schuman/Gale Research, 1982.*

Titles to Share with Young Adults

Ghosts, Horror, and Suspense Tales

Bierce, Ambrose. "Occurrence at Owl Creek Bridge." In *In the Midst of Life: Tales of Soldiers and Civilians* by Ambrose Bierce. Citadel, 1993. ISBN 0-80-650551-6

The Folktellers. *Chillers.* Mama-T Artists MTA-2

Jacobs, W. W. "The Monkey's Paw." In *The Oxford Book of English Ghost Stories*, chosen by Michael Cox and R. A. Gilbert. Oxford University Press, 1986. ISBN 0-19214163-5

Keding, Dan. *Stories from the Other Side.* Turtle Creek Recordings TC 1003

Lieberman, Syd. *The Tell-Tale Heart and Other Terrifying Tales.* SL Productions SL 105

"Mary Culhane and the Dead Man." In *The Goblins Giggle and Other Stories* by Molly Bang. Peter Smith, 1988. ISBN 0-8446-6360-3. Told by Carol Birch on *Nightmare Rising.* Frostfire 100; told by The Folktellers on *Chillers* Mama-T Artists MTA-2

"Mr. Fox." In *English Fairy Tales* by Joseph Jacobs. Dover, 1989. ISBN 0-486-21818-X. Told by Carol Birch on *Nightmares Rising.* Frostfire 100; told by the Folktellers on *Chillers* Mama-T Artists MTA-2

"The Phantom Black Carriage." Retold by Bob Dyer and Beth Horner on *An Evening at Cedar Creek.* Wellspring CS 4902

"The Skull." In *The Book of Ghosts and Goblins* by Ruth Manning-Sanders. Dutton, 1969, o.p. Told by Beth Horner on *An Evening at Cedar Creek* Wellspring CS 4902

"Sop Doll." In *Jack Tales* by Richard Chase. Houghton, 1943. ISBN 0-395-06694-8

"The Weeping Lass at the Dancing Place." In *Twelve Great Black Cats and Other Eerie Scottish Tales* by Sorche Nic Leodhas. Dutton, 1971, o.p.

Urban-Belief Tales

Brunvand, Jan Harold. *The Choking Doberman and Other "New" Urban Legends.* Norton, 1986. ISBN 0-393-30321-7

———. *The Vanishing Hitchhiker: American Urban Legends and Their Meaning.* Norton, 1989. ISBN 0-393-95169-3

Cohen, Daniel. *Southern Fried Rat and Other Gruesome Tales.* M. Evans, 1982. ISBN 0-87131-400-2

Schwartz, Alvin. *Scary Stories to Tell in the Dark: Collected from American Folklore.* HarperCollins, 1981. ISBN 0-397-31926-6 (See other titles in this series.) Also available on Harper Children's Audio CPN 1794.

Humor, Including Fractured Tellings of Well-Known Tales

Babbitt, Natalie. "The Very Pretty Lady." In *The Devil's Storybook.* Farrar, 1974. ISBN 0-374-31770-4

Brooke, William J. *A Telling of the Tales: Five Stories.* HarperCollins, 1990. ISBN 0-06-020688-8

————. *Untold Tales.* HarperCollins, 1992. ISBN 0-06-020271-8

Falk, Robert P., ed. *American Literature in Parody.* Greenwood, 1977. ISBN 0-8371-9741-4

Heide, Florence P. *Fables You Shouldn't Pay Any Attention To.* Lippincott, 1978, o.p.

Horner, Beth, reteller. "The Mousedeer and the Buffalo Chip." On *An Evening at Cedar Creek.* Wellspring, CS 4902

Mieder, Wolfgang. *Disenchantments: An Anthology of Modern Fairy Tale Poetry.* Univ. Press of England, 1985. ISBN 0-87451-440-1

Sexton, Anne. *Transformations.* Houghton Mifflin, 1972. ISBN 0-395-12722-X

Singer, Isaac Bashevis. *When Shlemiel Went to Warsaw and Other Stories.* Trans. by Isaac B. Singer and Elizabeth Shub. Illus. by Margot Zemach. Farrar, 1986. ISBN 0-374-48365-5

"Those Three Wishes." In *A Taste for Quiet and Other Disquieting Tales* by Judith Gorog. Putnam/Philomel, 1982, o.p. Also in *Ready-To-Tell Tales* by David Holt & Bill Mooney. August House, 1995. ISBN 0-87483-380-9. Told by Carol Birch on Frostfire *Careful What You Wish For.*

Thurber, James. *Fables for Our Time.* HarperCollins, 1983. ISBN 0-06-090999-4

"The Two Old Women's Bet." In *Grandfather Tales* by Richard Chase. Houghton Mifflin, 1973. ISBN 0-395-06692-1

Velde, Vivian Vande. *Tales from the Brothers Grimm and the Sisters Weird.* Harcourt, 1995. ISBN 0-15-200220-0

Viorst, Judith. "And Although the Little Mermaid Sacrificed Everything to Win the Love of the Prince, the Prince, Alas, Decided to Wed Another." In Viorst, *If I Were in Charge of the World and Other Worries.* Simon & Schuster, 1981. ISBN 0-689-30863-9

Yolen, Jane. *Sleeping Ugly.* Putnam, 1981. ISBN 0-698-20617-7. Told by Milbre Burch on *Touch Magic . . . Pass It On.* Weston Woods WW 741C

Myths, Hero Tales, and Legends

Beowulf. Told by Syd Lieberman on *The Tell-Tale Heart and Other Terrifying Tales.* SL Productions SL 105

Bulfinch, Thomas. *Bulfinch's Mythology.* Random House 1988. ISBN 0-517-27415-9

Frazer, Sir James George. *The Golden Bough.* Macmillan, 1985. ISBN 0-02-540980-8

Hamilton, Edith. *Mythology.* Little, Brown, 1942. ISBN 0-316-34114-2

McBride-Smith, Barbara. *Medusa and Other Good Ol' Greeks.* Pandora Productions 102

"The Return of Odysseus." In *Hero Tales from Many Lands* by Alice I. Hazeltine. Abingdon, 1961, o.p.

Folktales

Hooks, William H. *Moss Gown.* Illus. by Donald Carrick. Houghton Mifflin/Clarion, 1987. ISBN 0-89919-460-5

Louie, Ai-Ling. *Yeh-Shen: A Cinderella Story from China.* Illus. by Ed Young. Putnam/Philomel, 1982, 1990. ISBN 0-399-20900-X

Young, Ed, trans. and illus. *Lon Po Po: A Red Riding Hood Story from China.* Putnam/Philomel, 1989. ISBN 0-399-21619-7

Historical Tales

Webb, Sheyann, Rachel West Nelson, and Frank Sikora. *Selma, Lord, Selma: Girlhood Memories of the Civil Rights Days.* Univ. of Alabama Press, 1980. ISBN 0-8173-0031-7

"Where the Girl Rescued Her Brother." In *The Girl Who Married the Moon: Tales from Native North America* by Joseph Bruchac and Gayle Ross. BridgeWater, 1994. ISBN 0-8167-3480-1

Tales of Life's Conflicts and Issues

"The Apple Tree." Told by David Holt on *The Hairyman and Other Wild Tales.* High Windy Audio HW 1202

"Count Alaric's Lady." In *The Faun and the Woodcutter's Daughter* by Barbara Picard. Crowell, 1964, o.p. Also in *Storytelling: Art and Technique,* 3rd ed. by Ellin Greene. Bowker, 1996. ISBN 0-8352-3458-4

"Like Meat Loves Salt." In *Grandfather Tales* by Richard Chase. Houghton Mifflin, 1973. ISBN 0-395-06692-1

"Oliver Hyde's Dishcloth Concert." In *Richard Kennedy: Collected Stories.* HarperCollins, 1987. ISBN 0-06-023255-2

"Owl." In *The Magic Orange Tree and Other Haitian Folktales* collected by Diane Wolkstein. Schocken, 1984. ISBN 0-8052-0650-7

"Whitebear Whittington." In *Grandfather Tales* by Richard Chase. Houghton Mifflin, 1973. ISBN 0-395-06692-1

"The Young Woman of Vietnam." Told by Doug Lipman on *Folktales of Strong Women.* Also told by Beth Horner on *Encounter with a Romance Novel: Heroines in Everyday Life.* Beth Horner Productions BEB5301

Riddle Tales

"Clever Manka." In *The Shoemaker's Apron* by Parker Fillmore. Harcourt, 1920, o.p. Also in *Storytelling: Art and Technique,* 3rd ed. by Ellin Greene. Bowker, 1996. ISBN 0-8352-3458-4

Sir Gawain and the Loathly Lady retold by Selina Hastings. Illustrated by Juan Wijngaard. Lothrop, 1985. ISBN 0-688-05823-X

Jaffe, Nina, and Steve Zeitlin. *While Standing on One Foot: Puzzle Stories and Wisdom Tales from the Jewish Tradition.* Holt, 1993. ISBN 0-8050-2594-4

Shannon, George. *Stories to Solve: Folktales from Around the World.* Greenwillow, 1985. ISBN 0-688-04303-8 (See other titles in this series.)

"The Smuggler." In *Handbook for Storytellers* by Caroline Feller Bauer. Books on Demand. ISBN 0-7837-6153-8

Science Fiction

Asimov, Isaac. "The Ugly Little Boy." In *Tomorrow's Children: Eighteen Tales of Fantasy and Science Fiction.* Doubleday, 1966, o.p. Also in *The Ugly Little Boy & The Widget, the Wadget and Boff* by Isaac Asimov and Theodore Sturgeon. Tor Books, 1989. ISBN 0-8125-5966-5

Bradbury, Ray. "All Summer in a Day." In *Medicine for Melancholy–S Is for Space.* Bantam, 1990. ISBN 0-553-28638-2

10 Children and Young Adults as Storytellers

I never knew how much thought went into telling a story. It's hard, but it was fun. I was so nervous when I first got up to tell my story, but by the end of the week I actually enjoyed telling it. If I can do that I think I can do anything.
    —*Eighth grader[1]*

CHILDREN IN THE MIDDLE and upper grades enjoy telling stories to younger children, and younger children respond enthusiastically. The ten-year-old who shuns the library story hour as a program "for babies" may rediscover the power of stories as he or she relates them to peers or younger listeners.

The child as teller may seem a contemporary idea but in fact it was practiced in early library work with children. For instance, in 1917, the New York Public Library had 46 reading clubs with a membership of nearly 1,000 boys and girls. That year a special meeting was held to welcome Marie Shedlock to Staten Island. Each club sent a representative to the meeting. One young representative made this tribute to Marie Shedlock:

> Three or four years ago we were content to read stories and plays, but during the past two winters we have tried to tell stories ourselves and thus, Miss Shedlock, our ambition has been aroused to further your great work in reviving the art of storytelling.[2]

Across the country creative librarians and teachers are introducing children to the art of storytelling and reading aloud, and a cadre of professional storytellers are making possible more storytelling residences in schools.

Lucretia Lipper, Young Adult Librarian at East Brunswick (N.J.) Public Library, reports that the Teen Library Connection, or TLC, has been an exciting program since 1980. The program came about as a response to a patron's query for a meaningful activity for her daughter who was "too old for day camp and too young for a paying job." The library staff identified a sufficient number of teens in the same position to make offering a program worthwhile, and the Friends of the East Brunswick Library generously funded it. Teens volunteer for two-week periods to do a variety of tasks in the library, ranging from shelving books to taping a movie review for the cable local access station. The teens are supervised by the young adult librarian and a coordinator, usually a college student. They are encouraged to treat the program as a temporary job. At the end of the program they receive written evaluations, which they can discuss with the coordinator. Many of these volunteers apply for a paying job at the library when they come of age. One of the most desirable volunteer jobs involves producing a flannel-board storytelling show for toddlers and preschoolers. Creative volunteers are sought, usually three in number. They are supervised and directed by a library staff member, but the teens retain artistic control of the production. They create the flannel-board figures, choose simple folk tales or nursery rhymes to dramatize, and put the performance together, coordinating story reading and figure placement. The program, popular with moms and little ones, consists of two flannel-board stories interspersed with finger plays and songs.

For the past 25 years, Bob Rubinstein, a language and performing arts teacher at Roosevelt Middle School, Eugene, Oregon, has taught a class in "Folktales and Storytelling," and directed the Roosevelt Troupe of Tellers.[3] The Troupe of Tellers consists of 12 sixth to eighth graders, selected from students who have taken the storytelling course or who have had onstage acting experience. The troupe's training is 12 weeks long and is part of the school day. Two weeks are spent in preparation and ten weeks in performance. During the preparation period the students receive intensive training in audience presentation and learn a minimum of four stories—three short tales (each about three minutes long) suitable for listeners in kindergarten through second grades, and a longer story (five to eight minutes) suitable for older listeners.

During its 25 years of existence, the troupe has told stories and performed story-theater for over 70,000 children in classrooms, public libraries, camps, and hospitals in the Eugene-Springfield-Bethel area. They have presented workshop-performances to educators, librarians, and university students in Oregon and Washington, including the NSA National Storytelling Conference held in Seattle in 1993. In 1983, the troupe received one of the Oregon young people's public service awards.

For lack of funds, 1995 was the last year for this fine program, which has been "a national model for how young people can learn to tell and grow through telling as well as for how valuable storytelling can be in the school curriculum."[4] Fortunately, a video, *When the Troupe Tells Tales,* featuring members of the Roosevelt Middle School Troupe of Tellers and their director, Robert Rubinstein, is available (see Note 9).

Another well-known group was the Poetry Troupe, begun by Isabel Wilner when she was the librarian at the laboratory school at Towson

State (Md.) College. A group of elementary school children went into the campus classrooms to read aloud to the college students. The children's favorite poems, and information about the troupe, were published in *The Poetry Troupe: An Anthology of Poems to Read Aloud,* compiled by Wilner.

In the February 1995 issue of *Inside Story* (NSA), Debra Gordon-Zaslow describes her work with "at-risk" sixth graders in Ashland, Oregon. Inspired by Bob Rubinstein's work, Gordon-Zaslow has met with 12 selected students for 20 sessions over a five-week period for each of the past two years. She also meets privately with each student for a half-hour session. The training includes storytelling techniques, such as eye contact, vocal projection and control, and dramatic improvisation. These troubled students are "extremely shy or withdrawn," says Gordon-Zaslow.[5] Graduates of the program—seventh and eighth graders—help the sixth graders. Each student selects a story and at the end of the sessions, the students perform in a "Story-Theatre" assembly for elementary schools in the area. Original funding for the program came from a federal Drug Free Schools grant. It is now funded by an Ashland School foundation made up of local businesses and individuals.

"Reach for a Story" Project

Several years ago, Emily Holman, Coordinator of Children' Services at the Ocean County (N.J.) Library, and the author (serving as a consultant) planned and directed a storytelling project for the children's staff and for fourth to sixth graders in the county. The project, called "Reach for a Story," had ten goals:

1. To introduce children to the art of storytelling for their own enjoyment and for the entertainment of others
2. To motivate children to read and to use the resources of the library
3. To nurture the child's creative imagination
4. To increase the child's communication skills—listening, speaking, reading, and writing
5. To introduce children to folk literature and modern imaginative stories
6. To guide children in the selection of tellable tales
7. To teach children the techniques of learning and telling stories
8. To build appreciation of cultural differences and similarities
9. To encourage parents, teachers, librarians, and other professionals to use storytelling in their work with children
10. To increase the visibility of the library and its program for children

It was decided that each of the seven regions in the county system would hold a mini-festival, rather than a "contest," at which time *all* the children participating in the project would tell a story. The regional librarians, the storytelling consultant, the coordinator of children's services, and the young tellers would then select a representative from each region to tell at a grand festival to be held at the main library during Children's Book Week. The selections were made on the basis of the requirements for a good program (variety in theme, length of stories, and styles of telling) as well as on the proficiency of the teller. Every child who participated in the project received a certificate of recognition and a copy of the consultant's story anthology, *Midsummer Magic*. In addition, the seven representatives at the grand festival were presented with a book bag imprinted with a specially designed logo, "Reach for a Story," and a copy of Virginia Haviland's *Favorite Fairy Tales Told Around the World*, to encourage continuation of their newly learned craft. Three of the seven tellers later appeared on local cable television to talk about their experience in learning to be a storyteller and each told a story. Many of the children also told stories to classes in their schools.

The storytelling consultant presented two workshops for the children in each region. In between the workshops the regional librarians met with the young tellers. Interesting and colorful facts about medieval storytellers (such as those presented in Chapter 1) stirred the children's imagination.

After asking the children why they thought people told stories and where they thought stories came from, the consultant told them *A Story, A Story*, using only the text of Gail Haley's picture book. Then the consultant and the children talked about the "pictures" people see in their mind's eye as they listen to a story and the children shared some of their "pictures" before looking at Haley's illustrations. It is always surprising to hear the many different images the same words evoke.

Next the consultant told a variant of a familiar folktale, such as "Cinderella" or "Rumpelstiltskin." Time permitting, the children were encouraged to become "folklorist-detectives," a term coined by Professor Jane Bingham of Oakland University. In this activity the children find variants of a tale or compare several picture-books editions of the same story. Thus the children learn that storytelling is a way of seeing. To help the children visualize the happenings in a story, the consultant told "Hafiz, the Stonecutter," from Marie Shedlock's *The Art of the Story-Teller*, and asked the children to list the happenings in the story in their proper order. (The unillustrated Shedlock version was chosen over the more familiar picture-book version by Gerald McDermott primarily because the Shedlock version encourages children to make their own images, but also because it has an upbeat ending and a message that strikes a sympathetic chord with young tellers—"Be Yourself.") The children and the consultant discussed the story's circular pattern and the repetition of important phrases—the children were becoming aware of story form and the necessity of events occurring in logical sequence. Then the children made storyboards by drawing pictures of the happenings on their lists (Figure 20).

The storytelling consultant and the children talked about the many different kinds of stories—folktales, literary fairy tales, myths and legends, hero tales, tall tales, humorous stories, jokes, and ghost stories—and the qualities that make a story tellable (see Chapter 4). The children browsed in collections of tellable tales pulled from the folktale shelves before the workshop began. Individual consultations concluded the workshop.

Some children immediately found a story to work with; others took home one or two story collections to read before the next workshop. To find a story they would enjoy telling required browsing through several collections and reading many stories, one of the goals of the project. A few children found stories in places not anticipated by the staff. For instance, one girl chose a story about Detective Mole from Robert Quackenbush's easy-to-read mysteries. Another chose a short humorous tale, "What Hershel's Father Did," from *Cricket Magazine*.

The storyboard was presented as a memory jogger. Another memory aid used was the cue card (see Chapter 5). The children were encouraged to make both a storyboard and a cue card for their story (cue card forms were provided). These were discussed the following week when the children met with their librarians. The librarians listened to the children's first attempts at storytelling and, when necessary, assisted them in finding a different story if the original choice wasn't working out.

At the second workshop the children worked on vocal tone and facial expression, language, and the use of kinesics in storytelling. They practiced phrasing, or what Kathryn Farnsworth calls "where to take a breath," by marking up a story to indicate the shortest possible phrases.[6] They said tongue twisters and "acted out" their stories. Bob Barton, in his *Tell Me Another*, recommends the use of call and response stories, chanting word play, drama games, and the like. Such approaches offer fun as well as opportunities for practice. The children enjoyed relaxation and voice exercises—jumping jacks, head and shoulder rolls, yawning, "ugly exercises," and imagining themselves as puppets (see Chapter 4).

The children and the consultant talked about the importance of the beginning and ending of a story. With everyone speaking at the same time, to avoid self-consciousness, they said the first and last lines of each of their stories to suggest different states of emotion—surprise, boredom, sadness, anger, anxiety, pleasure. Then they listened to each teller say the lines as he or she thought they should be said.

The teller identified the most important moment in the story and pantomimed the emotion of that moment, with the group guessing the emo-

FIGURE 20. *Storyboard by Colleen Dolcy, Ocean County Library, New Jersey. Used by permission.*

tion. They talked about effective—and ineffective—use of gestures, facial expressions, and body movements (Figure 21).

Finally, the group gave a critique of the tellings. By asking, "What did you like about the way (storyteller's name) told the story?" and "Can you suggest anything (storyteller's name) might do to make the telling even better?" the consultant kept the group's criticism positive. Negative criticism, if any, should be offered by the group leader in private—and gently. Children, like adults, learn through experience.

The librarians met with the children a week later to hold a rehearsal for the mini-festivals. As often as possible the rehearsal took place in the same room as the mini-festival. In this way the children became familiar with the size and seating arrangement of the room and could practice projecting their voices in the more formal setting. They asked themselves, "Can the person sitting in the last row hear my story? Did I tell my story slowly enough so that the listeners had time to see the happenings in the story?" In several schools the librarian or media specialist arranged for the children to tell their stories during a class visit to the library. These experiences helped to polish the tellings. The regional librarians were astonished at the progress the young tellers made in such a short period of time, and at their poise and pleasure in telling before a group. Incidentally, the girls outnumbered the boys two to one, but the boys told with vigor and obviously enjoyed the experience. Parents noted an increase in self-confidence and in reading for pleasure. The children learned courtesy and how to be good listeners as well as good tellers.

Were there negative features? A few. Despite early resolutions to discourage competitiveness, a few teachers and librarians still conceived of the festivals as "contests." The author agrees with educator Bryon Padgett that "competitiveness that makes most kids feel anxious, unloved, and defeated, or vainly victorious" has no place in storytelling.[7]

The biggest problem was the uneven size of the groups in the regions. Some groups had as few as 4 children while others had as many as 22. The ideal size is 10 to 12 tellers. But public transportation is almost nonexistent in Ocean County and redistribution would have created a hardship. The regional librarian and the consultant each worked with half of the larger groups during the workshop tellings and critiques. The rewards far outnumbered the "problems."

Storytelling Residencies in Schools

Many state arts councils sponsor Artists in Education programs and storytellers are eligible to participate. The "storyteller in residence" arranges with the school principal and the teachers involved to meet with a specified number of classes over a specified number of weeks. Fourth and fifth graders are an especially responsive group to work with. The program

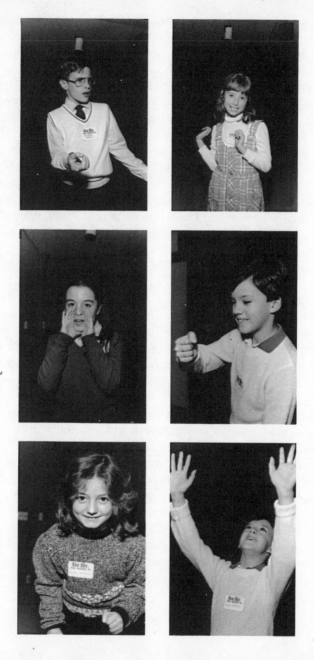

FIGURE 21. *Tale-tellers of Ocean County (N.J.): Christopher Anderson (top left), Christina Estlow (top right), Lurana Brown (middle left), Dylan Cadalzo (middle right and bottom right), and Aimee Amodio (bottom left). (Photographs © John van Campenhout.)*

requires a strong literature collection. The basic approach is similar to the one used in "Reach for a Story." However, school administrators often request some tie-in with the school curriculum. For instance, the children might study the folktales of a particular county or geographical region, or stories from different regions of the United States to fit in with a social studies program. Children can learn research skills and how to use the library's resources as they select, research, and learn a tale. Hearing a story and then having the children write the images they remember most is a technique used by storyteller-in-residence Susan Danoff to demonstrate that we all choose different moments in a story, and even if we choose the same moment we see it differently—a natural lead-in to creative writing in the language arts curriculum. In another storytelling residency, Beth Horner worked with a class of learning-disabled children to develop skills of verbal expression through telling stories that the children collected from members of their family.

Support from the faculty and agreement on possible residency activities (for example, workshops and classes for teachers, workshops and classes for students, consultation to teachers, performances and festivals) are essential for success. Scheduling can be complicated and working it out is time-consuming. The program usually runs over a period of six to eight weeks. Weekly lunchtime workshops for the teachers during that time have proved popular. One storytelling technique is discussed each week and exercises are given for the teachers to try with the students. The teachers are encouraged to read aloud or to tell stories to the children *every day*. If it is not possible to hold short weekly workshops, hold a longer (60- to 90-minute) workshop at the beginning of the residency. This workshop should cover the values of storytelling, resources for the storyteller, techniques of learning and telling, what to expect of the young tellers, and a demonstration of storytelling.

The children first tell in their classrooms, then to younger children or peers in their schools. Schools may sponsor a festival night for parents and teachers featuring the young tellers. Storytellers who have worked in inner-city schools have noticed that the children develop a more positive self-image and increase their skills in communicating their thoughts and feelings. A fifth grader in one of Susan Danoff's storytelling residencies wrote:

> During these past few months in the storytelling group I have learned that anything that you put your mind to you can do. I realized that with the help of Ms. Danoff and the other members of the storytelling group. Before I used to think I was hopeless in telling stories. But with encouragement from Ms. Danoff and the rest of the group not laughing every time I made a mistake, I made a remarkable achievement. Now my mother

is proud of me, my teacher is proud of me, and most of all, I'm proud of myself.[8]

Storytelling Builds Communications Skills and Self-Esteem

In learning to tell stories, children improve their communication skills. Bob Rubinstein, director of the Roosevelt Troupe of Tellers, comments: "Unlike theater or drama where they may be on stage and have a fixed situation where people come to them and they have other people with them on stage, each member of the troupe must learn to deal with different audiences and different stories and different situations. At the end of those ten weeks the growth in self-confidence and self-assurance is just amazing. They can handle just about anything in terms of public speaking and this lasts the rest of their life as I've learned when I've spoken to tellers from the past 15 or 20 years who have come back and told me what storytelling has meant to them."[9] Their story writing improves, too, as the children gain an understanding of story structure and the storyteller's "voice."

In some schools, storytelling has become a part of the language arts curriculum. When storytelling is part of the curriculum, and not a voluntary activity, it is especially important that the teacher establish a supportive environment. Some teachers designate "a storyteller's chair," and whoever is in that chair has the floor. In this way the children learn respect for each other and for the art of storytelling.

Fun Activities for Teaching Storytelling Skills

Start with group activities to relax the children, such as "And Then What Happened." The children and teacher or leader sit in a circle; the leader holds a soft ball and begins a story. Then he or she passes the ball to the next person and that person takes up the tale. This continues until the last person in the circle receives the ball and brings the story to its conclusion. A variation of this activity is done with a ball of yarn. The person who starts the story (and each teller who follows) tosses the ball, at an appropriate moment, to anyone in the circle to continue the story. Before tossing the ball, however, each person keeps hold of the yarn as it unwinds. At the end of the story each person is holding a piece of the yarn, symbolizing that each part of the story belongs to a teller. If anyone drops his or her strand, the pattern is broken, showing the importance of each element in the story.

Another fun activity is to have the group tell a story, using the "good/bad" pattern. The first child tells something good that happened to him or her that day. The group responds, "That's good!" The second child continues the tale, turning the good fortune to bad, and the group responds, "That's bad!" The story goes on, alternating good and bad fortune, while maintaining a logical sequence of events. Before doing this activity, you might want to read aloud Margery Cuyler's *That's Good! That's Bad!*

Teach the children strategies for learning a story, such as visualization, story webs (circles of keywords or brief phrases from the story) connected with lines to show the story sequence, story maps to show the setting and where events take place, or storyboards (to show the events of the action). A storyboard may contain dialogue, but usually consists of simple line drawings.

Have the children work in pairs. First, they can tell each other about their story. Encourage the listener to ask questions about the characters, setting, and action. Then have the children tell the story without words, by miming it. Lastly, each child can tell the story to his or her partner, and the partner can act as a "coach" or "prompter" if the teller forgets any part of the story.

Sometimes it helps to have the children outline their story. Folktales, the easiest stories to learn because they have a tight structure, consist of a beginning in which the main character(s) and the problem are introduced, a middle that tells what happens to the character(s), and an ending that tells how the character(s) solved the problem.

Children need to know how to introduce a story, and how to end it. They need to know that it's all right to have the story end in silence, with the listeners still in the story world; how to bring the listeners back to the present; and to accept applause when it is given.

Story Sources and Resource Guides

Good stories for children to tell are short, are easy to sequence, and have lots of dialogue. Anne Pellowski interviewed many children and teenagers who were doing storytelling when she wrote *The Storytelling Handbook: A Young People's Collection of Unusual Tales and Helpful Hints on How to Tell Them.* Her book contains the type of stories young people like to tell—stories with an unusual twist. In *Stories in My Pocket: The Kids' Storytelling Handbook,* Beauty and the Beast storytellers Martha Hamilton and Mitch Weiss have arranged stories in four sections, beginning with short "starter" stories and increasing in difficulty, with specific suggestions for telling each tale. In addition to storytelling tips for the kids there are guidelines for the adults who will be helping children tell stories. Two excellent guides addressed to anyone teaching storytelling in the classroom or other group situations are *Children Tell Stories: A Teaching Guide* by Martha Hamilton and Mitch Weiss, and *Children as Storytellers* by Kerry

Mallan. Also worth looking at (though the emphasis is on story theater) is the video *When the Troupe Tells Tales,* in which members of the Roosevelt Troupe of Tellers discuss storytelling techniques and what being a member of the troupe has meant to them.

NOTES

1. Martha Hamilton and Mitch Weiss, *Children Tell Stories: A Teaching Guide.* Richard C. Owen, 1990, p. 15.
2. Report in the files of the Office of Children's Services, New York Public Library.
3. Robert E. Rubinstein, "Much More Than Just a Tale!" *National Storytelling Journal* (Fall 1986): 16
4. Jimmy Neil Smith, Director, National Storytelling Association.
5. Debra Gordon-Zaslow, "Showcase: Former Teacher Turns At-Risk Students into Raconteurs Through Unique Program," *Inside Story* (February 1995): 5.
6. Kathryn Farnsworth, "Storytelling in the Classroom—Not an Impossible Dream." *Language Arts* 58 (February 1981): 165.
7. Bryon Padgett, "The Care and Feeding of a Child's Imagination," *Ms.* (May 1976): 61.
8. John Marshall, P. J. Hill School, Trenton, New Jersey. From the personal files of Susan Danoff.
9. Robert Rubinstein, *When the Troupe Tells Tales,* by the Roosevelt Middle School Tellers directed by Robert Rubinstein, 1993. 49 min. Video. $25.00 Available from Robert Rubinstein, 90 E. 49th Ave., Eugene, OR 97405.

Program Planning

At its simplest, program building is relating appropriate materials, within a given period of time, to reach a predetermined goal.
      —Dorothy De Wit[1]

CAREFUL PLANNING, FLEXIBILITY, AND creativity are required for a successful storytelling program.

Planning ahead allows the storyteller to select stories to learn and to arrange them in a program that is a satisfying whole. Know the number of programs you are going to give during the year and the types of programs, such as regular story hours, holiday and special celebrations, family story hours, and any others.

In planning the story hour consider the ages and interests of the children, their cultural or racial heritage, their listening capacity, and the scheduled length of the program. Selecting stories for children of similar background is not difficult, but often story-hour groups are composed of children of varying ages and interests. Although the story hour may consist of a single story, one that includes a variety of types of stories will appeal to the greatest number of children and make for a more interesting program. It will also provide a change of pace. Now is the time to go back to the cue cards that you made from your readings. You have the titles, types of stories, sources, and synopses at your fingertips. In building your repertoire you have chosen different types of stories, stories of varying lengths and moods, and stories of universal appeal.

The storyteller learns with experience to judge the mood of the children and to adjust the program accordingly. Sometimes the choice of stories, though planned in advance, must be changed at the last minute. The public librarian does not always know who will be at the story hour and, therefore, must be prepared to make changes.

Because it is more difficult to establish a listening mood for the imaginative literary fairy tale than for the robust action of the folktale, it is usually best to tell the folktale first if your program includes both types of stories.

If possible, schedule separate story hours for the younger children (5- to 7-year-olds), the middle-age children (8- to 10-year-olds), and the older children (11 years and older).

If you must, of necessity, tell to a group of children of mixed ages, plan to tell a story for the younger children first. The older children will be receptive if you explain that the story was chosen especially for the younger children. Then tell your main story and end with a short humorous tale. Take care that the story chosen for the younger children is not so simple in concept that it causes the older children to feel that they are too old for the entire program. The story for the older children must meet their interests and yet not be so far above the heads of the younger ones that they get nothing out of it. One storyteller, caught in a situation where the schedule was changed just prior to his arrival, found himself facing an audience of first and sixth graders. He carried it off by first telling a story that appealed to a mixed age group. Next he invited the sixth graders to learn "Mr. Wiggle and Mr. Waggle," an action story for young children, "to tell to your younger brothers and sisters or when you babysit." He ended the program with a story for the older children that contained elements familiar to the younger listeners. It is also possible to explain at the beginning of the program that the first story is for the younger children and that they may leave, if they wish, after it is told (providing, of course, that the adults responsible for the children are in the building).

Three shorter stories seem to work well with younger children or children who are not used to listening to stories. The first story should catch the children's fancy; the second story may ask for a more thoughtful response or be more moving emotionally; the third should be easily comprehended and satisfying. If the children seem to need a break between the second and third stories, tell a short participatory story or simply have the children stretch. Sometimes a participatory story at the end provides a welcome release of any built-up tension. With older children who are used to listening, try two longer stories with some riddles or a stretch in between the tales.

The program may be centered around a theme, such as "courage," a country, an author, or a subject. Or it may simply consist of stories that are unrelated in theme and yet balanced by type and mood. Other programs may focus on the birthdays of folklorists or writers of modern imaginative literature with the telling of their stories and poems.

Occasionally a teacher may request a story on a curriculum-related subject. Do this whenever you can; however, the storyteller must be free to select material for the story hour rather than to tell a story for didactic purposes. Although storytelling may be used legitimately to support and enhance the curriculum, the teacher should respect the librarian-storyteller's right to choose the story.

How Long Should the Story Hour Be?

The phrase "story hour" is misleading because the story hour usually lasts less than 60 minutes. The age of the children, their past experience in story listening, and the library's or center's schedule all influence the length of the program. It may be as short as 15 minutes or as long as an hour. The length of time should be stated to eliminate the "coming and going" that breaks the mood, and as a courtesy to parents who are providing transportation to and from the story hour. Begin on time and end as close to the announced time as possible. Many parents do not want their children to be out after dark; during the winter months the program may have to be shortened, held at an earlier hour, or held on a Saturday or Sunday.

Sample Story Hours

Story Hour for Children Ages 5 to 7

"The Crab and the Jaguar," in *Picture Folk-Tales* by Valery Carrick. Also in *Storytelling: Art and Technique,* 3rd ed. by Ellin Greene

"The Impudent Little Bird," in *The Singing Tortoise and Other Animal Folktales* by John Yeoman and Quentin Blake

"The Freedom Bird," in *Ready-to-Tell Tales* edited by David Holt and Bill Mooney

"Grandmother Rabbit and the Bossy Lion," in *Tortoises's Flying Lesson: Animal Stories* by Margaret Mayo

Story Hour for Children Ages 8 to 10

"The Shining Princess," in *The Shining Princess and Other Japanese Legends* retold by Eric Quayle

"The Pumpkin Child," in *Persian Folk and Fairy Tales* retold by Anne Sinclair Mehdevi. Also in *Storytelling: Art and Technique,* 3rd ed. by Ellin Greene

"The Princess on the Pea," in *Twelve Tales: Hans Christian Andersen* trans. by Erik Blegvad

Story Hour for a Mixed Age Group

Billy Beg and His Bull: An Irish Tale retold by Ellin Greene

"Cap o'Rushes," in *English Fairy Tales* by Joseph Jacobs

Caribbean Story Hour

The Cat's Purr by Ashley Bryan

"I'm Tipingee, She's Tipingee, We're Tipingee, Too," in *The Magic Orange Tree and Other Haitian Folktales* by Diane Wolkstein

"Uncle Bouqui Rents a Horse," in *Uncle Bouqui of Haiti* by Harold Courlander

Spanish Story Hour

"The Little Half Chick," in *Señor Cat's Romance and Other Favorite Stories from Latin America* retold by Lucía M. González. Also in *Storytelling: Art and Technique,* 3rd ed. by Ellin Greene
Perez y Martina by Pura Belpré
(Pura Belpré recorded "Perez and Martina" in Spanish and in English on CMS 505; the children would enjoy hearing all or part of this recording.)

Story Hour for Young Adults

"Whitebear Whittington," in *Grandfather Tales* by Richard Chase
"Mr. Fox," in *English Fairy Tales* by Joseph Jacobs
"The Yellow Ribbon," in *The Rainbow Book of American Folk Tales and Legends* by Maria Leach. Also in *Juba This and Juba That* by Virginia Tashjian

Family Story Hour 1

Briefly talk about the tradition of riddling and pose a few riddles from *Lightning Inside You: And Other Native American Riddles* edited by John Bierhorst, or a story from George Shannon's Stories to Solve series
"Clever Manka," in *The Shoemaker's Apron* by Parker Fillmore. Also in *Storytelling: Art and Technique,* 3rd ed. by Ellin Greene
"The Court Jester's Last Wish," in *While Standing on One Foot: Puzzle Stories and Wisdom Tales from the Jewish Tradition* by Nina Jaffe and Steve Zeitlin

Family Story Hour 2

"The Woman Who Flummoxed the Fairies," in *Heather and Broom: Tales of the Scottish Highlands* by Sorche Nic Leodhas
"The Mixed-Up Feet and the Silly Bridegroom," in *Zlateh the Goat and Other Stories* by Isaac B. Singer

Story Hour in Honor of an Author

Speak briefly about Eleanor Farjeon
Read from *Eleanor Farjeon's Poems for Children*
Tell "Elsie Piddock Skips in Her Sleep," in *Martin Pippin in the Daisy Field* by Eleanor Farjeon

The Multimedia Program

The multimedia program combines two or more art forms, each of which can stand on its own (storytelling, film, music, dance), into a creative whole. This type of program appeals to many storytellers, especially the librarian or school library media specialist who feels there is not enough time to learn a sufficient number of stories to sustain a regularly scheduled storytelling program. In truth, it takes as much time to plan and

FIGURE 22. *Children at the Spanish story hour, West Kendall Regional Library, Miami-Dade Public Library System, enjoy a puppet presentation of* Perez and Martina *by* Pura Belpré, *told by children's librarian Lucía González.*

select materials for a multimedia program as it takes to learn more stories. However, some people prefer the varied activity involved in preparing this type of program (such as previewing films and listening to recordings) to selecting and learning a story. The cultural experience that this kind of program offers children justifies the choice.

Storytelling can combine very well with other art forms, provided the program is carefully thought out and the various parts are related. The most effective programs usually are those that center around a theme, subject, or person. A school library media specialist planned a multimedia program with a spring theme for kindergarten children. She read *When the Root Children Wake Up* by Helen D. Fish, using the opaque projector to show the pictures on the center of three screens. On the side screens she showed slides of buds bursting and flowers in bloom as she played a recording of "The Waltz of the Flowers" from Tchaikovsky's *Nutcracker Suite*. Spontaneously, these young children went up to the screen to touch the flowers—they looked so real—and began to dance to the music. It was a beautiful experience for both the librarian and the children.

The preparation of this kind of program involves careful selection of materials. For a multimedia program to be successful, there must be a flow, a rhythm. The parts should complement each other, but each segment should be strong enough to stand on its own. If you use a film, choose one that is artistic. Remember that the story is as important as the film, dance, or other art form used; generally, it is best for the story to come first unless the other material helps to establish a listening mood for the story.

A recording can be used to set the mood, for a change of pace, or to hear an author's voice. Music usually is used to introduce or conclude the program and sometimes to enhance the narrated story, a technique that has been perfected by storyteller Spencer Shaw. Storytellers interested in using this technique should read Shaw's article "Recorded Magic for Story Hours" and should be prepared to spend many hours in practice. The music must be "integrated artistically. . . . [It] blends with the words and mood so that it never becomes a foreign, musical intrusion. The story is the thing. The music merely heightens the emotional impact in certain passages or makes specific word pictures more meaningful."[2]

Preparing a well-balanced program is not sufficient in the case of a multimedia story hour. The storyteller must also pay careful attention to the physical and mechanical requirements of the program. Check the condition of any films and recordings to be used.

Reserve any audiovisual equipment needed. Arrange for a competent projectionist if you need help. Be prepared for equipment failure.

Arrange for a room that can be darkened if you plan to show a film. Check electrical outlets. Allow time to set up the equipment before the program begins.

Arrange the seating so that you will be able to switch from one medium to another without having the children move.

Just before the program, check the audiovisual equipment again. Focus any film or filmstrip you plan to show.

Now relax, and enjoy the program with the children.

Sample Multimedia Programs

Program in Honor of an Author

Speak briefly about Carl Sandburg.

Read the poem and show the book *Arithmetic* by Carl Sandburg.

Play recording of Carl Sandburg reading from his poetry.

Tell "The White Horse Girl and the Blue Wind Boy," in *Rootabaga Stories* by Carl Sandburg.

Program in Celebration of Black History Month

As audience assembles, distribute photocopies of "Lift Every Voice and Sing," words by James Weldon Johnson and music by J. Rosamond Johnson.

Give a brief biography of James Weldon Johnson, based on the introduction in *God's Trombones*, by James Weldon Johnson.

Show the film "The Creation," narrated by James Earl Jones.

Read "Go Down Death," in *God's Trombones* by James Weldon Johnson.

End program with audience singing "Lift Every Voice and Sing."

Program with a Midsummer Theme

Introductory music: Incidental music from "A Midsummer Night's Dream," by Felix Mendelssohn.

Talk about the folklore of Midsummer Festival.

Tell "Count Alaric's Lady" or a story of your choice from *Midsummer Magic: A Garland of Stories, Charms, and Recipes* by Ellin Greene.

Dance Program for a Mixed Age Group

Play "Waltz of the Flowers," from *Nutcracker Suite* by Peter Ilich Tchaikovsky, as the children enter the story-hour room.

Tell "Nella's Dancing Shoes," from *Italian Peepshow* by Eleanor Farjeon.

Introduce the children to books on dance, such as *The Firebird, Swan Lake*, and *My Ballet Class* by Rachel Isadora, *A Very Young Dancer* by Jill Krementz, and *Of Swans, Sugar Plums, and Satin Slippers: Ballet Stories for Children* by Violette Verdy and Marcia Brown.

Tell *The Dancing Man* by Ruth Bornstein.
Play "Arabian Dance" from *Nutcracker Suite* by Peter Ilich Tchaikovsky, as the children leave the story-hour room.

NOTES

1. Dorothy De Wit, *Children's Faces Looking Up: Program Building for the Storyteller.* American Library Assn., 1979, p. ix.
2. Spencer Shaw, "Recorded Magic for Story Hours," *Top of the News* 15 (October 1958): 43–47.

12 Administration of the Story-Hour Program and In-Service Education

People who work with children need to understand the importance of stories in the lives of children and the unique contribution that library storytelling can make in bringing children and books together, in helping children acquire language and literacy skills, and in giving children an appreciation of their literary and cultural heritage.
     —*Augusta Baker*[1]

QUESTIONS HAVE BEEN RAISED about the role of the story hour and its importance in a time of budget cuts and diminishing staff. Public librarians and school library media specialists may need to convince their administrators as well as other members of their staffs that the story hour is a basic part of library service to children.

How Are Nonstorytellers Convinced of the Value of the Story Hour?

Unmeasurable intangibles, felt by the storyteller, are difficult to convey to others. Exposure to the art is one of the best ways to win over nonbelievers. Invite administrators, librarians who serve adults, principals, and teachers to observe a story hour where they can see for themselves the response of the children.

Both public librarians and school library media specialists can reach parents at PTO meetings. Family story hours (discussed later in this chapter), held in the evening, will convince many parents of the value of the story hour, and they will voice support of this program to both administrators and board members.

Suggest to your administrator the possibility of presenting a storytelling workshop at a staff or faculty meeting.

Plan a storytelling festival as a special event of the public library children's department and invite both staff and community. Be sure to invite school administrators and faculty.

Seek invitations to tell stories to community groups of adults, and then describe your program. Be alert to the possibility of inclusion in community programs.

Should the Art of Storytelling Be Included in the Administrator's In-Service Education Plans?

Administrators of public libraries, schools, and recreation centers recognize the need for the in-service education of their staffs, both professional and nonprofessional. Librarians, teachers, and recreational workers should insist that storytelling be one of the subjects covered in these sessions. Even graduates of library schools and colleges of education need this extra instruction, because storytelling is not fully covered in most universities. The administrator of a public library with a storytelling specialist on the staff can offer this specialist's services to other organizations in the community. Likewise, school administrators can share the expertise of their school library media specialists with teachers, aides, and others interested in storytelling.

Should Preparation Time Be Given During the Workday for Selecting and Learning Stories?

Administrators often raise the question about the time needed to prepare for a story hour. Much depends on the storyteller's ability to learn and retain. Some storytellers will find this easy and quick, whereas others will need a great deal of time. Certainly time should be allotted to search for the stories, because the reading of many books adds to the librarian's expertise in guiding readers. This reading cultivates and deepens the critical ability of the storyteller, who then gains in the appreciation of literary values. Books are important tools of the librarian's profession, and therefore, some time should be given to their examination and use. Realistically, much of the storytellers' preparation is done on their own time, but so is that of other professionals.

Should the Budget Include Noncirculating Books to Support the Storytelling Program?

Books from which the storyteller has selected stories or poems need to be available at all times for planning and learning. The absence of a storytelling collection means that the choice of stories will be governed by the books that are on the shelves. This usually means that the popular books will not be available to the storyteller.

A strong collection of reference books about storytelling and its related subjects is necessary for the storyteller's background reading (see Appendix). Such basic collections as Asbjørnsen and Møe's *East of the Sun and West of the Moon*, edited and illustrated by Ingri and Edgar Parin d'Aulaire; *The Glass Slipper: Charles Perrault's Tales of Times Past*, translated by John Bierhorst; the Lucy Crane, Lore Segal, and Ralph Manheim translations of the collected tales of the Brothers Grimm; and the M. R. James and Erik Haugaard translations of Hans Christian Andersen stories are necessary for comparative judgments of other translations. Clean books are necessary for the story-hour table and for display. These extra copies are not luxuries. They are part of the storyteller's professional library and are as necessary as the administrator's books on school or public library administration. You may have to refer to these books as "the storyteller's professional shelf" in order to justify the expenditure.

What Is the Best Day and Hour to Schedule the Story Hour?

In scheduling the story hour, consider the availability of space and staff. The story hour should be part of the entire programming plan, and so the day of the week as well as the frequency of the program is often governed by the overall schedule of events. It is also necessary to be aware of events in the community so that there is not too much scheduled at the same time for the same audience. Each organization will select the best day and hour for its users.

It is often necessary to experiment with days until the best one evolves. Public library story hours are often scheduled when the most children are in the library, and that time of day is usually at 4:00 P.M. (after school hours) or at an appropriate time on Saturday or Sunday. The school library media specialist usually schedules story hour within the school day. It might be possible to have a story hour during lunchtime for those children who do not go home for lunch. Busing presents a problem for after-school activities, but there may be enough children who are not bused to have a story hour in the library media center after school hours. The classroom teacher can schedule a time for storytelling or reading aloud within the school day and should also be alert to every opportunity for informal, spur-of-the-moment storytelling.

How Often Should Story Hours Be Held?

Many factors enter into the decision to have weekly, monthly, semi-monthly, or occasional special story hours. A neighborhood with few organized activities for children might very well need more frequent story hours for the six- to ten-year-olds than one with highly organized recreational and school activities and overscheduled children—those whose after-school hours are mostly taken up with dancing lessons, violin lessons, choir practice, scouts, and other activities. The number of available storytellers is an important factor because it is practically impossible for one storyteller to learn well two or three stories every week and, at the same time, carry out other library responsibilities. What should be an enjoyable experience becomes a chore, the quality of storytelling suffers, and attendance at story hours begins to drop because of the lack of careful planning and good preparation. A weekly story hour should be undertaken only when more than one storyteller is available.

Public libraries with more than one branch children's librarian can consider the feasibility of "swapping" storytellers. The easiest way to do this is to have all the story hours in the branches scheduled at the same time. Then the storytellers can plan together a schedule of rotation. The administration must agree to this schedule before it is made final, because different librarians will be covering each children's room during this period. The administrator may object to this plan if the children's librarian also is called upon to be in charge of the branch when the administrator is absent. In other words, the storyteller's schedule should fit into the administrator's schedule.

One of the benefits of the swapping plan is that each storyteller involved has an opportunity to tell the same stories more than once. Even though each storyteller is telling stories weekly, there is more time to prepare new stories. This schedule also brings "guest storytellers" to the children. The planner should ask that a "home" person be scheduled in the children's room, if possible, in order to familiarize the visiting storyteller with the physical aspects of the room as well as to introduce the visitor to the children. If this schedule is carried over for a reasonable length of time, the visitor ceases to be a visitor and is accepted as a "home staffer."

The school library media specialist can often find parents, teachers, and even older children (see Chapter 10) who can be trained in storytelling and so enable more story hours to be scheduled. One high school library media specialist who enjoys telling stories is released periodically from her regular schedule to go into elementary schools in her midwestern community to share her love of storytelling with the younger children and their teachers.

Why Is It Best to Plan in Advance?

The storyteller can be more creative in programming if plans are made in advance. There is time to select stories and other materials carefully and to learn the stories well enough to be comfortable with them. If one plans an entire storytelling program, perhaps from October to May, the decision can be made, for example, to celebrate Hans Christian Andersen's birthday (April 2), and selection and preparation of the stories can begin in the fall.

Should Adults Be Permitted to Attend the Story Hour?

If you are a stranger to the group, it can be helpful to have the group leader settle the children. Teachers who bring their classes to the library for story hour should stay to *listen*; they should not grade papers or perform other chores during storytelling. The teacher sets a model for listening.

Occasionally, a visiting storyteller or a student observer will be in the group. Observing experienced storytellers is an important part of the training of beginners and should be permitted. Too many adults in the group, however, may affect the mood; the presence of adults can be threatening to children and can suppress their spontaneous responses to the story. If adults are curious about what takes place in the story hour, it is better to videotape a story hour for them or to schedule a family story hour. The sensitive librarian or teacher will know when to make an exception. In a predominantly Spanish-speaking community in New York City, adults were allowed to sit at the back of the story-hour room. By permitting them to stay, the librarian was able to establish a rapport with parents recently arrived from Puerto Rico and to help them feel at home in the library. The parents in turn enriched the library by sharing their culture and strongly supporting the library's storytelling program.

What Is the Purpose of the Story-Hour Ticket?

Story-hour tickets—free, of course—are a means of publicizing the story hour and of controlling the size of the group. Some storytellers in public libraries issue a seasonal ticket to the story-hour program. The ticket is punched each time the child attends. Older children who are familiar with series tickets to concerts and theatrical performances like the idea of a seasonal story-hour ticket. Seasonal tickets are issued at the beginning of the season, which usually runs from October to May.

Tickets for individual story hours usually are distributed a day or two before the program or just before the story hour begins, at the place of the program. These tickets are collected as the children enter or leave the story-hour area.

What Other Kinds of Publicity Are Effective?

Storytellers soon learn what is the most effective publicity for both the adult community and the children. Fliers can be placed in restaurants, barber shops, beauty salons, grocery stores, staff rooms of schools and recreation centers, churches, and other public places frequented by adults. Storytellers can distribute fliers to children if they trust the children to take them home and not litter. Each librarian, teacher, or recreation worker is the best judge of distribution to children. A well-designed poster, placed in a library, school, recreation center, or playground, is an attention getter.

Important facts must be presented in both posters and fliers. These should include such items as the ages for which the story hour is planned, the place and time of the program, where tickets, if used, and additional information are available. It is best to specify a time limit, such as 4:00 P.M. to 4:45 P.M.; this enables children and parents to have some idea of the length of the program.

In designing the fliers and posters, make them as simple as possible, but eye-catching. In her article "Storytelling Programs for the Family," Carol Birch includes examples of an effective publicity poster and one that does not project a positive image of storytelling (Figure 23).

> Note the two posters created for the story-hour. The poster of the girls listening to a read story . . . [implies that] storytelling and reading are the same; stories attract (and are reserved for?) sweet, young, old-fashioned, white girls—not active children, not older children, not modern children, not other races, not even boys; stories are shared by bland, featureless girls/children/women who seem inconsequential at best.
>
> The second poster with the image of Pegasus offers a much more positive representation of storytellers. The graphic was adapted from a photograph of a painting by Susan Hefernan, an artist in New York City, and communicates the promise and strength inherent in stories.
>
> It suggests that stories are strong; stories illuminate like the sun, creating sharp contrasts of darkness and light; stories are winged things like Pegasus himself. Stories take one to a precipice where rationalistic explanations fall away—a place to soar or fall; stories exist at the very edge of night and day—at the edge of unconscious and conscious mind. The graphic is bold and the image evocative, drawing on the rich legacy of myth.[2]

Consider using books of designs and illustrations that are meant to be traced or even cut out, such as *The Dover Pictorial Archives*, a collection of out-of-copyright illustrations. If an illustration from a copyrighted book is desired, it is necessary, of course, to get permission for its use from the publisher. Explore and use the artistic talents of your co-workers and friends. Invite the art class in a school to submit designs. The use of chalk-walks, sandwich boards, balloons, and other fun publicity is described in Caroline Bauer's *New Handbook for Storytellers*.[3]

Another source of free publicity is the local radio station. Radio stations are usually willing to make spot announcements about community programs.

One-to-one publicity is always effective, and children seem to remember this better than printed forms of publicity. Personal urging to attend the next story hour makes the child feel especially wanted. The same "over-the-desk" conversation with parents also is effective. Some storytellers use free tickets as a reminder of the story hour.

If there is a public relations officer on the staff of the library or recreation center, publicity probably will be handled by that person. It then

FIGURE 23. *Example of an effective publicity poster (bottom) and one that does not project positive image of storytelling (top). From* The National Storytelling Journal, *Summer 1984, p. 17.*

becomes the responsibility of the storyteller to get the necessary information to the public relations officer as early as possible.

What Is the Importance of a Community File?

The dissemination of publicity depends largely upon your knowledge of key people in the community and your ability to gain their interest and cooperation. An up-to-date file of community organizations and people, complete with addresses, phone numbers, and any other necessary information, is a necessity. Generally speaking, the response is best when publicity is directed to one person in the organization—the principal or school library media specialist, the director of the day-care center or recreation center, the president of the parents' organization, the minister of the church. Newspapers and television and radio stations also respond best when the publicity is sent to a specific person with whom you have established contact. Fliers, posters, and letters should be sent to this person with a request for posting, distribution, and public announcements.

Do Personal Relationships Enter into Good Publicity?

A personal visit with the key people in an organization is very important. This is an opportunity to describe the storytelling program and the philosophy behind it. Some people must be convinced of the importance of story hours before they will publicize them. Invite these adults to attend a family story hour or an outdoor story hour for a mixed age group so that they will feel more knowledgeable and involved. Building good personal relationships will gain support for your program and can save time, too, as it often makes it possible to ask for publicity for future story hours over the phone.

In-Service Education

In the following sections, you will find suggestions for planning storytelling workshops, a storytelling festival, and family evening story hours.

Planning a Storytelling Workshop

Establish the objectives of the storytelling workshop. What do you want to happen to the participants as a result of attending the workshop?

Define the audience you want to reach. Are they librarians, teachers, recreational leaders, staff, volunteers?

Plan a budget. How much money is needed? Will participants be charged a registration fee?

How much time is available—a half day, a full day, several half-day sessions, a weekend?

How many leaders are available? Will it be a one-leader workshop? One leader plus an inspirational keynote speaker? One leader and several resource persons?

Will the participants meet as one large group or will the group be divided into smaller interest groups?

What aspects of storytelling will be covered?

What kinds of presentation and involvement methods would be most effective in achieving the objectives?

Hour-and-a-half or two-hour sessions are long enough to get into a topic and cover major points without tiring the audience. Keep the workshop groups reasonably small (10–25 persons). Larger groups can be accommodated, but the presentations will tend to be lectures. It is hard to have a good discussion in a large group and impossible for everyone to tell a story and receive feedback.

Provide an opportunity for the participants to hear good storytelling. If possible, arrange for children to be present at one of the storytelling demonstrations so that beginning storytellers can see an experienced storyteller interacting with children and handling some of the typical situations that arise.

Design an attractive flier stating the time, place, program, and registration information. Mail the flier to the expected audience in ample time to complete registration at least two weeks before the date of the workshop. Publicize your workshop through direct mail, professional journals, local organizations, library systems, newspapers, and radio.

If you plan to sell any storytelling materials at the workshop, order the materials on consignment from the publishers or a jobber far in advance of the workshop date. Arrange for at least two persons to handle the sales table, and be sure to have cash, including change, on hand.

Allow enough time to order any audiovisual materials you plan to use, to gather exhibit materials, and to prepare a bibliography. If you plan to use a film, reserve the projector well in advance. Be sure to have a projectionist available so that the workshop leader does not have this responsibility. Set up the equipment, and adjust the focus and sound before the workshop begins.

Arrange for comfortable meeting rooms. If a meal is to be served, plan an attractive but light menu. Coffee, tea, and juice served during the registration period is always welcome.

Have an attractive exhibit of books and other storytelling materials prominently displayed in a comfortable area. The exhibit should extend the participants' knowledge of storytelling literature. Allow time for browsing.

The introduction by the workshop leader or keynote speaker sets the tone for the workshop. The atmosphere should be relaxed, friendly, and supportive so that the participants are at ease when they tell a story or participate in discussion. The workshop leader should outline to participants what they will be doing and the time schedule.

Plan some form of evaluation. Evaluation is concerned with how well the objectives were reached.

Any workshop—and especially one planned for 100 or more persons—takes a tremendous amount of planning and coordination with all departments involved, from maintenance staff to top administration. The hard work that goes into a workshop should not show on the day of the workshop. Take care of the nitty-gritty beforehand so that the workshop runs as smoothly as possible, but always be prepared for the unexpected.

In-Staff Workshop for Beginning Storytellers

An in-staff workshop for beginning storytellers can be held once a week over a period of four to five weeks with each session approximately two hours long. The workshop leader should be an experienced storyteller.

Session 1 Purpose and values of storytelling
Selection of materials
Demonstration of storytelling
Bibliography of storytelling literature distributed
Participants asked to read widely from books listed on bibliography and to select stories they want to learn

Session 2 Selection of materials (continued)
Discussion of stories selected by participants
Preparation and presentation—techniques of learning and telling stories
Demonstration of storytelling
Participants asked to prepare a short, traditional tale (3–5 minutes) for presentation at next session

Session 3 Stories told by participants
General and constructive criticism offered by workshop leader and other participants (the leader must see that comments or criticisms are constructive and of such a nature that everyone can learn from them)
Discussion of any problems arising from participants' experience in preparing their stories

Session 4 Program planning
Administration
Model story hour by workshop leader
Participants asked to prepare a longer and more complex story (7–10 minutes) for presentation at next session

Session 5   Participants tell their stories and discuss their programs
            General and constructive criticism offered by workshop leader
               and participants
            Evaluation of workshop

Depending on the size of the group, it may be necessary to have additional sessions so that everyone has a chance to tell a story. If possible, the workshop leader should observe each participant as he or she tells a story to a group of children. This also presents an opportunity for the workshop leader to discuss in private any specific criticisms or suggestions for the beginning storyteller.

One-Day Workshop

One-day workshops planned for a larger audience with a wider range of experience often include several resource persons in addition to the workshop leader (Figure 24). A suggested program for such a workshop follows.

Morning Session

Have an inspirational keynote speaker who will set the tone. Divide the audience into small interest groups, such as:

1. Multicultural Stories
2. The Black Heritage in Storytelling
3. Poetry in the Story Hour
4. The Illustrator as Storyteller
5. The Literary Fairy Tale

Assign a specialist to each group to direct the discussion and act as resource person and demonstration storyteller. Allow an hour and a half for the morning interest groups.

Luncheon
Afternoon Session

The interest groups can be repeated so that each participant can hear about two aspects of storytelling, or the workshop can be arranged so that participants stay in the same group all day. This allows groups to go into greater depth of subject matter and also gives more time for demonstration and audience participation. Allow time for a question-and-answer period. An alternative plan is to have shorter afternoon interest groups and to end the workshop with a storytelling demonstration by the various specialist leaders to the entire audience.

FIGURE 24. *Ellin Greene presents "The Illustrator As Storyteller" to students at Louisiana State University School of Library and Information Science. (Photograph courtesy of LSU Public Relations Office.)*

Storytelling Workshop for Day-Care or Head Start Staff

This kind of workshop is often held at the day-care or Head Start center. As part of your preparation, look at the video *The Library Head Start Partnership* (40 min.), available in many public libraries or from the Center for the Book in the Library of Congress. The video has four segments: "Library–Head Start Partnership," "Entering the World of Books," "Evaluation and Selection of Materials," and "Library Assistance to Adults." You may want to show one or more segments during the workshop. Also, if possible, arrange for members of the agency's staff to observe you tell stories to the children in the center some time before the workshop.

Introduce yourself as a representative of the library and talk about the library/day-care or Head Start partnership in helping children develop a love of books and reading. Briefly describe the variety of services available to the organization from the library.

Emphasize the connection between hearing stories in early childhood and language development. Cite some of the supporting research.

Talk about the criteria for selecting stories to read aloud or to tell and illustrate your points with a variety of Mother Goose books, picture books, and simple folktales.

Demonstrate techniques of reading aloud and storytelling. If time allows, have the participants practice reading aloud in small groups.

Leave time for questions and for looking at the books and other materials you have brought with you.

Workshop for First-Time Parents

Welcome the parents to the library.

Talk about the importance of sharing literature with children from birth on, mentioning the connection between hearing stories in early childhood and language development (see Chapter 8).

Ask the parents if they remember a favorite book, story, or nursery rhyme from their own childhood.

Show examples of the kinds of books published for young children today: board books, cloth books, concept books, wordless picture books, Mother Goose and nursery rhymes, finger plays, and picture storybooks.

Read all or part of some books in different categories to model how to read aloud.

Show the video *Read to Me: Libraries, Books, and Your Baby.* Allow time for questions and answers about the library's services for parents and young children.

Display books on parenting and books for babies and toddlers and encourage the parents to browse.

If you have a two- or three-part workshop, show the film/video *The First Three Years. Program #9. Summary* (55 min.) at one of the sessions and follow the showing with discussion.

Planning a Storytelling Festival

Storytelling festivals are inspirational in nature and are usually planned for a large audience with varying storytelling experience. They may or may not include workshops for the audience.

Selection of Storytellers and Stories

Consider only the best storytellers. They may be members of the library staff or invited guests. (The latter may require additional funds.) Select storytellers who have different styles and techniques, so that the program will have variety both in content and length of stories. The stories should represent the best versions of folktales and the finest literature.

The Physical Setting

Select a quiet room that can be made attractive and that has good acoustics. Use flowers and beautifully illustrated books as background. Arrange the books in groups, perhaps by theme, and vary the sizes and colors within each group. Simplicity and an uncluttered appearance are important.

Arrange the books from which the stories will be told on the story-hour table with fresh flowers and the wishing candle, if one is to be used.

Arrange the chairs so that everyone can see the storyteller. Avoid using small, juvenile chairs for adult audiences; this is not "cute"—it is very uncomfortable for adults and makes some of them self-conscious.

The Program

Plan each segment of the program to last no longer than an hour and a half. Open with a few remarks about storytelling and the program. Introduce each storyteller by a short characterization of either the story to be told or the storyteller. Give the program dignity and integrity—no coy "let's pretend we are children" remarks.

Plan time at the end of the program for the audience to chat informally with the storytellers.

Family Evening Story Hours

The family story hour is usually planned for early evening, about 7:30 or 8:00 P.M., so that the family has time to complete dinner and arrive at the story hour without feeling pressured and rushed. The early hour allows time for a few minutes of visiting, browsing, and selecting books to take home, because this audience often leaves immediately after the program.

The family story hour is planned for children ages seven and older—and their parents. Younger children must be brought at times, but parents should be encouraged to leave them at home with a baby-sitter whenever possible. Older children need this occasional family excursion where they are the important members of the group.

Some families find it difficult to leave the younger children at home, however, and so the storyteller should be prepared to adjust to some "younger child" distractions. If there are quite a few younger children in the audience and if a second staff member can be assigned to the program, this person can take the younger children aside and have a picture-book hour. Another possibility is to have volunteers—high school students or other parents—who will read to the younger children.

Allow about 40 minutes for the actual storytelling. A program of two stories with some poetry or music, or three short stories, allows flexibility for creative planning. A mixture of story types is advisable—literary and folk, serious and humorous, quiet and active, are all to be considered. Choose stories that can be appreciated on both a child and an adult level. Spencer Shaw, an internationally known storyteller, held groups spellbound with his telling of "A Lover of Beauty," the story of Pygmalion and Galatea, from *Greek Myths* by Olivia Coolidge, when he conducted his family evening story hours in the Nassau County (N.Y.) libraries. In speaking of the values of these story hours, Shaw said, "Parents experience a new relationship with their children: an emotional bond which finds release in shared laughter, shared adventure, shared confidences. Children experience a new understanding of the parents' concerns. Together, they enjoy a storyteller's art."[4]

In "Storytelling Programs for the Family," Carol Birch shares the obstacles and solutions she experienced during the "Family Storytelling Hour with Carol" at the Craft and Folk Art Museum in Los Angeles, a program she conducted monthly for two years. The pattern Carol established was (1) a ritualistic, opening story, (2) a specific sharing time, (3) a story with broad appeal, (4) a more difficult story, (5) a participation story, and (6) a short scary or funny story to close. Carol had families sit together during the story hour, rather than the usual "children in front, adults in the back." This arrangement encouraged family members to touch and interact and to share the experience.[5]

NOTES

1. Augusta Baker, "Foreword" to *Storytelling: Art and Technique*, 3rd ed.
2. Carol L. Birch, "Storytelling Programs for the Family," *National Storytelling Journal* 1(Summer 1984): 14–18.

3. Caroline Feller Bauer, *New Handbook for Storytellers: With Stories, Poems, Magic and More* (American Library Assn., 1993), pp. 29–39.
4. Spencer G. Shaw, "A Story Falls in the Silence," *Wilson Library Bulletin* (October 1964): 179.
5. Birch, "Storytelling Programs for the Family," pp. 14–18.

Ninth Annual A(ugusta) Baker's Dozen
Schedule of Events

Friday, April 28

Storytelling for area fourth grade classes by invitation
Robert Mills Historic House and Park
1616 Blanding Street, 9:30 A.M.–11:30 A.M.

Colloquium Presentation

Tom Feelings presents
"The Picture Book: Reaching for the Child within the Adult"
Illustrator of over 20 books and
winner of the Coretta Scott King award for *Soul Looks Back in Wonder*
Currell College Auditorium
(on the Horseshoe near Davis College)
University of South Carolina
4:00 P.M.

Ninth Annual Augusta Baker Lecture

Children's author Bill Brittain presents
"The Perfect Children's Book"
Author of Newbery Honor Book *The Wish Giver*
Bostick Auditorium, Main Library
8:00 P.M.

Saturday, April 29

Storytelling for families featuring Ellin Greene and area storytellers
Free and open to the public
Bostick Auditorium, Main Library
10:30 A.M.–1:00 P.M.

FIGURE 25. *A(ugusta) Baker's Dozen—A Celebration of Stories, sponsored by Richland County Public Library, the College of Library and Information Science at the University of South Carolina, and the South Carolina State Library with support from the Friends of the Richland County Public Library, April 28–29, 1994.*

FESTSCHRIFT
for Augusta Baker

A Baker's Dozen:
13 Tales Worth Telling

Uncle Bouqui Rents a Horse

The Little Half-Chick

The Crab and the Jaguar

Jazzy Three Bears

The Cat's Purr

The Pumpkin Child

How the Farmer's Wife Took Care of Things

How the Lizard Lost and Regained His Farm

Clever Manka

The Voyage of the Wee Red Cap

Count Alaric's Lady

The Wise Old Woman

A Handful of Mustard Seed

Contributors and Stories

Augusta Baker. "Uncle Bouqui Rents a Horse," from *Uncle Bouqui of Haiti* by Harold Courlander. Morrow, 1942. Copyright © 1942 by Harold Courlander. Reprinted by permission.

Carol Birch. "The Voyage of the Wee Red Cap," from *This Way to Christmas* by Ruth Sawyer. HarperCollins, 1952.

Jane Botham. "How the Lizard Lost and Regained His Farm," from *The Hat-Shaking Dance and Other Ashanti Tales from the Gold Coast* by Harold Courlander with Albert Kofi Prempehj. Harcourt, 1957. Copyright © 1957 by Harold Courlander. Reprinted by permission.

Carolyn Field. "The Crab and the Jaguar," from *Picture Folk-Tales* by Valery Carrick. Stokes, 1926. Dover reprint, 1967.

The Folktellers. "Jazzy Three Bears," told to The Folktellers by Shoshana Lewis when she was five years old. Copyright © 1992 by The Folktellers. Used by permission.

Lucía M. González. "The Little Half-Chick," from *Señor Cat's Romance and Other Favorite Stories from Latin America* retold by Lucía M. González. Copyright © 1997 by Lucía M. González. Reprinted by permission of Scholastic Press/Scholastic Inc.

Ellin Greene. "Count Alaric's Lady," from *The Faun and the Woodcutter's Daughter*. Copyright © 1964 by Barbara Picard. Also in *Midsummer Magic* by Ellin Greene. Lothrop, 1977. Used by permission of HarperCollins Publishers.

Marilyn Berg Iarusso. "The Pumpkin Child," from *Persian Folk and Fairy Tales* by Anne Sinclair Mehdevi. Copyright © 1995 and renewed 1993 by Anne Sinclair Mehdevi. Reprinted by permission of Alfred A. Knopf, Inc.

Anne Pellowski. "Clever Manka," from *The Shoemaker's Apron* by Parker Fillmore. Harcourt, 1920.

George Shannon. "A Handful of Mustard Seed," from *Still More Stories to Solve: Fourteen Tales from Around the World*. Illustrated by Peter Sis. Copyright ©1994 by George W. B. Shannon. Published by Greenwillow Books. Reprinted by permission.

Spencer G. Shaw. "The Wise Old Woman," from *The Sea of Gold and Other Tales from Japan*. Copyright © 1965 by Yoshiko Uchida. Courtesy Scribners, an imprint of Simon & Schuster Children's Publishing Division.

Henrietta M. Smith. "The Cat's Purr," from *The Cat's Purr*. Text and illustration copyright 1985 by Ashley Bryan. Courtesy Atheneum Books for Young Readers, an imprint of Simon & Schuster Children's Publishing Division.

Carole Walton. "How the Farmer's Wife Took Care of Things: An Icelandic Folktale." Copyright © 1977 by Mary Buckley. Reprinted by permission of Tony Buckley.

FIGURE 26. *Augusta Baker.*

Uncle Bouqui Rents a Horse
Selected by Augusta Baker

Source: *Uncle Bouqui of Haiti* by Harold Courlander. Morrow, 1942, o.p.

Culture: Haitian

Telling time: 11 minutes

Audience: Age 7 to adult

Notes on telling: Uncle Bouqui is the perennial clown in Haitian folklore. He is the caricature of the slow-witted, usually well-meaning mountain man who is always getting into difficulties of his own making. These difficulties are usually complicated by the assistance of his nemesis, Ti Malice, who is the caricature of the sharp-witted city slicker. Both characters are derived from West African tradition whose prototypes were, for the most part, animal characters, notably Anansi, the spider. In Haiti the characteristics of the spider trickster hero, a combination of greed, gluttony, cleverness and stupidity, have been divided between the two Haitian characters.

As a storyteller, Augusta Baker was a master of comic timing (only Jack Benny could best her!). She always gave her listeners time to visualize what was taking place in the story and to anticipate the punch line with glee. When she told "Uncle Bouqui Rents a Horse" to younger children, she emphasized the comic aspects of putting so many people on the horse. With older children and adults, she emphasized the interplay between Uncle Bouqui and Ti Malice and between Uncle Bouqui and Madame Bouqui. (E.G.)

■

UNCLE BOUQUI decided he had to have a burro for a few days to carry his stuff to market. For weeks he had gone around singing a little song as he worked:

> "I'm not a mule, oh!
> I'm not a horse, oh!
> Uncle Bouqui makes me carry his coffee!"

It was really a complaint, but since there was no one else to complain about, he complained about the way he mistreated himself.

"I carry enough for six men," he told Madame Bouqui. "Whatever it is, Uncle Bouqui carries it. Any old scraggly mule would be ashamed to be seen with so many yams and beans piled on top of him."

"You eat enough for six men," Madame Bouqui said. "So you have to work like six men."

"Well, I can carry it all right," Bouqui said. "But it isn't dignified."

"Everybody carries things on his head," Madame Bouqui said. "Except maybe the President's wife."

"It isn't that," Bouqui said. "It's mostly my teeth."

"What do your teeth have to do with it?" Madame Bouqui asked.

"Look," Bouqui said. "My front teeth are gone. When I put a load on my head it pushes my gums together. When my gums come together my lips get pushed out in front. It's not very good looking."

"Wye!" Madame Bouqui said, putting her hand over her face to keep from laughing.

"I think I'll borrow Moussa's burro for a while. It can pasture in my banana grove and fatten itself up."

Bouqui went out in the garden and dug up a big pile of yams.

"Now that I have a burro I might as well get a *big* load ready," he said, and he dug up some more yams. After that he went over to Moussa's for the burro.

"Oh-oh!" Moussa said when he heard what Bouqui wanted. "Uncle Bouqui, my burro ran off yesterday and we haven't been able to find her. We've looked as far as the top of the hill, and there isn't even a track."

"Woy!" Bouqui said. "What about my yams?"

Moussa shook his head.

"First I lose my teeth," Bouqui wailed, "then my burro runs away! What luck I have!"

"Why don't you borrow a horse from Mr. Toussaint?" Moussa suggested.

"Toussaint! That stingy old man! He'll charge me rent. He'll charge me for even talking to him!"

"Well, you've got to get your stuff to market," Moussa said. "If my burro were here I'd lend her to you, but she isn't."

Bouqui frowned and sulked and pushed out his lips, but finally he went to Toussaint's place to rent a horse.

"It will cost you fifteen gourds," Toussaint said. "And you'd better take care of him! Don't try to make him carry as much as you put on your own head, either. This is a good horse."

"I only have five gourds now," Bouqui said.

"I'll take it," Toussaint said, snatching the money. "You can give me ten more tomorrow when you come for the horse."

All the way home Bouqui mumbled and grumbled. But he had to have a horse, that was all there was to it.

In the morning when he arose to get ready for market he heard a faint *ka-lip ka-lop* coming along the trail, and when he stuck his head out of the door he saw Uncle Moussa riding up on his burro.

"*Bonjou'*, Bouqui," Moussa said. "Here is the burro. In the middle of last night she came home. I heard a-snorting and a-squealing, and when I went out to look there she was rolling in the coffee plants to scratch her back."

"Wah!" Bouqui said. "I already rented a horse from Mr. Toussaint!"

"Take him back and use mine," Moussa said.

"I don't have him yet," Bouqui said, "but I already gave Toussaint five gourds! He'll never give it back! He sticks to money like a fly to fresh meat!"

While Bouqui was carrying on, Ti Malice came along the trail and stopped by the gate to listen. After a while he came into the yard.

"Take me along," Malice said to Bouqui. "I'll get your money back from Toussaint."

Bouqui's face broke into happy little wrinkles.

"What a wonderful idea! You could get money out of a coconut!" he said.

So Uncle Bouqui and Ti Malice went together to Mr. Toussaint's house.

"We've come for the horse," Malice said to Toussaint. "And he'd better be fed, too."

"There he is under the mango tree," Toussaint said. "But first give me the ten gourds."

"Just a minute," Malice said. "We have to check up to see if he's big enough."

"He's big enough. A horse is a horse," Toussaint said. "Don't try to back out of this deal. Uncle Bouqui rented him for fifteen gourds, and that's that."

"Just a minute," Ti Malice said. "We have to measure him." And he took a measuring tape out of his pocket and started to measure the horse's back.

"Let's see, now," he said to Uncle Bouqui. "You'll need about eighteen inches and you can sit here in the middle. Then I'll need about fifteen inches, and I'll sit here. Madame Malice can sit behind me, and she'll need about eighteen inches. Madame Bouqui can sit in the front, and she'll have to have about twenty inches. . . ."

"What's going on?" Toussaint said. "You can't put four people on that horse!"

"Don't bother us for a minute," Malice said, still measuring with his tape. "We have to figure where the children will sit. Jean Bouqui can go here on the horse's neck. Bouquino can sit in his lap, and we can strap Bouquinette right here if we're careful. . . ."

"Listen," Toussaint said, the perspiration starting to run down his face. "You must be crazy! A horse can't carry so many people!"

"He can try," Malice said. "At least, that's *his* end of the job. *Our* problem is how to get the whole party on him for the trip to Saut d'Eau for the festivities."

"You're not going to ride him all the way to Saut d'Eau!" Toussaint moaned. "He'll wear his feet off right down to his knees!"

"We can put my children *here,*" Malice said, measuring behind the horse's ears. "There's ten inches for Bobo and ten more for Toto, but they'll have to push together pretty tight."

"You're absolutely *coucou*, both of you!" Toussaint said. "You can't have the horse at all!"

"A bargain's a bargain!" Malice said. "You rented him to us and now we're going to use him. Uncle Bouqui, where will I put the baby?"

"Baby?" Bouqui said. He closed his mouth and licked his dry lips, but he just looked at Malice in bewilderment.

"Here, we'll put the baby here!" Malice said. "Madame Malice can hold him. But we may have to stretch the horse a bit. Then we can put the two pigs and the goats in the saddle bags. . . ."

Toussaint wiped the perspiration from his bald head.

"Pigs and goats!" he said. "Are you trying to *kill* the horse? The deal is off! This animal isn't a steamship!"

"A bargain's a bargain," Malice said firmly, and Bouqui nodded his head vigorously. "We'll take the matter to court."

"Here!" Toussaint said. "Here's your five gourds back!"

"You rented him out for fifteen gourds, and now you want to give five back," Malice said. "What do you take us for?"

"Yes, what for?" Bouqui echoed.

"All Bouqui gave me was five."

"You admit you rented him for fifteen, don't you?" Malice said.

"Yes, but . . ."

"Well, if you don't give the fifteen back we'll take you to the police post for not keeping your contract."

"Where'll we put grandmother?" Bouqui asked, looking at the horse.

"Here!" Toussaint panted, thrusting fifteen gourds in Malice's hands. "And get away from that horse!" He jumped on its back and rode away at a wild gallop.

Bouqui and Malice began to laugh. They fell on the ground and laughed until their stomachs hurt and the tears ran down their faces. They snorted and choked and gasped for breath thinking about Toussaint. They rolled and held their sides. When they were so weak they couldn't laugh any more they got up and returned to Bouqui's house.

Madame Bouqui served them coffee, and all through it they were snorting and sputtering.

"Wah!" Bouqui wailed. "I've never seen anything so funny in my life!"

"Wye! It was a scream!" Malice said. He put on his hat and went down the trail toward the city.

"This is certainly a day I'll remember," Bouqui said. "I gave him *five,* and he gave *fifteen* back! The stingiest man in Haiti!"

Uncle Bouqui was beaming. He giggled and put his hand in his pocket. Slowly the rosy look went out of his face. He pushed out his lips and tried another pocket. He got darker and darker and began to scowl.

"What's the matter?" Madame Bouqui said.

"Wah," Bouqui said in a faint voice, a little absentmindedly. He kept going through his pockets over and over again.

For a moment he stood very still. Then he let out a roar. *"Wye!"* Where's that thief Malice! He didn't give me the fifteen gourds!"

He bounded to the trail and looked up and down, but there was no sign of Malice. Bouqui's roaring died down into a feeble whimper. He came back and sat down.

"It's certainly a day to remember," Madame Bouqui said.

Uncle Bouqui was silent a long time.

"I don't think we could have done it," he said at last.

"Done what?" Madame Bouqui said.

"Put grandmother on the horse," Bouqui said.

■

Augusta Baker

Augusta Baker has played many roles in her lifetime—children's librarian, administrator, teacher, author, anthologist, reviewer, speaker, consultant, radio and television presenter. But the first word that comes to mind to all who know her is *storyteller.*

Born April 1, 1911, in Baltimore, Maryland, Augusta grew up surrounded by books and stories. After attending the University of Pittsburgh for two years, she transferred to the State University of New York at Albany and received her B.A. in education in 1934. But teaching wasn't for her. She went on to earn a B.S. in library science and began her career as a children's librarian at the New York Public Library in 1937. In 1953 she went to Trinidad to organize children's work in the Trinidad Public Library. That same year she was appointed assistant coordinator of children's services and storytelling specialist at the New York Public Library. She served in that position until 1961 when she became coordinator of children's services, supervising 80 children's rooms.

During her 37 years at the New York Public Library, Augusta founded the James Weldon Johnson Memorial Collection (books about black history and culture for children), located at the Countee Cullen Regional Branch; conceived and edited the first six editions of *The Black Experience in Children's Books*; co-authored *Storytelling: Art and Technique* with Ellin Greene; and edited three books: *The Talking Tree, The Golden Lynx,* and *Young Years.* She is the author of numerous articles, reviews, and forewords.

Augusta served on the board of directors and, in 1968, as president of the Children's Services Division (now ALSC) of the American Library Association. She also served on the ALA Council and executive board, and chaired several committees.

She retired from the New York Public Library in 1974, and in 1980 moved to Columbia, South Carolina, to be near her son and granddaughters. Almost immediately the University of South Carolina created the position of storyteller-in-residence for her. In addition to teaching a course in storytelling, she gave state workshops for the Department of Social Services, nursery schools, and area colleges. She retired from this position in 1994.

Since 1985 the Richland County Public Library and the College of Library and Information Science, University of South Carolina, have sponsored "A(ugusta) Baker's Dozen," a two-day storytelling festival held in April to honor this extraordinary woman. On the Friday morning, fourth-grade students are bused in from all over the Columbia area to hear stories. A program of interest to adults is held in the afternoon and another in the evening. The next morning there is a storytelling program for families (see Figure 25).

Augusta has been a popular instructor in storytelling at many universities, including Columbia, the New School for Social Research, New York University, Rutgers, Syracuse University, and the Universities of Nevada, South Florida, and South Carolina. She holds honorary doctorates from St. John's University and the University of South Carolina.

Author Betsy Byars once said that Augusta Baker was like the lace snail who left a trail of silken white lace behind, wherever she went. In recognition of her achievements Augusta has received many awards, including the first Dutton-Macrae Award (for advanced study in the field of library work with children and young people); the Parents Magazine Medal for Outstanding Service to the Nation's Children; the ALA Grolier Award (for outstanding achievement in guiding and stimulating the reading of children and young people); the Constance Lindsay Skinner Award, Women's National Book Association; the Clarence Day Award (for leadership given to the world of children's books); the Regina Medal, Catholic Library Association; and the Distinguished Service Award, Association for Library Service to Children, American Library Association.

Augusta often spoke of the impact that storytellers have on children. "I meet adults on the street and they say, 'I was at your story hours,' and they turn to their children and say, 'This is the woman who used to read me stories when I was little.'" In her acceptance for the 1971 Constance Lindsay Skinner Award, she returned the compliment: "Through the years boys and girls have strengthened my love for storytelling as they have settled in their seats, fixed their eyes on me, and settled down as I have said 'Once upon a time.' This has been one of my best rewards and I give thanks for it."

The Little Half-Chick

Selected by Lucía M. González

Source: Señor Cat's Romance and Other Favorite Stories from Latin America retold by Lucía M. González. Illustrated by Lulu Delacre. Scholastic, 1997 (forthcoming).

Culture: Hispanic/Cuban

Telling time: 8 minutes

Audience: Age 4 to 8

Notes on telling: The story of Medio-Pollito, the Little Half-Chick of the weather vane, is widely known in Spain and Latin America. As a child I was always delighted by the story of this willful and adventurous little chick who in spite of his many limitations sets out to see the world and meet the king. In his quest he learns a very important lesson the hard way, but grows up to become a very helpful and important half-chick.

"The Little Half-Chick" is a fun story to tell. I always invite the audience to join in and clap their hands on their knees as the Little Half-Chick skips away making the characteristic *Tipi-Tap-Tipi-Tap-Tipi-Tap* sound. Sometimes I use black cardboard to cut out the shape of the weather vane with the little rooster on top and use it as a prop.

■

ONCE UPON a time, a little half-chick named Medio-Pollito lived on a farm near the mill. He had only one wing and only one leg, and he did very well with these.

The other animals on the farm felt so sorry for him that they always gave in to his every whim. Because of this, he had grown to be a spoiled little chick who was always demanding his own way, and nearly always got it. In fact, he was as naughty and vain as two whole chicks rolled into one.

One day he told his mother: "Mama, I am tired of living on the same farm all my life. I am going to Madrid to meet the king! He will be very pleased to see me." And off he went:

Tipi-Tap-Tipi-Tap-Tipi-Tap

hopping on his only one leg.

On his way, Medio-Pollito came to a small brook. Its waters were choked with weeds.

"Medio-Pollito, help me!" coughed the brook. "Would you be so kind as to remove these weeds with your beak so that I may run free?"

But Medio-Pollito was in much too much of a hurry.

"I have no time to waste on anything so unimportant as water," said he. "I am going to Madrid to see the king!" And he hurried away:

Tipi-Tap-Tipi-Tap-Tipi-Tap

hopping across the field on his only one leg.

Later on that day, he found a fire that was dying for lack of air. The fire gasped, "Medio-Pollito, fan me with your wing so that I may breathe and live."

But the half-chick answered, "I have no time to waste on anything so unimportant as a fire! I am gong to Madrid to see the king!" And he hopped:

Tipi-Tap-Tipi-Tap-Tipi-Tap

a little faster on his only one leg.

At last, Medio-Pollito reached the outskirts of Madrid, from where he could see the palace gates. He grew so excited when he saw this, that he hopped even faster. And as he rushed along, he passed by some bushes.

From among the branches came the voice of the wind calling, "Medio-Pollito, I am trapped in these branches. Please, come and set me free!"

This time the little half-chick did not even stop as he replied, "I have no time to waste on anything so unimportant as the wind," said he. "I am going to Madrid to see the king!" And he went on hopping:

Tipi-Tap-Tipi-Tap-Tipi-Tap

down the road that led to the palace.

In no time, Medio-Pollito arrived at the palace. He slipped quickly through the gates, past the guards, and found himself in a great courtyard. *"Oh surely the king will be thrilled to see me now,"* thought the little half-chick.

But just as he passed under the kitchen window, one of the royal cooks grabbed him.

"Just what I needed," said the cook. "A little chick for the king's soup!" And he threw Medio-Pollito into a big pot of water that was boiling over the kitchen fire. As the water bubbled and rose, Medio-Pollito screamed, "Oh Water! Oh Water! My very good friend! Don't bubble, don't rise, or you'll drown me!"

But the water said simply, "You did not help me when I was in need!" And the water went right on bubbling.

The fire crackled and blazed beneath the pot. Medio-Pollito yelled, "Oh Fire! Oh Fire! My very good friend. Have pity, have mercy, don't burn me!"

But the fire said, "You did not help me when I was in need!" And the fire went right on burning.

Just then, the king came and looked into the pot. All he saw was a half-burnt half-chick. He reached inside, grabbed Medio-Pollito by his only one leg, and tossed him out the window saying, "This half-chick is not fit for a king's meal!"

But before Medio-Pollito could hit the ground, the wind lifted him up, up, up, over the roofs of Madrid and over the trees. Medio-Pollito shouted, "Wind, oh Wind, my good friend. Don't blow me, don't toss me, don't drop me! Just let me drift slowly down before I hit the ground."

But the wind exclaimed, "You did not help me when I was in need!" And he went right on blowing.

Higher and higher the wind carried the frightened Medio-Pollito. Then, at last, the wind swooped him down from the clouds and planted him right on top of the mill near the little farm that was once the little half-chick's humble home.

There Medio-Pollito stands to this day! He has had plenty of time to think about how he did not help his friends when they were in need. And to make up for it, he stands on top of that mill, on his only one leg, with his only one wing, watching from which direction the wind blows. And to this day, he helps farmers and travelers by telling them what kind of day it is going to be.

■

Tribute to Augusta Baker

I met Augusta Baker in the spring of 1990 through the teachings and anecdotes of my dear professor Henrietta Smith. Professor Smith transmitted to her class her knowledge of Augusta Baker with such care, admiration, and vivacity that I feel as if I had sat at one of her many story hours and seen the attentive and eager faces of the children in the audience enjoying each word, each expression, each story. I learned from Augusta Baker to trust the wonder of the story, its patterns, and its own power. I also learned to help my audience of children cross that imaginary line between the real world and the magical ecstasy of the world of the story hour.

Now that part of my job involves training other librarians in children's services and programming, I find myself retelling many of Professor Smith's anecdotes about Augusta Baker and her art of telling—the "Augusta Baker way."

Lucía González works for the Miami-Dade Public Library as a children's librarian, storyteller, and puppeteer. She is the reteller/compiler of *Señor Cat's Romance and Other Favorite Stories from Latin America,* illustrated by Lulu Delacre, and the reteller of *The Bossy Gallito/El Gallo de Bodas: A Traditional Cuban Folktale,* also illustrated by Delacre. Lucía grew up in Cuba and, like Pura Belpré, was inspired to translate her favorite stories remembered from childhood so that she could share them with children in the United States.

The Crab and the Jaguar

Selected by Carolyn Field

Source: *Picture Folk-Tales* by Valery Carrick. Illustrated by the author. Dover reprint, 1967. (Originally published by Frederick A. Stokes Co., 1926.) Also in *Twenty Tellable Tales* by Margaret Read MacDonald. H. W. Wilson, 1986.

Culture: The Russian writer Valery Carrick gives no source for the tale. Margaret Read MacDonald found a German-language version in *Indianermärchen aus Südamerica* by Theodor Koch-Grünberg. Koch-Grünberg ascribes the tale to the Taulipang Indians and places this group near the border of Brazil and British Guyana.

Telling time: 5 minutes

Audience: All ages from kindergarten children to adults

Notes on telling: I have told my favorite story, "The Crab and the Jaguar," hundreds of times in the past 58 years. It all began in 1938 when I did my two weeks' practice work at the Aguilar branch of the New York Public Library. Katherine Love was the children's librarian and asked me to tell a *short* story at the weekly library story hour. Since 1938, I have told "The Crab and the Jaguar" to adults and children throughout the United States and in Trinidad. During World War II, while serving in the American Red Cross, I told the story to servicemen on trains in the United States and to members of the Air Force in England. It is still my favorite story, and I can tell it at the drop of a hat!

■

ONE DAY a crab sat on a stone and was having a game with his eyes. He would say to them:

"Eyes, little eyes of mine! Fly away to the blue sea, quick-quick-quick-quick-quick!"

And the eyes would leap from his head and fly off to the blue sea. Then he would say:

"Eyes, little eyes of mine! Fly back to me from the blue sea, quick-quick-quick-quick-quick!"

Then his eyes would come flying back and settle down again in their proper place. And in this way the crab used to play endless games and keep himself amused.

One day a jaguar came to that place and looked at the crab and was very much astonished and said, "Whatever are you doing, my friend?"

"What am I doing?" repeated the crab. "I'm just having a game with my eyes. I tell them to fly away, and they fly away. Then I tell them to fly back, and they come back to their proper place."

"What a wonderful thing!" said the jaguar. "Do, please, do it again!"

"All right!" answered the crab. "I will. Eyes, little eyes of mine! Fly away to the blue sea, quick-quick-quick-quick-quick!"

And his eyes flew away. Then he said:

"Eyes, little eyes of mine! Fly back from the blue sea, quick-quick-quick-quick-quick!"

And his eyes flew back and settled in their proper place.

"What a lovely game that is!" said the jaguar. "Tell me, could you play it with my eyes?"

"Well, yes, I could," answered the crab; "but you know, just now, the terrible Animale-Podole, father of the Trahira-fish, is swimming about in the blue sea, and I'm very much afraid he might eat your eyes!"

"Oh, I don't suppose he will! Anyway, I'll risk it! Come, now, do make my eyes fly away!"

"Very well, I will!" said the crab. "Eyes of Mr. Jaguar! Fly away to the blue sea, quick-quick-quick-quick-quick!"

And the eyes leapt out of the jaguar's head and flew off to the blue sea. Then the jaguar said, "Now tell them to come back again!"

"Eyes of Mr. Jaguar!" said the crab. "Fly back here from the blue sea, quick-quick-quick-quick-quick!"

And his eyes came flying back and settled back in their proper place. And the jaguar said, "Oh, but you know that's really wonderfully funny! Please do it again!"

"Mind!" answered the crab. "I've told you the terrible Animale-Podole, father of the Trahira-fish, is swimming about in the sea. If he does eat up your eyes you'll be left without any!"

"Oh, never mind. Please do it again!" said the jaguar.

"Very well," answered the crab. "Eyes of Mr. Jaguar! Fly away to the blue sea, quick-quick-quick-quick-quick!"

And the jaguar's eyes flew off again to the blue sea. And it so happened that just in that spot and just at that time, the terrible Animale-Podole, father of the Trahira-fish, was swimming about, and he saw the eyes of the jaguar and swallowed them.

Then the crab called them back again, "Eyes of Mr. Jaguar! Fly back from the blue sea, quick-quick-quick-quick-quick!"

But the eyes never flew back. And the crab called them again and again; but it was no good. The terrible Animale-Podole, father of the Trahira-fish, had eaten them! And the jaguar got very angry with the crab and wanted to kill him, but couldn't catch him, for the crab crept under the stone. So there was no help for it, and the jaguar went off without his eyes. And after he had been walking a long time he met a King-vulture. And the King-vulture said to the jaguar, "Where are you going, my friend?"

"I don't know where I'm going; that's just it!" replied the jaguar. "The crab sent my eyes away to the blue sea, and there the terrible Animale-Podole, father of the Trahira-fish, swallowed them. So now I have to go about without eyes! Couldn't you make me some new ones?"

"Well, yes, I can! But you must make a promise and keep it: whatever beast you kill while hunting, always give me a share!"

"I promise!" said the jaguar.

So the King-vulture made the jaguar some new eyes, even better than his old ones. And ever since then, whatever beast the jaguar kills while out hunting, he always leaves a piece for the King-vulture.

■

Tribute to Augusta Baker

On graduating from Simmons College, I returned to the New York Public Library as a children's librarian. At the Library's Storytelling Symposium in 1939, I was honored to be asked to be one of the storytellers, and chose "The Crab and the Jaguar." Augusta Baker was there, heard it, liked it, and took it for her own. I did not know this until I heard her tell it in Philadelphia in 1959. She had never realized that I was the young librarian with dark hair in a bun who had told it at Storytelling Symposium twenty years before!

No tribute is too extravagant to pay to Augusta Baker, a dedicated children's librarian and storyteller. Her influence has been felt throughout the children's book world by librarians, teachers, parents, editors, authors, and illustrators. She has devoted her life, not only to library work with children, but to the many professional organizations related to children and books. She was a superb instructor at several universities, and a role model for persons who believe that quality children's books and caring librarians can help children develop into mature, intelligent, and caring adults.

Carolyn W. Field was coordinator of work with children at the Free Library of Philadelphia from 1953 to 1983. She is the recipient of numerous honors for her outstanding contribution to the library profession and served as president of the Association for Library Service to Children in 1960. In 1965 she organized the Philadelphia Children's Reading Round Table, which recently celebrated its thirtieth anniversary. She is the editor of *Special Collections in Children's Literature* (American Library Association, 1969, 1982) and wrote the Foreword to the 1995 edition.

Jazzy Three Bears

Selected by The Folktellers

Source: We learned this story from Shoshana Lewis, now a graduate of Georgetown University, when she was just five years old. She learned it in her day-care center. We had to fill in a few missing parts and we varied the rhythm a bit.

Culture: American/English

Telling time: 3 minutes

Audience: All ages from kindergarten children to adults

Notes on telling: This is a great story to use at the close of a program because it is so upbeat. You can hear it on our video *Pennies, Pets & Peanut Butter* or on our cassette "Stories for the Road."

■

ONCE UPON a time in a nursery rhyme,
There were three bears, umm, I said three bears, umm.
They all went a-walking through the green woods a-talking,
'Long come a little girl with long shiny golden hair,
Her name was Goldilocks,
Her name was Goldilocks.
Upon the door she knocked,
Ba-boom, ba-boom, ba-boom, boom, boom.
But no one was there,
No, no one was there.
She walked right in, had herself a ball,
Eating and a-rocking, and a-sleeping and all.

She didn't care,
No one was there,
She didn't care.
Wow, wow, wow,
Home came the three bears,
Tired from the woods,
Ready to sit down to some home-cooked goods,
Yeah, slurp.
"Someone's been eating my porridge," said the Papa Bear,

Said the Mama Bear.
"Hey, Mama She Bear," cried the Little Wee Bear,
"Someone has broken my chair, waa."
Well, they went upstairs,
To see what they could find,
Saw Goldilocks in bed,
Asleep all the time.
She woke up,
Broke up the party and boogied on out of there.
"Bye," said the Papa Bear,
"Bye," said the Mama Bear.
"Hey, Mama She Bear," said the Little Wee Bear,
"What kind of bear was that there, huh?"
And that is the story of the three bears,
I said the three bears,
I said the three,
I said the three,
I said the three bears.

■

Tribute to Augusta Baker

We first met Augusta Baker at a storytelling conference in Westchester County, New York, in 1975. We had heard about her, of course, and respected and appreciated her work in storytelling when we were on the staff of the public library in Chattanooga, Tennessee, in the early 1970s. We were thrilled to meet her—a "star" in our eyes—yet she was so down-to-earth. We sat on the tailgate of our little yellow Datsun pickup truck and someone took a photo. Then we all went out to eat and had a great time. Throughout our careers, Augusta has been encouraging and supportive of our work. As a featured teller at the NAPPS storytelling festival in 1983 and at the Asheville "Tell It in the Mountains" storytelling festival four years ago, she has continued to inspire younger storytellers and to entertain us all.

Barbara Freeman. From the library world to festival stages, Barbara Freeman and her Folkteller partner, Connie Regan-Blake, have been captivating audiences for over 20 years. Best known for her humorous tellings of Appalachian tales and, more recently, for her performance of parables and true stories of Christian saints and martyrs, Barbara's talents have been recognized in such diverse media as ABC's *Good Morning America, School Library Journal,* and National Public Radio's *All Things Considered.*

Connie Regan-Blake. Connie Regan-Blake is known for her entertaining yet powerfully absorbing performances and workshops. With Barbara Freeman she was a founding member of the National Storytelling Association (formerly, NAPPS), and she served as chair of the NAPPS board from 1983 to 1985. When she isn't performing in tandem, she tours solo, most recently with the Kandinsky Chamber Music Trio as a featured storyteller, bringing the folk arts to the classical crowd and drawing storytelling listeners into chamber music.

The Cat's Purr
Selected by Henrietta Smith

Source: *The Cat's Purr* written and illustrated by Ashley Bryan. Atheneum, 1985. The story is based on a West Indian folktale, "Why Cat Eats Rat," recorded by Arthur H. Fauset and published in *Folklore of the Antilles, French and English, Part II* by Elsie Clews Parsons. American Folklore Society, G. E. Stechert & Co., 1936. Bryan includes the text of the original tale at the end of his book.

Culture: West Indian

Telling time: 12 minutes

Audience: All ages

Notes on telling: How do you choose a favorite story when there are so many that speak to you? Somehow, there is one that has an extra touch of magic, that certain appeal that invites listeners of all ages to share in its contents and that the teller enjoys with equal enthusiasm each time the tale is told. Such a story for me is the rhythmic and musical "The Cat's Purr."

When learning "The Cat's Purr," try to see each scene, and when the sequence is firm in your head, then concentrate on the wonderful "pit-tap-a-la-pats" and "purrums." The more you tell it, the more easily the rhymes will fall into place, and the pacing will become more and more comfortable. Sometimes, *but not always*, I will watch for a very intense listener, and *gently* pounce at him or her as Cat vents his anger on Rat.

ONCE UPON a time, Cat and Rat were the best of friends. Uh-huh, they really were! They lived in huts right next to each other. And since Rat liked to copy Cat, their huts matched.

Cat planted a coconut palm tree by his hut. Rat planted one, too. Cat wove a straw mat for the corner of his hut. Rat wove one, too. When Rat visited Cat, he'd sit on Cat's mat; and on visits to Rat, Cat sat on Rat's mat.

Cat made a bamboo flute and played sweet tunes. "Let me play a tune, too," said Rat. Cat let Rat play a tune, too: *too-de-loo, too-de-loo.*

Cat and Rat farmed their land together. They worked in the field each day and took good care of their vegetable patch. After work they headed home, each with his hoe.

"When the vegetables are ready, let's have a big feast," said Cat one day.

"A grand party with dancing and singing," said Rat, "uh-huh, uh-huh!"

They laughed and talked of the feast as they walked along singing, "Ho for a feast and hi for a song."

One night, Cat's old uncle visited and brought Cat a present. Cat unwrapped the package. There, inside, was a small drum, the smallest drum Cat had ever seen.

"It's a cat's drum," the old uncle said, "passed down in the family. Now it's for you."

"It's so small. Can I play it?" asked Cat.

"Oh, yes!" said Cat's uncle. "It's small, and there's a special way to play it. Don't rap it or beat it or poke it or you won't get a good sound. Stroke it gently and listen." Cat stroked the drum gently. The drum went *purrum, purrum.*

"Oh, meow!" said Cat. "How soothing, how beautiful!"

"Take good care of the drum," Cat's old uncle said as he was leaving. "Remember now, don't rap it or beat it or tap it or poke it. Just stroke it gently. And don't let anyone else play it."

The next morning Rat called on Cat as he always did, on the way to work in the fields. He tapped on Cat's hut door: *rap-a-tap tap, rap-a-tap tap.*

Purrum, purrum, purrum, came the sound from inside Cat's hut. Rat had never heard such music before. He opened Cat's door and went in. There sat Cat on his bed playing a small drum.

"Pit-tap-a-la-pat," cried Rat. "What a big, sweet sound from such a small drum! It's so small you could swallow it whole! Squeek-eek, play it, Cat, uh-huh!"

Purrum, purrum, purrum, played Cat. *Purrum, purrum, purrum.*

Rat twirled about. He hummed and kicked up his feet to the purrum, purrum beat until Cat stopped drumming.

"Me now!" Rat cried.

"Oh no!" said Cat. "Meow! This is a Cat family drum from my uncle."

"Pit-tap-a-la-pat," said Rat. "So what? I played in the shade of your coconut tree; I sat on your mat, drank coconut milk, too. I played your flute, *too-de-loo, too-de-loo.*"

"That was different, Rat," Cat said. "My uncle said no one else plays this Cat drum. Anyway, this is not a time for drumming. Let's get to work in the fields." Cat set the drum down on the bed.

"I must think of a good plan so that I can play Cat's drum," Rat thought. "I'll need time to think."

"I'm hungry," Rat said. "Squee-eek! If I'm to work in the fields, I've got to eat food first. I'll faint if I go without breakfast."

Cat cooked cornmeal mush and served Rat. Rat ate, but couldn't keep his eyes off the drum. It still sang in his ears, *purrum, purrum*. His fingers itched to play it.

Rat ate slowly, bowl after bowl of cornmeal mush. Still not one good drum-playing plan popped into his head. He dawdled so long over the breakfast that it was teatime when he finished. His stomach was as tight as a drum.

"It's teatime," Rat said. "Squee-eek, and I'm still hungry. We'll work better after tea, Cat. Don't you agree?"

"Meow, I'm not hungry now," said Cat. "How can you still be hungry after swallowing so much mush?"

"It just wasn't enough mush, I guess," said Rat.

"Oh, meow," said Cat, and he served Rat the tea. "Now don't get sick. Remember, we have lots of work to do for our feast."

"Sick!" Rat thought. "That's it!" Cat had given Rat the idea he needed. Now he knew just what to do.

"Pit-tap-a-la-pat," Rat cried as he pushed aside his cup and plate. "I'm full now and ready for work. Squee-eek."

"Pit-tap-a-la-po," Cat cried. "Here's your hoe. Meow, let's go!"

Rat was almost to the door when he moaned and fell to the ground. He turned and tossed at Cat's feet. "Ooo-ooo," Rat groaned. "My belly's hurting me too bad. Squeak, Squee-eek."

"I knew you'd be sick," Cat said. Cat helped Rat to his feet. "Ah, poor Rat. Don't lie on the floor. Come lie on the bed."

"Ooo-ooo. Thank you. Squee-eek, ooo-ooo."

Cat put Rat to bed and spread a coverlet over him. "Rest," said Cat. "When your belly is cool, come and help me out in the fields."

"I will come, oh-ooo, when I'm well. We two do work so well together. Oh-ooo, oh-ooo."

Though Rat wailed well, he was not ill at all, uh-uh! He stretched out on Cat's bed till his toes touched the drum. His plan was working, and he felt happy.

Cat left Rat to rest and set out for their vegetable patch. Rat waited until he was sure that Cat had reached the field. Then Rat threw off the coverlet, sat up and began to sing:

Pit-tap-a-la-pat
Pit-tap-a-la-ping
Eat off Cat's food
And don't pay a thing

Rat reached for Cat's drum and hugged it. "I'd rather hug a drum than do hum-drum hoeing," Rat laughed. "Now it's my turn to play Cat's drum."

Rat danced while Cat drummed, so he had not learned Cat's secret of how best to beat it. Rat tapped the drum—no purrum. Rat beat the drum—no purrum. He poked it—no-no, no purrum! Instead of hugging Cat's drum now, Rat was so mad he could have pounded it. But by chance he stroked it. And there it was: *purrum, purrum, purrum.*

"Pit-tap-a-la-pat!" cried Rat. "What a thing, this drum. Rap it, tap it, beat it, poke it—no loud, sweet purrum. But when you stroke it—*purrum, purrum, purrum.*"

Far off in the field, Cat heard the sound. It was his drum—*purrum, purrum, purrum.* He dropped his hoe and ran toward his hut.

Rat saw Cat coming across the field. Quickly he replaced the drum at the foot of the bed. He stretched out and drew the coverlet up to his chin. He closed his eyes and pretended to be asleep. Cat ran into the room, shook Rat awake and shouted:

Pit-tap-a-la-pat
Pit-tap-a-la-pum
Who's that knocking
On my drum?

"I fell asleep," said Rat. "I didn't hear a thing. Squee-eek, oh-ooo! My belly's still hurting me too bad."

"You mean your belly's not cool yet, Rat?" Cat asked. "Well, lie down, but keep your eyes open."

"I will do as well as I can, Cat, even though I'm ill."

Cat set out alone to till the fields.

And Rat could hardly wait to play the drum again. When Cat was well out of sight, he sat up in bed and sang:

Pit-tap-a-la-pat
Pit-tap-a-la-ping
Eat off Cat's food
And don't pay a thing.

Rat shook with excitement when he took up the drum. First he hugged it, then he stroked it more lightly than before. An even louder *purrum, purrum, purrum,* came from the drum.

As Cat hoed a row of vegetable he heard *purrum, purrum, purrum.* At once he dropped his hoe and headed for home.

Rat was again in bed and under the coverlet when Cat ran in. Cat shook Rat and cried:

"Pit-tap-a-la-pat
Pit-tap-a-la-pum
Who's that knocking
On my drum?"

You make my belly ache more when you shake me up so," said Rat. "Oo-ooo, my belly's hurting me too bad. I didn't hear a thing."

"But, Rat, I tell you someone is knocking on my drum. I hear it in the field—*purrum, purrum, purrum.* Come now, help me, Rat."

"How can I?" said Rat. "I'm lying down, and my belly is hurting me."

"Stay in my bed till your belly's cool. But keep your eyes open. Find out who's knocking on my drum and tell me."

Cat left and closed the door. This time though, Cat didn't go far along the path to the field. He doubled back, ducked down, and crept to the side of the hut. There he climbed in through the kitchen window and hid under the table.

When Rat thought that Cat was far out of sight, he sat right up in bed.

"What's this?" Cat asked himself. "Maybe Rat's belly is cool now." He watched Rat from the hiding place under the table. He saw Rat take up the drum. Cat did not move. Rat began to sing:

"I fooled Cat once"

Cat kept quiet.

"I fooled Cat twice"

Cat blinked his eyes.

"I play Cat's drum"

Cat's ears twitched.

"Purrum, purrum, purrum."

"Drop that drum, Rat," cried Cat. "I've caught you at it. Meow."
"You haven't caught me yet," cried Rat.

Rat dodged and scampered down as Cat leaped onto the bed. So Cat jumped off the bed and trapped Rat in the corner. All Rat saw was Cat's wide-open mouth and Cat's very sharp teeth. And that gave Rat a new idea.

As Cat flung himself at Rat, Rat plunged the drum into Cat's open mouth and fled.

Cat fell against the bed. He gulped and swallowed. Down went the drum. To his surprise, Cat realized that instead of swallowing Rat, he had swallowed his drum. Cat stroked his stomach to settle the drum. A muffled sound came from within: *purrum, purrum, purrum.*

Rat ran out of Cat's hut and past his own. He didn't stop to pack a thing, uh-huh! He kept on going, and he didn't look back. By the time Cat finally ran out-of-doors, Rat was long gone.

"That's that for our vegetable feast." Cat cried. "If I ever catch that Rat, I'll feast on him. Meow!"

Since that day, Cat carries his drum safely within. You can't fool Cat anymore with belly cool this and belly cool that. Uh-huh! Cat always knows now who's playing his drum because Cat alone chooses whom he'll let play.

If you're kind to Cat, he'll let you play his drum. Remember, though, don't tap it or beat it, don't rap it or poke it. Just stroke Cat gently—very, very gently. Uh-huh, uh-huh!

Listen now. Can you hear Cat purring—*purrum, purrum, purrum?* That's Cat's drum! *Purrum, purrum, purrum.*

■

Tribute to Augusta Baker

When I was hired as a clerk in the New York Public Library system, little did I dream that my life would be so enriched by one person—Augusta Baker. As my supervisor, she showed me by example the most effective way truly to serve the public—with courtesy and interest and patience. As I pursued a degree in library science, Augusta Baker was one of my teachers. She taught me not only the *art* of storytelling, but also the *joy.* Even today when I might ask "why am I doing this," I hear her voice saying "Storytelling is a way to preserve the history and culture of all people, so go forth and tell."

And then this master storyteller taught me *how* to tell. She taught me to allow time for laughter, to include provocative pauses, and, without dramatic gestures or flamboyant histrionics, quietly to share with listeners the details of an "event" to which they were not privy. Because of her training I have been privileged to tell in places far and wide, and it is always as if Augusta were by my side reminding me of the importance of what I am trying to do and the value of the tradition being carried on. Finally, from "boss" to teacher and mentor to friend, we have come full cycle, and may this note say "Thank You, Gusta, for giving such vibrant life to the *art* of storytelling." How lucky I am to have been able to learn from *you*!

Henrietta M. Smith. After many years' experience as a children's librarian at the New York Public Library and in the public schools of Broward (Fla.) County, Henrietta M. Smith joined the faculty of the School of Library and Information Science, University of South Florida-Tampa, where she teaches youth services courses, including storytelling. She has served on several ALA and ALSC committees; and as chair of the Coretta Scott King Task Force, she edited the highly praised volume *The Coretta Scott King Awards Book: From Vision to Reality*.

The Pumpkin Child

Selected by Marilyn Berg Iarusso

Source: *Persian Folk and Fairy Tales* retold by Anne Sinclair Mehdevi. Illustrated by Paul E. Kennedy. Knopf, 1965, o.p.

Culture: Persian/Iranian

Telling time: 8 minutes

Audience: Age 5 to adult

Notes on telling: I've been telling "The Pumpkin Child" since 1983. At that time I was telling a lot of folktales with cannibals, witch babies, and troll hags, and I was looking for a medium length story with no violence in it. It is one of the tales recommended on the *Stories* list which I edited in 1977. Coincidentally, when I was a child I loved to read and reread a book Mehdevi wrote about a girl growing up in Persia.

"The Pumpkin Child" is long enough to be satisfying and short enough to be easily tucked into almost any program. I think what my audiences like about it is the comfort of hearing about the good mother who will not abandon her child and the feeling of being accepted and loved for what you are. They also like the story's humor and are pleased to recognize the elements from "Cinderella." I don't really change the story from the printed text, but I think the mother has grown more long-suffering and devoted over the years as I have grown more aware of how heroic women are in adversity.

■

THERE WAS a time and there wasn't a time in the long ago when a good wife lived with her husband in a small, neat house at the edge of town. She had everything she wanted except one thing. She longed to have a daughter. Year after year, she prayed for a daughter, but year after year, she and her husband remained childless. One day, she said to her husband, "I would like a little girl so much that I wouldn't even care if she looked like a pumpkin."

Not long after she spoke these words, a beautiful girl child was born, with eyes like sapphires and lips like pomegranate seeds. Both the woman and her husband were very happy until, one morning, when the mother went to pick up her child from its cradle, she found a pumpkin there instead. When the husband saw that his daughter had turned into a pumpkin, he ran away from town and never came back. But the good woman felt sorry for the little pumpkin and took care of it and loved it.

Year by year, the pumpkin grew bigger and fatter until it became too big to carry. Then it began to roll around the house and out into the street. All the neighbors laughed and mocked the poor wife because she had a pumpkin instead of a child.

Many more years passed, and the good wife continued to take care of her pumpkin child. She dressed it in pretty dresses which she sewed herself. When the pumpkin child was fifteen, the wife decided to send it to school with the other girls of the town so it could learn the arts of needlework and spinning. She gave the pumpkin a little kiss and told it to be good and not to mind if people laughed at it, and then the pumpkin rolled off to school.

The school for young ladies happened to be next door to a rich merchant's house. The merchant's son, Murad, used to delight in watching the young ladies as they spun and sewed in the school courtyard beneath his father's windows. One day, he saw a yellow pumpkin rolling around among the young ladies and he said to himself, "Why is a pumpkin going to a school for young ladies?"

Then, he began to notice that every day at noon, when the young ladies ate their meal under the fig trees, the pumpkin rolled off into a far corner of the garden and disappeared.

So, Murad went up to the roof of his father's house. From there he could see the entire garden. He watched the pumpkin as it rolled away by itself at noontime. After the pumpkin had rolled under a currant bush, so that it was hidden from everyone in the garden, it stopped rolling. The top of the pumpkin flew off and out stepped a young girl as beautiful as the moon on its fourteenth night. She climbed up a grapevine and began to pick grapes and eat them for her meal. When she had eaten her fill, she climbed back down the grapevine and stepped into the pumpkin and the top of the pumpkin flew into place again.

Every day after that, Murad went to the roof at noon and watched the beautiful girl as she emerged from the pumpkin, ate her lunch of grapes, and then returned to the pumpkin. Before a week had passed, Murad had fallen in love with her, not with one beat of his heart but with a hundred beats.

One day, he crept to the edge of his father's roof, which was near the top of the grapevine. When the girl in the pumpkin climbed up the vine, Murad leaned out and grasped her hand. He was just going to ask her to be his bride, when she quickly withdrew her hand, hurried down the grapevine, and disappeared inside the pumpkin. Then she rolled back to join the other young ladies.

Murad was very sad. But he found that the girl's ring had slipped off her middle finger into his hand. He went downstairs and said to his mother, "It is time I were married, Mother. I want a wife who can wear this ring on her middle finger and I will marry no other."

His mother was happy for she had long wanted Murad to be married and start his own life. She gave the ring to faithful Nana, an old servant, and said, "Go to each house in the town and find a young girl whose middle finger fits the ring. Then bring her to our house as a bride for Murad."

So, the gray-haired Nana went from house to house, trying the ring on the middle fingers of all the young girls in town. When people asked her what she was doing, she said, "My mistress, the merchant's wife, has sent me to find a wife for Murad. He wishes to marry the girl, rich or poor, whose middle finger fits this ring."

When the young girls in town heard this news, they were very excited. Some tried to starve themselves so their fingers would grow slender enough to fit the ring. Others tried to stuff themselves with butter and honey so their hands would grow plump enough to fit the ring. But the ring did not fit any of them. Finally, the gray-haired Nana came to the house of the good wife at the edge of town. She knocked and asked, "Is there a young girl living in this house?"

"Don't mock me, don't laugh at me," cried the good wife. "Because I wished too hard for a daughter, I was sent a pumpkin instead."

The servant Nana was amazed and said, "Let me see the pumpkin."

So, the pumpkin came rolling out of the kitchen and Nana started laughing.

"Don't mock me," cried the good wife. "Why do you want to see my pumpkin child?"

Nana said, "My mistress, the merchant's wife, has sent me to find a wife for her son Murad. He wishes to marry the girl, rich or poor, whose middle finger fits this ring." And Nana held out the ring Murad's mother had given her.

At this moment, to the amazement of the good wife and Nana, a slender, delicate hand poked out of the side of the pumpkin. When they tried the ring on its middle finger, they saw that the ring fitted exactly. Nana ran back to her mistress in a fright and explained what had happened.

The merchant and his wife were angry. "Our son cannot marry a pumpkin," they said. But Murad answered, "Nana, bring the pumpkin to me."

So, Nana ran back to the good wife's house, and soon the pumpkin came rolling into the merchant's house. Everyone laughed, but Murad said, "The middle finger of this pumpkin's hand fits the ring, and so I shall marry the pumpkin." Murad's mother wept, Murad's father shouted, but Murad insisted. And so the wedding was held, and all the town laughed because the richest and handsomest young man in town was marrying a fat, yellow pumpkin.

After the wedding, Murad took the pumpkin to a house far away on a hill where he cared for her and never allowed others to laugh at her. Then one night, when Murad was asleep, the top of the pumpkin flew off, and out climbed the young girl who was as beautiful as the moon on its fourteenth night. She kissed Murad gently and he woke up. He cried out, "It is the girl in the pumpkin. How were you released?"

"Your love released me," she said. "If you had not loved me when I was a pumpkin, then I would never have been set free."

And so, Murad and his pumpkin wife lived happily for many years. They kept the pumpkin shell in a corner of their house to remind them of the days when Murad had loved his wife even though everyone else had laughed at her.

■

Tribute to Augusta Baker

Augusta Baker was a master at giving her children's librarians a sense of mission and community. When she spoke to us she always told us stories. She used to tell us that we wouldn't be remembered for how up-to-date our files were by the people who used our libraries. She liked to tell us about the people who recognized her on the street years after they had been to her library story hours. They always had warm memories. She pointed out that they never said, "Aren't you the wonderful administrator who ran children's services at the New York Public Library?" It was always the storytelling they remembered.

What I remember most vividly was her timing, and the amazing pauses during which we watched her expressive face and anticipated the foolishness that was sure to come in stories of Uncle Bouqui and Ti Malice, or the stubborn woodcutter of Gura and his exasperated wife. It was not just that she took her time in telling a story, but that she used the time to allow every nuance to emerge. She gave the audience the opportunity to experience the story as she told it and to make their own discoveries. I find I tell stories more slowly year by year and, more and more, I watch the children's faces to see if they will guess what is coming next in the story before I say it. Being able to recognize the patterns in stories, and in human nature, is one of the joys of listening to stories. It is one of the things Augusta Baker taught me.

Marilyn Berg Iarusso has been the assistant coordinator of children's services and the storytelling and group work specialist at the New York Public Library since 1974. She is the editor of *Stories: A List of Stories to Tell and Read Aloud,* 8th edition. Marilyn has served on the board of The Storytelling Center, Inc., in New York City since 1984 and became its director in 1994. A frequent contributor to the professional literature, her "How to Promote the Love of Reading" won the John Brubaker Award for best article published in *Catholic Library World* in 1988.

How the Farmer's Wife Took Care of Things
Selected by Carole Walton

Source: An Icelandic folktale translated and adapted by Mary Buckley. Illustrated by Jocelyn Wild and Robin Wild. *Cricket* 4 (January 1977): 26-30.

Culture: Icelandic

Telling time: 9 minutes

Audience: Age 7 to adults

Notes on telling: The very first time I told this story was at the Princeton Storytelling Residency that Ellin Greene and Susan Danoff taught in 1986. They made me feel as if I'd just discovered and opened a chest of diamonds. I remember Ellin responding to a question that I had about voices: "Shall I make the little man in the thimble squeak in a high-pitched voice?" Ellin replied, "Why don't you give him a gruff whisper instead." That worked wonderfully, and I still use Ellin's advice.

When I tell the story to children I always bring a thimble with me, because so many children have never seen such a device. Wagging my finger, I tell them the German word for thimble, *Fingerhut,* and they laugh at the appropriateness of the word. Then I put the thimble away and say they will have to imagine the farmer's wife holding it and transferring it to her husband in the story. The ploy always works. One little boy saw me some months after he'd heard the story and told me he loved it, but couldn't think of the title. All he could do was rock the imaginary thimble between his thumb and forefinger, as he'd seen me to do when the dangerous little man was getting seasick. We just beamed at each other with appreciation.

One of the reasons I wanted to become a storyteller was to tell this story *well.* It was translated and adapted from the Icelandic by a dear college friend. She died young, but her story remains, the farmer's wise wife just as strong and unforgettable as Mary Buckley herself.

■

ON A LONELY farm in the mountains lived a farmer and his wife. They were neither rich nor poor, and the pride of the farmer's life was his herd of black and white cows.

One day in the late summer, the farmer decided to go down the mountain to the fair. As he was leaving, he said to his wife, "I may be very late, and you will be all alone. Can you take care of things by yourself?"

"Certainly," said his wife. So the farmer went on his way, and the wife went about her business. She did not mind being alone. She was busy all day, and, as night drew on, she built the fire and took up her sewing. Suddenly, she was startled to see a man standing in the doorway. He was stout, had straw-colored hair, and—though he did not think she saw it—he had a long knife under his jacket.

"Good evening," said the farmer's wife.

"Where is your husband?" asked the stranger.

"Busy in the barn, but he will be back shortly."

"I will wait," said the stranger and sat down on a stool by the fire.

"Very well," said the wife calmly and went on with her sewing.

"Your husband thinks he is a great man hereabouts?" asked the stranger, in a voice that showed he thought otherwise.

"Great enough," said the wife. "Are you planning to be a great man, too?"

"I could be, if I chose," said he.

"Indeed?" said the wife, in a voice that showed she thought otherwise of *that*.

"Indeed," said the stranger, and he suddenly grew until he was thirteen feet, seven inches tall, and his straw-colored hair brushed the roof beam.

If the wife was surprised, she didn't show it. She smiled and said, "Good trick. And yet," she went on thoughtfully, "growing big is easy. Even flowers can grow. But shrinking is another matter. Quite uncommon. I don't suppose you can shrink?"

"Can I shrink?" said the stranger scornfully. "How about this?" And he dwindled to the size of a squirrel. The wife chuckled and picked him up and held him at arm's length.

"Not a bad trick," she agreed. "It would be even better if you could make yourself small enough to fit in my thimble, but I suppose this is the best you can do."

"We'll see about that," said the little man contemptuously, and he shrank to the size of a bumblebee. When the farmer's wife saw that, she popped her thimble over him.

"Let me out!" he squeaked.

"I don't think I'd better do that," said she. "I think I'll wait until my husband comes home and see what he says." So she sat with her thumb held firmly over the thimble's opening and waited. Presently, home came the farmer, feeling very jolly.

"Did you have a good time at the fair?" asked his wife.

"Yes," said he, "and I brought you some ribbons."

"Thank you," said she, "and I have a present for you."

"What is it?"

"Guess what I have in my thimble."

"Your thumb?"

"No," said she. "I have a little man in there. If I hold the thimble up to your ear, you can hear him."

Sure enough, the farmer could hear the stranger swearing fiercely in a tiny voice.

"How did he get in there?" asked the farmer.

His wife told him all about the stranger's arrival and about his hidden knife. The farmer thought that his wife had been very clever, but he could not for the life of him think of what to do with a little man in a thimble.

At last he tapped politely on the thimble and said, "Sir, are you quite happy in there?"

"No," said the stranger.

"I thought not," said the farmer. "Shall we make a bargain?"

"What sort of bargain?" asked the stranger sulkily.

"If I let you out, will you promise to go away and never come near our farm again?"

"No," said the stranger. "As soon as I get out of here, I am going to grow eighteen feet tall, and then we shall see who makes bargains."

"Oh," said the farmer, and he began idly to shake the thimble between his thumb and forefinger, while he pondered what to do next.

Presently the stranger spoke again, sounding very seasick. "Farmer, I have changed my mind. Let me out, and I promise to go away and never come near your farm again."

"And do you promise not to grow until you are far away from here?"

"Yes," said the stranger.

"Good," said the farmer. Then he took the thimble out to the meadow and turned the stranger loose.

Next morning the farmer and his wife went out to milk their cows, but the animals were nowhere to be seen. The farmer's wife had an idea and hurried out to the meadow. There, under a blackberry bush, she found the whole herd of black and white cows grazing peacefully. The largest of them was only three inches high, and the smallest calf was no bigger than her thumbnail. She gathered the whole herd into her apron and went back to the house.

"I have found the cows," she said, and set the herd on the kitchen table before her startled husband.

"Dear me," said the farmer. "My precious cows! What shall I do with a herd of three-inch cows? That stranger certainly got the best of us!"

The farmer's wife thought for a minute; then she smiled and whispered something in her husband's ear.

That very day, the farmer went down the mountain to display his rare collection of three-inch cows at the fair. From near and far, people came to see the remarkable miniature cattle—especially the tiny calf—and the farmer and his wife became very rich.

What became of the stranger, I never heard.

■

Tribute to Augusta Baker

Although I've never met Augusta Baker, I feel I know her through Ellin Greene and through their book, *Storytelling: Art and Technique.* As an instructor of children's literature, I especially value the book's emphasis on traditional stories and the importance of introducing children to the pleasures of literature. My students appreciate the book's practical advice, especially the chapters on selection, preparation, and presentation, and this shows as they tell a ten-minute folktale at the end of the course. And they are quick to remind me if ever my recommendations during practice sessions differ from those in this helpful resource!

Carole Walton is a lecturer in the Department of English at Saint Mary's College, Notre Dame, where she has taught children's literature for 15 years. She has presented workshops on storytelling in museums and tells stories to audiences of all ages during regular programs in the galleries of Notre Dame's Snite Museum of Art as well as in elementary schools, libraries, and at college events. Carole also hosts "The Children's Hour," a Saturday morning radio program broadcast live in South Bend, Indiana, with a wide listening audience, including adults.

How the Lizard Lost and Regained His Farm

Selected by Jane Botham

Source: The Hat-Shaking Dance and Other Tales from the Gold Coast by Harold Courlander. Harcourt, 1957.

Culture: West African

Telling time: 10 minutes

Audience: Age 8 and older

Notes on telling: This story explains two natural phenomena—why the lizard moves his head the way he does, and why the spider endlessly spins and captures flies. The repetitive actions of this trickster spider story are enjoyed by younger children, while older children enjoy the complexity of the adventure. As it has plenty of action, the story can be told with children acting out the parts.

■

IT WAS a time of famine, and Kwaku Anansi was wondering how he would be able to fill his storehouse with food. He heard from his son Intikuma that Abosom, the lizard, had a fine garden, so he went to see for himself. As Intikuma had described it, so it was. The lizard's garden was green and flourishing.

Anansi said to himself, "If I had this garden, I'd have no more worries." So he went home and planned how to get it from the lizard.

One night when Abosom's crop was ready for harvesting, Anansi collected all his children together, saying, "Follow me and do whatever I do." He walked from the doorway of his house to the lizard's garden, the children walking behind him. Then he turned and walked back to his doorway. He walked back to lizard's place. Then he walked back to his house. The children began to complain, asking whether Anansi couldn't make up his mind. But he said angrily, "Don't question your elders! Follow me and do as I do!"

Back and forth they went. All night they marched. When the sun began to return and things became visible, they saw that where they had been marching there was now a trail, where formerly there had been only tall grass. Then Anansi gave his children baskets and digging knives, and they began to dig up the yams and harvest the other crops on the lizard's land.

When lizard came, he saw Anansi's family taking all his crops, and he cried out, "What are you doing on my land?"

Anansi replied, "Your land? It is my land. And why do you stand there in my garden without asking my permission?"

They argued this way for a long while, until the lizard said, "We shall go to the chief of the district and ask for a judgment."

They went to the chief and presented their cases. First Anansi said, "It is my land." Then Abosom said, "It is my land." And each one gave his reasons.

The chief listened. At last he went to the garden to see for himself. He said to Abosom, "Where is your house?" The lizard showed him his house. The chief then asked him, "Where is the path from your house?" The lizard was surprised at such a question. He answered, "There is no path. Among my people, when we go from one place to another, we rarely go twice the same way. Sometimes we go on top of the grass. Sometimes we go between the grass. Sometimes we jump from tree to tree."

When the chief heard this, he shook his head. "This is unheard of," he said. "Whenever someone goes from somewhere that is his to something that is his, he makes a path." Then the chief turned to Anansi, asking, "Where is your path?" And Anansi showed him.

"This is my judgment," the chief declared. "As Anansi has a path from his house to the garden, the garden is his."

When the lizard heard this, he lost the power of words. He could not say anything, because the judgment had been so false. He simply moved his head up and down without making a sound, calling on the Sky God Nyame to witness his misfortune.

The chief went home, and the lizard went home. As for Anansi, he and his children carried away all the food and put it in their storehouse.

But the lizard made a plan. First he dug a deep hole, far into the ground. Then he plastered mud around the top to make the hole look small. When he was through, the opening was no bigger than a man's hand.

The lizard made another thing. He made a cape of flies. He sat before his house catching the blue and green flies that alighted, and with fine threads he wove them into a beautiful cloth. When it was finished, the cape was like nothing that had ever been seen in the country. Whenever the cape was moved a little, the flies buzzed and made a lovely musical sound.

Abosom put the cape on and went through the marketplace of the village. Everyone who saw the cape and heard it buzz wanted to buy it. But the lizard said, "This is all that I have left. My crops and my farm are gone. This is all I own. Why should I sell it?" They offered him many things in exchange, but he refused.

Word came to Anansi about the cape, and he went to the market place to see it. He said to himself, "I will buy this cape. Such elegance is only for me." That night he went to lizard's house, saying, "How much will you take for your cloth of flies?"

Abosom replied, "Since you have outwitted me and taken all my food, I am hungry. I will give you the cape if you will fill up the small hole in my yard with yams and okra."

Anansi went and looked at the hole. He said to himself, "The lizard is sillier than I imagined. I will give him back a few of his yams and get the cape." Then he said to Abosom, "It is a bargain. I will fill the hole, and you will give me the cloth of flies." They called on the chief to be witness to the deal. Then Anansi went home for the food.

He brought a small basket of yams and okra. He put the yams and okra into the hole, but it wasn't yet full. He went home for another basket, but when he emptied it, the hole still wasn't full. Many baskets were brought. Anansi's children were called up to help. They carried the baskets full to the lizard's place, and they carried them back empty. Everything they brought went into the hole without filling it. They worked and carried all night. When morning came, the hole still wasn't full. Finally Anansi brought the last of the yams and okra and put them into the hole the lizard had made, and he cried out, "I have given everything! I have no more!"

The lizard looked into the hole, saying: "You haven't even begun to fill it."

But Anansi complained, "I have nothing more. My house is empty!"

The chief is our witness," the lizard said. "You promised to fill the hole. You haven't kept the bargain."

Anansi groaned in misery. But the lizard said, "I will discharge the debt if you return my garden to me."

Anansi cried, "It is yours. It is yours."

"It has been witnessed," Abosom said. "The land is mine. Here is the cloak."

The lizard took the cloak and put it forward for Anansi. Anansi took it and put it over his shoulders and was very proud. But just at that moment a strong wind came, and the flies buzzed, and before Anansi knew what was happening the cloak of flies flew away. Anansi ran after it through the bush country, but it was useless.

This is the way Abosom, the lizard, got back his garden and his crops.

Ever since then Anansi has been trying to make a cloak of flies like the one the lizard made. He spins his cloth and catches flies in it. For a while they buzz, but then Anansi gets hungry and eats them one at a time. And never has he been able to complete the cloak he is trying to make.

As for the lizard, whenever he remembers the false judgment of the chief that gave his farm to Anansi, he moves his head up and down helplessly, calling upon the Sky God to take note of this miscarriage of justice.

■

Tribute to Augusta Baker

Augusta Baker was the storytelling specialist at the New York Public Library when I first told stories. That was in 1960, and I barely remember her criticism, except that I kept giving the wrong names to the characters in the story, and she was as tactful as possible in telling me how confusing this made the story!

I can never think of Augusta without thinking of her many facial expressions. I remember them as intense, mischievous, malevolent (yes, she has that look too!), incredible, and delighted, with that wonderful smile. It is the latter expression that most of us know, but in my early years of knowing Augusta, it was a surprise to me to discover how very much she listened. Her intense look was the one I most prized. I remember we met to discuss children's libraries when I was the public library children's consultant with the New York State Library. Her concentration on the subject, her careful selection of phrases in framing her conversation, gave me not only a sense of the remarkable overview she had of library service to children, but provided me with the ability to clarify issues and concerns with which I was grappling.

Augusta is one of the greatest storytellers of her time, perhaps because of her sensitivity to people and her utter delight in meeting and knowing people—anyone and everyone. Her practical, down-to-earth storytelling techniques, combined with her analysis of storytelling, have encouraged many an eager but inexperienced storyteller to continue to tell stories. She is one in a million—ask anyone who knows her!

Jane Botham is coordinator of children's services at the Milwaukee Public Library. She has told stories to thousands of boys and girls in her positions at the New York, San Francisco, Madison, and Milwaukee public libraries. Her love of poetry inspired her to create an annual Poetry Concert, held for eight years, in which well-known poets, among them Ashley Bryan and Eve Merriam, were featured. The children also wrote and read poems they had written. You can read about the program in "Art, Literature and Poetry: Milwaukee Public Library Supports Culture," *School Library Journal* 33 (June/July 1987): 32-36.

Clever Manka

Selected by Anne Pellowski

Source: The Shoemaker's Apron by Parker Fillmore. Harcourt, 1920, o.p.

Culture: Czechoslovakian

Telling time: 15 minutes

Audience: Age 8 to adult

Notes on telling: I began telling this story as a children's librarian in New York and I still tell it. Because it is fairly long, I often choose to tell it as the centerpiece story in a family storytelling hour in a public library, with short, catchy stories preceding it and following it.

My version closely follows the one by Parker Fillmore except that I repeat the riddle and I don't give Manka's suggested answers to the burgomaster ahead of time—I wait until the moment in the story when they are given directly to him. This helps build a bit of suspense and momentum. I slow down and emphasize each word when the shepherd gives the answers to the three-part riddle.

Because today's audiences rarely know what the term burgomaster implies, I generally add a sentence or two at the beginning, explaining that a burgomaster was often like a judge and jury rolled into one. He also had some duties similar to a mayor.

"Clever Manka" is known throughout Europe, with variants found as far away as Asia, the Middle East, and South America. It is very old. Joseph Jacobs remarked that the plan by which the clever wife becomes reconciled with her husband is found in the Midrash, probably as early as the eighth century. And the Brothers Grimm noted a striking parallel in the saga of Aslaug, the daughter of Brunhild and Sigurd. King Ragnar demanded that Aslaug come to him "naked yet clothed, eating yet not eating, not alone but without companion." Aslaug wrapped herself in a fishnet, bit into an onion, and took along her dog.

∎

THERE WAS once a rich farmer who was as grasping and unscrupulous as he was rich. He was always driving a hard bargain and always getting the better of his poor neighbors. One of these neighbors was a humble shepherd who in return for service was to receive from the farmer a heifer. When the time of payment came the farmer refused to give the shepherd the heifer and the shepherd was forced to lay the matter before the burgomaster.

The burgomaster, who was a young man and as yet not very experienced, listened to both sides and when he had deliberated he said,

"Instead of deciding this case, I will put a riddle to you both and the man who makes the best answer shall have the heifer. Are you agreed?" The farmer and the shepherd accepted this proposal and the burgomaster said, "Well then, here is my riddle: What is the swiftest thing in the world? What is the sweetest thing? What is the richest? Think out your answers and bring them to me at this same hour tomorrow."

The farmer went home in a temper. "What kind of a burgomaster is this young fellow!" he growled. "If he had let me keep the heifer I'd have sent him a bushel of pears. But now I'm in a fair way of losing the heifer, for I can't think of any answer to his foolish riddle."

"What is the matter, husband?" his wife asked.

"It's that new burgomaster. The old one would have given me the heifer without any argument, but this young man thinks to decide the case by asking us riddles."

When he told his wife what the riddle was, she cheered him greatly by telling him that she knew the answers at once.

"Why, husband," said she, "our gray mare must be the swiftest thing in the world. You know yourself nothing ever passes us on the road. As for the sweetest, did you ever taste honey any sweeter than ours? And I'm sure there's nothing richer than our chest of golden ducats that we've been laying by these forty years."

The farmer was delighted. "You're right, wife, you're right! That heifer remains ours!"

The shepherd when he got home was downcast and sad. He had a daughter, a clever girl named Manka, who met him at the door of his cottage and asked, "What is it, father? What did the burgomaster say?"

The shepherd sighed. "I'm afraid I've lost the heifer. The burgomaster set us a riddle and I know I shall never guess it."

"Perhaps I can help you," Manka said. "What is it?"

So the shepherd gave her the riddle and the next day, as he was setting out for the burgomaster's, Manka told him what answers to make.

When he reached the burgomaster's house, the farmer was already there rubbing his hands and beaming with self-importance.

The burgomaster again propounded the riddle and then asked the farmer his answers.

The farmer cleared his throat and with a pompous air began, "The swiftest thing in the world? Why, my dear sir, that's my gray mare, of course, for no other horse ever passes us on the road. The sweetest? Honey from my beehives, to be sure. The richest? What can be richer than my chest of golden ducats!"

And the farmer squared his shoulders and smiled triumphantly.

"H'm," said the young burgomaster, dryly. Then he asked, "What answers does the shepherd make?"

The shepherd bowed politely and said, "The swiftest thing in the world is thought, for thought can run any distance in the twinkling of an eye. The sweetest thing of all is sleep, for when a man is tired and sad what can be sweeter? The richest thing is the earth, for out of the earth come all the riches of the world."

"Good!" the burgomaster cried. "Good! The heifer goes to the shepherd!"

Later the burgomaster said to the shepherd, "Tell me, now, who gave you those answers? I'm sure they never came out of your own head."

At first the shepherd tried not to tell, but when the burgomaster pressed him he confessed that they came from his daughter, Manka.

The burgomaster, who thought that he would like to make another test of Manka's cleverness, sent for ten eggs. He gave them to the shepherd and said, "Take these eggs to Manka and tell her to have them hatched out by tomorrow and to bring me the chicks."

When the shepherd reached home and gave Manka the burgomaster's message, Manka laughed and said, "Take a handful of millet and go right back to the burgomaster. Say to him, 'My daughter sends you this millet. She says that if you plant, grow it, and have it harvested by tomorrow, she'll bring you the ten chicks and you can feed them the ripe grain.'"

When the burgomaster heard this, he laughed heartily. "That's a clever girl of yours," he told the shepherd. "If she's as comely as she is clever, I think I'd like to marry her. Tell her to come to see me, but she must come neither by day nor by night, neither riding nor walking, neither dressed nor undressed."

When Manka received this message she waited until the next dawn when night was gone and day not yet arrived. Then she wrapped herself in a fishnet and, throwing one leg over a goat's back and keeping one foot on the ground, she went to the burgomaster's house.

Now I ask you, did she go dressed? No, she wasn't dressed. A fishnet isn't clothing. Did she go undressed? Of course not, for wasn't she covered with a fishnet? Did she walk to the burgomaster's? No, she didn't walk for she went with one leg thrown over a goat. Then did she ride? Of course she didn't ride for wasn't she walking on one foot?

When she reached the burgomaster's house she called out, "Here I am, Mr. Burgomaster, and I've come neither by day nor by night, neither riding nor walking, neither dressed nor undressed."

The young burgomaster was so delighted with Manka's cleverness and so pleased with her comely looks that he proposed to her at once and in a short time married her.

"But understand, my dear Manka," he said, "you are not to use that cleverness of yours at my expense. I won't have you interfering in any of my cases. In fact if you ever give advice to anyone who comes to me for judgment, I'll turn you out of my house at once and send you home to your father."

All went well for a time. Manka busied herself in her housekeeping and was careful not to interfere in any of the burgomaster's cases.

Then one day two farmers came to the burgomaster to have a dispute settled. One of the farmers owned a mare which had foaled in the marketplace. The colt had run under the wagon of the other farmer and thereupon the owner of the wagon claimed the colt as his property.

The burgomaster, who was thinking of something else while the case was being presented, said carelessly, "The man who found the colt under his wagon is, of course, the owner of the colt."

As the owner of the mare was leaving the burgomaster's house, he met Manka and stopped to tell her about the case. Manka was ashamed of her husband for making so foolish a decision and she said to the farmer, "Come back this afternoon with a fishing net and stretch it across the dusty road. When the burgomaster sees you he will come out and ask you what you are doing. Say to him that you're catching fish. When he asks you how you can expect to catch fish in a dusty road, tell him it's just as easy for you to catch fish in a dusty road as it is for a wagon to foal. Then he'll see the injustice of his decision and have the colt returned to you. But remember one thing: you mustn't let him find out that it was I who told you to do this."

That afternoon when the burgomaster chanced to look out the window he saw a man stretching a fishnet across the dusty road. He went out to him and asked, "What are you doing?"

"Fishing."

"Fishing in a dusty road? Are you daft?

"Well," the man said, "it's just as easy for me to catch fish in a dusty road as it is for a wagon to foal."

Then the burgomaster recognized the man as the owner of the mare and he had to confess that what he said was true.

"Of course the colt belongs to your mare and must be returned to you. But tell me," he said, "who put you up to this? You didn't think of it yourself."

The farmer tried not to tell but the burgomaster questioned him until he found out that Manka was at the bottom of it. This made him very angry. He went into the house and called his wife.

"Manka," he said, "do you forget what I told you would happen if you went interfering in any of my cases? Home you go this very day. I don't care to hear any excuses. The matter is settled. You may take with you the one thing you like best in my house for I won't have people saying that I treated you shabbily."

Manka made no outcry. "Very well, my dear husband, I shall do as you say. I shall go to my father's cottage and take with me the one thing I like best in your house. But don't make me go until after supper. We have been very happy together and I should like to eat one last meal with you. Let us have no more words but be kind to each other as we've always been and then part as friends."

The burgomaster agreed to this and Manka prepared a fine supper of all the dishes of which her husband was particularly fond. The burgomaster opened his choicest wine and pledged Manka's health. Then he set to, and the supper was so good that he ate and ate and ate. And the more he ate the more he drank, until at last he grew drowsy and fell sound asleep in his chair. Then without awakening him Manka had him carried out to the wagon that was waiting to take her home to her father.

The next morning when the burgomaster opened his eyes, he found himself lying in the shepherd's cottage.

"What does this mean?" he roared out.

"Nothing, dear husband, nothing!" Manka said. "You know you told me I might take with me the one thing I liked best in your house, so of course I took you! That's all."

For a moment the burgomaster rubbed his eyes in amazement. Then he laughed loud and heartily to think how Manka had outwitted him.

"Manka," he said, "you're too clever for me. Come on, my dear, let's go home."

So they climbed back into the wagon and drove home.

The burgomaster never again scolded his wife, but thereafter whenever a very difficult case came up he always said, "I think we had better consult my wife. You know she's a very clever woman."

■

Tribute to Augusta Baker

In her book *Folktales and Society*, the folklorist Linda Degh states that it is often during childhood that "it is decided then and there who will become, sometimes after many decades, a good storyteller." I did hear and read good stories as a child, but I certainly never consciously thought of telling them. Many persons ask me how I, a farm girl from a very rural part of Wisconsin, got to New York City.

It was a college teacher, Sister Eone, who set me on the road to storytelling, and who directed me to New York. Sister Eone had been a librarian with the New York Public Library before becoming a nun. When she saw my interest in storytelling, she stated flat out, in a voice that brooked no argument, "To get good storytelling training and experience you must go to New York and work with Augusta Baker." So I went.

The in-service course that I took from Mrs. Baker was very important in my development as a storyteller, but I count as most valuable the opportunities she gave me to tell stories in many, many different situations. I was still a library intern, with my professional degree not quite completed, when I did my first storytelling session in Central Park at the Hans Christian Andersen statue, under her watchful eye. Those sessions usually drew a good crowd of children, parents, nannies, and curious passers-by. At that session, a distinctly inebriated man lay down in the grass at the side of the storytelling area. During my first story, "The Crab and the Jaguar," he began echoing the refrain "Eyes, little eyes of mine!" but at very inappropriate moments. Mrs. Baker simply moved her chair closer to him and gave him one of her inimitable, silent stares. He subsided and fell asleep.

It was in many subtle lessons, such as that occasion, that I learned from Mrs. Baker how to handle audience response in the smoothest way possible. They are lessons I have used throughout my storytelling career.

Anne Pellowski is an internationally known consultant, storyteller, writer, and lecturer. From 1966 to 1982, following several years on the staff of the New York Public Library, Anne was director of the Information Center on Children's Cultures, U.S. Committee for UNICEF. She is the author of two distinguished texts, *The World of Storytelling* and *The World of Children's Literature,* as well as many books for children, including her latest, *The Storytelling Handbook: A Young People's Collection of Unusual Tales and Helpful Hints on How to Tell Them.*

The Voyage of the Wee Red Cap

Selected by Carol Birch

Source: The Long Christmas by Ruth Sawyer. Illustrated by Valenti Angelo. Viking, 1941, o.p.

Culture: Irish

Telling time: 12–15 minutes

Audience: Age 8 to adult

Notes on telling: Teig is one character from a long list of stories I like to tell about feisty, difficult characters who learn their lessons but do not lose their spunk. Like the character of Ebenezer Scrooge, Teig is miserly about money, empathy, and feelings of being connected to others with love. And like Scrooge he is altered forever by a night of wandering and of witnessing. In my telling, Teig is not evil or malevolent. I see humor in his querulousness and feel compassion for his all-too-human rationalizing that not actively doing "evil" can be equated with actively doing "good." Here is my introduction to this tale:

■

As long as there have been celebrations where people give gifts and share what they have with others, there have been people who want to keep what they have for themselves. At Christmas we might think of Scrooge but, long before Charles Dickens created Scrooge, in Ireland there was a man named Teig.

IT WAS the Eve of Saint Stephen, and Teig sat alone by his fire with naught in his cupboard but a pinch of tea and a bare mixture of meal, and a heart inside of him as soft and warm as the ice on the water-bucket outside the door. The turf was near burnt on the hearth—a handful of golden cinders left, just; and Teig took to counting them greedily on his fingers.

"There's one, two, three, an' four an' five," he laughed. "Faith, there be more bits o' real gold hid undther the loose clay in the corner."

It was the truth; and it was the scraping and scrooching for the last piece that had left Teig's cupboard bare of a Christmas dinner.

"Gold is betther nor eatin' an' dthrinkin'. An' if ye have naught to give, there'll be naught asked of ye." And he laughed again.

He was thinking of the neighbors, and the doles of food and piggins of milk that would pass over their thresholds that night to the vagabonds and paupers who were sure to come begging. And on the heels of that thought followed another: Who would be giving old Barney his dinner? Barney lived a stone's throw from Teig, alone in a wee tumbled-in cabin; and for a score of years past Teig had stood on the doorstep every Christmas Eve and, making a hollow of his two hands, had called across the road:

"Hey, there, Barney, will ye come over for a sup?"

And Barney had reached for his crutches—there being but one leg to him—and had come.

"Faith," said Teig, trying another laugh, "Barney can fast for the once; 'twill be all the same in a month's time." And he fell to thinking of the gold again.

A knock came at the door. Teig pulled himself down in his chair where the shadow would cover him, and held his tongue.

"Teig, Teig!" It was the Widow O'Donnelly's voice. "If ye are there, open your door. I have not got the pay for the spriggin' this month, an' the childher are needin' food."

But Teig put the leash on his tongue, and never stirred till he heard the tramp of her feet going on to the next cabin. Then he saw to it that the door was tight barred. Another knock came, and it was a stranger's voice this time:

"The other cabins are filled; not one but has its hearth crowded; will ye take us in—the two of us? The wind bites mortal sharp, not a morsel o' food have we tasted this day. Masther, will ye take us in?"

But Teig sat on, a-holding his tongue; and the tramp of the strangers' feet passed down the road. Others took their place—small feet, running. It was the miller's wee Cassie and she called out as she ran by:

"Old Barney's watchin' for ye. Ye'll not be forgettin' him, will ye, Teig?"

And then the child broke into a song, sweet and clear, as she passed down the road:

Hearken all ye, tis the Feast o' Saint Stephen,
Mind that ye keep it this holy even.
Open your door an' greet ye the stranger,
For ye mind that the wee Lord had naught but a manger.
Mhuire as traugh!

Feed ye the hungry an' rest ye the weary,
This ye must do for the sake of Our Mary.
'Tis well that ye mind—ye who sit by the fire—
That the Lord He was born in a dark and cold byre.
Mhuire as traugh!

Teig put his fingers deep in his ears. "A million murdthering curses on them that won't let me be! Can't a man try to keep what is his without bein' pesthered by them that has only idled and wasted their days?"

And then the strange thing happened: hundreds and hundreds of wee lights began dancing outside the window, making the room bright; the hands of the clock began chasing each other round the dial; and the bolt of the door drew itself out. Slowly, without a creak or a cringe, the door opened, and in there trooped a crowd of the Good People. Their wee green cloaks were folded close about them, and each carried a rush candle.

Teig was filled with a great wonderment, entirely, when he saw the fairies, but when they saw him they laughed.

"We are takin' the loan o' your cabin this night, Teig," said they. "Ye are the only man hereabouts with an empty hearth an' we're needin' one."

Without saying more, they bustled about the room making ready. They lengthened out the table and spread and set it; more of the Good People trooped in bringing stools and food and drink. The pipers came last, and they sat themselves around the chimney-piece a-blowing their chanters and trying the drones. The feasting began and the pipers played, and never had Teig seen such a sight in his life. Suddenly, a wee man sang out:

"Clip clap, clip clap, I wish I had my wee red cap!" And out of the air there tumbled the neatest cap Teig ever laid his two eyes on. The wee man clapped it on his head, crying:

"I wish I was in Spain!" and—whist—up the chimney he went, and away out of sight.

It happened just as I am telling it. Another wee man called for his cap, and away he went after the first. And then another and another, until the room was empty and Teig sat alone again.

"By my soul," said Teig, "I'd like to travel that way myself! It's a grand savin' of tickets an' baggage; an' ye get to a place before ye've had time to change your mind. Faith, there's no harm done if I thry it."

So he sang the fairies' rhyme, and out of the air dropped a wee cap for him. For a moment the wonder had him, but the next he was clapping the hat on his head and crying:

"Spain!"

Then—whist—up the chimney he went after the fairies, and before he had time to let out his breath he was standing in the middle of Spain, and strangeness all about him.

He was in a great city. The doorways of the houses were hung with flowers and the air was warm and sweet with the smell of them. Torches burned along the streets, sweetmeat-sellers went about crying their wares, and on the steps of the cathedral crouched a crowd of beggars.

"What's the meanin' o' that?" asked Teig of one of the fairies.

"They are waiting for those that are hearing the Mass. When they come out, they give half of what they have to those that have nothing, so on this night of all the year there shall be no hunger and no cold."

And then far down the street came the sound of a child's voice, singing:

Hearken all ye, 'tis the Feast o' Saint Stephen,
Mind that ye keep it this holy even.

"Curse it!" said Teig. "Can a song fly afther ye?" And then he heard the fairies cry, "Holland!" and cried, "Holland!" too.

In one leap he was over France, and another over Belgium, and with the third he was standing by long ditches of frozen water, and over them glided hundreds upon hundreds of lads and maids. Outside each door stood a wee wooden shoe, empty. Teig saw scores of them as he looked down the ditch of a street.

"What is the meanin' o' those shoes?" he asked the fairies.

"Ye poor lad!" answered the wee man next to him. "Are ye not knowing anything? This is the Gift Night of the year, when every man gives to his neighbor."

A child came to the window of one of the houses, and in her hand was a lighted candle. She was singing as she put the light down close to the glass, and Teig caught the words:

Open your door an' greet ye the stranger,
For ye mind that the wee Lord had naught but a manger.
        Mhuire as traugh!

"'Tis the devil's work!" cried Teig, and he set the red cap more firmly on his head. "I'm for another country."

I cannot be telling you a half of the adventures Teig had that night, nor half the sights he saw. But he passed by fields that held sheaves of grain for the birds and doorsteps that held bowls of porridge for the wee creatures. He saw lighted trees, sparkling and heavy with gifts; and he stood outside the churches and watched the crowds pass in, bearing gifts to the Holy Mother and Child.

At last the fairies straightened their caps and cried, "Now for the great hall in the King of England's palace!"

Whist—and away they went, and Teig after them; and the first thing he knew he was in London, not an arm's length from the King's throne. It was a grander sight than he had seen in any other country. The hall was filled entirely with lords and ladies; and the great doors were open for the poor and the homeless to come in and warm themselves by the King's fire and feast from the King's table. And many a hungry soul did the King serve with his own hands.

Those that had anything to give gave it in return. It might be a bit of music played on a harp or a pipe, or it might be a dance or a song; but more often it was a wish, just for good luck and safekeeping.

Teig was so taken up with the watching that he never heard the fairies when they wished themselves off; moreover, he never saw the wee girl that was fed and went laughing away. But he heard a bit of her song as she passed through the door:

Feed ye the hungry an' rest ye the weary,
This ye must do for the sake of Our Mary.

Then the anger had Teig. "I'll stop your pestherin' tongue, once an' for all time!" and, catching the cap from his head, he threw it after her.

No sooner was the cap gone than every soul in the hall saw him. The next moment they were about him, catching at his coat and crying, "Where is he from, what does he here? Bring him before the King!" And Teig was dragged along by a hundred hands to the throne where the King sat.

"He was stealing food," cried one.

"He was robbing the King's jewels," cried another.

"He looks evil," cried a third. "Kill him!"

And in a moment all the voices took it up and the hall rang with, "Aye, kill him, kill him!"

Teig's legs took to trembling, and fear put the leash on his tongue; but after a long silence he managed to whisper, "I have done evil to no one— no one!"

"Maybe," said the King; "but have ye done good? Come, tell us, have ye given aught to anyone this night? If ye have, we will pardon ye."

Not a word could Teig say. Fear tightened the leash, for he was knowing full well there was no good to him that night.

"Then ye must die," said the King. "Will ye try hanging or beheading?"

"Hanging, please, your Majesty," said Teig.

The guards came rushing up and carried him off. But as he was crossing the threshold of the hall a thought sprang at him and held him, just.

"Your Majesty," he called after him, "will ye grant me a last request?"

"I will," said the King.

"Thank ye. There's a wee red cap that I'm mortal fond of, and I lost it a while ago; if I could be hung with it on, I would hang a deal more comfortable."

The cap was found and brought to Teig.

"Clip clap, clip clap, for my wee red cap, I wish I was home," he sang.

Up and over the heads of the dumbfounded guards he flew—whist—and away out of sight. When he opened his eyes again, he was sitting close by his own hearth, with the fire burnt low. The hands of the clock were still, the bolt was fixed firm in the door. The fairies' lights were gone, and the only bright thing was the candle burning in old Barney's cabin across the road.

A running of feet sounded outside, and then a snatch of a song:

'Tis well that ye mind—ye who sit by the fire—
That the Lord He was born in a dark and cold byre.
    Mhuire as traugh!

"Wait ye, whoever ye are!" And Teig was away to the corner, digging fast at the loose clay, as a terrier digs at a bone. He filled his hands full of the shining gold, then hurried to the door, unbarring it.

The miller's wee Cassie stood there, peering at him out of the darkness.

"Take those to the Widow O'Donnelly, do ye hear? And take the rest to the store. Ye tell Jamie to bring up all that he has that is eatable an' dthrinkable; and to the neighbors ye say, 'Teig's keepin' the feast this night.' Hurry, away!"

Teig stopped a moment on the threshold until the tramp of her feet had died away; then he made a hollow of his two hands and called across the road:

"Hey, there, Barney, will ye come over for a sup?"

∎

Tribute to Augusta Baker

Augusta Baker was telling "Mr. Rabbit and Mr. Bear," from *The Knee-High Man and Other Tales* by Julius Lester. She savored each word as she described how Mr. Rabbit "had never tasted such delicious, scrumptious, crispy, luscious, delectable, exquisite, ambrosial, nectareous, yummy lettuce in aaaaaaall of his life." Some of the adjectives were spoken with great dignity in slightly different tones. The grandeur of some of the words was *slightly* mocked by a tilt of her chin, an arch in her brow, or other subtle—and quite delightful—nonverbal cues. Mrs. Baker spoke so sensuously, my mouth watered. She capitalized on the inherent humor in both Lester's list of inflated adjectives and the colloquial delivery of "yummy" which abruptly deflates the list. The contrasts of tone and mood brought an appreciative roar of laughter and midstory applause from the audience. In an entertainment-saturated age, her passion for the power and primacy of words is tangible.

She may represent a singular standard of dedication to discipline and rigorous training in her attention to detail and quality in the world of contemporary storytelling. Yet when she tells stories, effort is never visible. What is visible is her sure and authentic voice, so that when she tells a story, you know "who says." To my mind, Augusta Baker's greatest talent is her unique ability to leaven the dignity of her presence with equal measures of warmth and humor.

Carol Birch is a gifted, vibrant storyteller and an award-winning recording artist. She is respected as an insightful teacher of both children and adults, in classrooms and workshops, and at Wesleyan University where she is an adjunct professor of storytelling and children's literature. In addition to being a featured performer many times at the National Storytelling Festival in Jonesborough (Tenn.), Carol has performed in Singapore, Australia, and Europe. She is a contributor to storytelling collections and is coeditor of *Across the Great Divide of Orality to Print in the Continuum of Storytelling* (forthcoming).

Count Alaric's Lady

Selected by Ellin Greene

Source: The Faun and the Woodcutter's Daughter by Barbara Picard. Crowell, 1964, o.p. Also in *Midsummer Magic* by Ellin Greene. Lothrop, 1977, o.p.

Culture: English

Telling time: 23–25 minutes

Audience: Age 9 to adult

Notes on telling: Truthfully, I was telling stories for quite some time before I attempted to learn this one. Picard's story is a kind of reverse "Tam Lin," about a mortal man who falls in love with a fairy woman. It is a story of loss and of the true meaning of love. I first told it to a small circle of fourth graders, with some hesitancy as I wondered if the children would understand its deeper meaning. The children listened intently throughout the long tale and sat in stillness at the end of the telling. This is one time when I observed the five minutes of complete silence recommended by Marie Shedlock! Then I asked, gently, if they had ever lost someone or something they loved, and the children began to talk, the first child telling me about losing his dog. There was never any doubt about telling the story to children after that experience. Since then I have told the story to thousands of children and adults and it never fails to move the listeners.

The writing is very literary and requires judicious cutting so as not to lose the lyrical flow. Picard's long sentences sometimes run to nine lines of print. As you read the story with a discerning eye, you will see that many of these sentences can be shortened without loss of meaning and still keep the rhythm by retaining Picard's language. Of course, there is no need for all the "he says, she says" in an oral rendering of a written tale. Even the wordy description of a character (for example, the wise woman Magda) can be conveyed by the storyteller's posture and voice alone.

Sometimes when telling the tale, I play (very softly) part of Mendelssohn's *Incidental Music to "A Midsummer Night's Dream" Opus 61* at the point where Alaric comes upon his lady dancing in the meadow with the fairy people.

■

EARLY IN the morning of one midsummer's day, young Count Alaric rode out of his castle alone. His gay doublet was crimson and golden and there was gold thread on his gloves; and the trappings of his favourite white horse were silver and blue. The count sang as he rode over his fields, for he was happy and the sun was shining and life was good.

Half-way across a meadow he saw a maiden sitting on the grass. Her gown was of green with a silver girdle and she had flaxen hair so pale that it was almost white. Her chin was little and pointed and her eyes were a golden-green. Her feet were bare, and on her head she wore a wreath of moon daisies.

He reined in his horse and bade her good day, and she looked up at him. "Good day," she said, and her voice was low and very sweet.

"You are a stranger here, fair lady," said Count Alaric, dismounting. "Will you not tell me your name?"

She smiled a little, but distantly, as though she were smiling at something she remembered rather than at the young man who stood before her. "I do not know my name," she replied.

"But where do you come from?" asked the count, surprised.

"I do not know."

"Where are you going to, can you remember that?"

She shook her head, but did not seem distressed.

"Can you tell me nothing about yourself?" he asked.

"Nothing," she said, "save that for an hour or two I have been sitting here in this field, watching the sun rise higher in the sky and listening to the song of the lark."

Count Alaric was too courteous not to believe her story, though it seemed to him curious that she should know nothing about herself. "Is there any way I can help you?" he asked.

But all she said was, "You are very kind."

He looked down at her, at her pale, strange beauty; and she looked up and smiled, this time more deeply, and at him; and he knew that he wanted to help her more than anything in the world. But there was a look in her golden-green eyes that he had never seen in the eyes of any-one before; a look as though, even while she smiled and spoke to him, she were thinking of something else.

"My castle is yonder, behind those trees," he said. "Will you come to my castle with me?"

And after she had thought a while, she said, "I will go with you."

She rose, and he lifted her on to his horse and set her before him and rode back over the meadow and past the trees to his castle, where it stood with its lichen-covered walls all warm and golden in the morning sun.

And as she had no name he called her Catherine, because it had been his mother's name and he knew of none more beautiful. And since he loved her dearly and she was willing, he married her, and they were very happy together. Though she was usually silent when others were near, she laughed and talked with him; but whenever he looked into her golden-green eyes he saw that she was thinking of something else.

She knew neither how to spin nor weave, and she could not bake a loaf; but since she was Count Alaric's lady, with servants to wait on her, it mattered not. She could not play upon the lute or the harp, and had no skill in embroidery; but since, when she was alone, she was content to sit in the sun, hour after hour, with her hands folded on her lap and a little half-smile on her lips, it mattered not. She never talked to her women or made friends with them or gossiped pleasantly to while away the time, as even great ladies will, but kept herself reserved and distant; and they thought her strange and whispered so, but she cared nothing for what they said, so it mattered not.

When there were festivities at the castle, and everyone danced, Count Alaric's lady would never join in the merry-making; but sat instead by the wall and watched and smiled. And because it was her wish, though he longed to dance with her, Count Alaric did not try to persuade her otherwise. But one day he came upon her in a room of the castle, where a shaft of sunlight streamed through a window, dancing a strange measure alone, watched only by the stiff faded figures of the arras on the wall.

"You dance so lightly and so gracefully," he said, "why will you never dance with me?"

She looked at him with a puzzled frown. "I never want to dance," she said.

He laughed. "You were dancing a moment ago, dearest, I saw you as I came in."

Her face lightened. "Ah yes, I heard the music and I had to dance."

"But, dearest, there was no music."

"There was," she said with conviction, "I heard it plainly and I had to dance. Sometimes I hear it in the distance, but to-day it seemed quite near."

"Can you hear it now?" he asked.

She listened for a moment before shaking her head sadly. "No, it is all silent now."

Count Alaric took her hands in his. "Tell me, Catherine," he said, "tell me the truth, are you happy with me?"

She smiled and laughed and kissed him. "Of course I am happy with you," she said.

But his heart was heavy, even as he took her in his arms, for he saw still the look in her eyes, as though she thought of something else.

And when a year had passed, all but two days, since he had met his lady first, sitting alone in the meadow with moon daisies in her hair, the day before midsummer's eve, Count Alaric had to go on a journey.

"I shall be back within three days," he said to her as he mounted his horse, and she smiled and wished him Godspeed as he rode off with six retainers along the path that led from the castle, turning more than once to look back at her where she stood in the archway of the great door, her pale hair bright in the sunshine.

By the following evening, the count found that the matters to which he had travelled to attend were settled to his satisfaction; and because the next morning would be a year to the very day when he had first set eyes on his lady, and because he could not bear to be parted from her for even a moment, he left his men to rest for the night while he rode home alone, hoping to reach his castle by morning, so that he would be with her at the very same hour as that upon which he had found her, twelve months before.

He rode all through the night, and toward dawn, when the moon was beginning to fade, as he passed the meadow where he had first seen the maiden he had married, he heard strains of sweet music. He rode towards it over the grass, his horse's hooves making no sound on the soft green carpet, scattered with clover and buttercups. As he came nearer to the music he could see in the moonlight some twenty or thirty figures dancing. Pale faces with flying hair above gowns of green and bare white feet in the dew, as they trod a strange measure, daintily.

"It is the fairy people dancing on midsummer's eve," thought Count Alaric, and he rode a little closer to watch them. And then he became aware that one among them with hair so fair it might have been a moonbeam around her head, was wearing crimson with a golden girdle, instead of green. "That hair," he thought, "and that little pointed chin. And I have seen her wearing that gown before." But he could not believe it, and he watched for many minutes before he knew, beyond a doubt, that the dancer in crimson was the Lady Catherine.

"The fairy people have lured her from the castle to dance with them," he thought. "I must save her from their power. There is no time to lose," and he urged his horse forward toward the dancers, meaning to ride in among them and seize his lady and gallop home with her before he could be prevented. But at the nearness of the fairy people his horse suddenly took fright and bolted, fleeing like a mad creature back the way it had come. It had carried him three miles along the road before he finally calmed it and could turn its head for home again. But before he reached the place where the dancers had been, the cock crew for the dawn of a new day, and he found the meadow quite deserted.

He rode on past the trees to the castle and went straight to his lady's room, thinking to find it empty. But when he flung back the velvet curtains of her bed, by the light of the branched candlestick he held, he saw her there, asleep, her pale hair spread over the pillow. He had disturbed her, and she awoke and smiled.

"Dearest," he said, "is all well with you?"

"Of course it is well," she replied. "You are home sooner than I expected. I am glad."

"What did you do while I was away?" he asked.

"I waited for you. What else should I do?"

"What did you do last night?"

"I slept. What else should I have done?" She smiled again. "You ask so many questions. I am tired. Let me sleep. Wake me again when the sun is high." And she closed her eyes and slept once more.

"I must have been mistaken," thought the count. "It was not her I saw in the meadow." And reassured, he turned from the bed and walked softly away. But hanging over a chair he caught sight of her gown of crimson brocade, and he saw that the hem of it was dark and heavy with damp, as though it had been dragged in the dew.

But Count Alaric spoke no more to his lady about the matter. "For," he said to himself, "at the best she will have forgotten everything and my questions will only distress her, and at the worst she will remember and lie to me, and I could not bear a lie from her lips."

But though he said nothing, Count Alaric thought much on what had passed on midsummer's eve, and every time that he looked into the eyes of his lady and saw that still she thought of something else, his heart grew heavier. And at last there came a day when he said to himself, "I can bear this no longer, I must speak of it to someone who can give me advice." And he remembered old Magda, the wise woman who lived on the heath, and how, while his mother had lived, Magda had sometimes come to the castle and been received with kindness and respect. He remembered how once, when he had been only a child, he had fallen ill, and his mother had sent for Magda, and she had come and stood by his bed where he burnt in fever; and she had laid her hand on his head and it had grown cool under her touch, and she had smiled at him and given his mother some herbs she had gathered, with instructions how to prepare a healing drink of them; and from that moment he had grown better.

"I will go to Magda in her hovel on the moors," he thought. "If there is anyone who can tell me why there is that look in my Catherine's eyes, it is wise old Magda."

So Count Alaric rode across the heath, over the purple heather, where the harebells nodded their dainty cups and the little blue butterflies flitted; and when he came to the tumbledown hut where Magda lived, he dismounted and knocked on the door, and a voice bade him come in.

The door was low and he had to stoop his head to pass inside. After the bright sunshine on the heath he could see nothing at first; but as his eyes became accustomed to the dim light within, he saw Magda sitting by the wall plaiting a basket from rushes; and he stood waiting by the door until she should look up and notice him. She finally put her work aside and smiled. "Good day, Count Alaric. Sit you down." He sat on a stool opposite her and waited for her to speak again.

Magda was only a peasant woman, tall and lean, with broad shoulders and strong hands; her gown of rough frieze had seen many seasons come and go, and her feet were bare. Yet she had a dignity of bearing which many great ladies might have envied, and she treated Count Alaric as though he were her equal, while he treated her as though she were a queen; and that not because it was whispered that she could cast spells on those who displeased her, but for herself alone, because he thought of her as a queen among women.

She watched him with her shrewd, kindly eyes, and for a few moments she said nothing; and the count drew in peace and comfort from her gaze and thought how in all the years since he had seen her first she had not changed nor aged. She had still the same strong lines in her calm face that had been burnt by the summer suns, and the same grey eyes under the faded red cloth twisted round her head.

"You are in trouble, Alaric," she said at last, "or you would not have sought me out."

"I need your help," he said.

"You are lord of all the land for miles, your castle stands firm and mighty and your possessions are great. You have all a man could desire, and you have been married but fourteen months to a lady whose beauty, I hear, surpasses the beauty of all other women of these parts. And yet you need to ask my help."

"It is of my Catherine that I would speak with you."

"And what would you tell me about the Lady Catherine?" Magda folded her hands on her lap.

And Count Alaric told her of how he had found, sitting alone in a meadow, the strange maiden who could tell him nothing about herself; and of how his lady had none of the skill in homely crafts such as women usually possess; and of how he had seen her, on midsummer's eve, dancing with the fairy people in the fields. "And always," he said, "always when I watch in her eyes, I see there a strange look, as though she is thinking of something else. Tell me what ails her, Magda, for I love her dearly."

When he had done, Magda sat silent for a while in thought. Then she said, "I think I know what ails the Lady Catherine, but I would be sure before I speak. Come to me again to-morrow, and bring me a lock of her hair."

That night, while his lady lay sleeping, Count Alaric cut off a lock of her pale hair; and the next morning he rode again over the heath. When he knocked on the door of her hovel Magda was stirring a stew of herbs over the fire. "Come in and sit you down," she said.

The count drew the lock of hair from the pouch at his belt and gave it to her, and she took it without a word and rose and held it in her hands.

He watched her standing there, as tall as any man, in her grey frieze gown, holding the hair, like a faint imprisoned moonbeam, in her strong brown hands. She looked at it a long time, and then she went to the fire, and crouching down, dropped it on the embers. The lock burnt with a sigh and a greenish flame, and left a little wisp of smoke which hovered for a moment by the hearth before dissolving in the air.

Magda rose and looked at the count. "It is as I thought," she said, "your lady is one of the fairy people."

Count Alaric cried out, "She cannot be!" But he saw the pity and understanding in Magda's eyes and he knew that she spoke the truth.

"When you first found her she must have been dancing on midsummer's eve as the fairy people do, and for some reason remained in the meadow after dawn when her companions had returned to their other world. Away from her people she would forget much of her life with them, and that is why she could tell you nothing of how she came to be there. You have married one of the fairy people, Alaric."

He turned away. "Must I then lose her?" he asked.

"So long as she remembers anything of her fairy life she will never be wholly yours. She will always hear the fairy music borne to her on the wind, and on midsummer's eve she will always have to dance with her people; and one day she may not return from their revels. And even if she should come back to you each time, whenever you see into her eyes, there will always be that look as though she is thinking of something else."

"Is there no way by which I can win her completely for my own?" asked the count in despair. "No way I can make her forget the fairy people?"

"There is only one way," replied Magda, "by which a mortal can win one of the fairy people for himself, and that is by offering her a love so perfect that it leaves no room in her mind for memories of any other life. Only when your love for your lady is perfect will she forget entirely what she once was and whence she came, only then will she cease to hear the fairy music and wish to dance to it, and only then will you be able to look into her eyes and see that she is thinking of nothing but of you and of herself and of your life together."

"But my love for her is perfect," said the count. "I love her with all my heart. I give her everything she desires, I would toil and fight for her if need be, my whole life is hers. Oh, Magda, I would die for her."

Magda shook her head. "There must be something lacking. If your love for her were perfect, she would be wholly yours."

"Then what am I to do?" asked the count.

"My friend," replied Magda gently, "that is something I cannot know. Search your heart and ask it where you have failed, I cannot tell you what lies within yourself."

"My love for her could not be greater than it is. If she is not now wholly mine, she never will be."

"Do not despair," said Magda. "Go home and see what time will do to help you."

He mounted his horse and rode over the heather, and Magda came part of the way with him, striding beside the white horse, her head held proudly. Within sight of the castle she stopped. "Farewell and good luck, Alaric," she said. "My thoughts will be with you," and she left him to go on alone.

Count Alaric returned to his castle, and from that day on he was even kinder to his lady than he had been before, if that were possible. He sent over all the land for gifts to please her, and never a day went by without his offering her yet another proof of his affection, as if he hoped that thus his love might at last grow perfect. But though she was gay and happy enough, whenever he looked into her eyes he saw that still she thought of something else; and now that he knew what it was she was thinking of, he grew hourly more sad, though he hid his sorrow carefully.

And the days passed and joined together to make the months. The winter came and after winter the spring, and then spring was gone with its yellows and whites, and the summer was back again. And on midsummer's eve, as soon as it was dusk, Count Alaric's lady slipped out through the castle gates in a gown of blue velvet and ran to the fields; and the farther she went from the castle, the louder grew the fairy music in her ears. Count Alaric, who had been waiting and watching, saw her go, and he buckled on his sword and mounted his horse and followed her.

When he reached the meadow he heard the music and saw once again the fairy people dancing on the grass in their fluttering gowns of green. And his lady was among them, her feet as bare as theirs, with her pale hair hanging about her shoulders like a veil thrown over the blue velvet that looked gray by the light of the moon.

The count left his horse by the hazel bushes at the edge of the field and came nearer to the dancers, treading softly and keeping to the shadows where he could. And as he watched her whom he called Catherine dancing with her people and laughing aloud with the joy of it, he felt as though his heart would break. "She must be mine," he whispered. "I will take her from them no matter what it costs." And he drew his sword and stepped in among the dancers and seized her by the arm.

The fairy people scattered apart and fluttered into a group like a heap of leaves a little way off; white faces with piercing golden-green eyes watching him in the moonlight. His lady would have gone with them, but that he held her fast. "Catherine, it is I, Alaric, your husband. I have come to fetch you home." But she only struggled and turned her face to the fairy people and cried out to him to let her go. And the fairy people held out their arms to her like white moonbeams and called, "Come back to us, our sister."

And when Count Alaric's lady found that she could not break free from his hold, she became cunning and ceased to struggle. She smiled at him in the moonlight. "My people wait for me, dear husband. They wait for me to dance with them. Let me go and join in the dancing, and when it is over, I will come back to you."

"If I let you go, you may never come back to me."

She touched his cheek with her one free hand and stroked his hair. "Dear husband, I promise to come back to you."

He shook his head. "The promises of the fairy people are as a drop of water lost in a stream or as a breath blown with the wind. If I let you go, you may never come back."

The fairy people fluttered their arms and their gowns of green and called, "Come, our sister, come back to us."

She ceased her smiling and knelt at his feet and lifted her face to his, and her golden-green eyes were aswim with tears. "The fairy people have no tears," she said, "but you have taught me how to weep."

He turned away from her so that pity should not make him weak. But still he held her wrist and said, "If I let you go, I may never see you again."

The fairy people swayed closer in the moonlight and moaned, "O our sister, our sister, come back to us."

And when she saw that neither by cajoling nor entreaties could he be moved, Count Alaric's lady leapt to her feet and cried out, "Give me now your strength, my people." And they broke from their group like leaves blown by a breeze, whispering, "Be strong, our sister, be strong. Be strong and come back to us," and encircled the count and his lady.

And Count Alaric's lady became a sapling with the wind in its branches, and instead of her wrist his hand gripped its trunk and the wind bent it away from him to tear it from his hold. But he flung aside his sword and clung to the tree, and at last the wind died down and all was still.

The ring of fairy people moved nearer. "Be fierce, our sister, be fierce and come back to us."

And Count Alaric's lady became a red vixen which writhed in his hands and bit to the bone. But in spite of its struggles he held it, and at last it lay still in his arms.

The fairy circle drew closer. "Be wild, our sister, be wild. Be wild and come back to us."

And Count Alaric's lady became a silver salmon which twisted and turned and would have slipped from his grasp, but that he held it close till it lay gasping in his hands.

The fairy feet stepped nearer, coming over the grass. "Be formless, our sister, be formless. Be formless and come back to us."

And Count Alaric's lady became water which would have trickled through his fingers, but that he held it in his cupped hands, crouched low to the earth.

The fairy voices were closer, crying in the moonlit night. "Be swift, our sister, be swift. Be swift and come back to us."

And Count Alaric's lady became a breath of wind upon the air that sought to elude him and be lost for ever, but he clasped it in his hands and held it to his heart.

The white faces of the fairy people pressed nearer. "Be burning, our sister, be burning. Be burning and come back to us."

And Count Alaric's lady became a tongue of flame that burnt his hands as though it would scorch away the flesh. But the count thought, "If I can hold her until the dawn, she will be partly mine for at least another year." And he did not let go of the flame.

And Count Alaric's lady took once again her own shape and sank down upon the grass at his feet and hid her face with her one free hand while he kept hold of the other. "You are too strong for me," she whispered, "and I cannot leave you."

A wail rose up from the fairy people and the circle broke, and they scattered and joined again in a group a short way off. And the garments of the fairy people merged a little with the grass, and their hair was like a mist to hide them, and their voices came more faintly over the meadow.

The count looked up and saw a thin streak of saffron in the east. "It is almost dawn," he thought, "and she will be with me for another year." But he looked at her, where she crouched in the grass and moaned. "Catherine," he said gently, "if you stay with me, will you remember your people and be sad?"

She turned her head and looked upwards to him. "I shall only partly remember them. I shall regret them faintly, but not be sad. I shall always know that there is something which I have lost, but I shall not remember what."

"And if you went back to your people, would you remember me and our life together and regret that it was past?"

"I should remember nothing of our life together. I should forget you utterly, so I should have no regrets and be only happy."

"I would not wish you to have even a moment of sorrow. Dearest, go back to your people and be happy, without any memories." And Count Alaric let go of her wrist, and she rose and went to the fairy people where they held out their hands to her and fluttered their gowns of green; while in the distance the first cock crew for the dawning of a new day.

"It is dawn and they will take her away with them and I shall never see her again," thought the count, and he turned and ran to the hedge where his horse was tied; and he never looked back, for it was dawn and he could not bear to see no one in the meadow where the fairy people had been dancing.

He rode his horse blindly, over field and through woods, caring not where it carried him; and an hour later, when he turned for the first time from his bitter thoughts, it was to find that he was on the road for home. There before him was his castle, golden in the early sun; and between him and the castle, along the dusty road, trudged a solitary figure in a blue velvet gown. He urged on his horse and she heard it and turned and saw him and waited, joy and relief on her face. He reined in beside her. "Catherine," he said.

For all her joy and relief she was very near to tears. "Oh Alaric, I can almost not walk another step, I am so tired. And see," she raised her skirts a little, "I have somehow lost my shoes. I woke up and found myself in a meadow, all alone, and I was so afraid. I must have walked there in my sleep. Did you ride out to look for me? And were you afraid too?"

Count Alaric smiled. "I rode out to look for you," he said. "And I was afraid." He lifted her on to his horse before him, and when he looked into her golden-green eyes, he saw that she was no longer thinking of anything else, but only of him and of herself and of their life together, and that at last she was wholly his.

And in that moment Count Alaric knew that love is only perfect when it will give up even the thing which it loves, for that thing's sake.

■

Tribute to Augusta Baker

While I was a student in Mary Virginia Gaver's course in children's literature at Rutgers Graduate School of Library Service, Augusta Baker came to talk about storytelling and to tell stories. I was mesmerized by her expressive golden-brown eyes and vibrant telling. Upon graduation I was *invited* (yes, that was the word used at the time) to join the staff of The New York Public Library (spelled with a capital "T"). I refused (something quite unheard of) in order to accept a newly created position as group work specialist at the Elizabeth (N.J.) Public Library where I had been working while earning my M.L.S. degree. With the naiveté and boldness of youth I asked Mrs. Baker to help me with in-service training in storytelling for the EPL staff, one of my new responsibilities. Years later, after I became her assistant and was aware of her busy schedule, I asked, "Why ever did you agree to do it?" She replied, with her wonderful smile, "You were so enthusiastic, I couldn't refuse."

From Augusta, I learned to look for the potential in every new storyteller and to nurture that potential, no matter how small it seemed—and over the years I have seen small potential grow into consummate storytelling. She taught me to trust the story, to tell it in a simple, straightforward manner, how to arrange stories to make a pleasing program, and the elements that assure a successful workshop or conference.

Now in her eighties, she still displays that generosity of spirit, warmth, good humor, and common sense that captivated me 40 years ago. A legend in her time, Augusta Baker is truly America's first lady of storytelling.

Ellin Greene is a library educator, author, and storyteller. In addition to *Storytelling: Art and Technique,* 3rd edition, she is the author of the highly acclaimed *Books, Babies and Libraries: Serving Infants, Toddlers, Their Parents and Caregivers,* coauthor with George Shannon of *Storytelling: A Selected Annotated Bibliography*, compiler of three story anthologies, and reteller of seven tales for children. She has been a featured performer at the National Storytelling Festival in Jonesborough (Tenn.), and, since 1968, an adjunct professor of storytelling at Rutgers.

The Wise Old Woman

Selected by Spencer G. Shaw

Source: *The Sea of Gold and Other Tales from Japan* by Yoshiko Uchida. Illustrated by Marianna Yamaguchi. Scribners, 1965, o.p.

Culture: Japanese

Telling time: 12 to 15 minutes

Audience: Age 10 to 15 and adults, especially senior citizens

Notes on telling: In folk literature from the different cultures of the world, the *themes* relating to old age and the treatment of the elderly have been probed with poignancy. The inevitable *problem* that must be resolved in many of these stories is how to save the aged from an undeserved punishment or demise. Filled with sequences of *suspense* and *crises* as the protagonist and the antagonist enact their respective roles, the *plot* proceeds to a satisfying *climax* with justice prevailing.

In this beloved Japanese story, a young farmer, with the aid of his elderly mother, reveals to the arrogant, cruel lord of the village the wrongfulness of his edict to banish all who reach the age of 71, and provides satisfying images of filial devotion and the benefits of wisdom and experience.

■

MANY LONG years ago, there lived an arrogant and cruel young lord who ruled over a small village in the western hills of Japan.

"I have no use for old people in my village," he said haughtily. "They are neither useful nor able to work for a living. I therefore decree that anyone over seventy-one must be banished from the village and left in the mountains to die."

"What a dreadful decree! What a cruel and unreasonable lord we have," the people of the village murmured. But the lord fearfully punished anyone who disobeyed him, and so villagers who turned seventy-one were tearfully carried into the mountains, never to return.

Gradually there were fewer and fewer old people in the village and soon they disappeared altogether. Then the young lord was pleased.

"What a fine village of young, healthy and hard-working people I have," he bragged. "Soon it will be the finest village in all of Japan."

Now there lived in this village a kind young farmer and his aged mother. They were poor, but the farmer was good to his mother, and the two of them lived happily together. However, as the years went by, the mother grew older, and before long she reached the terrible age of seventy-one.

"If only I could somehow deceive the cruel lord," the farmer thought. But there were records in the village books and every one knew that his mother had turned seventy-one.

Each day the son put off telling his mother that he must take her into the mountains to die, but the people of the village began to talk. The farmer knew that if he did not take his mother away soon, the lord would send his soldiers and throw them both into a dark dungeon to die a terrible death.

"Mother . . .," he would begin, as he tried to tell her what he must do, but he could not go on.

Then one day the mother herself spoke of the lord's dread decree. "Well, my son," she said, "the time has come for you to take me to the mountains. We must hurry before the lord sends his soldiers for you." And she did not seem worried at all that she must go to the mountains to die.

"Forgive me, dear mother, for what I must do," the farmer said sadly, and the next morning he lifted his mother to his shoulders and set off on the steep path toward the mountains. Up and up he climbed, until the trees clustered close and the path was gone. There was no longer even the sound of birds, and they heard only the soft wail of the wind in the trees. The son walked slowly, for he could not bear to think of leaving his old mother in the mountains. On and on he climbed, not wanting to stop and leave her behind. Soon, he heard his mother breaking off small twigs from the trees that they passed.

"Mother, what are you doing?" he asked.

"Do not worry, my son," she answered gently. "I am just marking the way so you will not get lost returning to the village."

The son stopped. "Even now you are thinking of me?" he asked, wonderingly.

The mother nodded. "Of course, my son," she replied. "You will always be in my thoughts. How could it be otherwise?"

At that, the young farmer could bear it no longer. "Mother, I cannot leave you in the mountains to die all alone," he said. "We are going home and no matter what the lord does to punish me, I will never desert you again."

So they waited until the sun had set and a lone star crept into the silent sky. Then in the dark shadows of night, the farmer carried his mother down the hill and they returned quietly to their little house. The farmer dug a deep hole in the floor of his kitchen and made a small room where he could hide his mother. From that day, she spent all her time in the secret room and the farmer carried meals to her there. The rest of the time, he was careful to work in the fields and act as though he lived alone. In this way, for almost two years, he kept his mother safely hidden and no one in the village knew that she was there.

Then one day there was a terrible commotion among the villagers for Lord Higa of the town beyond the hills threatened to conquer their village and make it his own.

"Only one thing can spare you," Lord Higa announced. "Bring me a box containing one thousand ropes of ash and I will spare your village."

The cruel young lord quickly gathered together all the wise men of his village. "You are men of wisdom," he said. "Surely you can tell me how to meet Lord Higa's demands so our village can be spared."

But the wise men shook their heads. "It is impossible to make even one rope of ash, sire," they answered. "How can we ever make one thousand?"

"Fools!" the lord cried angrily. "What good is your wisdom if you cannot help me now?"

And he posted a notice in the village square offering a great reward of gold to any villager who could help him save their village.

But all the people in the village whispered, "Surely, it is an impossible thing, for ash crumbles at the touch of the finger. How could anyone ever make a rope of ash?" They shook their heads and sighed, "Alas, alas, we must be conquered by yet another cruel lord."

The young farmer, too, supposed that this must be, and he wondered what would happen to his mother if a new lord even more terrible than their own came to rule over them.

When his mother saw the troubled look on his face, she asked, "Why are you so worried, my son?"

So the farmer told her of the impossible demand made by Lord Higa if the village was to be spared, but his mother did not seem troubled at all. Instead she laughed softly and said, "Why, that is not such an impossible task. All one has to do is soak ordinary rope in salt water and dry it well. When it is burned, it will hold its shape and there is your rope of ash! Tell the villagers to hurry and find one thousand pieces of rope."

The farmer shook his head in amazement. "Mother, you are wonderfully wise," he said, and he rushed to tell the young lord what he must do.

"You are wiser than all the wise men of the village," the lord said when he heard the farmer's solution, and he rewarded him with many pieces of gold. The thousand ropes of ash were quickly made and the village was spared.

In a few days, however, there was another great commotion in the village as Lord Higa sent another threat. This time he sent a log with a small hole that curved and bent seven times through its length, and he demanded that a single piece of silk thread by threaded through the hole. "If you cannot perform this task," the lord threatened, "I shall come to conquer your village."

The young lord hurried once more to his wise men, but they all shook their heads in bewilderment. "A needle cannot bend its way through such curves," they moaned. "Again we are faced with an impossible demand."

"And again you are stupid fools!" the lord said, stamping his foot impatiently. He then posted a second notice in the village square asking the villagers for their help.

Once more the young farmer hurried with the problem to his mother in her secret room.

"Why, that is not so difficult," his mother said with a quick smile. "Put some sugar at one end of the hole. Then, tie an ant to a piece of silk thread and put it in at the other end. He will weave his way in and out of the curves to get to the sugar and he will take the silk thread with him."

"Mother, you are remarkable!" the son cried, and he hurried off to the lord with the solution to the second problem.

Once more the lord commended the young farmer and rewarded him with many pieces of gold. "You are a brilliant man and you have saved our village again," he said gratefully.

But the lord's troubles were not over even then, for a few days later Lord Higa sent still another demand. "This time you will undoubtedly fail and then I shall conquer your village," he threatened. "Bring me a drum that sounds without being beaten."

"But that is not possible," sighed the people of the village. "How can anyone make a drum sound without beating it?"

This time the wise men held their heads in their hands and moaned, "It is hopeless. It is hopeless. This time Lord Higa will conquer us all."

The young farmer hurried home breathlessly. "Mother, Mother, we must solve another terrible problem or Lord Higa will conquer our village!" And he quickly told his mother about the impossible drum.

His mother, however, smiled and answered, "Why, this is the easiest of them all. Make a drum with sides of paper and put a bumblebee inside. As it tries to escape, it will buzz and beat itself against the paper and you will have a drum that sounds without being beaten."

The young farmer was amazed at his mother's wisdom. "You are far wiser than any of the wise men of the village," he said, and he hurried to tell the young lord how to meet Lord Higa's third demand.

When the lord heard the answer, he was greatly impressed. "Surely a young man like you cannot be wiser than all my wise men," he said. "Tell me honestly, who has helped you solve all these difficult problems?"

The young farmer could not lie. "My lord," he began slowly, "for the past two years I have broken the law of the land. I have kept my aged mother hidden beneath the floor of my house, and it is she who solved each of your problems and saved the village from Lord Higa."

He trembled as he spoke, for he feared the lord's displeasure and rage. Surely now the soldiers would be summoned to throw him into the dark dungeon. But when he glanced fearfully at the lord, he saw that the young ruler was not angry at all. Instead, he was silent and thoughtful, for at last he realized how much wisdom and knowledge old people possess.

"I have been very wrong," he said finally. "And I must ask the forgiveness of your mother and of all my people. Never again will I demand that the old people of our village be sent to the mountains to die. Rather, they will be treated with the respect and honor they deserve and share with us the wisdom of their years."

And so it was. From that day, the villagers were no longer forced to abandon their parents in the mountains, and the village became once more a happy, cheerful place in which to live. The terrible Lord Higa stopped sending his impossible demands and no longer threatened to conquer them, for he too was impressed. "Even in such a small village there is much wisdom," he declared, "and its people should be allowed to live in peace."

And that is exactly what the farmer and his mother and all the people of the village did for all the years thereafter.

■

Tribute to Augusta Baker

In a span of more than five decades it has been a privilege to have shared with many colleagues professional responsibilities, duties, accomplishments, and dreams. Among such relationships there is one that shall always be deeply cherished, for it has been enriched with a personal gift of friendship as extended to me, without reservation, by Augusta Baker.

Through the years this personal link was crafted with our mutual interests in closely related spheres of library services for children and for adults who are concerned with this age group. Recognized as a distinguished librarian, administrator, educator, author, and raconteur, Augusta always shared her creative talents unselfishly and provided constant guidance to countless children's librarians. Preeminent in Augusta's career has been her intense advancement of the art of storytelling.

Exemplifying the highest standards of excellence in librarianship that are worthy of emulation, her invaluable contributions have become landmarks. National and international in scope, her influence has been widely extended through her publications, lectures, teaching, and radio and television commitments, and through her service in elected positions in library and educational associations.

In recognition of Augusta's gift of friendship to me with its many inherent benefits, I express my gratitude.

Spencer G. Shaw, professor emeritus, Graduate School of Library and Information Science, University of Washington, has served as a branch librarian in the Hartford (Conn.) Public Library; program coordinator and storytelling specialist, Brooklyn (N.Y.) Public Library; and consultant in library service to children, Nassau County (N.Y.) Library System. His teaching, lectureships, and program presentations have included national and international commitments in Australia, New Zealand, Japan, Hong Kong, Canada, Mexico, England, the Netherlands, and Cyprus.

A Handful of Mustard Seed

Selected by George Shannon

Source: Still More Stories to Solve: Fourteen Folktales from Around the World by George Shannon. Illustrated by Peter Sis. Greenwillow, 1994.

Culture: Buddhist

Telling time: 3 minutes

Audience: Upper elementary grades to adults

Notes on telling: "A Handful of Mustard Seed" is a Buddhist story retold from *Popular Tales and Fictions: Their Migrations and Transformations*, Volume 2, by W. A. Clouston. Clouston worked from *Buddhaghosha's Parables*, translated from the Burmese by Henry Thomas Rogers. The Greek satirist Lucien included a variant in "Demonax" written in the second century A.D.

To me, "A Handful of Mustard Seed" is best told as an overwhelming and mysterious memory. A dead child. A mother grieving toward craziness. A sliver of hope. And a resolution that seems—at first—as hard to fathom as the baby's death. Tell the tale through the mother's broken heart and you'll naturally share her pain and loneliness, *and* her final sense of communion. I think of this tale not so much as a story to solve as I do a poem that brings revelation.

■

A YOUNG woman gave birth to a son, and like all parents she and her husband loved their baby more than words could tell. Then tragedy came. Before their son was a year old, he became very ill and died. The mother cried for days, refusing to let anyone bury her child. She begged everyone to help her find some kind of medicine that would bring her son to life again.

Many people thought she'd gone mad, but a wise man told her to go ask Buddha.

"I have the medicine you need," said Buddha. "But one ingredient is missing."

"Tell me!" demanded the woman. "I'll find it today."

"You must bring me a handful of mustard seed," said Buddha. "But it *must* come from a house where no child or spouse or parent has died."

The woman began going from house to house. She searched for weeks and months but could not find a house that met Buddha's requirements. His request turned out to be impossible. The woman failed to find a medicine that could help her son, yet she returned with a different medicine that helped to ease *her* pain. What was the medicine she found?

How It Was Done

As she searched for a house where no child or spouse or parent had died, the woman began to realize that every household she visited had lost a loved one, yet they had all found ways to go on with their lives. Their words and stories helped the woman feel less alone.

Buddha's seemingly odd request helped her experience the healing value of stories shared—the only real medicine he could give her.

■

Tribute to Augusta Baker

The first time I saw Augusta Baker was at the 1976 ALA annual conference, when I was a library student in love with storytelling. When she took her seat among others in the crowded room my jaw dropped as surely as if I'd seen a movie star. Her! The name on the books. *The* name in library storytelling. When I learned several years later that I was to be on the same conference program as Mrs. Baker I felt honored and terrified. She'd hear my speech. She'd hear *me* tell a story. She couldn't have been more gracious and encouraging. I have no memory of what story I told that day, but I remember she told one of Kipling's literary tales. Even more, I recall the anecdote she told to a few of us in the hall at the end of small group sessions. It was a tale of another conference. When *that* conference broke into simultaneous sessions, so many raced to gaze at a handsome new writing star that not one soul came to *her* session. She laughed at the memory—an entertaining teller through and through. A teller who's always known that the *story* is the star.

George Shannon is a writer and storyteller. His integrity and lyrical style bring pleasure to the reader/listener whether it is a picture story book, one of the popular Stories to Solve books for children in the middle grades, a young adult novel, or a scholarly work. He is coauthor with Ellin Greene of *Storytelling: A Selected Annotated Bibliography* and the author of *A Knock at the Door, Folk Literature and Children: An Annotated Bibliography of Secondary Materials,* and *Arnold Lobel.* His many scholarly articles exploring folklore have gained him high regard in the library and education worlds.

Appendix: Sources for the Storyteller

Professional Reading

BOOKS AND EXCERPTS FROM BOOKS

Andersen, Hans Christian. *The Complete Fairy Tales and Stories.* Translated from the Danish by Erik Christian Haugaard. Doubleday, 1974. o.p.

————. *Hans Christian Andersen: Eighty Fairy Tales.* Translated by R. P. Keigwin. Introduction by Elias Bredsdorff. Illustrated by Vilhelm Pedersen and Lorenz Frolich. Pantheon, 1982. o.p.

Arnott, Kathleen. *African Myths and Legends.* Illustrated by Joan Kiddell-Monroe. Oxford Univ. Press, 1990. ISBN 0-19-274143-8

Ausubel, Nathan. *A Treasury of Jewish Folklore.* Crown, 1989. ISBN 0-517-50293-3

Barton, Bob. *Tell Me Another: Storytelling and Reading Aloud at Home, at School and in the Community.* Heinemann, 1986. ISBN 0-435-08231-0

Barton, Bob, and David Booth. *Stories in the Classroom: Storytelling, Reading Aloud and Roleplaying with Children.* Heinemann, 1990. ISBN 0-435-08527-1. This valuable guide is based on the authors' more than 30 years of experience as teachers, consultants, and storytellers. Though addressed to classroom teachers, it has much to offer anyone who works with children in a group setting. The authors discuss "why children need stories" and "why children need to story" and present ways of engaging children in storying.

Bauer, Caroline Feller. *New Handbook for Storytellers with Stories, Poems, Magic, and More.* Illustrated by Lynn Gates Bredeson. American Library Assn., 1993. ISBN 0-8389-0613-3. This revised and expanded edition of the author's popular storytelling handbook is filled with exciting ideas for multimedia story hours. It includes excerpts from the works of over 50 well-known writers, sample programs, and updated booklists.

————. *The Poetry Break: An Annotated Anthology with Ideas for Introducing Children to Poetry.* Illustrated by Edith Bingham. H. W. Wilson, 1994. ISBN 0-8242-0852-8. Part 1 of this fun-filled book explains the Poetry Break idea and suggests methods and activities to make poetry a natural part of a child's life. Part 2 is a collection of 240 poems, both classic and contemporary, for children ranging from preschool through elementary school.

Bauman, Richard. *Verbal Arts as Performance.* Waveland Press, 1984. ISBN 0-88133-048-5

Bettelheim, Bruno. *The Uses of Enchantment: The Meaning and Importance of Fairy Tales.* Knopf, 1976. ISBN 0-394-49771-6

Bierhorst, John. *Black Rainbows: Legends of the Incas and Myths of Ancient Peru.* Farrar, 1976. o.p.

————. *The Mythology of Mexico and Central America.* Morrow, 1990. ISBN 0-688-06721-2

————. *The Mythology of North America.* Morrow, 1986. ISBN 0-688-04145-0

————. *The Mythology of South America.* Morrow, 1988. ISBN 0-688-06722-0

A three-part series on the mythology of the New World by a distinguished folklorist. Scholarly *and* accessible.

Briggs, Katherine. *British Folk Tales.* Dorset Press, 1989. ISBN 0-88029-288-1. A selection from the four-volume work *A Dictionary of British Folk-tales*, published by Routledge & Kegan Paul Ltd., London, in 1970–1971, with new introductions.

Brown, Marcia. *Lotus Seeds: Children, Pictures, and Books.* Simon & Schuster, 1986. ISBN 0-684-18490-7. Thirteen perceptive essays by a distinguished artist.

Bryant, Sara Cone. *How to Tell Stories to Children.* Gordon Press, 1980. Reprint of 1924 edition. ISBN 0-8490-3176-1

Butler, Dorothy. *Babies Need Books.* Atheneum, 1982. o.p.

Calvino, Italo. *Italian Folktales.* Translated by George Martin. Harcourt, 1990. ISBN 0-15-145770-0. The Italian equivalent of *Grimm's Fairy Tales.*

Campbell, Joseph. "Folkloristic Commentary." In *The Complete Grimm's Fairy Tales,* pp. 833–863. Pantheon, 1976. ISBN 0-394-49415-6

Chambers, Aidan, "Storytelling and Reading Aloud," in Chambers's *Introducing Books to Children,* 2nd ed., pp. 129–156. Horn Book, 1983. ISBN 0-87675-284-9

Chukovsky, Kornei. *From Two to Five.* Revised edition. Translated and edited by Miriam Morton. Foreword by Frances Clarke Sayers. Univ. of California Press, 1968. ISBN 0-520-00238-5. A delightful and insightful book about language development in young children by a Russian scholar and poet of childhood.

Clarkson, Atelia, and Gilbert Cross. *World Folktales: A Scribner Resource Collection.* Macmillan, 1982. o.p.

Colum, Padraic. "Introduction." In *The Complete Grimm's Fairy Tales,* pp. xi–xvii. Pantheon, 1976. ISBN 0-394-49415-6

Cook, Elizabeth. *The Ordinary and the Fabulous: An Introduction to Myths, Legends, and Fairy Tales,* 2nd ed. Cambridge Univ. Press, 1976. o.p.

Cooper, Pamela, and Rives Collins. *Look What Happened to Frog: Storytelling in Education.* Gorsuch Scarisbrick, 1992. ISBN 0-89787-345-9. Aimed at elementary school teachers, this how-to book is full of zippy, specific advice and dozens of fresh activities, including ways to use puppets, shadow boxes, flannel boards, and the like, in storytelling.

Courlander, Harold. *Treasury of African Folklore.* Marlowe, 1995. ISBN 1-56924-816-8

———. *Treasury of African-American Folklore.* Marlowe, 1996. ISBN 1-56924-811-7

Cullinan, Bernice E., Marilyn C. Scala, and Virginia C. Schroder, with Ann K. Lovett. *Three Voices: An Invitation to Poetry Across the Curriculum.* Stenhouse, 1995. ISBN 1-57110-015-6. This book is organized into three sections: developing a love of poetry, helping students discover how poetry works, and using poetry in the content areas. Written by teachers for teachers, Strategy 5 "Poetry to Enrich Stories," Strategy 31 "Storytelling and Cultures," and Strategy 32 "Performance and Poetry," hold particular interest for storytellers.

Dailey, Sheila. *Putting the World in a Nutshell: The Art of the Formula Tale.* H. W. Wilson, 1994. ISBN 0-8242-0860-9. In separate chapters, Dailey discusses the nine basic types of formula tales—chain, cumulative, circle, endless, catch, compound triad, question, air castles, good/bad tales—and gives several examples of each type. Because formula tales are so easy to learn and tell, this is a good source book for new storytellers.

de la Mare, Walter. *Animal Stories.* Scribner, 1940. o.p. The introduction traces the development of the animal folk tale.

de Vos, Gail. *Storytelling for Young Adults: Techniques and Treasury.* Libraries Unlimited, 1991. ISBN 0-87287-832-5. Brief chapters on the values of storytelling to young adults, storytelling techniques, and suggestions for integrating storytelling into the classroom are followed by an annotated bibliography of 120 stories suitable for telling to ages 13–18. The annotations for the stories, which range from folk and fairy tales to urban legends, include a summary of the story, sources, and timing.

de Wit, Dorothy. *Children's Faces Looking Up: Program Building for the Storyteller.* American Library Assn., 1979. ISBN 0-8389-0272-3. This older but still valuable title explores the characteristics of a good storytelling program—balance, rhythm, pacing, and variety—and demonstrates with six sample programs.

Dundes, Alan, ed. *Cinderella: A Casebook.* Univ. of Wisconsin Press, 1988. ISBN 0-299-11864-9.

Favat, F. André. *Child and Tale: The Origins of Interest.* National Council of Teachers of English, 1977. o.p.

Freeman, Judy. *Books Kids Will Sit Still For: The Complete Read-Aloud Guide.* 2nd ed. Bowker, 1990. ISBN 0-8352-3010-4

———. *More Books Kids Will Sit Still For: A Read-Aloud Guide.* Bowker, 1995. ISBN 0-8352-3520-3. Both titles by Freeman contain helpful tips on how and what to read aloud and extensive bibliographies of picture books, fiction, poetry, folklore, and nonfiction, teacher- and child-tested for reading aloud to children from preschool age through sixth grade.

Gardner, Howard. "Literature." In *The Arts and Human Development,* pp. 198-215. Basic Books, 1994. ISBN 0-465-0040-7

Greene, Ellin. *Books, Babies, and Libraries: Serving Infants, Toddlers, Their Parents & Caregivers.* American Library Assn., 1991. ISBN 0-8389-0572-2. An overall view of library service to children under the age of three and their caregivers and the librarian's role in developing a love of books and reading. Covers early child development and learning, emergent literacy, library collections, program planning, networking and outreach, and planning, implementing, and evaluating library service to early childhood. Includes talks by Dorothy Butler and Jan Omerod presented at the New York Public Library's Early Childhood Conference, April 1989.

———. *Read Me a Story: Books & Techniques for Reading Aloud & Storytelling.* Preschool Publications, 1992. This concise, informative guide on storytelling and reading aloud was designed for use by early childhood teachers and caregivers. It includes a bibliography of more than 100 children's books arranged by genre or subject. Recommended for the library's parenting collection.

Grimm, Jacob. *The Complete Grimm's Fairy Tales.* Pantheon, 1976. ISBN 0-394-49415-6

Hamilton, Edith. *Mythology.* Little, Brown, 1942. ISBN 0-316-34114-2

Hamilton, Martha, and Mitch Weiss. *Children Tell Stories: A Teaching Guide.* Richard C. Owen, 1990. ISBN 0-913461-20-2. Here are many suggestions for adults seeking ways to encourage themselves and children to tell stories adeptly. This award-winning book particularly suits teachers because it has plans for a six-week unit and eight handouts. Includes 25 short tales for beginning tellers.

Harrell, John. *Origins and Early Traditions of Storytelling.* York House, 1983. ISBN 0-9615389-1-0

Hazard, Paul. *Books, Children and Men,* 5th ed. Horn Book, 1983. ISBN 0-87675-059-5

Huck, Charlotte S. *Children's Literature in the Elementary School.* Harcourt, 1993. ISBN 0-03-047528-7

Jeffery, Debby Ann. *Literate Beginnings: Programs for Babies and Toddlers.* American Library Assn., 1994. ISBN 0-8389-0640-0. This fine timesaver for librarians and others who do baby-toddler programs is divided into two parts. Part 1 covers the rationale for such programs, planning, selection of materials (book and non-book), and evaluation of baby-toddler programs. Part 2 consists of 52 theme-related program sheets with picture-book titles and the words to finger plays and songs.

Johnson, Edna, Evelyn Sickels, Carolyn Horovitz, and Frances Clarke Sayers. *Riverside Anthology of Children's Literature,* 6th ed. Houghton Mifflin, 1985. ISBN 0-395-35773-X

Kimmel, Margaret Mary, and Elizabeth Segal. *For Reading Out Loud! A Guide to Sharing Books with Children.* Revised ed. Dell, 1991. ISBN 0-440-50400-7

Lane, Marcia. *Picturing the Rose: A Way of Looking at Fairy Tales.* H. W. Wilson, 1994. ISBN 0-8242-0848-X. "A discussion of the nature and meaning of fairy tales with explanation of the process for preparing seven multicultural tales for telling."

Larrick, Nancy. *Let's Do a Poem: Introducing Children and Poetry Through Listening, Singing, Chanting, Impromtu Choral Reading, Body Movement, Dance, and Dramatization.* Delacorte, 1991. o.p. A practical handbook based on the author's extensive experience with poetry and children.

Lewis, Claudia. "Poetry and Young Children." In *Resources for Early Childhood: A Handbook,* pp. 331–333. Garland, 1995. ISBN 0-8240-7395-9

Livingston, Myra Cohn. *Climb into the Bell Tower: Essays on Poetry.* HarperCollins, 1990. ISBN 0-06-024015-6. Eleven essays addressed to librarians, teachers, authors, and other adults who work with children, by the recipient of the NCTE Award for Excellence in Poetry for Children.

Livo, Norma J., and Sandra A. Rietz. *Storytelling Folklore Sourcebook.* Libraries Unlimited, 1991. ISBN 0-87287-601-2. In brief entries, the authors show how the folklore of ancient times influences contemporary speech.

Lüthi, Max. *The European Folktale: Form and Nature.* Translated by John D. Niles. Indiana Univ. Press, 1986. ISBN 0-253-20393-7

————. *Once Upon a Time: On the Nature of Fairy Tales.* Indiana Univ. Press, 1976. ISBN 0-253-20203-5

MacDonald, Margaret Read. *Booksharing: 101 Programs to Use with Preschoolers.* Shoe String Press, 1988. ISBN 0-208-02159-0. Though the programs include films, music, drama, and crafts, the emphasis throughout is on picture books as the primary resource for introducing young children to literature.

————. *The Storyteller's Start-Up Book: Finding, Learning, Performing, and Using Folktales.* August House, 1993. ISBN 0-87483-304-3. A user-friendly basic text for the beginning teller, with 12 easy-to-learn tales.

————. *Twenty Tellable Tales.* H. W. Wilson, 1986. ISBN 0-8242-0719-X. The tales are short, contain chants, songs, or refrains, and are set down in an ethnopoetic style to emphasize their orality. Also see other collections in the ethnopoetic format by this prolific author.

Mallan, Kerry. *Children as Storytellers.* Heinemann, 1992. ISBN 0-435-08779-7. The author teaches children's literature, storytelling, and teacher-librarianship at Queensland University of Technology, Australia. Her book gives many pointers for uncovering the storyteller in children and for helping them to find and learn simple tales.

Mannheim, Ralph, trans. *Grimm's Tales for Young and Old: The Complete Stories.* Doubleday, 1983. ISBN 0-385-18950-8

Marino, Jane. *Sing Us a Story: Using Music in Preschool and Family Storytimes.* H. W. Wilson, 1994. ISBN 0-8242-0847-1. A librarian shares her love of music by suggesting ways to integrate songs into preschool and family storytimes. The first part of the book includes 38 songs for use with children ages 2½ to 4; the second part has 39 songs for use in programs where adults and children of all ages gather together. Musical arrangements are given for all of the songs.

Marino, Jane, and Dorothy F. Houlihan. *Mother Goose Time: Library Programs for Babies and Their Caregivers.* H. W. Wilson, 1992. ISBN 0-8242-0850-1. Written with warmth, enthusiasm, and the knowledge that comes from conducting baby and toddler library storytimes for over ten years, this practical guide covers the why, who, what, when, and where of getting started, 150+ "baby-tested and toddler approved" rhymes classified by developmental stage and activity level, music arrangements for the rhymes, a short list of picture books to use in the programs, and a bibliography of additional resources.

Nichols, Judy. *Storytimes for Two-Year-Olds.* Illustrated by Lora Sears. American Library Assn., 1987. ISBN 0-8389-0451-3. How to plan toddler storytimes, with 33 thematic programs, including program notes, suggested crafts, and follow-up ideas for parents to pursue at home.

Nuba, Hannah, Michael Searson, and Deborah Lovitky Sheiman, eds. *Resources for Early Childhood: A Handbook.* Garland, 1995. ISBN 0-8240-7395-9. A collection of essays on topics in early childhood education, from language development to social policy issues, by notable theorists in the field.

Opie, Iona, and Peter Opie. *The Classic Fairy Tales.* Oxford Univ. Press, 1980. ISBN 0-19-520219-8

Painter, William M. *Musical Story Hours: Using Music with Storytelling and Puppetry.* Foreword by Spencer Shaw. Shoe String, 1989. ISBN 0-208-02205-8. Music can enhance traditional storytelling programs provided that the music is compatible with the stories in theme, mood, and tempo. The author draws on his extensive knowledge of classical music (though other forms of music are also discussed) and personal experiences to offer guidelines for matching stories and music. The book consists of sample musical story programs, arranged under 21 topics, with a quick reference list of the pairings of the stories and music discussed.

————. *Story Hours with Puppets and Other Props.* Shoe String, 1990. ISBN 0-208-02284-8. A clear and encouraging guide for anyone interested in combining puppetry and story hours.

Pellowski, Anne. *The Family Storytelling Handbook: How to Use Stories, Anecdotes, Rhymes, Handkerchiefs, Paper, and Other Objects to Enrich Your Family Traditions.* Illustrated by Lynn Sweat. Macmillan, 1987. ISBN 0-02-770610-9. The why and how of storytelling within the family, with over a dozen entertaining stories ready to tell.

————. *The Story Vine: A Source Book of Unusual and Easy-to-Tell Stories from Around the World.* Illustrated by Lynn Sweat. Macmillan, 1984. ISBN 0-02-770590-0. Step-by-step instructions for telling stories that require objects, such as string, picture drawing, dolls, or musical instruments.

————. *The Storytelling Handbook: A Young People's Collection of Unusual Tales and Helpful Hints on How to Tell Them.* Illustrated by Martha Stoberock. Simon & Schuster, 1995. ISBN 0-689-80311-7. Addressed to children and young adults who want to learn the art of storytelling, this handbook will also serve as a guide for librarians and teachers working with young tellers.

————. *The World of Storytelling.* H. W. Wilson, 1990. ISBN 0-8242-0788-2. An indispensable resource for the serious student of storytelling. This expanded and revised edition covers history, types of storytelling, format and style of telling, and the training of storytellers, with emphasis on the importance of knowing something about the culture from which a story comes. Includes an extensive bibliography.

Richey, Cynthia K. *Programming for Serving Children with Special Needs.* American Library Assn., 1994. ISBN 0-8389-5763-3. This helpful booklet offers guidance on personnel, facilities, programs, etc., to make libraries more user-friendly for children with emotional or physical disabilities.

Rosen, Betty. *And None of It Was Nonsense: The Power of Storytelling in School.* Postscript by Harold Rosen. Scholastic, 1988. ISBN 0-435-08464-X. An extraordinary teacher describes her use of storytelling to bring about positive change among groups of multi-lingual, multiethnic boys, ages 8 to 18, at a school in Tottenham, northern London.

Sawyer, Ruth. *My Spain: A Storyteller's Year of Collecting.* Viking, 1967. o.p.

————. *The Way of the Storyteller,* rev. ed. Viking Penguin, 1977. ISBN 0-14-004436-1

Sayers, Frances Clarke. "From Me to You" and "The Storyteller's Art." In Sayers's *Summoned by Books: Essays and Speeches,* pp. 93–98, 99–106. Viking, 1965. o.p.

Shannon, George. "A Telling Look at Pictures." In *A Knock at the Door.* Oryx, 1992, pp. 155–161. ISBN 0-89774-733-X

Shedlock, Marie. *The Art of the Story-teller,* 3rd ed. Dover, 1951. ISBN 0-486-20635-1

Sherlock, Philip. *West Indian Folk Tales.* Illustrated by Joan Kiddell-Monroe. Oxford Univ. Press, 1988. ISBN 0-19-274127-6

Smith, Lillian. "The Art of the Fairy Tale." In *The Unreluctant Years: A Critical Approach to Children's Literature.* Introduction by Kay E. Vandergrift. American Library Assn., 1991, pp. 34–53. ISBN 0-8389-0557-9

Stilley, Cynthia, comp. *Ring a Ring o'Roses: Finger Plays for Pre-School Children,* 9th ed. Flint (Mich.) Public Library, 1988. Over 375 finger plays (33 in Spanish), arranged alphabetically by title with subject and first-line indexes.

Stotter, Ruth. *About Story: Writings on Stories and Storytelling 1980–1994.* Stotter Press, 1994. ISBN 0-943565-09-X. Twenty-one short articles, ranging in topic from a thoughtful discussion of the storyteller's responsibility when telling stories from other cultures to the kinesic component of storytelling performance.

Sutherland, Zena. *Children and Books,* 8th ed. HarperCollins, 1990. ISBN 0-673-46357-5

Tashjian, Virginia A., comp. *Juba This and Juba That: Stories to Tell, Songs to Sing, Rhymes to Chant, Riddles to Guess, and More!* Illustrated by Nadine Bernard Westcott. Little, Brown, 1995. ISBN 0-316-83234-0. Originally published in 1969, this collection quickly became a popular handbook with librarians and teachers who tell stories to children.

Taylor, Denny, and Dorothy S. Strickland. *Family Storybook Reading.* Heinemann, 1986. ISBN 0-435-08249-3. Though this book is addressed to parents, librarians and teachers will find it invaluable reading.

Teale, William H. "Reading to Young Children: Its Significance for Literacy Development." In *Awakening to Literacy,* edited by Hillel Goelman, Antoinette Oberg, and Frank Smith. Heinemen, 1984. ISBN 0-435-08207-8

Travers, P. L. "Only Connect." In *Only Connect: Readings on Children's Literature,* 2nd ed. Edited by Sheila Egoff, G. T. Stubbs, and L. F. Ashley. Oxford Univ. Press, 1980. ISBN 0-19-540309-6

Trelease, Jim. *Hey! Listen to This: Stories to Read Aloud.* Penguin, 1992. ISBN 0-670-83691-5. Read-aloud chapters selected from 48 books, arranged by theme or genre, to share with children ages five to nine. Each selection begins with an introduction that includes something about the author and about the book itself. At the end of each chapter Trelease suggests related materials to pursue.

————. *The New Read-Aloud Handbook.* 2nd rev. ed. Viking, 1991. ISBN 0-14-046881-1. The importance of reading aloud to children, tips on how to engage the listener, and a treasury of stories to share.

————. *The Read-Aloud Handbook,* 4th ed. Viking, 1995. ISBN 0-14-046971-0

Trousdale, Ann M., Sue A. Woestehoff, and Marni Schwartz, eds. *Give Us a Listen: Stories of Storytelling in School.* National Council of Teachers of English, 1994. ISBN 0-8141-

1846-1. Seventeen teachers from elementary through university levels relate their experiences with storying in their classrooms in this excellent collection of essays. Each reader will find a favorite (mine was the one about a three-year-old's interaction with "Jack and the Beanstalk").

Velleman, Ruth A. *Meeting the Needs of People with Disabilities: A Guide for Librarians, Educators and Other Service Professionals.* Oryx, 1990. ISBN 0-98774-521-3

Yolen, Jane. *Touch Magic: Fantasy, Faerie and Folklore in the Literature of Childhood.* Putnam, 1992. ISBN 0-399-21897-1

Zipes, Jack. *The Complete Fairy Tales of the Brothers Grimm.* Bantam, 1987. ISBN 0-553-05184-9. Zipes's idiomatic English respects the nineteenth-century flavor of the tales. Storytellers will appreciate the informative introduction.

———. *Creative Storytelling: Building Community, Changing Lives.* Routledge, 1995. ISBN 0-415-91272-5. Zipes urges schools to invite and employ storytellers to stir children's curiosity about folktales. By understanding, comparing, and altering characters and themes, children in the fourth grade and above can adapt the folktales to their own experiences.

———. *Spells of Enchantment: The Wondrous Fairy Tales of Western Culture.* Viking, 1991. ISBN 0-670-83053-4. The introduction presents the developmental history and current critical theories of the literary fairy tale. The body of the book contains literary fairy tales by 67 European and American authors, from Apuleius to Jane Yolen.

Ziskind, Sylvia. *Telling Stories to Children.* Wilson, 1976. ISBN 0-8242-0588-X

ARTICLES

Birch, Carol. "Storytelling Programs for the Family." *National Storytelling Journal* 1 (Summer 1984): 14-18.

Blankenship, M. E., J. E. Lokerson, and K. A. Verbeke. "Folk and Fairy Tales for the Learning Disabled: Tips for Enhancing Understanding and Enjoyment." *School Library Media Quarterly* 17 (Summer 1989): 200-205.

Cullinan, Bernice E., Ellin Greene, and Angela Jagger. "Books, Babies, and Libraries: The Librarian's Role in Literacy Development." *Language Arts* (November 1990): 750-755.

Greene, Ellin. "A Peculiar Understanding: Re-creating the Literary Fairy Tale." *Horn Book* 59 (June 1983): 270-278.

———. "There Are No Talent Scouts . . . " *School Library Journal* 29 (November 1982): 25-27.

Haley, Gale E. "Caldecott Award Acceptance." *Horn Book* 47 (1971): 363-368.

Hays, May Bradshaw. "Memories of My Father, Joseph Jacobs." *Horn Book* 28 (December 1952): 385-392.

Iarusso, Marilyn Berg. "How to Promote the Love of Reading." *Catholic Library World* (March/April 1988): 212-218.

Kupetz, Barbara N. "A Shared Responsibility: Nurturing Literacy in the Very Young." *School Library Journal* (July 1993): 28-30.

L'Engle, Madeleine. "What is Real?" *Language Arts* 55:4 (April 1978): 447-451.

Lewis, Claudia. "The Pleasant Land of Counterpane." *Horn Book* (October 1966): 542-547.

Lipman, Doug. "In Quest of the Folktale." *Yarnspinner* 14:4 (June 1990): 1-3.

Mellon, Constance A. "Promoting Cross-Cultural Appreciation Through Storytelling." *Journal of Youth Services in Libraries* 5:3 (Spring 1992): 306–307.

————. "Reflections on Technology, Books, and Children." *Journal of Youth Services in Libraries* 7 (Winter 1994): 207-210.

Nesbitt, Elizabeth. "Hold to That Which Is Good." *Horn Book* 16 (January-February 1940): 7-15.

"Oral Tradition" Issue. *Parabola* 17 (August 1992).

Rovenger, Judith. "Learning Differences/Library Directions: Library Service to Children with Learning Differences." *Library Trends* 35 (Winter 1987):427-435.

"Storytelling and Education" Issue. *Parabola* 4 (1979).

Stallings, Fran. "The Web of Silence: Storytelling's Power to Hynotize." *National Storytelling Journal.* (Spring/Summer): 6-19.

Stone, Kay, and Donald Davis, "To Ease the Heart: Traditional Storytelling." *National Storytelling Journal* 1 (Winter 1984): 3-6.

Teale, William H. "Positive Environments for Learning to Read: What Studies of Early Readers Tell Us." *Language Arts* 55 (November-December 1978): 922-932.

Travers, P. L. "Grimm's Women." *New York Times Book Review*, November 16, 1975, p. 59.

Wendelin, Karla H., and Kathy Everts Danielson. "New Twists on Old Tales: A Ten." *CLA Bulletin* 18 (Spring 1992): 11-14.

Werner, Craig. "A Blind Child's View of Children's Literature." *Children's Literature* 12 (1984): 209-216.

Wilson, Anne. "Magical Thought in Story." *Signal* 36 (September 1981): 138-151.

Wolkstein, Diane. "Twenty-Five Years of Storytelling: The Spirit of the Art." *Horn Book* 68 (November-December 1992): 702-708.

BIBLIOGRAPHIES AND INDEXES

Ashliman, D. L. *A Guide to Folktales in the English Language: Based on the Aarne-Thompson Classification System.* Greenwood, 1987. ISBN 0-313-25961-5

Brewton, John E., and Sara W. Brewton. *Index to Children's Poetry.* Wilson, 1942. First Supplement, 1954; Second Supplement, 1965; Third Supplement, 1975. ISBN 0-8242-0021-7

Briggs, Katherine M. *An Encyclopedia of Fairies.* Pantheon, 1978. ISBN 0-394-40918-3

Cathon, Laura, ed. *Stories to Tell Children: A Selected List,* 8th ed. Univ. of Pittsburgh Press for Carnegie Library of Pittsburgh, 1974.

Coughlan, Margaret, ed. *Folklore from Africa to the United States: An Annotated Bibliography.* Library of Congress, 1976. o.p.

Eastman, Mary. *Index to Fairy Tales, Myths and Legends.* Faxon, 1926. Supplements 1 and 2, 1937, 1952. o.p.

Greene, Ellin, and George Shannon. *Storytelling: A Selected Annotated Bibliography.* Garland, 1986. o.p.

Haviland, Virginia. "Storytelling," "Folktales, Myths and Legends," and "Poetry and Children." In her *Children's Literature: A Guide to Reference Sources,* pp. 183–201, 201–226, 235–241. Library of Congress, 1966. Also in the first supplement to her *Children's Literature: A Guide to Reference Sources,* pp. 121–122, 123–132, and 134–136. Library of Congress, 1972. o.p.

Iarusso, Marilyn Berg, ed. *Stories: A List of Stories to Tell and Read Aloud,* 8th ed. The New York Public Library, 1990. ISBN 0-87104-625-3

Ireland, Norma Olin, comp. *Index to Fairy Tales, 1949–1972, Including Folklore, Legends, and Myths in Collections,* Third Supplement. Scarecrow Press, 1973. ISBN 0-8108-2011-0

————. *Index to Fairy Tales, 1973–1977, Including Folklore, Legends, and Myths in Collections.* Fourth Supplement. Scarecrow Press, 1985. ISBN 0-8108-1855-8

Ireland, Norma Olin, and Joseph W. Sprug, comps. *Index to Fairy Tales, 1978–1986, Including Folklore, Legends, and Myths in Collections.* Fifth Supplement. Scarecrow Press, 1989. ISBN 0-8108-2194-X

Leach, Maria, ed. *Funk & Wagnall's Standard Dictionary of Folklore, Mythology and Legend.* 2 vols. Harper San Francisco, 1984. ISBN 0-06-250511-4

MacDonald, Margaret Read. *The Storyteller's Sourcebook: A Subject, Title and Motif Index to Folklore Collections for Children.* Neal-Schuman, Gale Research, 1982. o.p.

Marantz, Sylvia, and Kenneth A. Marantz. *The Art of Children's Picture Books: A Selective Reference Guide.* Garland, 1988. ISBN 0-8240-2745-0

Rooth, Anna Birgitta. *The Cinderella Cycle.* Ayer, 1981. ISBN 0-405-13322-7

Shannon, George W. B. *Folk Literature and Children: An Annotated Bibliography of Secondary Materials.* Greenwood Press, 1981. ISBN 0-313-22808-6

Ziegler, Elsie B. *Folklore: An Annotated Bibliography and Index to Single Editions.* Faxon, 1973. ISBN 0-87305-100-9

SERIES

Folktales of the World, edited by Richard Dorson, consists of individual volumes of folktales from many countries, prepared by a noted scholar from that country. Published by the University of Chicago Press in the 1960s and 1970s.

The Oryx Multicultural Folktale Series, published by Oryx Press, contains four collections of variants of well-known tales accompanied by essays about the tale types. The series is designed for teachers and others who work with children in the middle and upper grades and includes: *Beauties & Beasts* collected by Betsy Hearne. Oryx, 1993. ISBN 0-89774-729-1; *Cinderella* collected by Judy Sierra. Oryx, 1992. ISBN 0-89774-727-5; *A Knock at the Door* by George Shannon. Oryx, 1992. ISBN 0-89774-733-X; *Tom Thumb* collected by Margaret Read MacDonald. Oryx, 1993. ISBN 0-89774-728-3.

The Pantheon Fairy Tale and Folklore Library contains volumes of tales from individual countries. Each volume is edited by a scholar in the area: A sampling includes *African Folktales* selected and retold by Roger D. Abrahams. 1983. ISBN 0-394-72117-9; *Afro-American Folktales* selected and retold by Roger D. Abrahams. 1984. ISBN 0-394-72885-8; *American Indian Myths and Legends* selected and edited by Richard Erdoes and Alfonso Ortiz. 1985. ISBN 0-394-74018-1; *Favorite Folktales from Around the World* edited by Jane Yolen. 1988. ISBN 0-394-75188-4; *Irish Folktales* edited by Henry Glassie. 1987. ISBN 0-394-74637-6; *Japanese Tales* edited by Royall Tyler. 1989. ISBN 0-394-75656-0; *The Norse Myths* edited by Kevin Crossley-Holland. 1981. ISBN 0-394-74846-8; *Norwegian Folk Tales* by Peter Christian Asbjornsen and Jorgen Moe. 1982. ISBN 0-394-71054-1; *Russian Fairy Tales* collected by Alexander Afanasyev. 1976. ISBN 0-394-73090-9.

World Folklore series, published by Libraries Unlimited and edited by Heather McNeil, consists of individual volumes about the folklore of a particular culture and includes photographs and background material. To date, the series includes: No. 1 *Folk Stories of the Hmong: Peoples of Laos, Thailand, and Vietnam* by Norma J. Livo and Dia Cha. Libraries Unlimited, 1991. ISBN 0-87287-8546; No. 2 *Images of a People: Tlingit Myths and Legends* by Mary Helen Pelton and Jacqueline DiGennaro. Libraries Unlimited, 1992. ISBN 0-87287-918-6; No. 3 *Hyena and the Moon: Stories to Tell from Kenya* by Heather McNeil. Libraries Unlimited, 1994. ISBN 1-56308-169-5; No. 4 *The Corn Woman: Stories and Legends of the Hispanic Southwest* retold by Angel Vigil. Translated by Jennifer Audrey Lowell and Juan Francisco Marin. Libraries Unlimited, 1994. ISBN 1-56308-1194-6; No. 5 *Thai Tales: Folktales of Thailand* retold by Supaporn Vathanaprida. Edited by

Margaret Read MacDonald. Illustrations by Boonsong Rokitasuke. Libraries Unlimited, 1994. ISBN 1-56308-096-6.

Garland Publishing is noted for its scholarly output. Its *World Folktale Library, Folklore Library, Folklore Casebooks,* and *Folklore Bibliographies* are indispensable to the serious student of storytelling. The Folklore Library consists of master's theses and doctoral dissertations of merit, which for one reason or another, were not published. Folklorist Alan Dundes is the series editor. *African Folktales with Foreign Analogues* by May Augusta Kupple, a bibliography of over 5,000 individual African folktales with parallels found in Europe and Asia, is just one example. For additional titles, see the Garland Folklore Catalog.

Several publishing houses focus solely on storytelling materials, among them August House and Yellow Moon Press. Older houses associated with library publishing, such as the American Library Association, Libraries Unlimited, Inc., R. R. Bowker, and H. W. Wilson, are adding more storytelling titles to their lists.

Stotter Press, P.O. Box 726, Stinson Beach, CA 94970, publishes an annual *Storyteller's Calendar,* which notes storytelling events and the birthdays of well-known storytellers. Each month is illustrated with a photograph of artifacts related to storytelling, such as the "Strong Women" quilt raffled at the Bay Area Storytelling Festival in 1993, "Storyteller" figurines from the Southwest, and Balinese masks.

STORYTELLING ASSOCIATIONS

There are two national storytelling associations: the National Storytelling Association (NSA, formerly NAPPS) and the National Story League (NSL).

The National Storytelling Association publishes the *National Directory of Storytellers* which, in addition to a state-by-state directory of professional storytellers, lists educational opportunities, festivals and other storytelling events, organizations and centers, and over 55 periodicals devoted to storytelling. NSA also publishes books and tapes on storytelling and a bimonthly magazine, *Storytelling.* NSA holds an annual storytelling festival in October and an annual conference during the summer months. For further information, write to National Storytelling Association, P.O. Box 309, Jonesborough, TN 37659.

The National Story League, established in 1903, is an organization of people who volunteer their services as storytellers in children's hospitals, nursing homes, churches, schools, and at community events. NSL holds a biannual conference during the third week in October. In alternate years the state leagues hold their conferences. The National Story League sponsors Junior Leagues to train young people ages 11 to 18 in the art and technique of storytelling. The league publishes *Story Art,* a quarterly magazine. For further information, write to Marion O. Kiligas, 259 E. 41 St., Norfolk, VA 23504.

Folk and Fairy Tales

COLLECTIONS

Aardema, Verna, reteller. *Misoso: Once Upon a Time Tales from Africa.* Illustrated by Reynold Ruffins. Knopf, 1994. ISBN 0-679-83430-3. Twelve *misoso* ("Once upon a time") tales from a variety of African cultures, with a glossary and illuminating note for each story, and a bibliography of sources. **[African]**

Baker, Augusta. *The Golden Lynx and Other Tales.* Lippincott, 1960, o.p. A selection of folktales from many lands.

Baumgartner, Barbara, reteller. *Crocodile! Crocodile! Stories Told Around the World.* Illustrated by Judith Moffatt. Dorling Kindersly, 1994. ISBN 1-56458-463-1. A children's librarian and professional storyteller has chosen six less anthologized folktales suitable for younger listeners and retold them as she would perform them. In addition to giving her story sources, she has included a section, "Bringing the Stories to Life with Stick Puppets."

Belpré, Pura. *The Tiger and the Rabbit, and Other Tales.* Lippincott, 1965. o.p. Folk tales from Puerto Rico. **[Puerto Rican]**

Bierhorst, John. *The Monkey's Haircut and Other Stories Told by the Maya.* Morrow, 1986. ISBN 0-688-04269-4. An unusual collection of folktales which includes myths, just-so-stories, witch stories, and animal tales. Contains an excellent introduction, sources, variants and bibliography. **[Mayan]**

————. *The Naked Bear: Folktales of the Iroquois.* Morrow, 1987. ISBN 0-688-06422-1. A skillfully edited collection of excellent stories for telling. **[Native American]**

————. *The Whistling Skeleton: American Indian Tales of the Supernatural.* Collected by George Bird Grinnell. Four Winds, 1982, o.p. Stories from the Pawnee, the Blackfeet, and the Cheyenne. The informative foreword deepens understanding of the traditions and customs of the three tribes. **[Native American]**

Bruchac, Joseph, reteller. *The Boy Who Lived with the Bears and Other Iroquois Stories.* Illustrated by Murv Jacob. HarperCollins, 1995. ISBN 0-06-021287-X. Six Iroquois stories retold by a Native American (Bruchac also recorded the tales on Parabola's Storytime Series) and illustrated by an award-winning Native American artist. **[Native American]**

————. *Flying with the Eagle, Racing the Great Bear.* Illustrated by Murv Jacob. BridgeWater, 1993. ISBN 0-8167-3026-1. **[Native American]**

Bruchac, Joseph, and Gayle Ross, retellers. *The Girl Who Married the Moon.* Illustrated by S. S. Burrus. BridgeWater, 1994. ISBN 0-8167-3480-1. These companion books (the first focuses on boys, the second on girls) each contain 16 coming-of-age stories from as many different Native American nations. The stories emphasize the need for courage and resourcefulness during the journey to adulthood. **[Native American]**

Bryan, Ashley. *Beat the Story Drum, Pum-Pum.* Retold and illustrated by Ashley Bryan. Simon & Schuster, 1987. ISBN 0-689-31356-X. African tales told with rhythm, humor, and vigor. **[African]**

————. *Lion and the Ostrich Chicks.* Illustrated by Ashley Bryan, 1996. ISBN 0-689-80713-9. Four stories that represent different African peoples—Masai, Bushman, Angola and Hausa. **[African]**

————. *The Ox of the Wonderful Horns and Other African Folktales.* Simon & Schuster, 1993. ISBN 0-689-31799-9. **[African]**

Caduto, Michael J., and Joseph Bruchac. *Keepers of the Animals: Native American Stories and Wildlife Activities for Children.* Illustrated by John K. Fadden. Fulcrum, 1991. ISBN 1-55591-088-2. **[Native American]**

————. *Keepers of the Earth: Native American Stories and Environmental Activities for Children.* Illustrated by John K. Fadden and Carol Wood. Introduction by N. Scott Momaday. Fulcrum, 1988. ISBN 1-55591-027-0. **[Native American]**

————. *Keepers of Life: Discovering Plants Through Native American Stories and Earth Activities for Children.* Illustrated by John Kahionhes Fadden and David Kanietakeron Fadden. Fulcrum, 1994. ISBN 1-55591-186-2. Companion volumes of Native American stories and activities that teach children respect for the environment and all living creatures. **[Native American]**

Carrick, Valery. *Picture Folk-Tales.* Dover, 1967. o.p. Ten short animal tales, including "The Crab and the Jaguar."

Chase, Richard. *Grandfather Tales.* Houghton, 1973. ISBN 0-395-06692-1. Tales collected from the southern Appalachian folk and retold with local idioms. **[North American/Appalachian]**

————. *Jack Tales.* Houghton, 1943. ISBN 0-395-06694-8. Appalachian tales centered around the character Jack. **[North American/Appalachian]**

Courlander, Harold. *Cow-Tail Switch and Other West African Stories.* Holt, 1947, 1988. ISBN 0-8050-0288-X. **[African]**

Courlander, Harold, and Wolf Leslau. *The Fire on the Mountain and Other Stories from Ethiopia and Eritrea.* Illustrated by Robert Kane. Holt, 1995. ISBN 0-8050-3652-0. An outstanding collection of sophisticated folktales, originally published in 1950 and out of print since 1968. **[African]**

Crossley-Holland, Kevin, ed. *British Folk Tales: New Versions.* Orchard, 1987. ISBN 0-531-05733-X. In the first comprehensive retelling in a long time, here are 55 stories of all types. Includes sources and a commentary for each tale. **[British]**

D'Aulaire, Edgar Parin, and Ingri D'Aulaire. *East of the Sun and West of the Moon: Twenty-One Norwegian Folk Tales.* Viking, 1969. o.p. **[Norwegian]**

DeArmond, Dal, reteller and illus. *The Boy Who Found the Light.* Sierra, 1990. ISBN 0-316-17787-3. Three traditional stories from Alaska: "The Boy Who Found the Light," "The Doll," and "The Raven and the Marmot." **[Inuit]**

Durrell, Ann, comp. *The Diane Goode Book of American Folk Tales & Songs.* Illustrated by Diane Goode. Dutton, 1989. ISBN 0-525-44458-0. Nine stories and seven songs from various regions and ethnic groups in the United States. **[North American]**

Fang, Linda. *The Ch'i-lin Purse: A Collection of Ancient Chinese Stories.* Illustrated by Jeanne M. Lee. Farrar, 1995. ISBN 0-374-31241-9. A collection of nine stories with substantial notes about the origins of the retellings and a pronunciation guide. **[Chinese]**

Faulkner, William J. *The Days When the Animals Talked: Black American Folk Tales and How They Came to Be.* Illustrated by Troy Stowell. Africa World Press, 1993. ISBN 0-86543-373-9. Slave tales as well as animal stories told without dialect. Introductions are a good base for the storyteller. **[African American]**

Finger, Charles. *Tales from Silver Lands.* Doubleday, 1924, 1965. Scholastic, 1989. ISBN 0-590-42447-5. Contains several chilling stories from South America that are excellent for the Halloween story hour. A Newbery Award book. **[South American]**

Gág, Wanda. *Tales from Grimm* and *More Tales from Grimm.* Coward, 1936, 1947. o.p.

Garner, Alan. *Alan Garner's Book of British Fairy Tales.* Illustrated by Derek Collard. Delacorte, 1985, o.p. Both familiar and unfamiliar folktales told and illustrated with strength and power. **[British]**

————. *A Bag of Moonshine.* Illustrated by Patrick James Lynch. Delacorte, 1986. Stories of boggarts and hobgoblins chosen from the folklore of England and Wales. **[English/Welsh]**

————. *The Lad of the Gad.* Philomel, 1981. o.p. Five Gaelic stories, four drawn from *Popular Tales of the West Highlands,* by J. F. Campbell, and one based on an Irish manuscript, "The Adventures of the Children of the King of Norway." **[British]**

Gatti, Anne, reteller. *Tales from the African Plains.* Illustrated by Gregory Alexander. Dutton, 1995. ISBN 0-525-452826. Twelve stories of wisdom collected from different cultural groups from Africa, told with humor. **[African]**

Greene, Ellin. *Midsummer Magic: A Garland of Stories, Charms, and Recipes.* Lothrop, 1977. o.p. (A limited number of copies are available from the author. To order, send a self-addressed mailing label and $15 in check or money order to Ellin Greene, 113 Chatham Lane, Point Pleasant, NJ 08742.)

Grimm, Jacob, and Wilhelm Grimm. *About Wise Men and Simpletons.* Translated from the German by Elizabeth Shub. Simon & Schuster, 1986. ISBN 0-02-737450-5 **[German]**

————. *The Brothers Grimm: Popular Folk Tales.* Newly translated by Brian Alderson. Illustrated by Michael Foreman. Doubleday, 1978. o.p. **[German]**

————. *Household Stories of the Brothers Grimm*. Translated from the German by Lucy Crane. Dover, 1986. ISBN 0-486-21080-4 **[German]**

————. *The Juniper Tree and Other Tales from Grimm*. Selected by Lore Segal and Maurice Sendak. Translated from the German by Lore Segal and Randall Jarrell. Farrar, 1973, ISBN 0-374-51358-9 **[German]**

Haley, Gail E., reteller. *Mountain Jack Tales*. Dutton, 1992. ISBN 0-525-44974-4. In a sly, colloquial style, the narrator, Poppyseed, relates nine adventures of Jack. Haley's background information and bibliography about the Jack tales will be of special interest to storytellers. **[North American/Appalachian]**

Hamilton, Virginia, reteller. *Her Stories: African American Folktales, Fairy Tales, and True Tales*. Illustrated by Leo Dillon and Diane Dillon. Scholastic, 1995. ISBN 0-590-47370-0. This stunning book "brings together narratives about females from the vast treasure store of traditional black folklore." The collection of 19 stories is divided into five sections: Animal Tales, Fairy Tales, Tales of the Supernatural, Folkways and Legends, and True Tales, with sources and notes. **[African American]**

————. *The People Could Fly: American Black Folktales*. Illustrated by Leo Dillon and Diane Dillon. Knopf, 1992. ISBN 0-679-84336-1. Twenty-four selections that represent the main body of American black folklore. Includes animal stories, John stories, and slave tales. **[African American]**

Harris, Christie. *Mouse Woman and the Mischief-Makers*. Atheneum, 1977. o.p. **[Native American]**

Harris, Joel Chandler. *Jump! The Adventures of Brer Rabbit*. Adapted by Van Dyke Parks and Malcolm Jones. Illustrated by Barry Moser. Harcourt-Brace, 1986. ISBN 0-15-241350-2. The adapters-retellers have eliminated the fictional character Uncle Remus and used standard English in this collection for younger children. **[African American]**

————. *Jump Again! More Adventures of Brer Rabbit*. Adapted by Van Dyke Parks. Illustrated by Barry Moser. Harcourt, 1987. ISBN 0-15-241352-9 **[African American]**

————. *Jump on Over! The Adventures of Brer Rabbit and His Family*. Adapted by Van Dyke Parks. Illustrated by Barry Moser. Harcourt, 1989. ISBN 0-15-241354-5. The second and third collections in this series maintain the same high quality as the first, both in narrative style and illustration. **[African American]**

Haviland, Virginia, ed. *The Fairy Tale Treasury*. Coward, 1972. o.p. Thirty-two of the best loved tales for young children.

————. *Favorite Fairy Tales Told Around the World*. Illustrated by S. D. Schindler. Little, Brown, 1985. ISBN 0-316-35044-3. A selection from the 16-volume series. Retold in simple language for children to read for themselves.

He, Liyi. *The Spring of Butterflies: And Other Folktales of China's Minority Peoples*. Translated by He Liyi. Edited by Neil Philip. Paintings by Pan Aiquing and Li Zhao. Lothrop, 1985. o.p. Traditional stories of the Tibetan, Thai, Uighur, and Bai peoples who live in China. **[Chinese]**

Jacobs, Joseph. *English Fairy Tales*. Dover, 1898. ISBN 0-486-21818-X **[English]**

Jaffe, Nina, reteller. *Patakin: World Tales of Drums and Drummers*. Illustrated by Ellen Eagle. Holt, 1994. ISBN 0-8050-3005-0. Ten folktales featuring drums, with notes, information about types of drums, and the historical importance of drums in the societies from which the stories come.

Jaffe, Nina, and Steve Zeitlin. *While Standing on One Foot: Puzzle Stories and Wisdom Tales from the Jewish Tradition*. Illustrated by John Segal. Holt, 1993. ISBN 0-8050-2594-4. Seventeen stories involving a riddle or question. **[Jewish]**

Jaquith, Priscilla, reteller. *Bo Rabbit Smart for True: Folktales from the Gullah*. Illustrated by Ed Young. Putnam, 1994. ISBN 0-399-22668-0. Hilarious stories told on the Sea Islands of

Georgia and South Carolina, using a modified version of a poetic, lilting pattern of speech. **[African American]**

Lang, Andrew. *Blue Fairy Book.* Edited by Brian Alderson. Dover, 1969. ISBN 0-486-21437-0

——. *Green Fairy Book.* Edited by Brian Alderson. Illustrated by Anthony Maitland. Dover, 1969. ISBN 0-486-21439-7

——. *Pink Fairy Book.* Edited by Brian Alderson. Illustrated by Colin McNaughton, Dover, 1966. ISBN 0-486-21792-2

——. *Red Fairy Book.* Edited by Brian Alderson. Illustrated by Faith Jacques. Dover, n.d. ISBN 0-486-21673-X

——. *Yellow Fairy Book.* Edited by Brian Alderson. Illustrated by Erik Blegvad. Dover, n.d. ISBN 0-486-21674-8

——. *A World of Fairy Tales.* Selected and introduced by Neil Philip. Illustrated by Henry Justice Ford. Dial, 1994. ISBN 0-8037-1250-2. Philip has chosen 24 of the lesser-known tales from Lang's 12-volume color fairy tale collections. The source of each story is given as well as the name of the fairy book from which it was taken. This beautiful edition, with the original artwork by Ford, is a treasure.

Lattimore, Deborah Nourse, reteller and illus. *Arabian Nights: Three Tales.* HarperCollins, 1995. ISBN 0-06-024585-9. Includes "Aladdin," "The Queen of the Serpents," and "The Lost City of Ubar." **[Middle East]**

Leach, Maria. *Whistle in the Graveyard: Folk Tales to Chill Your Bones.* Illustrated by Ken Rinciari. Puffin, 1982. o.p.

Lester, Julius. *How Many Spots Does a Leopard Have? And Other Tales.* Illustrated by David Shannon. Scholastic, 1989. ISBN 0-590-41973-0. A master storyteller retells ten African and two Jewish folktales. **[African/Jewish]**

——. *The Knee-High Man and Other Tales.* Dial, 1972, 1985. ISBN 0-8037-4593-1 **[African American]**

——. *The Tales of Uncle Remus: The Adventures of Brer Rabbit.* Illustrated by Jerry Pinkney. Dial, 1987. ISBN 0-8037-0271-X **[African American]**

——. *More Tales of Uncle Remus: Further Adventures of Brer Rabbit, His Friends, Enemies, and Others.* Illustrated by Jerry Pinkney. Dial, 1988. ISBN 0-8037-0419-4 **[African American]**

——. *Further Tales of Uncle Remus: The Misadventures of Brer Rabbit, Brer Fox, Brer Wolf, the Doodang, and Other Creatures.* Illustrated by Jerry Pinkney. Dial, 1989. ISBN 0-8037-0610-3 **[African American]**

——. *The Last Tales of Uncle Remus.* Illustrated by Jerry Pinkney. Dial, 1994. ISBN 0-8037-1303-7. Lester uses modified contemporary southern black English, "which is a combination of standard English and black English," and includes some contemporary references, such as shopping malls, in his spirited retelling of Uncle Remus tales, but the story lines have not changed. His introductions are *must* reading for the storyteller. **[African American]**

Lottridge, Celia Barker. *Ten Small Tales.* Illustrated by Joanne Fitzgerald. Macmillan/McElderry, 1994. ISBN 0-689-50568-X. Folktales from different cultures, suitable for telling to younger children.

MacManus, Seumas. *Donegal Fairy Stories.* Dover, 1968. ISBN 0-486-21971-2 **[Irish]**

Martin, Eva, and László Gál. *Tales of the Far North.* Dial, 1986. o.p. Twelve Canadian fairy tales, born of the marriage of French and English traditions. **[North American/Canadian]**

Manitonquat (Medicine Story), reteller. *The Children of the Morning Light: Wampanoag Tales.* Illustrated by Mary F. Arquette. Macmillan, 1994. ISBN 0-02-765905-4. Stories of the southeastern Massachusetts Wampanoag told in a colloquial style. **[Native American]**

Mayo, Margaret, reteller. *Magical Tales from Many Lands.* Illustrated by Jane Ray. Dutton, 1993. ISBN 0-525-45017-3. Fourteen tales from a variety of cultures, from Arabic to Peruvian, with source notes.

National Association for the Preservation and Perpetuation of Storytelling. *Best-Loved Stories Told at the National Storytelling Festival.* Introduction by Jane Yolen. National Storytelling Press, 1991. ISBN 1-879991-01-2. Published on the occasion of the twentieth anniversary of the National Storytelling Festival, founded by Jimmy Neil Smith, the 37 tales offer a sampler drawn from the hundreds of stories told over the years. Also see *More Best Stories Told at the National Storytelling Festival.* National Storytelling Press, 1992. ISBN 1-879991-09-8

Nic Leodhas, Sorche. *Heather and Broom: Tales of the Scottish Highlands.* Holt, 1960. o.p. **[Scottish]**

Norman, Howard, reteller. *How Glooskap Outwits the Ice Giants: And Other Tales of the Maritime Indians.* Illustrated by Michael McCurdy. Little, Brown, 1989. ISBN 0-316-61181-6. Six Glooskap stories. **[Native American]**

O'Brien, Edna. *Tales for the Telling: Irish Folk and Fairy Stories.* Illustrated by Michael Foreman. Puffin, 1988. ISBN 0-14-032293-0 **[Irish]**

Oodgeroo. *Dreamtime: Aboriginal Stories.* Illustrated by Bronwyn Bancroft. Lothrop, 1993. ISBN 0-688-13296-0. About half of the stories are based on the author's childhood memories of growing up on Stradbroke Island off the Queensland coast. The other half are aboriginal tales and new stories written in traditional aboriginal form. Both the author and artist are aboriginals. **[Australian/Aboriginal]**

Osborne, Mary Pope. *Mermaid Tales from Around the World.* Illustrated by Troy Howell. Scholastic, 1993. ISBN 0-590-44377-1. Twelve mermaid tales, mostly from tradition (an exception is Hans Christian Andersen's "The Little Mermaid"), with an author's note on sources and an artist's note on his approach to illustrating the stories.

Oxenbury, Helen, reteller and illus. *The Helen Oxenbury Nursery Story Book.* Knopf, 1992. ISBN 0-394-87519-2. An appealing collection of ten nursery tales, including such favorites as "Henny-Penny," "The Turnip," and "Goldilocks and the Three Bears."

Philip, Neil, reteller. *The Arabian Nights.* Illustrated by Sheila Moxley. Orchard, 1994. ISBN 0-531-06868-4. This handsome edition of a literary classic includes such favorites as "Aladdin" and "Ali Baba and the Forty Thieves." **[Middle East]**

————. *Fairy Tales from Eastern Europe.* Illustrated by Larry Wilkes. Houghton, 1991. ISBN 0-395-57456-0. Twenty-two stories from Eastern Europe and the former Soviet Union. **[Eastern Europe]**

Ransome, Arthur. *Old Peter's Russian Tales.* Viking, 1975. ISBN 0-14-030696-X **[Russian]**

Riordan, James. *The Woman in the Moon and Other Tales of Forgotten Heroines.* Illustrated by Angela Barrett. Dial, 1985. ISBN 0-8037-0194-2

Rockwell, Anne. *The Three Bears and 15 Other Stories.* HarperCollins, 1975. ISBN 0-690-00598-9

Ross, Gayle, reteller. *How Rabbit Tricked Otter and Other Cherokee Trickster Stories.* Illustrated by Murv Jacob. Foreword by Chief Wilma Mankiller. HarperCollins, 1994. ISBN 0-06-021285-3. Fifteen tales centered around Rabbit, retold by a descendant of John Ross, a chief of the Cherokee nation. **[Native American]**

Schram, Peninnah, reteller. *Jewish Stories One Generation Tells Another.* Jason Aronson, 1987. ISBN 0-87668-9675. **[Jewish]**

———, ed. *Chosen Tales: Stories Told by Jewish Storytellers.* Jason Aronson, 1995. ISBN 1-56821-352-2. Two outstanding collections by a master storyteller. The stories will appeal to a wide age range, from children to adults. **[Jewish]**

Schwartz, Alvin, reteller. *Scary Stories to Tell in the Dark.* Collected from American folklore. Drawings by Stephen Gammel. Harper, 1986. ISBN 0-397-31926-6. See other collections by this author.

Schwartz, Howard. *Elijah's Violin and Other Jewish Fairy Tales.* Illustrated by Linda Heller. Oxford Univ. Press, 1994. ISBN 0-19-509200-7 **[Jewish]**

Schwartz, Howard, and Barbara Rush, retellers. *The Diamond Tree: Jewish Tales from around the World.* Illustrated by Uri Schulevitz. HarperCollins, 1991. ISBN 0-06-025239-1. Fifteen familiar and unfamiliar Jewish tales from Africa, the Middle East, and Eastern Europe. **[Jewish]**

Serwadda, W. Moses. *Songs and Stories from Uganda.* Transcribed and edited by Hewitt Pantaleconi. Illustrated by Leo Dillon and Diane Dillon. World Music Press, 1987. ISBN 0-937203-17-3 **[African]**

Serwer-Bernstein, Blanche. *Let's Steal the Moon.* Illustrated by Trina S. Hyman. Shapolsky Pubs., 1987. ISBN 0-933503-27-X

Shannon, George, reteller. *More Stories to Solve: Fifteen Folktales from around the World.* Illustrated by Peter Sis. Greenwillow, 1991. ISBN 0-688-09161-X

———. *Still More Stories to Solve: Fourteen Folktales from around the World.* Illustrated by Peter Sis. Greenwillow, 1994. ISBN 0-688-04619-3. As in *Stories to Solve: Folktales from around the World* (Greenwillow, 1985) Shannon presents the tales in the form of challenging riddles.

Sherlock, Philip M. *West Indian Folk Tales.* Oxford Univ. Press, 1988. ISBN 0-19-274127-6 **[West Indian]**

Singer, Isaac B. *The Fools of Chelm and Their History.* Translated from the Yiddish by Elizabeth Shub. Illustrated by Uri Shulevitz. Farrar, 1973. ISBN 0-374-32444-1 **[Jewish]**

———. *When Shlemiel Went to Warsaw and Other Stories.* Illustrated by Margot Zemach. Farrar, 1992. ISBN 0-374-38316-2. Eight Yiddish tales, some traditional, some original. **[Jewish]**

Stoutenburg, Adrien. *American Tall Tales.* Puffin, 1976. ISBN 0-14-030928-4 **[North American]**

Vuong, Lynette Dyer. *The Brocaded Slipper and Other Vietnamese Tales.* Illustrated by Vo-Dinh Mai. Harper, 1992. ISBN 0-06-440440-4. Vietnamese variants of familiar folktales such as "Cinderella" and "The Frog Prince." **[Vietnamese]**

———. *The Golden Carp: And Other Tales from Vietnam.* Illustrated by Manabu Saito. Lothrop, 1993. ISBN 0-688-12514-X. Six fairy tales from the Vietnamese oral tradition, with source notes and a pronunciation guide. **[Vietnamese]**

Walker, Barbara K., reteller. *The Dancing Palm Tree and Other Nigerian Folktales.* Illustrated by Helen Siegl. Texas Tech, 1990. Reissue. ISBN 0-89672-216-3. Within each of these 11 tales from the Yoruba people there is a moral, for an important purpose of storytelling in Nigeria is to teach. Walker's excellent glossary provides insight into the culture. **[African]**

Walker, Paul Robert, reteller. *Giants!* Illustrated by James Bernardin. Harcourt, 1995. ISBN 0-15-200883-7. There is great variety in the type of giant stories in this collection, from the biblical story of David and Goliath to the Greek myth of the Cyclops and the nursery tale of Jack and the Beanstalk.

Williams-Ellis, Amabel, sel. *Tales from the Enchanted World*. Illustrated by Moira Kemp. Little, 1988. ISBN 0-316-94133-6. Twenty-two stories from around the world, some old favorites, others less well-known, chosen from earlier collections by Williams-Ellis, who died in 1984. A rich source for the storyteller.

Williamson, Duncan. *Fireside Tales of the Traveller Children. Twelve Scottish Stories*. Illustrated by Alan B. Herriot. Trafalgar, 1994. o.p. **[Scottish]**

Windham, Sophie, reteller. *Read Me a Story: A Child's Book of Favorite Tales*. Scholastic, 1991. ISBN 0-590-44950-8. Fifteen familiar nursery tales.

Wolkstein, Diane. *The Magic Orange Tree and Other Haitian Folktales*. Drawings by Elsa Henriqueg. Schocken, 1987. ISBN 0-8052-0650-7 **[Haitian]**

Yeats, W. B. *Fairy Tales of Ireland*. Selected by Neil Philip. Illustrated by P. J. Lynch. Delacorte, 1990. ISBN 0-385-30249-5. Twenty folk and fairy tales chosen from Yeats's *Fairy and Folk Tales of the Irish Peasantry* and *Irish Fairy Tales*, with a brief commentary on Yeats and notes about the stories. **[Irish]**

Yellow Robe, Rosebud. *Tonweya and the Eagles and Other Lakota Tales*. Illustrated by Jerry Pinkney. Dial, 1992. ISBN 0-8037-8973-4. Ten tales of the Lakota Sioux people. **[Native American]**

Yeoman, John. *The Singing Tortoise and Other Animal Folktales*. Illustrated by Quentin Blake. Tambourine, 1994. ISBN 0-688-13366-5. These 11 animal folktales capture the flavor of the cultures from which they come, from Tibet to Papua New Guinea. Some of the tales are hilarious, others are poignant. All are very tellable and will appeal to a wide age range.

Yep, Laurence, reteller. *The Rainbow People*. Illustrated by David Wiesner. HarperCollins, 1989. ISBN 0-06-026760-7. **[Chinese]**

———. *Tongues of Jade*. Illustrated by David Wiesner. HarperCollins, 1991. ISBN 0-06-022470-3. These companion volumes of traditional tales were brought to America and collected in the 1930s from Chinese immigrants living in Oakland, California. They are filled with magic and mystery. **[Chinese]**

Yolen, Jane. *Favorite Folktales from Around the World*. Pantheon, 1988. ISBN 0-394-75188-4. One hundred sixty tales from over 40 different cultures. Excellent introduction.

PICTURE-BOOK EDITIONS

Aardema, Verna. *Bimwili and the Zimwi*. Illustrated by Susan Meddaugh. Dial, 1985. ISBN 0-8037-0212-4. A tale from Zanzibar in which the little girl Bimwili outwits an ogre. **[African]**

———. *Borreguita and the Coyote: A Tale from Ayutla, Mexico*. Illustrated by Petra Mathers. Knopf, 1991. ISBN 0-679-80921-X. A clever little lamb outwits a hungry coyote. **[Mexican]**

———. *How the Ostrich Got Its Long Neck*. Illustrated by Marcia Brown. Scholastic, 1995. ISBN 0-590-48367-6. A *pourquoi* story from Kenya, reminiscent of "The Elephant's Child" by Rudyard Kipling. **[African]**

———. *Jackal's Flying Lesson*. Illustrated by Dale Gottlieb. Knopf, 1995. ISBN 0-679-85813-X. Clever Blue Crane rescues Mother Dove's babies by making Jackal think he can fly. **[South African]**

———. *Traveling to Tondo: A Tale of the Nkundo of Zaire*. Illustrated by Will Hillenbrand. Knopf, 1991. ISBN 0-679-80081-6. A comical tale about a civet cat traveling with friends to his wedding. Whenever unexpected delays take place, the friends agree to wait for each other. By the time the bridegroom arrives, the bride has married and has two kittens! The cumulative action and chantable refrain invite audience participation. **[African]**

————. *Who's in Rabbit's House?* Illustrated by Leo Dillon and Diane Dillon. Dial, 1979. ISBN 0-8037-9551-3. A humorous Masai tale for younger children. **[African]**

————. *Why Mosquitoes Buzz in People's Ears.* Illustrated by Leo Dillon and Diane Dilllon. Puffin, 1978. ISBN 0-8037-6089-2. **[African]**

Arnold, Katya, reteller and illus. *Baba Yaga.* North-South, 1993. ISBN 1-55858-208-8. With the help of a hungry gosling, young Tishka escapes from the witch Baba Yaga. Based on the story "Tereschichka," collected by Alexander Afanasyev. The illustrations by the Russian-born artist were inspired by traditional Russian *lubola* pictures, hand-colored wood engravings. **[Russian]**

Asbjørnsen, Peter C., and Jørgen E. Moe, *The Three Billy Goats Gruff.* Illustrated by Marcia Brown. Harcourt, 1991. ISBN 0-15-690150-1. **[Norwegian]**

Bang, Molly Garrett. *Wiley and the Hairy Man.* Adapted from an American folktale. Macmillan, 1976. ISBN 0-02-708370-5. How Wiley and his mother trick the Hairy Man. **[African American]**

Belpré, Pura, reteller. *Perez and Martina: A Puerto Rican Folktale.* Illustrated by Carlos Sanchez. Viking, 1991. Reissue (Warne, 1932). ISBN 0-670-84166-8. A favorite with Puerto Rican children, who recognize and appreciate the humor in the tragic romance between the beautiful cockroach Martina and the gallant mouse Perez. Also available in Spanish. ISBN 0-670-84167-6. **[Puerto Rican]**

Birdseye, Tom, reteller. *Soap! Soap! Don't Forget the Soap! An Appalachian Folktale.* Illustrated by Andrew Glass. Holiday House, 1993. ISBN 0-8234-10005-6. A much-loved tale from North Carolina about a boy who has trouble remembering and the hilarious situations he gets himself into as a result. **[North American/Appalachian]**

Brett, Jan, adapter and illus. *Goldilocks and the Three Bears.* Dodd, Mead, 1987. ISBN 0-399-22004-6. Adapted from *The Green Fairy Book* by Andrew Lang. **[English]**

————. *The Mitten: A Ukrainian Folktale.* Putnam, 1989. ISBN 0-399-21920-X. When too many forest creatures seek shelter in a mitten, they all tumble out onto the snow. **[Ukrainian]**

Brooke, L. Leslie, illus. *The Golden Goose Book.* Houghton Mifflin, 1992. ISBN 0-395-61303-5

Brown, Marcia, reteller and illus. *Once a Mouse.* Simon & Schuster, 1972. ISBN 0-684-12662-1. A fable from the Hitopadésa about big and little, set in India. **[Indian]**

Bruchac, Joseph, and Gayle Ross, retellers. *The Story of the Milky Way: A Cherokee Tale.* Illustrated by Virginia A. Stroud. Dial, 1995. ISBN 0-8037-1737-7. With the help of Beloved Woman, the people frighten away the spirit dog who has been stealing their cornmeal. The white cornmeal spills from the dog's mouth as he flees across the sky— and that is how the Milky Way came to be! **[Native American]**

Bryan, Ashley, reteller and illus. *The Cat's Purr.* Simon & Schuster, 1985. ISBN 0-689-31086-2. How Cat lost his drum and got his purr. **[West Indian]**

————. *The Dancing Granny.* Simon & Schuster, 1987. ISBN 0-689-71149-2. Granny Anika and Spider Ananse become dancing partners. **[West Indian]**

————. *Turtle Knows Your Name.* Simon & Schuster, 1989. ISBN 0-689-31578-3. Turtle helps a little boy remember his long name. As always, Bryan's storytelling is full of rhythm and vitality. **[West Indian]**

Climo, Shirley. *The Egyptian Cinderella.* Illustrated by Ruth Heller. HarperCollins, 1989. ISBN 0-690-04822-X. Set in Egypt in the sixth-century B.C.E., this mixture of fact and fable is one of the earliest versions of the Cinderella story. A falcon steals the tiny rose-red slippers of a Greek slave girl and carries them to the pharaoh. The pharaoh searches until he find Rhodopis, the beautiful owner, and makes her his queen. **[Egyptian]**

————. *The Korean Cinderella.* Illustrated by Ruth Heller. HarperCollins, 1993. ISBN 0-06-020432-X. Pear Blossom is helped by a frog, sparrows, and an ox, rather than by a fairy godmother, in the Korean version of a favorite tale. Children will enjoy discovering other parallels—a straw sandal substitutes for the glass slipper, a handsome young magistrate for the prince. **[Korean]**

Cole, Joanna, reteller. *It's Too Noisy!* Illustrated by Kate Duke. HarperCollins, 1989. ISBN 0-690-04735-5. A humorous story about a farmer's attempts to find quiet in his noisy cottage. **[Jewish]**

Compton, Patricia A., reteller. *The Terrible EEK: A Japanese Tale.* Illustrated by Sheila Hamanaka. Simon & Schuster, 1991. ISBN 0-671-73737-6. A funny cumulative tale that begins when an eavesdropping thief misunderstands the words "terrible leak" for "terrible eek." **[Japanese]**

Conover, Chris, reteller and illus. *Froggie Went A-Courting.* Farrar, 1986. ISBN 0-374-32466-2. A retelling of an Elizabethan nursery rhyme. **[British]**

Cooper, Susan, reteller. *The Selkie Girl.* Simon & Schuster, 1986. ISBN 0-689-50390-3. A fine retelling in words and pictures that captures the bittersweet quality of this ancient tale about a mortal man wed to a seal woman. **[Irish]**

————. *The Silver Cow: A Welsh Tale.* Illustrated by Warwick Hutton. Simon & Schuster, 1983. ISBN 0-689-50236-2. A story about the crafty greed of a farmer and the revenge of the magic people, the Tylwyth Teg. **[Welsh]**

————. *Tam Lin.* Illustrated by Warwick Hutton. Simon & Schuster, 1991. ISBN 0-689-50505-1. The last in the author's and artist's Celtic trilogy is a lyric prose retelling of the old ballad about a young girl who rescues a lad under the enchantment of the Elfin Queen. **[Scottish]**

Croll, Carolyn, reteller and illus. *The Three Brothers.* Putnam, 1991. ISBN 0-399-22195-6. A farmer offers the family farm to the son who can fill the barn by the end of the day. With the help of his imagination—and a candle—the youngest son succeeds. **[German/Latvian]**

Czernecki, Stefan, and Timothy Rhodes. *The Singing Snake.* Illustrated by Stefan Czernecki. Hyperion, 1993. ISBN 1-56282-399-X. Old Man said he would make a musical instrument in the shape of the creature with the most beautiful singing voice. To win the contest, Snake carefully swallows Lark so that when Lark sings it appears as if her song is coming from Snake. When Snake is found out, he hides in the grass, which is why people today call someone who can't be trusted "a snake in the grass." The instrument that Old Man made is called a didgeridoo. **[Australian]**

Dasent, George Webbe, trans. *East o' the Sun and West o' the Moon.* Introduction by Naomi Lewis. Illustrated by P. J. Lynch. Candlewick, 1992. ISBN 1-56402-049-5. The much-loved fairy tale about a girl and an enchanted white bear. **[Norwegian]**

Day, Nancy Raines, reteller. *The Lion's Whiskers: An Ethiopian Folktale.* Illustrated by Ann Grifalconi. Scholastic, 1995. ISBN 0-590-45803-5. A kind stepmother finds a way to win the heart of her new husband's son. For a different treatment of this Ethiopian folktale, see *Pulling the Lion's Tail* by Jane Kurtz. Illustrated by Floyd Cooper. Simon & Schuster, 1995. ISBN 0-671-88183-3 **[African]**

Dayrell, Elphinstone. *Why the Sun and Moon Live in the Sky.* Illustrated by Blair Lent. Houghton, 1990. ISBN 0-395-53963-3 **[African]**

deFelice, Cynthia, reteller. *The Dancing Skeleton.* Illustrated by Robert Andrew Parker. Macmillan, 1989. ISBN 0-02-726452-1. A funny ghost story about a deceased husband who tries to frustrate his wife's new romance. **[Native American]**

deFelice, Cynthia, and Mary DeMarsh, retellers. *Three Perfect Peaches: A French Folktale.* Illustrated by Irene Trivas. Orchard, 1995. ISBN 0-531-06872-2. The princess is very near death and only three perfect peaches can save her. A romantic tale told with tongue-in-cheek humor. **[French]**

deGerez, Toni. *Louhi, Witch of North Farm: A Story from Finland's Epic Poem the Kalevala.* Illustrated by Barbara Cooney. Viking, 1986. ISBN 0-670-80556-4. A vividly retold tale from "the Land of Heroes." **[Finnish]**

deGerez, Tree. *When Bear Came Down from the Sky.* Illustrated by Lisa Desimini. Viking, 1994. ISBN 0-670-85171-X. All the things that happened, including the first snowfall, when Sky Father let Bear visit Earth. An unusual myth that will appeal to younger children, told with simplicity and charm. **[Finnish]**

Demi, reteller and illus. *The Stonecutter.* Crown, 1995. ISBN 0-517-59864-7. A stonecutter learns wisdom when an angel grants his everchanging wish to be something else. **[Chinese]**

de Regniers, Beatrice Schenk. *Little Sister and the Month Brothers.* Illustrated by Margot Tomes. Lothrop, 1994. ISBN 0-688-05293-2. The 12 month brothers befriend little sister when her cruel stepmother and sister send her out to find strawberries in the snow. **[Czech]**

Ehlert, Lois, illus. *Moon Rope: A Peruvian Folktale/Un lazo a la luna: Una leyenda peruana.* Translated into Spanish by Amy Price. Harcourt, 1992. ISBN 0-15-255343-6. How fox ended up on the moon, told in Spanish and English. Illustrated with striking collages inspired by pre-Columbian artifacts. **[South American/Peruvian]**

Faulkner, William J., reteller. *Brer Tiger and the Big Wind.* Illustrated by Roberta Wilson. Morrow, 1995. ISBN 0-688-12985-4. When Brer Tiger refuses to let the other animals eat from the pear tree and drink from the spring during a time of famine and drought, Brer Rabbit devises a scheme to teach Tiger the importance of sharing. **[African American]**

Galdone, Joanna. *The Tailypo: A Ghost Story.* Illustrated by Paul Galdone. Houghton, 1984. ISBN 0-395-30084-3 **[African American]**

Galdone, Paul. *What's in Fox's Sack?* Houghton Mifflin, 1987. ISBN 0-89919-062-6. A retelling, for younger children, of an old English folktale. **[English]**

Gershator, Phillis, reteller. *Tukama Tootles the Flute: A Tale from the Antilles.* Illustrated by Synthia Saint James. Orchard, 1994. ISBN 0-531-06811-0. Through the power of his magic song, Tukama escapes from a two-headed giant who planned to have him for supper. **[West Indian]**

Gerson, Mary-Joan, reteller. *How Night Came from the Sea: A Story from Brazil.* Illustrated by Carla Golembe. Little, Brown, 1994. ISBN 0-316-30855-2. An African sea goddess brings the gift of night to the land of bright sunshine. **[South American]**

―――. *Why the Sky Is Far Away: A Nigerian Folktale.* Illustrated by Carla Golembe. Little, Brown, 1992. ISBN 0-316-30852-8. In the beginning the sky was close to earth and the people did not have to grow their own food. Anyone who was hungry could cut off a piece of sky and eat it. But there was one woman who was never satisfied. **[African]**

Goble, Paul, reteller and illus. *Adopted by the Eagles: A Plains Indian Story of Friendship and Treachery.* Simon & Schuster, 1994. ISBN 0-02-736575-1. When two Lakota friends fall in love with the same maiden, one turns treacherous and leaves the other to die. The deserted friend is rescued by eagles and returns to marry the maiden. **[Native American]**

―――. *Iktomi and the Berries: A Plains Indian Story.* Orchard, 1989. ISBN 0-531-05819-0 **[Native American]**

―――. *Iktomi and the Boulder: A Plains Indian Story.* Orchard, 1988. ISBN 0-531-05760-7 **[Native American]**

————. *Iktomi and the Buffalo Skull.* Orchard, 1991. ISBN 0-531-05911-1 **[Native American]**

————. *Iktomi and the Ducks: A Plains Indian Story.* Orchard, 1990. ISBN 0-531-05883-2. Four tales about the Plains Indian trickster Iktomi, told in a style that invites audience participation. **[Native American]**

González, Lucía M., reteller. *The Bossy Gallito/El Gallo de Bodas: A Traditional Cuban Folktale.* Illustrated by Lulu Delacre. Scholastic, 1994. ISBN 0-590-46843-X. This cumulative folktale is reminiscent of "The Old Woman and Her Pig." On his way to his uncle's wedding, a bossy little rooster cannot resist eating some corn near a mud puddle and dirties his beak. Only his friend the Sun can cause a chain of events that will make the grass clean his beak so he can go to the wedding. A bilingual picture book. **[Cuban]**

Greene, Ellin, reteller. *Billy Beg and His Bull.* Illustrated by Kimberly Bulcken Root. Holiday, 1994. ISBN 0-8234-1100-1. With the help of magical gifts from his bull, Billy Beg kills three multiheaded giants and a fiery dragon, and wins the hand of a princess. A male Cinderella tale. **[Irish]**

————. *Ling-Li and the Phoenix Fairy: A Chinese Folktale.* Illustrated by Zong-Zhou Wang. Houghton Mifflin, 1996. ISBN 0-395-71528-8. Ling-Li's beautiful wedding robe, made by her own hand, is stolen and torn into pieces, which become the flower known as impatiens. **[Chinese]**

Greene, Jacqueline Dembar, reteller. *What His Father Did.* Illustrated by John O'Brien. Houghton, 1992. ISBN 0-395-55042-4. Herschel, a raggedy vagabond, tricks an innkeeper into providing supper by threatening to do "what my father did when he was given no supper." After he has eaten everything the innkeeper can gather from the neighbors, Herschel tells her his father "went to bed with an empty stomach"! **[Jewish]**

Grimm, Jacob, and Wilhelm Grimm. *The Bremen Town Musicians.* Illustrated by Bernadette Watts. Translated by Anthea Bell. North-South, 1992. ISBN 1-55858-140-5. A simple but lively retelling of an old favorite. **[German]**

————. *The Devil and the Three Golden Hairs.* Retold and illustrated by Nonny Hogrogian. Knopf, 1983. ISBN 0-394-95560-9 **[German]**

————. *The Elves and the Shoemaker.* Retold and illustrated by Bernadette Watts. North-South, 1986. ISBN 1-55858-035-2. Another favorite with younger children. **[German]**

————. *The Frog Prince or Iron Henry.* Translated by Naomi Lewis. Illustrated by Binette Schroeder. North-South, 1989. ISBN 1-55858-015-8. Ideal for sharing in the picture-book hour. **[German]**

————. *Little Red Riding Hood.* Retold and illustrated by Trina Schart Hyman. Holiday House, 1983. ISBN 0-8234-0653-9 **[German]**

————. *The Seven Ravens.* Translated by Elizabeth D. Crawford. Illustrated by Lisbeth Zwerger. Simon & Schuster, 1991. ISBN 0-88708-092-8 **[German]**

————. *The Sleeping Beauty.* Retold and illustrated by Trina Schart Hyman. Little, Brown, 1983. ISBN 0-316-38708-8 **[German]**

————. *Snow White and Rose Red.* Retold and illustrated by Barbara Cooney. Delacorte, 1991. ISBN 0-385-30175-8. A newly designed edition of a book first published in 1965. Two loving sisters befriend a bear (a prince bewitched by a wicked dwarf) who, in turn, brings them good fortune. **[German]**

————. *Snow-White and the Seven Dwarfs.* Illustrated by Nancy Burkert. Translated by Randall Jarrell. Farrar, 1972. ISBN 0-374-37099-0 **[German]**

————. *The Wolf and the Seven Little Kids.* Illustrated by Felix Hoffman. Harcourt, 1959. o.p. **[German]**

Haley, Gail E. *Jack and the Bean Tree.* Crown, 1986. ISBN 0-517-55717-7 **[North American/Appalachian]**

————. *Jack and the Fire Dragon.* Crown, 1988. ISBN 0-517-56814-4. A dramatic picture-book version of the Appalachian story known as "Old Fire Dragaman" in *Jack Tales* by Richard Chase. **[North American/Appalachian]**

————. *A Story, A Story: An African Tale.* Simon & Schuster, 1970. ISBN 0-689-20511-2 **[African]**

Han, Suzanne Crowder, reteller. *The Rabbit's Escape.* Illustrated by Yumi Heo. Holt. 1995. ISBN 0-8050-2675-4 **[Korean]**

————. *The Rabbit's Judgment.* Illustrated by Yumi Heo. Holt, 1994. ISBN 0-8050-2674-6. Two folktales about a clever rabbit, from the author's collection, *Korean Folk and Fairy Tales.* Told in English and Korean. **[Korean]**

Hastings, Selina, reteller. *The Firebird.* Illustrated by Reg Cartwright. Candlewick, 1993. ISBN 1-56402-096-7. With the advice of his valiant horse, a brave lad wins the Princess Vasilisa. This simplifed retelling of the famous Russian tale is a pleasing introduction to the ballet. Another inviting picture book is *Firebird* (Putnam,1994) by Rachel Isadora, a former ballerina who used George Balanchine's version of the ballet as her inspiration. ISBN 0-399-22510-2 **[Eastern Europe]**

————. *Sir Gawain and the Loathly Lady.* Illustrated by Juan Wijngaard. Lothrop, 1985. ISBN 0-688-05823-X. "What is it that women most desire?" is the question that stumps King Arthur and his knights. A hideous lady has the correct answer but the price seems almost unbearably high. **[British]**

Heyer, Marilee. *The Weaving of a Dream: A Chinese Folktale.* Viking, 1986. ISBN 0-670-80555-6. A devoted and brave son retrieves his mother's beautiful tapestry, stolen by the fairies, and is justly rewarded. **[Chinese]**

Hodges, Margaret. *The Little Humpbacked Horse.* Farrar, 1987. ISBN 0-374-44495-1. Based on a story by the Russian writer Peter Pavlovich Yashov. **[Russian]**

Hong, Lily Toy, reteller and illus. *Two of Everything.* Whitman, 1993. ISBN 0-8075-8157-7. Mr. Haktak finds a pot that duplicates whatever is put into it. The Haktaks become rich, but then Mrs. Haktak falls into the pot! What will Mr. Haktak do? **[Chinese]**

Hooks, William H. *Moss Gown.* Illustrated by Donald Carrick. Houghton Mifflin, 1987. ISBN 0-89919-460-5. A traditional English tale which preserves elements of the King Lear story and "Cinderella," as told in the tidewater section of eastern North Carolina. **[North American]**

————. *The Three Little Pigs and the Fox.* Illustrated by S. D. Schindler. Macmillan, 1989. ISBN 0-02-744431-7. An Appalachian version of "The Three Little Pigs." **[North Amerian/Appalachian]**

Hort, Lenny, reteller. *The Fool and the Fish.* Illustrated by Gennady Spirin. Dial, 1990. ISBN 0-8037-0861-0. Based on Alexander Afanasyev's folktale about Ivan and a wish-granting fish. Ivan is so lazy that all he wants is to escape from work, but his wishes bring him unexpected good fortune and marriage to the tsar's daughter. **[Russian]**

Howe, John, reteller and illus. *Jack and the Beanstalk.* Little, 1989. ISBN 0-316-37579-9. More subdued and with more realistic illustrations than Kellogg's version, but equally satisfying. **[English]**

Ishii, Momoko, reteller. *The Tongue-cut Sparrow.* Translated from the Japanese by Katherine Paterson. Illustrated by Suekichi Akaba. Dutton, 1987. ISBN 0-525-67199-4. This retelling makes use of onomatopoeic words to bring out the pathos and humor of the much-loved folktale. **[Japanese]**

Jacobs, Joseph. *King of the Cats.* Illustrated by Paul Galdone. Houghton, 1980. ISBN 0-395-29030-9. A story for Halloween shivers. **[English]**

————. *Tom Tit Tot.* Illustrated by Evaline Ness. Scribner, 1965. o.p. The English variant of "Rumpelstiltskin." **[English]**

Jaffe, Nina, reteller. *Older Brother, Younger Brother: A Korean Folktale.* Illustrated by Wenhai Ma. Viking, 1995. ISBN 0-670-85645-2. The story of two brothers as different as day and night and of the swallow and magic gourds that bring each brother his just reward. **[Korean]**

Kellogg, Steven, reteller and illus. *Jack and the Beanstalk.* Morrow, 1991. ISBN 0-688-10250-6. The text closely follows that of its nineteenth-century collector, Joseph Jacobs, but Kellogg's energetic illustrations add much gusto to the old tale. **[English]**

Kimmel, Eric A., reteller. *Anansi and the Moss-Covered Rock.* Illustrated by Janet Stevens. Holiday, 1990. ISBN 0-8234-0689-X. When Anansi discovers a magic rock, he is able to trick the other animals out of their fruits and vegetables until little Bush Deer turns the tables on him and Anansi loses everything. (See other stories about Anansi by this author/illustrator team). **[African]**

————. *Hershel and the Hanukkah Goblins.* Illustrated by Trina Schart Hyman. Holiday House, 1989. ISBN 0-8234-0769-1. An original story based on Yiddish folklore about Hershel Ostropolier.

————. *The Three Princes: A Tale from the Middle East.* Illustrated by Leonard Everett Fisher. Holiday House, 1994. ISBN 0-8234-1115-X. A story from *The Arabian Nights* about a princess who was as wise as she was beautiful. **[Middle East]**

Knutson, Barbara. *Sungura and Leopard: A Swahili Trickster Tale.* Little, 1993. ISBN 0-316-50010-0. Sungura. the clever little hare, finds a way to save his family from the leopard with whom he shares a house. **[African]**

Kurtz, Jane, reteller. *Fire on the Mountain.* Illustrated by E. B. Lewis. Simon & Schuster, 1994. ISBN 0-671-88268-6. Challenged by his rich master to spend a night in the cold mountains alone and without shelter, Alemayu keeps himself alive by imagining the warmth of a distant fire. The master accuses the poor shepard lad of cheating because "looking at a fire on the mountain is the same as building a fire," but is shamed into honoring his promise. **[African]**

Lang, Andrew, reteller. *Aladdin and the Wonderful Lamp.* Illustrated by Errol Le Cain. Puffin, 1983. ISBN 0-14-050389-7 **[Middle East]**

Langton, Jane, reteller. *Salt: A Russian Folktale.* Translated by Alice Plume. Illustrated by Ilse Plume. Hyperion, 1992. ISBN 1-56282-178-4. Based on the folktale by Alexander Afanasyev. How Ivan the Fool discovers a mountain of salt, outwits his greedy brothers, and marries a beautiful tsarevna. **[Russian]**

Lee, Jeanne M. *Toad Is the Uncle of Heaven: A Vietnamese Folktale.* Holt, 1989. ISBN 0-8050-1147-1. How it came to be that one day the King of Heaven called an ugly toad "Uncle." **[Vietnamese]**

Levine, Arthur A., reteller. *The Boy Who Drew Cats: A Japanese Folktale.* Illustrated by Frédéric Clément. Dial, 1994. ISBN 0-8037-1172-7. Kenji's compulsion to draw cats saves his life when the cats come alive and battle with the Goblin Rat and its followers in the darkness of an abandoned temple. Key Japanese characters, their pronunciation and meaning are explained in a glossary. **[Japanese]**

Lewis, J. Patrick. *The Frog Princess: A Russian Folktale.* Paintings by Gennady Spirin. Dial, 1994. ISBN 0-8037-1623-0. The youngest son of the tsar, forced to marry a little green frog, discovers she is really a princess under an evil enchantment. **[Russian]**

Lottridge, Celia Barber, reteller. *The Name of the Tree: A Bantu Folktale.* Illustrated by Ian Wallace. Simon & Schuster, 1990. ISBN 0-689-50490-X. During a drought the animals hunger for the fruit "that smelled like all the fruits of the world," but it is on a tree too high for even the giraffe to reach. The tree will yield its fruit only to those who know its name. When Gazelle and Elephant fail to bring back the name from King Lion, it is determined little tortoise who makes the long journey and returns with the tree's name. **[African]**

McDermott, Gerald, reteller and illus. *Coyote: A Trickster Tale from the American Southwest.* Harcourt, 1994. ISBN 0-15-220724-4. Coyote's attempts to fly like the crows ends in disaster. A Zuni tale. **[Native American]**

———. *The Magic Tree: A Tale from the Congo.* Holt, 1994. ISBN 0-8050-3080-8. An unloved twin discovers a magic tree that brings him wealth and happiness, but when he forgets his pledge of silence, he loses everything. **[African]**

———. *Raven: A Trickster Tale from the Pacific Northwest.* Harcourt, 1993. ISBN 0-15-265661-8. Raven disguises himself as a human baby in order to steal the sun from the Sky God's house and bring light to the people of the world. **[Native American]**

———. *Zomo the Rabbit: A Trickster Tale from West Africa.* Harcourt, 1992. ISBN 0-15-299967-1. How Zomo the clever rabbit performs three impossible tasks set by the Sky God and earns wisdom. **[African]**

Maddern, Eric, reteller. *Rainbow Bird: An Aboriginal Folktale from Northern Australia.* Illustrated by Adrienne Kennaway. Little, 1993. ISBN 0-316-54314-4. Bird Woman steals Fire from Crocodile Man and puts it into the heart of every tree so that people can make fire from dry sticks and logs. Then she puts firesticks into her tail and becomes Rainbow Bird. **[Australian Aboriginal]**

Mahy, Margaret, reteller. *The Seven Chinese Brothers.* Illustrated by Jean Tseng and Mousien Tseng. Scholastic, 1990. ISBN 0-590-42055-0. The popular Chinese folktale of look-alike brothers who possess unique abilities. This retelling lacks the rhythm and humor of Claire Bishop's *The Five Chinese Brothers,* but avoids the stereotype images that made that book so controversial. **[Chinese]**

Marshak, Samuel, reteller. *The Month Brothers: A Slavic Tale.* Translated from the Russian by Thomas P. Whitney. Illustrated by Diane Stanley. Morrow, 1983. ISBN 0-688-01510-7. A traditional Czechoslovakian story about a little girl who sees all the 12 months of the year at once. **[Czech]**

Martin, Rafe, reteller. *The Rough-Face Girl.* Illustrated by David Shannon. Putnam, 1992. ISBN 0-399-21859-9. The Algonquin version of the Cinderella story. **[Native American]**

Mills, Lauren, reteller and illus. *Tatterhood and the Hobgoblins: A Norwegian Folktale.* Little, 1993. ISBN 0-316-57406-6. A girl with a mind of her own rescues her sister from the hobgoblins and proves the insignificance of appearances. **[Norwegian]**

Mollel, Tolowa M., reteller. *The Flying Tortoise: An Igbo Tale.* Illustrated by Barbara Spurll. Houghton Mifflin, 1994. ISBN 0-395-68845-0. This pourquoi tale from the Igbo people of southeastern Nigeria tells why the tortoise has a checkered shell. **[African]**

———. *The Orphan Boy.* Illustrated by Paul Morin. Houghton Mifflin, 1991. ISBN 0-89919-985-2. A star takes the shape of a young orphan boy in order to bring good fortune to an impoverished herdsman. As in "The Crane Maiden," curiosity leads to the revelation of the boy's true identity and the old man's loss. The boy returns to the sky where he appears as Venus, the morning star. A haunting story, beautifully told and illustrated. **[African]**

Mosel, Arlene, reteller. *The Funny Little Woman.* Illustrated by Blair Lent. Dutton, 1972. ISBN 0-525-30265-4. A woman who loves to laugh and to make rice cakes escapes from the wicked *oni* with a magic cooking paddle and becomes the richest woman in Japan. **[Japanese]**

Nunes, Susan, reteller. *Tiddalick the Frog.* Illustrated by Ju-Hong Chen. Simon & Schuster, 1989. ISBN 0-689-31502-3. When a giant frog drinks up all the fresh water in the world it is Noyang the eel who breaks the drought with his wild and wonderful dancing that makes Tiddalick laugh and release the water. **[Australian Aboriginal]**

O'Brien, Anne Sibley, reteller and illus. *The Princess and the Beggar: A Korean Folktale.* Scholastic, 1993. ISBN 0-590-46092-7. Exiled by the king for her disobedience, the "weeping princess" teaches the royal arts to her illiterate beggar husband and in the process regains her self-respect and that of her father. A feminist tale from the sixth century, retold by an American who spent most of her childhood in South Korea. **[Korean]**

Olson, Arielle North, reteller. *Noah's Cats and the Devil's Fire.* Illustrated by Barry Moser. Orchard, 1992. ISBN 0-531-05984-7. Why cats have eyes that gleam in the dark and fur that makes sparks. **[Rumanian]**

Ormerod, Jan, and David Lloyd, retellers. *The Frog Prince.* Illustrated by Jan Ormerod. Lothrop, 1990. ISBN 0-688-09568-2. This retelling of the familiar tale about an enchanted frog is based on the Grimm story and the English version known as "The Well of the World's End." **[German/English]**

Paterson, Katherine, reteller. *The Tale of the Mandarin Ducks.* Illustrated by Leo Dillon and Diane Dillon. Dutton, 1990. ISBN 0-525-67203-4. In this story of love and compassion, a pair of mandarin ducks repay the couple Yasubo and Skoza for their former kindness to the drake. **[Japanese]**

Percy, Graham, illustrator. *The Cock, the Mouse, and the Little Red Hen.* Candlewick, 1992. ISBN 1-56402-008-8. A favorite nursery tale with illustrations that capture all the humor and drama. **[English]**

Pitre, Felix, reteller. *Paco and the Witch: A Puerto Rican Folktale.* Illustrated by Christy Hale. Dutton, 1995. ISBN 0-525-67501-9. Paco must guess the name of the evil witch or be forever in her power. The storyteller's skill and the use of many Spanish words within the English text evoke a real sense of the land and culture of Puerto Rico. **[Puerto Rican]**

Poole, Josephine. *Snow White.* Illustrated by Angela Barrett. Knopf, 1991. ISBN 0-679-82656-4. Keeping to the plot, but not to the language of the Grimm's tale, Poole gives readers a more contemporary set of characters, providing a new look to an old story. **[German]**

Rogasky, Barbara. *The Water of Life: A Tale from the Brothers Grimm.* Holiday, 1986. ISBN 0-8234-0552-4. The youngest son finds the Water of Life and helps save his father. **[German]**

Root, Phyllis. *Coyote and the Magic Words.* Illustrated by Sandra Speidel. Lothrop, 1993. ISBN 0-688-10308-1. An original story based on southwestern Native American folklore that will have special appeal for storytellers. **[Native American]**

Ross, Gayle. *How Turtle's Back Was Cracked: A Traditional Cherokee Tale.* Illustrated by Murv Jacob. Dial, 1995. ISBN 0-8037-1728-8. When a wolf chokes to death on a persimmon, Turtle takes credit, convinced he is a mighty hunter. In revenge for Turtle flaunting "wolf spoons," the other wolves capture Turtle and mean to kill him. Turtle outwits his captors, but cracks his beautiful shell when the wolves throw him into the river and he lands on a rock. **[Native American]**

Roth, Susan L., reteller and illus. *The Story of Light.* Morrow, 1990. ISBN 0-688-08676-4. A pourquoi story inspired by a Cherokee tale that tells how Spider brought light to the animal people. **[Native American]**

Rounds, Glen, reteller and illus. *Three Little Pigs and the Big Bad Wolf.* Holiday, 1992. ISBN 0-8234-0923-6. Rounds's bold drawings and sparse text give this old tale an immediacy that will appeal to the K-3 crowd. **[English]**

San Souci, Robert D. *The Faithful Friend.* Illustrated by Brian Pinkney. Simon & Schuster, 1995. ISBN 0-02-786131-7. In this West Indian variant of Grimm's "Faithful John," set on the island of Martinique, an uncle hires three zombies to cast an evil spell over his niece and her betrothed. The emphasis throughout the story is on the friendship between two youths, one black, one white. **[West Indian]**

———. *Sukey and the Mermaid.* Illustrated by Brian Pinkney. Simon & Schuster, 1992. ISBN 0-02-778141-0. A mermaid befriends an unhappy girl in this haunting story from the Sea Islands, South Carolina. **[African American]**

Sawyer, Ruth. *Journey Cake, Ho!* Illustrated by Robert McCloskey. Puffin, 1978. ISBN 0-14-050275-0. The American variant of "The Gingerbread Boy." **[North American]**

———. *The Remarkable Christmas of the Cobbler's Sons.* Illustrated by Barbara Cooney. Viking, 1994. ISBN 0-670-84922-7. This story was first published in 1941 in Ruth Sawyer's *The Long Christmas* under the title "Schnitzle, Schnotzle, and Schnootzle." The story has been slightly changed, but this lovely edition is a treasure to share with younger children. **[Austrian]**

Sciezka, Jon. *The True Story of the Three Little Pigs,* by A. Wolf as told to Jon Scieszka. Illustrated by Lane Smith. Viking, 1989. ISBN 0-670-82759-2. The old nursery tale sounds entirely different when the wolf gives it his spin. A fractured tale for children already familiar with the traditional version.

Shannon, George. *The Piney Woods Peddler.* Illustrated by Nancy Tafuri. Greenwillow, 1981. ISBN 0-688-84304-2. An original tale that uses elements of traditional American swapping songs. **[North American]**

Shepard, Aaron, reteller. *The Gifts of Wali Dad: A Tale of India and Pakistan.* Illustrated by Daniel San Souci. Atheneum, 1995. ISBN 0-684-19445-7. A retelling of a story from Andrew Lang's *Brown Fairy Book* about a simple grass-cutter whose gift to a queen brings about an embarrassment of riches. **[Indian and Pakistani]**

Shute, Linda. *Momotaro, the Peach Boy: A Traditional Japanese Tale.* Lothrop, 1986. ISBN 0-688-05863-9 **[Japanese]**

Snyder, Dianne, reteller. *The Boy of the Three-Year Nap.* Illustrated by Allen Say. Houghton, 1988. ISBN 0-395-44090-4. A lazy boy gets more than he bargained for—a rich wife *and* a good job! **[Japanese]**

Steptoe, John. *Mufaro's Beautiful Daughters: An African Tale.* Morrow, 1993. ISBN 0-688-12935-8. An original story inspired by a folktale published in 1895 in Theal's *Kaffir Folktales.* **[African]**

Tadjo, Véronique, reteller and illus. *Lord of the Dance: An African Retelling.* HarperCollins, 1989. ISBN 0-397-32351-4. The Senufo people are known for their wood-carved masks that represent invisible spirits. In this poetic retelling the mask represents the Creator. **[African]**

Taylor, Harriet Peck, reteller and illus. *Coyote and the Laughing Butterflies.* Macmillan, 1995. ISBN 0-02-788846-0. "Even today butterflies remember the trick that was played on coyote. They flutter high and low, to and fro, laughing too hard to fly straight, all day long in the yellow sunshine." Based on a Tewa legend. **[Native American]**

Uchida, Yoshiko, reteller. *The Wise Old Woman.* Illustrated by Martin Springett. Simon & Schuster, 1994. ISBN 0-689-50582-5. An arrogant young lord decrees that everyone over the age of 70 must be taken into the mountains and left to die. But a septuagenarian is the only person able to solve the three impossible tasks that will save his village. **[Japanese]**

Whitney, Thomas P. *Vasilisa the Beautiful.* Illustrated by Nonny Hogrogian. Macmillan, 1970. o.p. The Russian Cinderella. **[Russian]**

Williams, Carol Ann. *Tsubu the Little Snail.* Illustrated by Tatsuro Kiuchi. Simon & Schuster, 1995. ISBN 0-671-87167-6. This ancient Japanese folktale has elements of "Tom Thumb," but the mood is spiritual with the emphasis on honoring the divine essence in every being. **[Japanese]**

Winthrop, Elizabeth, adapter. *Vasilissa the Beautiful.* Illustrated by Alexander Koshkin. HarperCollins, 1991. ISBN 0-06-021662-X. With the help of a magical doll given to her by her mother before her death, Vasilissa overcomes the witch Baba Yaga and marries a tsar. **[Russian]**

Wolkstein, Diane. *White Wave: A Chinese Tale.* Illustrated by Ed Young. Harcourt, 1996. ISBN 0-15-200293-6 **[Chinese]**

Yacowitz, Caryn, reteller. *The Jade Stone: A Chinese Folktale.* Illustrated by Ju-Hong Chen. Holiday, 1992. ISN 0-8234-0919-8. The emperor sends Chan Lo a perfect piece of jade from which to carve a dragon, but the artist listens to the stone and carves three carp. **[Chinese]**

Yagawa, Sumiko. *The Crane Wife.* Translation from the Japanese by Katherine Paterson. Illustrated by Suekichi Akaba. Peter Smith, 1992. ISBN 0-8446-6589-4. A man rescues a wounded crane and soon after marries an elegant stranger. Three times his wife weaves exquisite cloth but begs her husband not to watch. His curiosity brings about his sorrow when she resumes her crane shape and departs. **[Japanese]**

Yep, Laurence, reteller. *The Man Who Tricked a Ghost.* Illustrated by Isadore Seltzer. Bridgewater, 1993. ISBN 0-8167-3030-X. An amusing ghost story said to have been written down by an emperor of China in the third century A.D. **[Chinese]**

Yolen, Jane. *Tam Lin.* Illustrated by Charles Mikolaycak. Harcourt, 1990. ISBN 0-15-284261-6. A longer prose rendering of the ancient Scottish ballad with dramatic and romantic illustrations. (See also Susan Cooper's version.) **[Scottish]**

Young, Ed, trans. and illus. *Lon Po Po: A Red-Riding Hood Story from China.* Putnam, 1989. ISBN 0-399-21619-7. Three brave young girls outwit a wolf in this smooth retelling of the Red Riding Hood story, set in China. **[Chinese]**

Zelinsky, Paul O., reteller and illus. *Rumpelstiltskin: From the German of the Brothers Grimm.* Dutton, 1986. ISBN 0-525-44265-0 **[German]**

Zemach, Harve. *Duffy and the Devil: A Cornish Tale.* Illustrated by Margot Zemach. Farrar, 1973. ISBN 0-374-31887-5 **[Cornish]**

Zemach, Margot. *The Little Red Hen: An Old Story.* Farrar, 1993. ISBN 0-374-44511-7. The classic nursery story reinterpreted through humorous pictures.

Tall Tales, Fables, Myths, Legends, and Hero Tales

COLLECTIONS

Bader, Barbara. *Aesop & Company, with Scenes from His Legendary Life.* Etchings by Arthur Geisert. Houghton, 1991. ISBN 0-395-50597-6. This handsome edition of 19 favorite Aesop fables includes a scholarly introduction and facts and legends about Aesop's life. **[Greek]**

Belting, Natalie M. *Moon Was Tired of Walking on Air.* Illustrated by Will Hillenbrand. Houghton, 1992. ISBN 0-395-53806-8. Fourteen strikingly differerent myths from ten South American tribes. **[South American]**

Bierhorst, John. *Doctor Coyote: A Native American Aesop's Fables.* Illustrated by Wendy Watson. Simon & Schuster, 1987. ISBN 0-02-709780-3 **[Native American]**

————. *The Hungry Woman: Myths and Legends of the Aztecs.* Morrow, 1993. ISBN 0-688-12301-5. Contains an important and scholarly introduction that is background for the storyteller. **[Mexican]**

Clark, Margaret, reteller. *The Best of Aesop's Fables.* Illustrated by Charlotte Voake. Little, Brown, 1990. ISBN 0-316-14499-1. These 27 fables, with their morals left unsaid and their lively illustrations, will appeal to younger children. **[Greek]**

Cohn, Amy L. *From Sea to Shining Sea: A Treasury of American Folklore and Folk Songs.* Illustrated by 11 Caldecott Medal and four Caldecott Honor Book artists. Scholastic, 1993. ISBN 0-590-42868-3. American history connected through music and folklore. This outstanding anthology is divided into 15 chapters, each representing a period in American history and illustrated by a different artist. **[North American]**

Colum, Padraic. *The Children's Homer: The Adventures of Odysseus and the Tale of Troy.* Macmillan, 1982. ISBN 0-02-042520-1 **[Greek]**

Courlander, Harold. *The Crest and the Hide: And Other African Stories of Heroes, Chiefs, Bards, Hunters, Sorcerers and Common People.* Coward, 1982. o.p. Twenty legends collected by the noted folklorist. With notes and sources. **[African]**

d'Aulaire, Ingri, and Edgar d'Aulaire. *Book of Greek Myths.* Doubleday, 1980. ISBN 0-440-40694-3. **[Greek]**

————. *Norse Gods and Giants.* Doubleday, 1986. ISBN 0-385-23692-1. **[Scandinavian]** These reissued classics contain most of the famous gods, goddesses, mortals and animals that children find fascinating.

DeArmond, Dale. *Berry Woman's Children.* Greenwillow, 1985. ISBN 0-688-05815-9. Fables based on Eskimo myths and folklore. **[Inuit]**

Hamilton, Virginia. *In the Beginning: Creation Stories from Around the World.* Illustrated by Barry Moser. Harcourt, 1988. 0-15-238740-4. Hamilton's comments after each of these 25 myths reveal curious similarities.

Hazeltine, Alice. *Hero Tales from Many Lands.* Abingdon, 1961. o.p.

Heins, Ethel, reteller. *The Cat and the Cook: And Other Fables of Krylov.* Illustrated by Anita Lobel. Greenwillow, 1995. ISBN 0-688-12310-4. Twelve droll fables from the Russian writer (1768-1844) with notes on the fabulist and sources for this collection. **[Russian]**

Jaffrey, Madhur. *Seasons of Splendour: Tales, Myths, and Legends of India.* Illustrated by Michael Foreman. Puffin, 1992. ISBN 0-14-034699-6 **[Indian]**

Kanawa, Kiri Te. *Land of the Long White Cloud: Maori Myths, Tales and Legends.* Illustrated by Michael Foreman. Arcade, 1990. ISBN 1-55970-046-7. These authentic tales, based on the author's childhood memories, need the storyteller's voice to make them come alive. **[New Zealander]**

Leach, Maria. *How the People Sang the Mountain Up.* Viking, 1967. o.p.

Low, Alice. *The Macmillan Book of Greek Gods and Heroes.* Illustrated by Arvin Stewart. Macmillan, 1994. ISBN 0-689-71874-8. A fine interweaving of stories and characters. **[Greek]**

McCaughrean, Geraldine, reteller. *Greek Myths.* Illustrated by Emma Chichester Clark. Simon & Schuster, 1993. ISBN 0-689-50583-3. Sixteen epic stories, retold in a contemporary style suitable for telling or reading aloud. **[Greek]**

Osborne, Mary Pope, reteller. *American Tall Tales.* Wood engravings by Michael McCurdy. Knopf, 1991. ISBN 0-679-80089-1. Nine magnificent heroes, including Johnny Appleseed; Mose, the New York fireman; and a fantastic woman, Sally Ann Thunder Ann Whirlwind, stomp across the pages of this outsized book. **[North American]**

————. *Favorite Greek Myths.* Illustrated by Troy Howell. Scholastic, 1989. ISBN 0-590-413338-4. Twelve myths, their straightforward events enhanced by imaginative details, are followed by a list clarifying the roles of the deities and mortals, as well as useful word origins. **[Greek]**

Picard, Barbara Leonie, reteller. *French Legends, Tales & Fairy Stories.* Illustrated by Joan Kiddell-Monroe. Oxford Univ. Press, 1992. ISBN 0-19-274149-7. This fine collection of stories for older children includes four hero tales, six courtly tales of the Middle Ages, and 13 folktales or legends. **[French]**

————. *The Iliad of Homer.* Illustrated by Joan Kiddell-Monroe. Oxford Univ. Press, 1991. ISBN 0-19-274147-0. **[Greek]**

————. *The Odyssey of Homer.* Illustrated by Joan Kiddell-Monroe. Oxford Univ. Press, 1991. ISBN 0-19-274146-2. Distinguished retellings of these companion stories. **[Greek]**

Pyle, Howard. *The Merry Adventures of Robin Hood of Great Renown in Nottinghamshire.* Dover, 1968. ISBN 0-486-22043-5 **[English]**

————. *The Story of King Arthur and His Knights.* Dover, 1965. ISBN 0-486-21445-1 **[British]**

Quale, Eric, reteller. *The Shining Princess and Other Japanese Legends.* Illustrated by Michael Forman. Arcade, 1989. ISBN 0-55970-039-4. Among the ten stories in this collection may be found such storytellers' favorites as "The Tongue-cut Sparrow," "Momotaro—The Peach Warrior," and "The Matsuyama Mirror." **[Japanese]**

Robinson, Gail. *Raven the Trickster: Legends of the North American Indians.* Illustrated by Joanna Troughton. Atheneum, 1982. o.p. Nine unusual and tellable tales about the mischeivous "animal-god" of the early people of the northwest coast of the Pacific Ocean. **[Native American]**

San Souci, Robert D. *Cut from the Same Cloth: American Women of Myth, Legend, and Tall Tale.* Illustrated by Brian Pinkney. Putnam, 1993. ISBN 0-399-21987-0. All 15 female heroes in this collection are wily and bold, like Sal Fink, Sweet Betsey from Pike, Hiiaka (from Hawaii), and the others whose names are not well known. The introductory comments for each tale establish the geographical and literary contexts, and the 11 pages of folklore sources and bibliography at the end of the book are valuable for scholars. **[North American]**

Sawyer, Ruth. *Joy to the World: Christmas Legends.* Little, Brown, 1966. o.p.

Schwartz, Howard. *Next Year in Jerusalem: 3,000 Years of Jewish Stories.* Illustrated by Neil Waldman. Viking 1996. ISBN 0-670-86110-3. This outstanding anthology includes rabbinic and hassidic legends, folktales, fairy tales, and even a vampire story. Schwartz gives sources of the 11 stories, historical facts, and background. **[Jewish]**

Synge, Ursula. *The Giant at the Ford and Other Legends of the Saints.* Macmillan, 1980. o.p.

————. *Land of Heroes: Retelling of the Kalevala.* Macmillan, 1978. o.p. **[Finnish]**

Young, Ella. *The Tangle-Coated Horse.* Longmans, 1927. o.p.

PICTURE-BOOK EDITIONS

Barber, Antonio. *The Mousehole Cat.* Illustrated by Bayley Nicola. Macmillan, 1990. ISBN 0-02-708331-4. With his singing and purring, Mowzer the cat lulls the Great Storm-Cat so that the old fisherman Tom can bring in his boatload of fish for the starving townspeople. Based on a Cornish legend. **[Cornish]**

Begay, Shonto, reteller and illus. *Ma'ii and Cousin Horned Toad: A Traditional Navajo Story.* Scholastic, 1992. ISBN 0-590-45391-2. Ma'ii the Coyote eats his little cousin Horned Toad and claims Horned Toad's farm for his own. But Horned Toad plays tricks on Ma'ii from inside his stomach and makes him so uncomfortable that "even to this day, Ma'ii leaves his cousin Horned Toad alone." **[Native American]**

Bierhorst, John, reteller. *The Woman Who Fell from the Sky: The Iroquois Story of Creation.* Illustrated by Robert Andrew Parker. Morrow, 1993. ISBN 0-688-10680-3. After Sky Woman creates the natural world, she gives birth to two sons, Sapling and Flint. This unusual creation myth explains why "there are two minds in the universe, one that is hard like Flint and one that is gentle like Sapling." **[Native American]**

Bruchac, Joseph, reteller. *The Great Ball Game: A Muskogee Story.* Illustrated by Susan L. Roth. Dial, 1994. ISBN 0-8037-1539-0. The birds and animals play a stickball game to decide who is better. This legend from the Muskogee, or Creek, Indian Nation explains why birds fly south in winter. **[Native American]**

————. *The First Strawberries: A Cherokee Story.* Illustrated by Anna Vojtech. Dial, 1993. ISBN 0-8037-1331-2. When first man and first woman quarrel, the sun creates the sweet strawberry to bring the couple together again. **[Native American]**

————. *Gluskabe and the Four Wishes.* Illustrated by Christina Nyburg Shrader. Dutton, 1995. ISBN 0-525-65164-0. Four men, each with a different wish, are granted their wish (in startling ways), by Gluskabe, helper of the Great Spirit. A Native American Wabanaki teaching story. **[Native American]**

Calhoun, Mary. *Jack and the Whoopee Wind.* Illustrated by Dick Gackenbach. Morrow, 1987. ISBN 0-688-06137-0. Jack sets out to tame the wind. A tall tale. **[North American]**

Chaucer, Geoffrey. *Chanticleer and the Fox.* Adapted and illustrated by Barbara Cooney. Harper, 1982. ISBN 0-690-18561-8. The story of the proud cock and the wily fox. Adapted from "Nun's Priest's Tale" in *The Canterbury Tales.* **[English]**

Climo, Shirley, reteller. *Atalanta's Race: A Greek Myth.* Illustrated by Alexander Koshlein. Houghton, 1995. ISBN 0-395-67322-4. Raised by a bear after being abandoned by her royal father for not being the son he prayed for, Atalanta becomes a great hunter and athlete. **[Greek]**

Cohen, Caron Lee. *The Mud Pony.* Illustrated by Shonto Begay. Scholastic, 1988. ISBN 0-590-41525-5. In this hero story from the Pawnee Indians, a poor boy shapes a pony out of clay and cares for it as if it were real. In time of trouble the pony comes alive and helps the boy achieve greatness. **[Native American]**

Crespo. George. *How the Sea Began: A Taino Myth.* Houghton, 1993. ISBN 0-395-63033-9. The devoted parents of a missing hunter place his bow and arrows in a large gourd. The gourd provides fish, and when it is accidentally broken, tears flow out to form the sea. One of the few stories we have from the people first seen by Columbus. **[Puerto Rican]**

Cooper, Susan. *The Selkie Girl.* Illustrated by Warwick Hutton. Simon & Schuster, 1986. ISBN 0-689-50390-3. The Celtic legend of the marriage and parting of a seal maiden and her mortal husband.

de Poala, Tomie. *The Clown of God: An Old Story.* Harcourt, 1978. ISBN 0-15-219175-5. The author-illustrator has given the thirteenth-century story of the juggler of Notre Dame an Italian setting.

————. *The Legend of the Poinsettia.* Putnam, 1994. ISBN 0-399-21692-8. Lucinda, a child who has nothing else to offer, brings an armful of weeds to church for her Christmas gift. Miraculously, the weeds blossom into the flaming red stars of the poinsettia. **[Mexican]**

Emberley, Barbara. *The Story of Paul Bunyan.* Illustrated by Ed Emberley. Simon & Schuster, 1994. ISBN 0-671-88557-X **[North American]**

Esbensen, Barbara Juster, reteller. *Ladder to the Sky: How the Gift of Healing Came to the Ojibway Nation.* Illustrated by Helen K. Davie. Little, Brown, 1989. ISBN 0-316-24952-1. When an old woman disobeys the Great Spirit, sickness and death come into the world. Then the Great Spirit's helpers teach the people the healing power of herbs and flowers. **[Native American]**

———. *The Star Maiden: An Ojibway Tale.* Little, Brown, 1988. ISBN 0-316-24951-3. The origin of water lilies. **[Native American]**

Goble, Paul. *Buffalo Woman.* Simon & Schuster, 1984. ISBN 0-02-737720-2. The origin of the Buffalo dance. **[Native American]**

———. *The Great Race of the Birds and Animals.* Bradbury, 1985. ISBN 0-02-736950-1. This Cheyenne and Sioux myth explains how humans won power over the other animals and were made the guardians of creation. **[Native American]**

———. *Her Seven Brothers.* Bradbury, 1988. ISBN 0-02-737960-4. How the Big Dipper was created. A Cheyenne legend. **[Native American]**

———. *The Lost Children: The Boys Who Were Neglected.* Bradbury, 1993. ISBN 0-02-736555-7. A Blackfoot Indian legend about the creation of the constellation of the Pleiades. **[Native American]**

———. *Love Flute.* Bradbury, 1992. ISBN 0-02-736261-2. Among the Plains Indians, it was the custom for a young man to court the girl he wished to marry with a love flute. This is the story of the very first love flute, given to a shy young man by the birds and animals. **[Native American]**

Greene, Ellin, reteller. *The Legend of the Cranberry: A Paleo-Indian Tale.* Illustrated by Brad Sneed. Simon & Schuster, 1993. ISBN 0-671-75975-2. This bittersweet Lenape legend explains the demise of the mastodon and the origin of the cranberry. **[Native American]**

Haley, Gail E. *The Green Man.* Scribner, 1979. o.p. The legend of the lord of the forest. **[British]**

Harrell, Beatrice Orcutt, reteller. *How Thunder and Lightning Came to Be: A Choctaw Legend.* Illustrated by Susan L. Roth. Dial, 1995. ISBN 0-8037-1748-2. An amusing story about two foolish but lovable birds to whom the Great Sun Father gives the job of warning people of coming storms. **[Native American]**

Hastings, Selina. *Sir Gawain and the Green Knight.* Illustrated by Juan Wijngaard. Lothrop, 1981. ISBN 0-688-00592-6 **[British]**

Hodges, Margaret, reteller. *Brother Francis and the Friendly Beasts.* Illustrated by Ted Lewin. Scribner, 1991. ISBN 0-684-19173-3. Biography and legend combine for a good read-aloud. **[Christian]**

———, reteller. *The Golden Deer.* Illustrated by Daniel San Souci. Simon & Schuster, 1992. ISBN 0-684-19218-7. In this Jataka tale, Buddha, in the form of a deer, persuades the king to stop killing not only the deer, but all the animals. **[Indian]**

———. *The Hero of Bremen.* Illustrated by Charles Mikolaycak. Holiday, 1993. ISBN 0-8234-0934-1. The legendary knight Roland returns to help a lame cobbler become the hero of Bremen. **[German]**

———. *The Kitchen Knight: A Tale of King Arthur.* Illustrated by Trina Schart Hyman. Holiday, 1990. ISBN 0-8234-0787-X. A retelling of "The Tale of Sir Gareth of Orkney" from Malory's *Le Morte d' Arthur.* **[British]**

———. *Saint George and the Dragon.* Illustrated by Trina Schart Hyman. Little, Brown, 1984. ISBN 0-316-36789-3 **[British]**

————. *Saint Jerome and the Lion.* Illustrated by Barry Moser. Orchard, 1991. ISBN 0-531-05938-3. The story of Saint Jerome, translator of the Bible into Latin, and his friendship with a lion. **[Christian]**

Hutton, Warwick, reteller and illus. *Odysseus and the Cyclops.* Simon & Schuster, 1995. ISBN 0-689-80036-3

————. *Persephone.* Simon & Schuster, 1994. ISBN 0-689-50600-7

————. *Perseus.* Simon & Schuster, 1993. ISBN 0-689-50565-5

————. *Theseus and the Minotaur.* Simon & Schuster, 1989. ISBN 0-689-50473-X

————. *The Trojan Horse.* Simon & Schuster, 1992. ISBN 0-689-50542-6 Hutton's simplified but elegant retellings and expressive watercolors bring new life to these ancient Greek myths. **[Greek]**

Isaacs, Anne. *Swamp Angel.* Illustrated by Paul O. Zelinsky. Dutton, 1994. ISBN 0-525-45271-0. The amazing feats of Angelica Longrider, the greatest woodswoman in Tennessee. **[North American]**

Keats, Ezra Jack, reteller and illus. *John Henry: An American Legend.* Knopf, 1987. ISBN 0-394-99052-8. The heroic legend told in a simple, balladlike style. **[African American]**

Kellogg, Steven, reteller and illus. *Johnny Appleseed.* Morrow, 1988. ISBN 0-688-06417-5. The careful illustrations describe the gentle hero's life almost as well as the words in this unsentimental tale about the man who planted apple orchards as far west as Indiana. **[North American]**

————. *Paul Bunyan.* Morrow, 1992. ISBN 0-688-03849-2. Kellogg's energetic storytelling in words and paintings introduces this popular folk hero. **[North American]**

————. *Pecos Bill.* Morrow, 1986. ISBN 0-688-05871-X. A simplified telling of the tall tale that is part of our American heritage. **[North American]**

Kesey, Ken. *Little Tricker the Squirrel Meets Big Double the Bear.* Illustrated by Barry Moser. Viking, 1990. ISBN 0-670-81136-X. A wily squirrel outwits a big hungry bear in this Ozark tall tale. **[North American]**

Lagerlöf, Selma. *The Legend of the Christmas Rose.* Retold by Ellin Greene. Illustrated by Charles Mikolaycak. Holiday House, 1990. ISBN 0-8234-0821-3. See under Literary Fairy Tales: Single Editions. **[Swedish]**

Lester, Julius. *John Henry.* Illustrated by Jerry Pinkney. Dial, 1994. ISBN 0-8037-1606-0. Lester adds contemporary details and poetic similes in this wonderful retelling of the original legend. **[African American]**

Lobel, Arnold. *Fables.* Harper, 1980. ISBN 0-06-023973-5

Mikolaycak, Charles, reteller and illus. *Babushka: An Old Russian Folktale.* Holiday, 1984. ISBN 0-8234-0520-6. A classic Christmas story about an old woman's search for the Christ Child. **[Russian]**

Ober, Hal, reteller. *How Music Came to the World: An Ancient Mexican Myth.* Illustrated by Carol Ober. Houghton, 1994. ISBN 0-395-67523-5. The story of how the sky god and the wind god worked together to bring music to the world is illustrated with pre-Columbian Aztec and Mayan motifs. **[Mexican]**

Orgel, Doris, reteller. *Ariadne, Awake!* Illustrated by Barry Moser. Viking, 1994. ISBN 0-670-85158-2. Ariadne is at the center of this retelling of the Greek myth of Theseus and the Minotaur. **[Greek]**

Oughton, Jerrie, reteller. *How the Stars Fell into the Sky: A Navajo Legend.* Houghton, 1992. ISBN 0-395-58798-0. First Woman wanted to write the laws in the sky with her jewels so that all the people could read them. She accepted Coyote's offer to help, but Coyote was so impatient he tossed the jewels (stars) into the sky, shattering First Woman's careful patterns. That is why there is confusion in the world today. **[Native American]**

San Souci, Robert D., reteller. *The Samurai's Daughter: A Japanese Legend.* Illustrated by Stephen T. Johnson. Dial, 1992. ISBN 0-8037-1135-2. The brave heroine of this medieval legend slays a sea monster and restores the sanity of the deranged ruler who unjustly punished her father. **[Japanese]**

Sloat, Teri, reteller and illus. *The Eye of the Needle.* Dutton, 1990. ISBN 0-525-44623-0. This amusing tall tale about a hungry Eskimo boy who swallows some fish, a salmon, a seal, a whale, and a whole stream of water, delights young story-hour listeners. Based on a Yupik tale as told by Betty Huffman. **[Inuit]**

Stamm, Claus, reteller. *Three Strong Women: A Tall Tale from Japan.* Illustrated by Jean Tseng and Mou-sien Tseng. Viking, 1990. ISBN 0-670-88323-1. A new edition of a book first published in 1962. A grandmother, mother, and daughter teach Forever Mountain, the greatest wrestler in Japan, the meaning of true strength. **[Japanese]**

Steptoe, John, reteller and illus. *The Story of Jumping Mouse.* Lothrop, 1984. ISBN 0-688-01902-1 **[Native American]**

Stevens, Janet, reteller and illus. *Coyote Steals the Blanket: A Ute Tale.* Holiday House, 1993. ISBN 0-8234-0996-1. Coyote gets his comeuppance in this lively tale about the irrepressible trickster. **[Native American]**

Tanaka, Beatrice, reteller. *The Chase: A Kutenai Indian Tale.* Illustrated by Michael Gay. Crown, 1991. ISBN 0-517-58623-1. When Coyote sees Rabbit running, he thinks hunters are coming and begins running too, starting a chain reaction among the animals. A funny cumulative tale from the Pacific Northwest. **[Native American]**

Thomassie, Tynie. *Feliciana Feydra Le Roux: A Cajun Tall Tale.* Illustrated by Cat Bowman Smith. Little, Brown, 1995. ISBN 0-316-84125-0. When Grampa won't let her go alligator hunting with "all the men-children" in the family, Feliciana sneaks out to follow them and finds herself face-to-face with an alligator! This riotous tale about a spunky little girl is sure to please the picture-book crowd. **[North American]**

Van Laan, Nancy, reteller. *Buffalo Dance: A Blackfoot Legend.* Illustrated by Beatriz Vidal. Little, 1993. ISBN 0-316-89728-0. A different but equally satisfying rendering of the origin of the buffalo dance (see also *Buffalo Wife* by Paul Goble). Based on one of the earliest recorded versions of this myth. **[Native American]**

Waldherr, Kris. *Persephone and the Pomegranate: A Myth from Greece.* Dial, 1993. ISBN 0-8037-1191-3. A simple, straightforward telling of the familiar myth, to share with younger children. **[Greek]**

Yep, Laurence, reteller. *The Junior Thunder Lord.* Illustrated by Robert Van Nutt. BridgeWater, 1994. ISBN 0-8167-3454-2. In this retelling of a seventeenth-century Chinese tale, a young merchant befriends a huge man (the mortal shape of an exiled thunder lord) with a frighteningly hairy face. His kindness brings much-needed rain. **[Chinese]**

Young, Ed. *Seven Blind Mice.* Philomel, 1992. ISBN 0-399-22261-8. When seven blind mice meet a "strange Something," six come to the wrong conclusion about what he has found, based on partial information. Only the seventh mouse, who examines the whole creature, knows it is an elephant. This fable from India appeals to a wide age range, and Young's vibrant cut-paper artwork invites further exploration. **[Indian]**

Zeman, Ludmila, reteller and illus. *Gilgamesh the King.* Tundra, 1992. ISBN 0-88776-283-2

Literary Fairy Tales

COLLECTIONS

Andersen, Hans Christian. *Favorite Tales of Hans Andersen.* Translated from Danish by M. R. James. Checkerboard Press, 1988. ISBN 1-56288-253-8

————. *Hans Andersen: His Classic Fairy Tales.* Translated by Erik Haugaard. Illustrated by Michael Foreman. Doubleday, 1978. o.p. Eighteen favorite stories.

————. *Seven Tales by H. C. Andersen.* Translated by Eva Le Gallienne. Illustrated by Maurice Sendak. HarperCollins, 1959. ISBN 0-06-023790-2

————. *Twelve Tales.* Selected, translated, and illustrated by Erik Blegvad. Simon & Schuster, 1994. ISBN 0-689-50584-1

Babbitt, Natalie. *The Devil's Storybook.* Farrar, 1974. ISBN 0-374-31770-4

Banks, Lynne Reid. *The Magic Hare.* Illustrated by Barry Moser. Morrow, 1993. ISBN 0-688-10896-2. Ten unusual stories about a winsome hare.

Bianco, Margery Williams. *A Street of Little Shops.* Grigg Press, 1981. o.p. Delightful original stories set in a little country village in the 1920s.

Chaucer, Geoffrey. *Canterbury Tales.* Adapted, selected, and translated from Middle English by Barbara Cohen. Illustrated by Trina Schart Hyman. Lothrop, 1988. ISBN 0-688-06201-6. These four well-chosen tales offer a good introduction to Chaucer. Includes "The Nun's Priest's Tale," "The Pardoner's Tale," "The Wife of Bath's Tale," and "The Franklin's Tale."

Cummings, e. e. *Fairy Tales.* Harcourt, 1975. ISBN 0-15-629895-6

de la Mare, Walter. *Tales Told Again.* Faber, 1980. o.p. Nineteen classic fairy tales retold by a literary genius.

Farjeon, Eleanor. *The Little Bookroom.* Godine, 1984. o.p. The author's selection of the favorite of her own short stories for children.

Housman, Laurence. *The Rat-Catcher's Daughter: A Collection of Stories by Laurence Housman.* Selected by Ellin Greene. Atheneum, 1974. o.p.

Hughes, Richard. *The Wonder Dog: The Collected Children's Stories of Richard Hughes.* Morrow, 1977. o.p.

Kennedy, Richard. *Richard Kennedy: Collected Stories.* Illustrated by Marcia Sewall. HarperCollins, 1987. ISBN 0-06-023255-2. Sixteen stories for older children, originally published separately as picture books.

Kipling, Rudyard. *Just So Stories.* Illustrated by David Frampton. HarperCollins, 1991. ISBN 0-06-023294-3. A handsome edition with richly colored woodcuts in harmony with the tales.

————. *Just So Stories.* Illustrated by Safaya Salter. Holt, 1987. ISBN 0-8050-0439-4

Peretz, I. L. *The Seven Good Years and Other Stories of I. L. Peretz.* Translated and adapted by Esther Hautzig. Jewish Publication Society of America, 1984. o.p.

Perrault, Charles. *The Complete Tales of Charles Perrault.* Translated by Neil Philip and Nicolette Simborowski. Illustrated by Sally Holmes. Clarion, 1993. ISBN 0-395-57002-6. A new translation of all 11 of Perrault's tales, with an introduction and afterword by Neil Philip.

————. *The Glass Slipper: Charles Perrault's Tales of Times Past.* Translated by John Bierhorst. Illustrated by Mitchell Miller. Macmillan, 1981. o.p.

Pyle, Howard. *The Wonder Clock.* Dover, 1887, 1915. ISBN 0-486-21446-X. Twenty-four original stories in the tradition of folktales.

Sandburg, Carl. *More Rootabagas.* Collected and with a foreword by George Hendrick. Illustrated by Paul O. Zelinsky. Knopf, 1993. ISBN 0-679-80070-0. A Sandburg scholar has collected ten of the "many dozens" of unpublished "Rootabaga Stories."

————. *Rootabaga Stories.* Harcourt, 1951, 1988. ISBN 0-15-269061-1

Singer, Isaac B. *Stories for Children.* Farrar, 1984. ISBN 0-374-37266-7. Thirty-six tales chosen from former collections.

————. *Zlateh the Goat and Other Stories.* Illustrated by Maurice Sendak. Harper, 1966, 1984. ISBN 0-06-025698-2

Wilde, Oscar. *The Fairy Tales of Oscar Wilde.* Illustrated by Isabelle Brent. Introduction by Neil Philip. Viking, 1994. ISBN 0-670-85585-5. This edition, distinguished by its beautiful Persian-style artwork, includes all nine of Wilde's fairy tales for children.

————. *The Happy Prince and Other Stories.* Illustrated by Charles Robinson. Morrow, 1991. ISBN 0-688-10390-1. Part of the Books of Wonder series. Includes five stories, "The Happy Prince," "The Nightingale and the Rose," "The Selfish Giant," "The Devoted Friend," and "The Remarkable Rocket," with Robinson's famous illustrations.

Yolen, Jane. *The Girl Who Cried Flowers and Other Tales.* Crowell, 1974. o.p.

Zipes, Jack, ed. *The Outspoken Princess and the Gentle Knight: A Treasury of Modern Fairy Tales.* Illustrated by Stephane Poulin. Bantam, 1994. ISBN 0-553-09699-0. An anthology of stories by 15 modern writers, including Ernest Hemingway, Richard Kennedy, Jack Sendak, Catherine Storr, and Jane Yolen.

PICTURE-BOOK EDITIONS

Alexander, Lloyd. *The Fortune-Tellers.* Illustrated by Trina Schart Hyman. Dutton, 1992. ISBN 0-525-44849-7. An unhappy carpenter who consults a fortune-teller, and hears only what he wants to hear, achieves wealth and fame when he is mistaken for a fortune-teller himself.

————. *The House Gobbaleen.* Illustrated by Diane Goode. Dutton, 1995. ISBN 0-525-45289-3. Gladsake, a wise and cunning cat, teaches his master how to make his own luck instead of relying on "the Friendly Folk." An amusing story made even funnier by the droll illustrations.

Andersen, Hans Christian. *The Emperor's New Clothes.* Illustrated by Dorothée Duntze. Retold by Anthea Bell. North-South, 1986. ISBN 1-55858-036-0

————. *The Fir Tree.* Illustrated by Nancy Burkert. Harper, 1986. o.p.

————. *The Fir Tree.* Illustrated by Bernadette Watts. North-South Books, 1990. ISBN 1-55858-093-X

————. *The Nightingale.* Translated from the Danish by Eva Le Gallienne. Illustrated by Nancy Burkert. Harper, 1965. ISBN 0-06-443070-7

————. *The Nightingale.* Translated by Anthea Bell. Illustrated by Lisbeth Zwerger. Simon & Schuster, 1991. ISBN 0-907234-57-7

————. *The Princess and the Pea.* Illustrated by Dorothée Duntze. North-South, 1985. ISBN 1-55858-034-4

————. *The Steadfast Tin Soldier.* Illustrated by Marcia Brown. Scribner, 1953. o.p.

————. *The Steadfast Tin Soldier.* Translated by Naomi Lewis. Illustrated by P. J. Lynch. Harcourt, 1992. ISBN 0-15-200599-4

————. *The Swineherd.* Translated from the Danish by Anthea Bell. Illustrated by Lizbeth Zwerger. North-South, 1995. ISBN 1-55858-428-5

————. *The Swineherd.* Translated by Naomi Lewis. Illustrated by Dorothee Duntze. Holt, 1987. o.p.

————. *Thumbelina.* Retold by Amy Ehrlich. Illustrated by Susan Jeffers. Dial, 1979. o.p.

————. *The Tinderbox.* Illustrated by Warwick Hutton. Simon & Schuster, 1988. ISBN 0-689-50458-6

————. *The Ugly Duckling.* Retold by Lilian Moore. Illustrated by Daniel San Souci. Scholastic, 1987. ISBN 0-590-40957-3.

————. *The Wild Swans.* Illustrated by Marcia Brown. Scribner, 1963. o.p.

————. *The Wild Swans.* Retold by Amy Ehrlich. Illustrated by Susan Jeffers. Dial, 1987. ISBN 0-8037-9381-2

Chekov, Anton. *Kashtanka.* Adapted from a new translation by Ronald Meyer. Illustrated by Gennady Spirin. Harcourt, 1995. ISBN 0-15-200539-0. Kashtanka, a young chestnut-colored dog, becomes separated from her master during a heavy snowfall. She is adopted by a kindhearted circus clown and learns to perform in his act. On opening night there is a wonderful surprise and Kashtanka is reunited with her family. Spirin's paintings are a perfect match for this heartwarming story. A good read-aloud.

de la Mare, Walter, reteller. *The Turnip.* Illustrated by Kevin Hawkes. Godine, 1992. ISBN 0-87923-934-4. Not the familiar Russian nursery tale, but a story from Grimm about two brothers, one kind and generous, the other selfish and greedy, and how their lives are changed by a turnip.

French, Fiona. *Anancy and Mr. Dry-Bone.* Little, Brown, 1991. ISBN 0-316-29298-2. This original trickster tale based on characters from African and Caribbean folklore is told in street-smart, jazzy language.

Gogol, Nikolai. *The Nose.* As retold for children by Catherine Cowan. Illustrated by Kevin Hawkes. Lothrop, 1994. ISBN 0-688-10464-9. The high-spirited words and pictures make a romp of Gogol's absurd satire about a nose with a life of its own.

Goldin, Barbara Diamond. *The Magician's Visit: A Passover Tale.* Illustrated by Robert Andrew Parker. Viking, 1993. ISBN 0-670-84840-9. Adapted from a story by I. L. Peretz.

Gregory, Valiska. *Through the Mickle Woods.* Illustrated by Barry Moser. Little, Brown, 1992. ISBN 0-316-32779-4. A king honors his dying queen's last request: "Into the dark and mickle woods go forth to find the bear. . ." And the bear gives him three stories that both sadden and help to heal him. A picture storybook for older readers.

Hodges, Margaret. *Gulliver in Lilliput.* Retold by Margaret Hodges from *Gulliver's Travels* by Jonathan Swift. Illustrated by Kimberly Bulcken Root. Holiday, 1995. ISBN 0-8234-1147-8. Hodges retells Part I as Gulliver might have told the first of his adventures to children. Root's marvelous watercolor paintings are as riveting as the tale.

Kipling, Rudyard. *The Elephant's Child.* North-South, 1995. ISBN 1-55858-369-6

Lagerlöf, Selma. *The Legend of the Christmas Rose.* Retold by Ellin Greene. Illustrated by Charles Mikolaycak. Holiday, 1990. ISBN 0-8234-0821-3. Once, long ago in Sweden, there was a garden that bloomed every Christmas Eve in remembrance of the Christ Child. The garden was destroyed by evil in the human heart, but a bulb was rescued and from it grew the flower we call the Christmas Rose. Based on Swedish folklore and written by the first woman to receive the Nobel Prize for Literature.

LeGuin, Ursula K. *A Ride on the Red Mare's Back.* Illustrated by Julie Downing. Orchard, 1992. ISBN 0-531-05991-X. With the help of an inspired toy horse, a girl rescues her younger brother from trolls. A journey story reminiscent of Hans Christian Andersen's story "The Snow Queen."

MacDonald, George. *Little Daylight.* Adapted by Anthea Bell. Illustrated by Dorothee Duntze. North-South, 1987. ISBN 0-200-72912-8. The princess is doomed to wax and wane with the cycles of the moon until she is kissed by a prince who does not know who she is.

Peretz, I. L. *The Magician.* Illustrated by Uri Shulevitz. Macmillan, 1985. ISBN 0-02-782770-4

Perrault, Charles. *Cinderella, or the Little Glass Slipper.* Illustrated by Marcia Brown. Simon & Schuster, 1971. ISBN 0-684-12676-1

———. *Puss in Boots.* Translated by Malcolm Arthur. Illustrated by Fred Marcellino. Farrar, 1990. ISBN 0-374-36160-6

Pyle, Howard. *King Stork.* Illustrated by Trina Schart Hyman. Little, Brown, 1973, 1986. o.p.

Ray, Jane. *The Happy Prince.* Dutton, 1994. ISBN 0-525-45367-9. An abridged version of Oscar Wilde's fairy tale, with shimmering illustrations.

Stockton, Frank R. *The Bee Man of Orn.* Illustrated by Maurice Sendak. Harper, 1964, 1986. ISBN 0-06-025818-7. The Bee Man sets out to find his original form and has many adventures.

———. *The Griffin and the Minor Canon.* Illustrated by Maurice Sendak. Harper, 1963, 1986. ISBN 0-06-025816-0. Middle-grade children will enjoy this highly imaginative story.

Thurber, James. *The Great Quillow.* Illustrated by Steven Kellogg. Harcourt, 1994. ISBN 0-15-232544-1. Kellogg's ebullient paintings are a perfect match for Thurber's story about a clever toymaker who outwits a giant.

———. *Many Moons.* Illustrated by Marc Simont. Harcourt, 1990. ISBN 0-15-251872-X. First published in 1943 with pictures by Louis Slobodkin for which he received the 1944 Caldecott Medal. This new edition has been illustrated with charming pastel watercolors by an artist who knew Thurber personally and has included him in one of the drawings.

———. *Many Moons.* Illustrated by Louis Slobodkin. Harcourt, 1943. ISBN 0-15-251873-8

Walter, Mildred Pitts. *Brother to the Wind.* Illustrated by Diane Dillon and Leo Dillon. Lothrop, 1985. ISBN 0-688-03812-3. An original story that draws on many beliefs and symbols of the African culture.

Wilde, Oscar. *The Happy Prince.* Illustrated by Ed Young. Simon & Schuster, 1992. ISBN 0-671-77819-6. The complete text with exquisite impressionistic artwork.

———. *The Nightingale and the Rose.* Illustrated by Freire Wright and Michael Foreman. Oxford, 1981. ISBN 0-19-520231-7

Willard, Nancy. *The Sorcerer's Apprentice.* Illustrated by Leo Dillon and Diane Dillon. Scholastic, 1993. ISBN 0-590-473298. This modern version of the magical tale is told in rhyming text and features a contemporary heroine.

Yolen, Jane. *The Girl in the Golden Bower.* Illustrated by Jane Dyer. Little, Brown, 1994. ISBN 0-316-96894-3. A sorceress obsessed with finding a powerful charm does not know that a little girl possesses it—a brown comb that shimmers for a moment as the child puts it into her hair, and then turns to gold. And "no one could tell where the hair ended and the comb began."

———. *The Sleeping Beauty.* Illustrated by Ruth Sanderson. Knopf, 1986. ISBN 0-394-55433-7. A beautiful retelling of a classic love story.

Poetry and Song

Adoff, Arnold. *The Poetry of Black America: Anthology of the Twentieth Century.* Introduction by Gwendolyn Brooks. Harper, 1973. o.p.

Bauer, Caroline Feller. *Rainy Day: Stories and Poems.* Harper, 1986. ISBN 0-397-32105-8

———. *Snowy Day: Stories and Poems.* Harper, 1986. ISBN 0-397-32177-5

Begay, Shonto. *Navajo: Visions and Voices Across the Mesa.* Scholastic, 1995. ISBN 0-590-46153-2. Begay has written original poetry and prose to accompany 20 of his painting to make a portrait of Navajo life. The result is a stunning, moving experience.

Berry, James. *When I Dance.* Illustrated by Karen Barbour. Harcourt, 1991. ISBN 0-15-295568-2. A collection of poems for young people by the celebrated Jamaican poet. The poems reflect two cultures: the rural Caribbean and inner-city life in Britain.

Bierhorst, John, comp. *On the Road of Stars: Native American Night Poems and Sleep Charms.* Illustrated by Judy Pederson. Macmillan, 1994. ISBN 0-02-709735-8. Lullabies and poems to bring good dreams.

————. *The Sacred Path: Spells, Prayers and Power Songs of the American Indians.* Morrow, 1983. ISBN 0-688-01699-5

Bober, Natalie S. *Let's Pretend: Poems of Flight and Fancy.* Illustrated by Bill Bell. Viking, 1986. ISBN 0-14-032132-2

Bodecker, N. M. *Hurry Hurry, Mary Dear! And Other Nonsense Poems.* Simon & Schuster, 1976. ISBN 0-689-50066-1. Nonsense poems that reflect a variety of moods from wistful to ridiculous.

Bontemps, Arna. *Hold Fast to Your Dreams.* Follett, 1969. o.p.

Booth, David, comp. *Til All the Stars Have Fallen: A Collection of Poems for Children.* Illustrated by Kady MacDonald Denton. Viking, 1990. ISBN 0-670-83272-3. The 76 poems in this diverse and delightful collection are by Native American and Canadian poets.

Brenner, Barbara, ed. *The Earth Is Painted Green: A Garden of Poems about Our Planet.* Illustrated by S. D. Schindler. Scholastic, 1994. ISBN 0-590-45134-0. Includes nearly 100 poems by such award-winning poets as Aileen Fisher, Myra Cohn Livingston, and Valerie Worth.

Bryan, Ashley. *All Night, All Day: A Child's First book of African-American Spirituals.* Musical arrangements by David Manning Thomas. Macmillan, 1991. ISBN 10-689-31662-3. The artist has selected 20 of the best-known and best-loved spirituals and captured their spirit in colorful double-spread paintings.

————. *Sing to the Sun.* HarperCollins, 1992. ISBN 0-06-020829-5. Bryan's first book of original poetry is a joyful celebration of life that sets the heart singing. Illustrated with jewel-colored paintings that look like stained glass windows.

Carroll, Lewis. *Lewis Carroll's Jabberwocky.* Illustrated by Jane Breskin Zalben. Boyds Mills, 1992. ISBN 1-56397-080-5. The poem and Humpty Dumpty's explanation to Alice of the meaning of portmanteau words.

————. *The Walrus and the Carpenter.* Illustrated by Jane Breskin Zalben. Holt, 1986. ISBN 0-8050-0071-2.

Carter, Anne, comp. *Birds, Beasts, and Fishes: A Selection of Animal Poems.* Illustrated by Reg Cartwright. Macmillan, 1991. ISBN 0-02-717776-9. This fine collection for middle-grade children features 53 poems in diverse voices, from Lear to Sandburg.

Cendrars, Blaise. *Shadow.* Translated and illustrated by Marcia Brown. Simon & Schuster, 1986. ISBN 0-689-71084-4. "The eerie, shifting image of Shadow appears where there is light and fire and a storyteller to bring it to life." Powerful imagery for older children.

Chorao, Kay. *The Baby's Bedtime Book.* Dutton, 1989. ISBN 0-525-44149-2

————. *The Baby's Good Morning Book.* Dutton, 1990. ISBN 0-525-44257-X

————. *The Baby's Lap Book.* Dutton, 1991. ISBN 0-525-44604-4. Three beautiful collections that contain traditional rhymes as well as poems by favorite authors like Christina Rossetti, Eleanor Farjeon, and Robert Louis Stevenson.

Clark, Ann Nolan. *In My Mother's House.* Illustrated by Velino Herrera. Viking, 1991. ISBN 0-14-054496-8. These poems reflect the world as seen through the eyes of five young children of Tesuque Pueblo, near Santa Fe, New Mexico. Originally published in 1941.

Clark, Emma Chichester, comp. and illus. *I Never Saw a Purple Cow and Other Nonsense Rhymes.* Little, Brown, 1991. ISBN 0-316-14500-9. An exuberant collection of over 100 nonsense rhymes about animals. With the exception of entries by Hilaire Belloc, Gelett Burgess, Lewis Carroll, and Samuel Goodrich, the selections come from tradition.

Cole, William. *A Zooful of Animals.* Illustrated by Lynn Munsinger. Houghton, 1992. ISBN 0-395-52278-1. A playful collection of 45 poems about animals, by American and British poets.

cummings, e. e. *hist whist.* Illustrated by Deborah Kogan Ray. Crown, 1989. ISBN 0-517-57360-1. Just scary enough to please children in the primary grades.

de Gasztold, Carmen Bernos. *Prayers from the Ark: Selected Poems.* Translated from the French by Rumer Godden. Illustrated by Barry Moser. Viking, 1992. ISBN 0-670-84496-9. A selection of 13 poems from an international bestseller first published in 1962 has been illustrated with hauntingly beautiful paintings.

de la Mare, Walter. *Peacock Pie.* Faber, 1988. ISBN 0-571-14963-4

————. *Peacock Pie: A Book of Rhymes.* Illustrated by Louise Brierley. Holt, 1989. ISBN 0-8050-1124-2. A newly illustrated edition of a classic work first published in 1913.

de Regniers, Beatrice Schenk, et al. *Sing a Song of Popcorn: Every Child's Book of Poems.* Illustrated by nine Caldecott Medal artists. Scholastic, 1988. ISBN 0-590-40645-0. A handsome collection, arranged by theme, such as "Mostly People," "Story Poems," "Spooky Poems," etc. Each section has been illustrated by a different artist.

Demi, comp. and illus. *In the Eyes of the Cat: Japanese Poetry for All Seasons.* Translated by Tze-si Huang. Holt, 1992. ISBN 0-8050-1955-3. Seventy-seven Japanese nature poems, arranged by the seasons.

Dunning, Stephen, et al. *Reflections on a Gift of Watermelon Pickle . . . And Other Modern Verse.* Lothrop, 1966. ISBN 0-688-41231-9

Elledge, Scott, comp. *Wider than the Sky: Poems to Grow Up With.* HarperCollins, 1990. ISBN 0-06-021786-3. An American literature professor emeritus compiled this anthology of 200 poems with his 10-year-old niece in mind.

Evans, Dilys, comp. *Monster Soup and Other Spooky Poems.* Illustrated by Jacqueline Rogers. Scholastic, 1992. ISBN 0-590-45208-8. Deliciously scary poems about monsters, ghosts, and other fabulous creatures.

Farjeon, Eleanor. *Eleanor Farjeon's Poems for Children.* Harper, 1984. The complete text of four volumes of verse by Eleanor Farjeon: *Sing for Your Supper, Over the Garden Wall, Joan's Door, Come Christmas,* and 20 poems from her *Collected Poems* heretofore published only in England.

Feelings, Tom, comp. and illus. *Soul Looks Back in Wonder.* Dial, 1993. ISBN 0-8037-1001-1. The artist has chosen poems by African American authors, including Maya Angelou, Lucille Clifton, and Langston Hughes, to accompany his stunning collages made from blueprints, colored pencils, spray paints, cutouts, and colored paper.

Fleischman, Paul. *I Am Phoenix: Poems for Two Voices.* Illustrated by Ken Nutt. HarperCollins, 1985. ISBN 0-06-021881-9

Giovanni, Nikki. *Spin a Soft Black Song.* Illustrated by George Martins. Hill and Wang, 1985. ISBN 0-8090-8796-0. Reissue of the 1971 edition in a new format.

Goldstein, Bobbye S., comp. *Inner Chimes: Poems on Poetry.* Boyds Mills, 1992. ISBN 1-56397-040-6. An anthology of poems about poetry, by such diverse writers as Eleanor Farjeon, Eve Merriam, and Nikki Giovanni.

Gordon, Ruth, comp. *Peeling the Onion: An Anthology of Poems.* HarperCollins, 1993. ISBN 0-06-021727-8. Thought-provoking poems on diverse subjects, for the middle grades and up.

————. *Pierced by a Ray of Sun: Poems About the Times We Feel Alone.* HarperCollins, 1995. ISBN 0-06-023613-2. These poems about feeling alone and different speak to all of us but especially to young adults.

Greenfield, Eloise. *Daydreamers.* Illustrated by Tom Feelings. Dial, 1981. ISBN 0-8037-2137-4

————. *Honey, I Love and Other Love Poems.* Illustrated by Diane Dillon and Leo Dillon. HarperCollins, 1978. ISBN 0-690-01334-5

————. *Under the Sunday Tree.* Illustrated by Amos Ferguson. HarperCollins, 1988. ISBN 0-06-022254-9. Poems and paintings that evoke native life in the Bahamas.

Grimes, Nikki. *Meet Danitra Brown.* Illustrated by Floyd Cooper. Lothrop, 1994. ISBN 0-688-12073-3. Thirteen spirited poems about Danitra Brown, "the most splendiferous girl in town."

Hall, Donald. *The Oxford Book of Children's Verse in America.* Oxford, 1985. ISBN 0-19-503539-9

Hart, Jane, ed. *Singing Bee! A Collection of Favorite Children's Songs.* Illustrated by Anita Lobel. Lothrop, 1989. ISBN 0-688-41975-5

Hopkins, Lee Bennett, comp. *Rainbows Are Made: Poems by Carl Sandburg.* Wood engravings by Fritz Eichenberg. Harcourt, 1982. ISBN 0-15-265480-1

————. *The Sky Is Full of Song.* Illustrated by Dirk Zimmer. Harper, 1983. ISBN 0-06-022583-1. An anthology that celebrates the changing of the seasons.

————. *Small Talk: A Book of Short Poems.* Illustrated by Susan Gaber. Harcourt, 1995. ISBN 0-15-276577-8. Moments of significance caught by such writers as Carl Sandburg, Langston Hughes, and Eve Merriam.

————. *Still As a Star: A Book of Nighttime Poems.* Illustrated by Karen Milone. Little, Brown, 1989. ISBN 0-316-37272-2. Lullabies and poems that reflect a quiet evening mood.

————. *Through Our Eyes: Poems and Pictures about Growing Up.* Photographs by Jeffrey Dunn. Little, Brown, 1992. ISBN 0-316-19654-1. Sixteen poems about growing up in contemporary America, accompanied by color photographs of children of diverse races engaged in a variety of activities.

Hughes, Langston. *The Dream Keeper and Other Poems.* Illustrated by Brian Pinkney. Knopf, 1994. ISBN 0-679-84421-X. A new edition, with seven additional poems (66 poems in all), a new introduction by Lee Bennett Hopkins, and scratchboard illustrations by Brian Pinkney. Originally published in 1932.

Janeczko, Paul B., comp. *The Place My Words Are Looking For: What Poets Say about and Through Their Work.* Bradbury, 1990. ISBN 0-02-747671-5. Thirty-nine leading American poets share their poems and thoughts about writing poetry.

————. *Poems of Youth.* Watts, 1991. ISBN 0-531-05901-4. Contemporary poems that speak to young adults.

————. *Strings: A Gathering of Family Poems.* Simon & Schuster, 1984. ISBN 0-02-747790-8

Johnson, James Weldon. *The Creation.* Illustrated by James E. Ransome. Holiday, 1994. ISBN 0-8234-1069-2. Johnson's powerful free-verse poem is based on the biblical story.

————. *God's Trombones: Seven Negro Sermons in Verse.* Illustrated by Aaron Douglass. Viking, 1990. ISBN 0-14-018403-1. Excellent introduction discusses the folk sermon. For older boys and girls and adults.

Jones, Hettie, comp. *The Trees Stand Shining: Poetry of the North American Indians.* Illustrated by Robert Andrew Parker. Dial, 1993. ISBN 0-8037-9083-X. "The poems in this book are really songs." They reflect the American Indian's closeness to nature.

Kennedy, X. J. *The Beasts of Bethlehem.* Illustrated by Michael McCurdy. Simon & Schuster, 1992. ISBN 0-689-50561-2. The thoughts of each of the animals present at the birth of Christ are expressed with quiet reverence in these 19 poems and drawings.

Kennedy, X. J., and Dorothy M. Kennedy, comps. *Talking Like the Rain: A First Book of Poems.* Illustrated by Jane Dyer. Little, Brown, 1992. ISBN 0-316-48889-5. The title of this joyous anthology comes from Isak Dinesen's *Out of Africa* ("Speak again. Speak like rain"). The more than 120 poems are about important moments in a child's life, from dressing up and birthday parties to splashing in puddles and discovering "the lovely whiteness of snow."

Koch, Kenneth, and Kate Farrell. *Talking to the Sun: An Illustrated Anthology of Poems for Young People.* Metropolitan Museum of Art and Holt, 1985. ISBN 0-8050-0144-1

Kuskin, Karla. *Dogs and Dragons, Trees and Dreams: A Collection of Poems.* Harper, 1980. ISBN 0-06-023544-6

Lalicki, Barbara. *If There Were Dreams to Sell.* Illustrated by Margot Tomes. Simon & Schuster, 1994. ISBN 0-02-751251-7. Reissue of an unusual alphabet poetry book. Originally published in 1984.

Larrick, Nancy, comp. *Cats Are Cats.* Illustrated by Ed Young. Philomel, 1988. ISBN 0-399-21517-4. "Truly these cats are cats that inspire wonder, the imagination, and a sensitivity to perfectly matched visual and verbal images" (from Kay E. Vandergrift's review in *School Library Journal,* December 1988).

————. *Mice Are Nice.* Illustrated by Ed Young. Philomel, 1990. ISBN 0-399-21495-X. A few cats have managed to find their way into this companion piece, in which we meet a meadow mouse, a house mouse, a mouse in a rocket, and others.

————. *Piping Down the Valleys Wild: Poetry for the Young of All Ages.* Illustrated by Ellen Raskin. Dell, 1982. ISBN 0-440-46952-X

————. *To the Moon and Back: A Collection of Poems.* Illustrated by Catharine O'Neill. Delacorte, 1991. ISBN 0-385-30159-6. Rhythmic verse that appeals to the imagination from such well-known poets as e. e. cummings and David McCord along with lesser-known selections from Native American and Inuit poetry.

Lawrence, Jacob. *Harriet and the Promised Land.* Simon & Schuster, 1993. ISBN 0-671-86673-7. The story of the daring black slave who led her people to freedom, told in rhythmic verse and powerful paintings by the acclaimed artist.

Lear, Edward. *Of Pelicans and Pussycats: Poems and Limericks.* Illustrated by Jill Newton. Dial, 1990. ISBN 0-8037-0728-2. These seven poems and six limericks are a pleasing introduction to Lear.

————. *The Owl and the Pussycat.* Illustrated by Jan Brett. Putnam, 1991. ISBN 0-399-21925-0. This beguiling rendition of a childhood favorite is set in the colorful tropics.

Lewis, Claudia. *Up in the Mountains and Other Poems of Long Ago.* Illustrated by Joel Fontaine. HarperCollins, 1991. ISBN 0-06-023810-0. A beloved teacher of children's literature recalls growing up in Oregon. Another evocative collection by this poet is *Up and Down the River: Boat Poems,* illustrated by Bruce Degan. Harper, 1979. ISBN 0-06-023812-7

Lewis, Richard. *In the Night, Still Dark.* Illustrated by Ed Young. Simon & Schuster, 1988. ISBN 0-689-31310-1. A skillful abridgment of the Hawaiian creation chant traditionally recited over a newborn child to help bond the new life to all other living things.

————. *Miracles: Poems by Children of the English-Speaking World.* Touchstone, 1966. ISBN 0-686-39707-X

————. *Out of the Earth I Sing: Poetry and Songs of Primitive Peoples of the Earth.* Norton, 1968. o.p.

Livingston, Myra Cohn, comp. *Animal, Vegetable, Mineral: Poems about Small Things.* HarperCollins, 1994. ISBN 0-06-023008-8. Langston Hughes, Karla Kuskin, William Carlos Williams, and other fine poets illuminate things in our everyday world that often go unnoticed.

————. *Call Down the Moon: Poems of Music.* Simon & Schuster, 1995. ISBN 0-689-80416-4. These traditional and contemporary poems "range in mood from amusing to moving, serious to sublime."

————. *How Pleasant to Know Mr. Lear! Edward Lear's Selected Works with an Introduction and Notes.* Stemmer House, 1994. ISBN 0-88045-126-2

————. *Worlds I Know and Other Poems.* Illustrated by Tim Arnold. Macmillan, 1985. ISBN 0-689-50332-6. Forty-two poems that reflect Livingston's own childhood experiences.

Livingston, Myra Cohn, and Leonard Everett Fisher, *Celebrations.* Holiday House, 1985. ISBN 0-8234-0550-8. Poems and paintings to mark 16 important days throughout the year, including Martin Luther King Day.

Lobel, Arnold. *The Random House Book of Mother Goose.* Random, 1986. ISBN 0-394-86799-8

Longfellow, Henry Wadsworth. *Paul Revere's Ride.* Illustrated by Ted Rand. Dutton, 1990. ISBN 0-525-44610-9. Full-color paintings capture the drama of the well-known poem.

McCord, David. *One At a Time.* Little, Brown, 1986. ISBN 0-316-55516-9. The collected poems of David McCord, with a subject index and index of first lines.

Merriam, Eve. *Fresh Paint: New Poems.* Simon & Schuster, 1986. ISBN 0-02-766860-6

————. *The Singing Green: New and Selected Poems for All Seasons.* Illustrated by Kathleen Collins Howell. Morrow, 1992. ISBN 0-688-11025-8. A joyous collection by a distinguished American poet. See other collections by this prolific author.

Millay, Edna St. Vincent. *Edna St. Vincent Millay's Poems Selected for Young People.* HarperCollins, 1951. o.p.

Moore, Lilian. *Something New Begins: New and Selected Poems.* Simon & Schuster, 1982. ISBN 0-689-30818-3

————. *Sunflakes: Poems for Children.* Illustrated by Jan Ormerod. Houghton Mifflin, 1992. ISBN 0-395-58833-2. The 82 verses in this appealing anthology were chosen with young children in mind.

Nye, Naomi Shihab, comp. *This Same Sky: A Collection of Poems from around the World.* Simon & Schuster, 1992. ISBN 0-02-768440-7. Older children and young adults will be pulled into the lives of these extraordinary, talented poets, none of whom were born in the United States. Nearly all of the 129 poems present common ideas in uncommonly fresh ways.

O'Neill, Mary. *Hailstones and Halibut Bones.* Illustrated by John Wallner. Doubleday, 1989. ISBN 0-385-24484-3. Reissue of a popular book, with fresh new illustrations.

Philip, Neil, ed. *Songs Are Thoughts: Poems of the Inuit.* Illustrated by Maryclare Foa. Orchard, 1995. ISBN 0-531-06893-5. Poems that introduce children to the Inuit way of life.

Plotz, Helen. *Imagination's Other Place: Poems of Science and Mathematics.* HarperCollins, 1987. ISBN 0-690-04700-2

Pomerantz, Charlotte. *Halfway to Your House.* Illustrated by Gabrielle Vincent. Greenwillow, 1991. ISBN 0-688-11804-6. Delicate watercolors illustrate these whimsical poems for the young child.

————. *The Tamarindo Puppy and Other Poems.* Illustrated by Byron Barton. Greenwillow, 1993. ISBN 0-688-80251-6. The inclusion of Spanish words within the predominately English text is a pleasing introduction to the Spanish language.

Prelutsky, Jack. *The Dragons Are Singing Tonight.* Illustrated by Peter Sis. Greenwillow, 1993. ISBN 0-688-09645-X. Seventeen poems about dragons, illustrated with colorful and witty paintings.

————, comp. *For Laughing Out Loud: Poems to Tickle Your Funnybone.* Illustrated by Marjorie Priceman. Knopf, 1991. ISBN 0-394-82144-0. An ebullient collection of nonsense verse by mostly contemporary poets, including Kennedy, Kuskin, Silverstein, Viorst, and Prelutsky himself.

————. *Poems of A. Nonny Mouse.* Illustrated by Henrik Drescher. Knopf, 1989. ISBN 0-394-88711-5. A good introduction for children who think they don't like poetry.

————. *Ride a Purple Pelican.* Illustrated by Garth Williams. Greenwillow, 1986. ISBN 0-688-04031-4. Delightful rhymes for the very young.

————. *Something Big Has Been Here.* Illustrated by James Stevenson. Greenwillow, 1990. ISBN 0-688-06434-5. This popular poet grabs children with his wacky sense of humor.

Radley, Gail, comp. *Rainy Day Rhymes.* Illustrated by Ellen Kandoian. Houghton, 1992. ISBN 0-395-59967-9. An appealing collection of 17 poems about rain by Rachel Field, Robert Louis Stevenson, Aileen Fisher, and others.

Read, Herbert. *This Way Delight.* Pantheon, 1956. o.p.

Rogasky, Barbara, comp. *Winter Poems.* Illustrated by Trina Schart Hyman. Scholastic, 1994. ISBN 0-590-42872-1. Twenty-five poems, some new, some more than a thousand years old, celebrate the winter season without reference to any holidays.

Rollins, Charlemae Hill, comp. *Christmas Gif': An Anthology of Christmas Poems, Songs, and Stories Written by and about African-Americans.* Illustrated by Ashley Bryan. Introduction by Augusta Baker. Morrow, 1993. ISBN 0-688-11667-1. Reissue of a classic anthology first published in 1963.

Rosen, Michael, comp. *Poems for the Very Young.* Illustrated by Bob Graham. Kingfisher, 1993. ISBN 1-85697-908-3. A collection of modern and traditional poems with pleasing wordplay and sounds.

Schwartz, Alvin. *And the Green Grass Grew All Around: Folk Poetry from Everyone.* Illustrated by Sue Truesdell. HarperCollins, 1992. ISBN 0-06-022757-5. Children's folk poetry—funny, irreverent, bursting with energy—collected in schoolyards and other places where children gather.

Service, Robert. *The Cremation of Sam McGee.* Paintings by Ted Harrison. Greenwillow, 1987. ISBN 0-688-06903-7. A classic poem about Gold Rush days.

Shaw, Alison, comp. *Until I Saw the Sea: A Collection of Seashore Poems.* Holt, 1995. ISBN 0-8050-2755-6. Nineteen poems with color photographs of seashore scenes taken on Martha's Vineyard by the compiler, an award-winning photographer.

Silverstein, Shel. *Where the Sidewalk Ends.* HarperCollins, 1974. ISBN 0-06-025667-2

Simon, Seymour, ed. *Star Walk.* Morrow, 1995. ISBN 0-688-1188-9. A collection of poetry (and some prose) about stars and space, accompanied by awe-inspiring photographs.

Sky-Peck, Kathryn. *Who Has Seen the Wind? An Illustrated Collection of Poetry for Young People.* Rizzoli, 1991. ISBN 0-8478-1423-8. Classic poems illustrated with reproductions of paintings from the Museum of Fine Arts in Boston.

Sneve, Virginia Driving Hawk, comp. *Dancing Teepees: Poems of American Indian Youth.* Illustrated by Stephen Gammell. Holiday House, 1989. ISBN 0-8234-0724-1. Selections from the oral tradition of North American Indians and contemporary tribal poets.

Soto, Gary. *Neighborhood Odes.* Illustrated by David Diaz. Harcourt, 1992. ISBN 0-15-256879-4. These 21 poems celebrate everyday life in a Hispanic neighborhood. For children in the middle grades.

Stevenson, Robert Louis. *A Child's Garden of Verses.* Illustrated by Henriette Willebeek le Mair. Philomel, 1991. ISBN 0-399-21818-1. A new edition of a book first published in 1926 with additional illustrations by this well-known artist.

Strickland, Michael R., comp. *Poems that Sing to You.* Illustrated by Alan Leiner. Boyds Mills, 1993. ISBN 1-56397-178-X. Poems that capture the rhythms of music.

Thomas, Joyce Carol. *Brown Honey in Broomwheat Tea.* Illustrated by Floyd Cooper. HarperCollins, 1993. ISBN 0-06-021087-7. Poems about family and pride of heritage.

———. *Gingerbread Days.* Illustrated by Floyd Cooper. HarperCollins, 1995. ISBN 0-06-023469-5. This companion volume to *Brown Honey in Broomwheat Tea* celebrates family love throughout the months of the year.

Treece, Henry. *The Magic Wood.* Illustrated by Barry Moser. HarperCollins, 1992. ISBN 0-06-020802-3. A ghost poem for children old enough to enjoy the macabre.

Volavkova, H., ed. *I Never Saw Another Butterfly: Children's Drawings and Poems from Theresienstadt Concentration Camp, 1942-1944.* Schocken 1994. ISBN 0-8052-1015-6.

Watts, Bernadette, sel. and illus. *Fly Away, Fly Away Over the Sea: And Other Poems for Children by Christina Rossetti.* North-South, 1992. o.p. Twenty-three short lyrical poems by a poet who understood early childhood.

Whipple, Laura, comp. *Eric Carle's Animals, Animals.* Illustrated by Eric Carle. Philomel, 1989. ISBN 0-399-21744-4. A wide range of poetry about the animal kingdom, selected from sources as diverse as the Bible, Shakespeare, Japanese haiku, Lewis Carroll, Ogden Nash, and Pawnee Indian. Illustrated with brilliantly colored tissue paper collages.

———. *Eric Carle's Dragons Dragons and Other Creatures That Never Were.* Illustrated by Eric Carle. Philomel, 1991. ISBN 0-399-22105-0. A companion volume with poems about dragons and other mythological creatures.

Wilner, Isabel. *The Poetry Troupe: An Anthology of Poems to Read Aloud.* Simon & Schuster, 1977. ISBN 0-684-15198-7

Worth, Valerie. *At Christmastime.* Illustrated by Antonio Frasconi. HarperCollins, 1992. ISBN 0-06-205019-2. A lovely collection for younger children.

Yolen, Jane, selector. *Mother Earth, Father Sky: Poems of Our Planet.* Illustrated by Jennifer Hewitson. Boyds Mills, 1995. ISBN 1-56397-414-2. This handsome anthology reminds us of our responsibilities as caretakers of planet Earth.

Stories to Tell

STORIES OF SPECIAL APPEAL TO 3-TO-5-YEAR-OLDS

"The Acorn Tree." In *The Acorn Tree and Other Folktales* by Anne Rockwell. Greenwillow, 1995. ISBN 0-688-10746-X

"The Bed." In *The Tiger and the Rabbit and Other Tales* by Pura Belpré. Lippincott, 1965. o.p.

"Budulinek." In *The Fairy Tale Treasury* selected by Virginia Haviland. Dell, 1986. o.p.

"The Cat and the Parrot." In *How to Tell Stories to Children* by Sara Cone Bryant. Omnigraphics, 1979. ISBN 1-55888-994-9

The Elves and the Shoemaker by Jacob Grimm and Wilhelm Grimm. Retold by Bernadette Watts. North-South, 1986. ISBN 1-55858-035-2

"The Gingerbread Boy." In *The Fairy Tale Treasury* selected by Virginia Haviland. Dell, 1986. o.p.

The Gunniwolf retold by Wilhelmina Harper. Dutton, 1970. ISBN 0-525-31139-4

"Henny Penny." In *Read Me a Story: A Child's Book of Favorite Tales* by Sophie Windham. Scholastic, 1991. ISBN 0-590-44950-8

"The Little Boy Who Turned Himself into a Peanut." In *Ten Small Tales* by Celia Lottridge. Simon & Schuster, 1994. ISBN 0-689-50568-X

The Little Old Lady Who Was Not Afraid of Anything by Linda Williams. HarperCollins, 1986. ISBN 0-690-04584-0

The Little Red Hen by Byron Barton. HarperCollins, 1993. ISBN 0-06-021675-1

Lizard's Song by George Shannnon. Illustrated by Jose Aruego and Ariane Dewey. Greenwillow, 1981. ISBN 0-688-80310-5

May I Bring a Friend? by Beatrice Schenk de Regniers. Illustrated by Beni Montressor. Simon & Schuster, 1971. ISBN 0-689-20615-1

Millions of Cats by Wanda Gág. Putnam, 1977. ISBN 0-698-20091-8

The Mitten: A Ukrainian Folktale retold and illustrated by Jan Brett. Putnam, 1990. ISBN 0-399-21920-X

The Old Woman and Her Pig: An Old English Tale by Rosanne Litzinger. Harcourt, 1993. ISBN 0-15-257802-1

The Owl and the Pussycat by Edward Lear. Illustrated by Jan Brett. Putnam, 1991. ISBN 0-399-21925-0

"Pooh Goes Visiting and Gets into a Tight Place." In *Winnie-the-Pooh* by A. A. Milne. Dutton, 1926. ISBN 0-525-45004-1

"Rabbit's Snow Dance." In *The Boy Who Lived with the Bears and Other Iroquois Stories* by Joseph Bruchac. HarperCollins, 1995. ISBN 0-06-021288-8

"Sody Saleratus." In *Crocodile! Crocodile! Stories Told Around the World* retold by Barbara Baumgartner. Illustrated by Judith Moffatt. Dorling Kindersley, 1994. ISBN 1-56458-463-1

"Star Money." In *The Three Bears and 15 Other Stories* by Anne Rockwell. HarperCollins, 1975. ISBN 0-690-00598-9

"The Story of the Three Little Pigs." In *English Fairy Tales* by Joseph Jacobs. Dover, 1898. ISBN 00-89190-076-4

"The Sweet Porridge." In *More Tales from Grimm* by Wanda Gág. Coward, 1947. o.p.

"The Three Bears." In *The Golden Goose Book* by L. Leslie Brooke. Houghton Mifflin, 1992. ISBN 0-395-61303-5

The Three Billy Goats Gruff by Peter C. Asbjørnsen and Jørgen E. Moe. Harcourt, 1991. ISBN 0-15-690150-1

"The Turnip." In *The Helen Oxenbury Nursery Story Book* by Helen Oxenbury. Harcourt, 1993. ISBN 0-517-13398-9

When the Root Children Wake Up by Sibylle von Olfers. Lippincott, 1941. o.p.

Who's in Rabbit's House? by Verna Aardema. Dial, 1979. ISBN 0-8037-9549-1

Why the Sun and Moon Live in the Sky by Elphinstone Dayrell. Houghton Mifflin, 1990. ISBN 0-395-53963-3

The Wolf and the Seven Little Kids by Jacob Grimm and Wilhelm Grimm. North-South, 1995. ISBN 1-55858-445-5

STORIES OF SPECIAL APPEAL TO 5-TO-8-YEAR-OLDS

"Alligator's Sunday Suit." In *Bo Rabbit Smart for True: Folktales from the Gullah* retold by Priscilla Jacquith. Putnam, 1994. ISBN 0-399-22668-0

Anansi and the Moss-Covered Rock by Eric Kimmel. Illustrated by Janet Stevens. Holiday House, 1988. ISBN 0-8234-0689-X

"Baba Yaga and the Little Girl with the Kind Heart." In *Old Peter's Russian Tales* by Arthur Ransome.Viking, 1975. ISBN 0-14-030696-X

Borreguita and the Coyote: A Tale from Ayutla, Mexico by Verna Aardema. Illustrated by Petra Mathers. Knopf, 1991. ISBN 0-679-80921-X

The Bossy Gallito/El Gallo de Bodas: A Traditional Cuban Folktale retold by Lucía M. González. Illustrated by Lulu Delacre. Scholastic, 1994. ISBN 0-590-46843-X

The Bremen Town Musicians by Jacob Grimm and Wilhelm Grimm. Translated by Anthea Bell. Illustrated by Bernadette Watts. North-South, 1992. ISBN 1-55858-140-5

The Cat's Purr by Ashley Bryan. Simon & Schuster, 1985. ISBN 0-689-31086-2. Also in *Storytelling: Art and Technique* 3rd ed., by Ellin Greene. Bowker, 1996. ISBN 0-8352-3458-4

"The Crab and the Jaguar." In *Picture Folk-Tales* by Valery Carrick. Dover, 1992. ISBN 0-486-27083-1. Also in *Storytelling: Art and Technique* 3rd ed., by Ellin Greene. Bowker, 1996. ISBN 0-8352-3458-4

The Eye of the Needle: Based on a Yupik Tale Told by Betty Hoffman. Retold and illustrated by Teri Sloat. Dutton, 1990. ISBN 0-525-44623-0

"The Frog Prince." In *Tales from Grimm* by Wanda Gág. Coward, 1936. o.p.

"How to Tell Corn Fairies When You See 'Em." In *Rootabaga Stories* by Carl Sandburg. Harcourt, 1988. ISBN 0-15-269061-1

"I'm Tipingee, She's Tipingee, We're Tipingee, Too." In *The Magic Orange Tree and Other Haitian Folktales* by Diane Wolkstein. Schocken, 1987. ISBN 0-8052-0650-7

"The Impudent Little Bird." In *The Singing Tortoise and Other Animal Folktales* by John Yeoman. Morrow, 1994. ISBN 0-688-13366-5

"Jazzy Three Bears." In *Storytelling: Art and Technique* 3rd ed., by Ellin Greene. Bowker, 1996. ISBN 0-8352-3458-4

"Koala." In *Magical Tales from Many Lands* by Margaret Mayo. Dutton, 1993. ISBN 0-525-45017-3

"Leelee Goro." In *Misoso: Once Upon a Time Tales from Africa* retold by Verna Aardema. Knopf, 1994. ISBN 0-679-83430-3

"The Little Half-Chick." In *Señor Cat's Romance and Other Favorite Stories from Latin America* retold by Lucía M. González. Scholastic, 1997. Also in *Storytelling: Art and Technique* 3rd ed., by Ellin Greene. Bowker, 1996. ISBN 0-8352-3458-4

The Little Red Hen by Paul Galdone. Houghton Mifflin, 1979. ISBN 0-395-28803-7

"The Little Rooster and the Turkish Sultan." In *The Good Master* by Kate Seredy. Puffin, 1986. ISBN 0-14-030133-X. See also Eric Kimmel's retelling, *The Valiant Red Rooster: A Story from Hungary.* Illustrated by Katya Arnold. Holt, 1995. ISBN 0-8050-2781-5

Little Sister and the Month Brothers by Beatrice Schenk de Regniers. Illustrated by Margot Tomes. Morrow, 1994. ISBN 0-688-05293-2

"The Magic Orange Tree." In *The Magic Orange Tree and Other Haitian Folktales* by Diane Wolkstein. Schocken, 1987. ISBN 0-8050-0650-7

Many Moons by James Thurber. Illustrated by Marc Simont. Harcourt, 1990. ISBN 0-15-251873-8

"Mr. Miacca." In *English Fairy Tales* edited by Joseph Jacobs. Dover, 1898. ISBN 0-486-21818-X

"Molly Whuppie." In *English Fairy Tales* edited by Joseph Jacobs. Dover, 1898. ISBN 0-486-21818-X.

"Mother Holle." In *More Tales from Grimm* by Wanda Gág. Coward, 1947. o.p.

"One-Eye, Two-Eyes, and Three-Eyes." In *The Complete Grimm's Fairy Tales* by Jacob Grimm and Wilhelm Grimm. Pantheon, 1976. ISBN 0-394-49415-6

Perez y Martina by Pura Belpré. Viking, 1991. ISBN 0-670-84167-6. Also available in English. ISBN 0-670-84166-8.

"Punia and the King of the Sharks." In *Twenty Tellable Tales* by Margaret Read MacDonald. Wilson, 1986. ISBN 0-8242-0719-X

"Puss in Boots." In *Puss in Boots and Other Stories* told and illustrated by Anne Rockwell. Simon & Schuster, 1988. ISBN 0-02-777781-2

Snow-White and the Seven Dwarfs: A Tale from the Brothers Grimm translated by Randall Jarrell. Farrar, 1972. ISBN 0-374-37099-0

"Soap, Soap, Soap." In *Grandfather Tales* by Richard Chase. Houghton Mifflin, 1973. ISBN 0-395-06692-1. Also see Tom Birdseye's retelling, *Soap! Soap! Don't Forget the Soap! An Appalachian Folktale* illustrated by Andrew Glass. Holiday House, 1993. ISBN 0-8234-1005-6

The Star Maiden: An Ojibway Tale retold by Barbara Juster Esbensen. Little, Brown, 1988. ISBN 0-316-24951-3

"The Steadfast Tin Soldier." In *Twelve Tales: Hans Christian Andersen* selected, translated, and illustrated by Erik Blegvad. Simon & Schuster, 1994. ISBN 0-689-50584-1. Also available in various picture-book editions.

"The Three Little Pigs." In *The Golden Goose Book* by L. Leslie Brooke. Houghton Mifflin, 1992. ISBN 0-395-61303-5

Tikki Tikki Tembo retold by Arlene Mosel. Holt, 1968. ISBN 0-8050-0662-1

"Unanana and the Enormous One-Tusked Elephant." In *Magical Tales from Many Lands* by Margaret Mayo. Dutton, 1993. ISBN 0-525-45017-3

The Wedding Procession of the Rag Doll and the Broom Handle and Who Was in It by Carl Sandburg. Harcourt, 1978. ISBN 0-15-695487-7

What's in Fox's Sack? by Paul Galdone. Houghton Mifflin, 1982. ISBN 0-89919-062-6

"Why the Waves Have Whitecaps." In *The Knee-High Man and Other Tales* by Julius Lester. Dial, 1985. ISBN 0-8037-4593-1

"Wiley, His Mama, and the Hairy Man." In *The People Could Fly: American Black Folktales* by Virginia Hamilton. Knopf, 1985. ISBN 0-394-86925-7

STORIES OF SPECIAL APPEAL TO 8-TO-11-YEAR-OLDS

"Anansi's Hat-Shaking Dance." In *The Hat-Shaking Dance and Other Ashanti Tales from Ghana* by Harold Courlander and Albert K. Prempeh. Harcourt, 1957. o.p.

"The Baker's Daughter." In *A Street of Little Shops* by Margery Bianco. Grigg, 1981. o.p.

"Bedtime Snacks." In *The Rainbow People* by Laurence Yep. HarperCollins, 1989. ISBN 0-06-026760-7

The Boy Who Drew Cats: A Japanese Folktale by Arthur A. Levine. Illustrated by Frédéric Clément. Dial, 1994. ISBN 0-8037-1172-7

Clever Tom and the Leprechaun by Linda Shute. Lothrop, 1988. ISBN 0-688-07488-X

"Don't Blame Me." In *The Wonder Dog: The Collected Short Stories of Richard Hughes.* Greenwillow, 1977. o.p.

"The Goat Well." In *The Fire on the Mountain and Other Stories from Ethiopia and Eritrea* by Harold Courlander and Wolf Leslau. Holt, 1995. ISBN 0-8050-3652-0

"The Graveyard Voice." In *The Ghost and I: Scary Stories for Participatory Telling* edited by Jennifer Justice. Yellow Moon Press, 1992. ISBN 0-938756-37-0

"Hafiz, the Stone-Cutter." In *The Art of the Story-teller* by Marie Shedlock. Dover, 1951. ISBN 0-486-20635-1

"He Lion, Bruh Bear, and Bruh Rabbit." In *The People Could Fly: American Black Folktales* by Virginia Hamilton. Knopf, 1985. ISBN 0-394-86925-7

"How Boots Befooled the King." In *The Wonder Clock* by Howard Pyle. Dover, 1887, 1915. ISBN 0-486-21446-X

"How to Break a Bad Habit." In *Twenty Tellable Tales* by Margaret Read MacDonald. Wilson, 1986. ISBN 0-8242-0719-X

"The Hungry Old Witch." In *Tales from Silver Lands* by Charles J. Finger. Scholastic, 1989. ISBN 0-590-42447-5

"Jack and Old Raggedy Bones." In *Mountain Jack Tales* by Gail E. Haley. Dutton, 1992. ISBN 0-525-44974-4

"King Arthur and His Sword." In *The Story of King Arthur and His Knights* by Howard Pyle. Peter Smith, n.d. ISBN 0-8446-2766-6

King of the Cats by Joseph Jacobs. Houghton Mifflin, 1980. ISBN 0-393-29030-9

"The Legend of the Bodhran." In *Patakin: World Tales of Drums and Drummers* by Nina Jaffe. Holt, 1994. ISBN 0-8050-3005-0

"The Magic Ball." In *Tales from Silver Lands* by Charles J. Finger. Scholastic, 1989. ISBN 0-590-42447-5

"The Magic Pomegranate." In *Jewish Stories One Generation Tells Another* retold by Peninnah Schram. Aronson, 1993. ISBN 0-87668-967-5

The Magic Tree: A Tale from the Congo by Gerald McDermott. Holt, 1994. ISBN 0-8050-3080-8

"Mary Culhane and the Dead Man." In *The Goblins Giggle and Other Stories* selected by Molly Bang. Peter Smith, 1988. ISBN 0-8446-6360-3

"Mouse Woman and Porcupine Hunter." In *Mouse Woman and Mischief-Makers* by Christie Harris. Atheneum, 1977. o.p.

"Paul Bunyan: The Winter of the Blue Snow." In *Paul Bunyan Swings His Axe* by Dell J. McCormick. Caxton, 1936. ISBN 0-87004-093-6

"The Princess Golden-Hair and the Great Black Raven." In *The Wonder Clock* by Howard Pyle. Dover, 1887, 1915. ISBN 0-486-21446-X

"Rabbit and Coyote." In *The Monkey's Haircut and Other Stories Told by the Maya* edited by John Bierhorst. Illustrated by Robert A. Parker. Morrow, 1986. ISBN 0-688-04269-4

"The Rat-Catcher's Daughter." In *The Rat-Catcher's Daughter: A Collection of Stories by Laurence Housman* selected by Ellin Greene. Atheneum, 1974. o.p.

"Robin Hood: The Shooting-Match at Nottingham Town." In *Some Merry Adventures of Robin Hood* by Howard Pyle. Scribner, 1954. o.p.

"The Rooster, the Hand Mill and the Swarm of Hornets." In *The Golden Lynx and Other Tales* selected by Augusta Baker. Lippincott, 1960. o.p.

The Rough-Face Girl by Rafe Martin. Illustrated by David Shannon. Putnam, 1992. ISBN 0-399-21859-9

"The Stinky Cheese Man." In *The Stinky Cheese Man and Other Fairly Stupid Tales* by Jon Scieszka. Illustrated by Lane Smith. Viking, 1992. ISBN 0-670-84487-X

"The Tailor." In *Just Enough to Make a Story* 3rd ed., by Nancy Schimmel. Sister's Choice, 1992. ISBN 0-932164-03-X

"The Talking Stone." In *The Hungry Woman: Myths and Legends of the Aztecs* edited by John Bierhorst. Morrow, 1993. ISBN 0-688-12301-5

Tatterhood and the Hobgoblins: A Norwegian Folktale retold and illustrated by Lauren Mills. Little, Brown, 1993. ISBN 0-316-57406-6

"Ticky-Picky Boom-Boom." In *Anansi, the Spider Man* Jamaican folktales retold by Philip M. Sherlock. Oxford Univ. Press, 1988. o.p.

"The Tinderbox." In *Twelve Tales: Hans Christian Andersen* selected, translated, and illustrated by Erik Blegvad. Simon & Schuster, 1994. ISBN 0-689-50584-1. The *Tinderbox* (Simon & Schuster, 1988) is beautifully illustrated by Warwick Hutton. ISBN 0-689-50458-6

"Turtle Goes Hunting." *In The Naked Bear: Folktales of the Iroquois* edited by John Bierhorst. Illustrated by Dirk Zimmer. Morrow, 1987. ISBN 0-688-06422-1

"Two Giants." In *Tales for the Telling: Irish Folk and Fairy Stories* by Edna O'Brien. Illustrated by Michael Foreman. Puffin, 1988. ISBN 0-14-032293-0

"Waukewa's Eagle." In *Twenty-four Unusual Tales* by Anna Cogswell Tyler. Harcourt, 1921. o.p.

"The Wonderful Brocade." In *The Spring of Butterflies and Other Chinese Folk Tales* by He Liyi. Lothrop, 1985. o.p.

Yeh-Shen: A Cinderella Story from China retold by Ai-Ling Louie. Illustrated by Ed Young. Putnam, 1990. ISBN 0-399-20900-X

STORIES OF SPECIAL APPEAL TO 11-TO-15-YEAR-OLDS

"The Babysitter." In *Things That Go Bump in the Night: A Collection of Original Stories* edited by Jane Yolen and Martin H. Greenberg. HarperCollins, 1989. ISBN 0-06-026802-6

"The Boy Punia and the King of the Sharks." In *Legends of Hawaii* by Padraic Colum. Yale Univ. Press, 1937. ISBN 0-300-00376-5

"The Cat Bride." In *Dream Weaver* by Jane Yolen. Collins, 1979. o.p.

"Childe Roland." In *English Fairy Tales* edited by Joseph Jacobs. Dover, 1898. ISBN 0-486-21818-X

"The Children of Lir." In *A Storyteller's Choice* by Eileen Colwell. Walck, 1964. o.p. See also the picture book *The Children of Lir* by Sheila MacGill-Callahan. Illustrated by Gennady Spirin. Dial, 1993. ISBN 0-8037-1121-2

"Clever Manka." In *The Shepherd's Nosegay* by Parker Fillmore, edited by Katherine Love. Harcourt, 1958. o.p. Also in *Storytelling: Art and Technique* 3rd ed., by Ellin Greene. Bowker, 1996. ISBN 0-8352-3458-4

"Count Alaric's Lady." In *Midsummer Magic* by Ellin Greene. Lothrop, 1977. o.p. Also in *Storytelling: Art and Technique* 3rd ed., by Ellin Greene. Bowker, 1996. ISBN 0-8352-3458-4

"The Cow-Tail Switch." In *The Cow-Tail Switch and Other West African Stories* by Harold Courlander and George Herzog. Holt, 1988. ISBN 0-8050-0288-X

"Cupid and Psyche." In *Greek Myths* by Olivia E. Coolidge. Houghton Mifflin, 1949. ISBN 0-395-06721-9

"Eyes of Jade." In *Tongues of Jade* by Laurence Yep. HarperCollins, 1991. ISBN 0-06-022470-3

"Finn and the Snakes." In *The Green Hero: Early Adventures of Finn McCool* by Bernard Evslin. Four Winds, 1975. o.p.

"The Fire on the Mountain." In *The Fire on the Mountain and Other Stories from Ethiopia and Eritrea* by Harold Courlander and Wolf Leslau. Holt, 1995. ISBN 0-8050-3652-0. Also see the picture book, *Fire on the Mountain,* retold by Jane Kurtz. Illustrated by E. B. Lewis. Simon & Schuster, 1994. ISBN 0-671-88268-6

"A Friend's Affection." In *The Golden Carp and Other Tales from Vietnam* by Lynette Dyer Vuong. Lothrop, 1993. ISBN 0-688-12514-X

"The Girl Who Cried Flowers." In *The Girl Who Cried Flowers and Other Tales* by Jane Yolen. Crowell, 1974. o.p.

"The Girl Who Married the Moon." In *The Girl Who Married the Moon* by Joseph Bruchac and Gayle Ross. BridgeWater, 1994. ISBN 0-8167-3480-1

"Hershel and the Nobleman." In *While Standing on One Foot: Puzzle Stories and Wisdom Tales from the Jewish Tradition* by Nina Jaffe and Steve Zeitlin. Holt, 1993. ISBN 0-8050-2594-4

"Jamie Freel and the Young Lady." In *Fairy Tales of Ireland* by W. B. Yeats. Illustrated by P. J. Lynch. Delacorte, 1990. ISBN 0-385-30249-5

"The King's Child" retold by Judith Black. In *Ready-to-Tell Tales* edited by David Holt and Bill Mooney. August House, 1994. ISBN 0-87483-380-9

"The Lass That Couldn't Be Frightened." In *Heather and Broom: Tales of the Scottish Highlands* by Sorche Nic Leodhas. Holt, 1960. o.p.

"The Magic Fruit." In *Magical Tales from Many Lands* retold by Margaret Mayo. Dutton, 1993. ISBN 0-525-45017-3

"Mr. Fox." In *English Fairy Tales* edited by Joseph Jacobs. Dover, 1898. ISBN 0-486-21818-X

"The Nightingale and the Rose." In *The Happy Prince and Other Stories* by Oscar Wilde. Morrow, 1991. ISBN 0-688-10390-1.

"Owl." In *The Magic Orange Tree and Other Haitian Folktales* by Diane Wolkstein. Schocken, 1987. ISBN 0-688-10390-1

"The Porcelain Man." In *Richard Kennedy: Collected Stories.* HarperCollins, 1987. ISBN 0-06-023255-2

"A Pretty Girl in the Road" by Vance Randolph. In *Favorite Folktales from Around the World* edited by Jane Yolen. Pantheon, 1986. ISBN 0-394-75188-4

"The Promise." In *Here There Be Witches* by Jane Yolen. Harcourt, 1995. ISBN 0-15-200311-8

"The Ranee and the Cobra." In *The Singing Tortoise and Other Animal Folktales* by John Yeoman. Morrow, 1993. ISBN 0-688-13366-5

Sir Gawain and the Loathly Lady retold by Selina Hastings. Illustrated by Juan Wijngaard. Lothrop, 1985. ISBN 0-688-05823-X

"Shrewd Todie and Lyzer the Miser." In *When Shlemiel Went to Warsaw and Other Stories* by Isaac B. Singer. Farrar, 1968. o.p.

"The Sloogey Dog and the Stolen Aroma: A Fang Tale." In *Misoso: Once Upon a Time Tales from Africa* retold by Verna Aardema. Knopf, 1994. ISBN 0-679-83430-3

"The Snowman." In *Hans Christian Andersen: The Complete Fairy Tales and Stories* translated by Erik C. Haugaard. Doubleday, 1983. ISBN 0-385-18951-6

"The Story of Washing Horse Pond." In *The Spring of Butterflies and Other Chinese Folktales* by He Liyi. Lothrop, 1985. o.p.

Tam Lin by Jane Yolen. Harcourt, 1990. ISBN 0-15-2284261-6

"The Tell-Tale Heart." In *The Pit and the Pendulum and Five Other Tales* by Edgar Allan Poe. Watts, 1967. o.p.

"Tia Miseri." In *From Sea to Shining Sea: A Treasury of American Folklore and Folk Songs* by Amy L. Cohn. Scholastic, 1993. ISBN 0-590-42868-3

"Those Three Wishes." In *A Taste of Quiet* by Judith Gorog. Philomel, 1982. o.p. Carol Birch's retelling can be found in *Ready-to-Tell Tales* edited by David Holt and Bill Mooney. August House, 1994. ISBN 0-87483-380-9

Tristan and Iseult by Rosemary Sutcliff. Peter Smith, 1994. ISBN 0-8446-6773-0. Tell as a cycle story, or read aloud a few chapters at a sitting.

"The Very Pretty Lady." In *The Devil's Storybook* by Natalie Babbitt. Farrar, 1974. ISBN 0-374-31770-4

"When the Girl Rescued Her Brother." In *The Girl Who Married the Moon* by Joseph Bruchac and Gayle Ross. BridgeWater, 1994. ISBN 0-8167-3480-1

"Whitebear Whittington." In *Grandfather Tales* by Richard Chase. Houghton Mifflin, 1973. ISBN 0-395-06692-1

"Wicked John and the Devil." In *Grandfather Tales* by Richard Chase. Houghton Mifflin, 1973. ISBN 0-395-06692-1

"The Wise Old Woman" from *The Sea of Gold and Other Tales from Japan* by Yoshiko Uchida. Scribners, 1965. o.p. Also in *Storytelling: Art and Technique* 3rd ed., by Ellin Greene. Bowker, 1996. ISBN 0-8352-3458-4. Also see the picture book, *The Wise Old Woman* by Yoshiko Uchida. Illustrated by Martin Springett. Simon & Schuster, 1994. ISBN 0-689-50582-5

"The Woodcutter of Gura." In *The Fire on the Mountain and Other Stories from Ethiopia and Eritrea* by Harold Courlander and Wolf Leslau. Holt, 1995. ISBN 0-8050-3652-0

"The Wooing of the Maze." In *The Rat-Catcher's Daughter: A Collection of Stories by Laurence Housman* selected by Ellin Greene. Atheneum, 1974. o.p.

"The Yellow Ribbon" by Maria Leach. In *Juba This and Juba That* 2nd ed., selected by Virginia A. Tashjian. Little, Brown, 1995. ISBN 0-316-83234-0

STORIES OF SPECIAL APPEAL TO A MIXED-AGE GROUP

"Aladdin." In *Arabian Nights: Three Tales* retold by Deborah Nourse Lattimore. HarperCollins, 1995. ISBN 0-06-024585-9

Billy Beg and His Bull: An Irish Tale retold by Ellin Greene. Holiday House, 1994. ISBN 0-8234-1100-1

The Cat's Purr by Ashley Bryan. Simon & Schuster, 1985. ISBN 0-689-31086-2. Also in *Storytelling: Art and Technique* 3rd ed., by Ellin Greene. Bowker, 1996. ISBN 0-8352-3458-4

"The Crab and the Jaguar." In *Picture Folk-Tales* by Valery Carrick. Dover, 1992. ISBN 0-486-27083-1. Also in *Storytelling: Art and Technique* 3rd ed., by Ellin Greene. Bowker, 1996. ISBN 0-8352-3458-4

"The Elephant's Child." In *Just So Stories* by Rudyard Kipling. Holt, 1987. ISBN 0-8050-0439-4

"The Freedom Bird." In *Ready-to-Tell Tales: Surefire Stories from America's Favorite Storytellers* edited by David Holt and Bill Mooney. August House, 1994. ISBN 0-87483-380-9

"How the Lizard Lost and Regained His Farm." In *The Hat-Shaking Dance and Other Tales from the Gold Coast* by Harold Courlander. Also in *Storytelling: Art and Technique* 3rd ed., by Ellin Greene. Bowker, 1996. ISBN 0-8352-3458-4

"How the Farmer's Wife Took Care of Things," an Icelandic folktale translated and adapted by Mary Buckley. Originally published in *Cricket* magazine. Also in *Storytelling: Art and Technique* 3rd ed., by Ellin Greene. Bowker, 1996. ISBN 0-8352-3458-4

How the Turtle's Back Was Cracked: A Traditional Cherokee Tale retold by Gayle Ross. Illustrated by Murv Jacob. Dial, 1995. ISBN 0-8037-1728-8

"The Huckabuck Family and How They Raised Pop Corn in Nebraska and Quit and Came Back." In *Rootabaga Stories* by Carl Sandburg. Harcourt, 1988. ISBN 0-15-269061-1

John Henry: An American Legend by Ezra Jack Keats. Knopf, 1987. ISBN 0-394-99052-8

"The Lion and the Rabbit . . . A Fable from India" adapted by Heather Forest. In *Joining In: An Anthology of Audience Participation Stories and How to Tell Them* compiled by Teresa Miller. Yellow Moon Press, 1988. ISBN 0-938756-21-4

"The Little Rooster and the Turkish Sultan." In *The Good Master* by Kate Seredy. Puffin, 1986. ISBN 0-14-030133-X

"Mr. Sampson Cat." In *Picture Tales from the Russian* by Valery Carrick. Dover, 1992. o.p.

The Month Brothers: A Slavic Tale by Samuel Marshak. Translated by Thomas P. Whitney. Illustrated by Diane Stanley. Morrow, 1983. ISBN 0-688-01510-7

"The Mosquito." In *The Story Vine* by Anne Pellowski. Simon & Schuster, 1984. ISBN 0-02-770590-0. (Another fascinating "string" story in this book is "The Farmer and the Yams.")

"Peterkin and the Little Grey Hare." In *The Wonder Clock* by Howard Pyle. Dover, 1887. ISBN 0-486-21446-X

"The Pumpkin Child." In *Persian Folk and Fairy Tales* retold by Anne Sinclair Mehdevi. Knopf, 1965. o.p. Also in *Storytelling: Art and Technique* 3rd ed., by Ellin Greene. Bowker, 1996. ISBN 0-8352-3458-4

Rikki-Tikki-Tavi by Rudyard Kipling. Illustrated by Lambert Davis. Harcourt, 1992. ISBN 0-15-267015-7

"The Seventh Princess." In *The Little Bookroom* by Eleanor Farjeon. Godine, 1984. o.p.

"Sody Sallyraytus." In *Grandfather Tales* by Richard Chase. Houghton Mifflin, 1973. ISBN 0-395-06692-1.

Stone Soup by Marcia Brown. Simon & Schuster, 1947. ISBN 0-684-92296-7

A Story, A Story: An African Tale by Gail Haley. Simon & Schuster, 1970. ISBN 0-689-20511-2

"The Three Sillies." In *English Fairy Tales* edited by Joseph Jacobs. Dover, 1898. ISBN 0-486-21818-X

What a Wonderful World by George David Weiss and Bob Thiele. Simon & Schuster, 1995. ISBN 0-689-80087-8

"White Wave." In *Homespun* edited by Jimmy Neil Smith. Crown, 1988. ISBN 0-517-56936-1. Also available as a picture book, *White Wave: A Chinese Tale* retold by Diane Wolkstein. Illustrated by Ed Young. Harcourt, 1996. ISBN 0-15-200293-6

"Why Dogs Hate Cats." In *The Knee-High Man and Other Tales* by Julius Lester. Dial, 1985. ISBN 0-8037-4593-1

"The Woman Who Flummoxed the Fairies" by Sorche Nic Leodhas. In *Womenfolk and Fairy Tales* edited by Rosemary Minard. Houghton Mifflin, 1975. ISBN 0-395-20276-0

STORIES OF SPECIAL APPEAL FOR THE FAMILY EVENING STORY HOUR

"The Boy Who Lived with the Bears." In *The Boy Who Lived with the Bears and Other Iroquois Stories* by Joseph Bruchac. HarperCollins, 1995. ISBN 0-06-021288-8

"Cap o' Rushes." In *English Fairy Tales* edited by Joseph Jacobs. Dover, 1898. ISBN 0-486-21818-X

"Clever Grethel." In *Tales Told Again* by Walter de la Mare. Knopf, 1959. o.p.

"Clever Manka." In *The Shoemaker's Apron* by Parker Fillmore. Harcourt, 1920. Also in *Storytelling: Art and Technique* 3rd ed., by Ellin Greene. Bowker, 1996. ISBN 0-8352-3458-4

The Dancing Granny by Ashley Bryan. Simon & Schuster, 1987. ISBN 0-689-71149-2

"Don't Blame Me." In *The Wonder Dog: The Collected Children's Stories of Richard Hughes.* Morrow, 1977. o.p.

"Elsie Piddock Skips in Her Sleep." In *Martin Pippin in the Daisy Field* by Eleanor Farjeon. Lippincott, 1937. o.p.

"Gubrand-on-the-Hillside." In *East o' the Sun and West o' the Moon* by George W. Dasent. Dover, 1970. ISBN 0-486-22521-6

"A Handful of Mustard Seed." In *Still More Stories to Solve: Fourteen Folktales from Around the World* by George Shannon. Greenwillow, 1994. ISBN 0-688-04619-3. Also in *Storytelling: Art and Technique* 3rd ed., by Ellin Greene. Bowker, 1996. ISBN 0-8352-3458-4

"Kaleeba." In *Songs and Stories from Uganda* by W. Moses Serwadda. Illustrated by Leo Dillon. World Music Press, 1987. ISBN 0-937203-17-3

The Little Juggler by Barbara Cooney. Hastings, 1961. o.p.

"Living in Wales." In *The Wonder Dog: The Collected Children's Stories of Richard Hughes.* Morrow, 1977. o.p.

"A Lover of Beauty." In *Greek Myths* by Olivia E. Coolidge. Illustrated by E. Sandoz. Houghton Mifflin, 1949. ISBN 0-395-06721-9

"The Mixed-Up Feet and the Silly Bridegroom." In *Zlateh the Goat and Other Stories* by Isaac B. Singer. HarperCollins, 1966. ISBN 0-06-025699-0

"Oranges and Lemons." In *Italian Peepshow* by Eleanor Farjeon. Stokes, 1926. o.p.

"The Palace on the Rock." In *The Wonder Dog: The Collected Children's Stories of Richard Hughes.* Morrow, 1977. o.p.

"Perfection." In *The Devil's Storybook* by Natalie Babbitt. Farrar, 1974. ISBN 0-374-31770-4

"The Pixie at the Grocer's." In *Twelve Tales* by Hans Christian Andersen. Selected, translated, and illustrated by Erik Blegvad. Simon & Schuster/McElderry, 1994. ISBN 0-689-50584-1

"Prince Rooster." In *While Standing on One Foot: Puzzle Stories and Wisdom Tales from the Jewish Tradition* by Nina Jaffe and Steve Zeitlin. Holt, 1993. ISBN 0-8050-2594-4

"The Princess on the Pea." In *Fairy Tales of Hans Christian Andersen.* Illustrated by Isabelle Brent. Collected and with an introduction by Neil Philip. Viking, 1995. ISBN 0-670-85930-3. Also see the picture book *The Princess and the Pea* illustrated by Dorothee Duntze. North-South, 1985. ISBN 0-03-005738-8

The Remarkable Christmas of the Cobbler's Sons by Ruth Sawyer. Illustrated by Barbara Cooney. Viking, 1994. ISBN 0-670-84922-7. Also in *The Long Christmas* by Ruth Sawyer under the title "Schniztle, Schnotzle, and Schnootzle." Viking, 1941, o.p.

"The Sleeping Beauty." In *Told Under the Green Umbrella* by the Literature Committee of the Association for Childhood Education International. Macmillan, 1935. o.p.

"The Snooks Family" by Harcourt Williams. In *Juba This and Juba That* 2nd ed., selected by Virginia A. Tashjian. Little, Brown, 1995. ISBN 0-316-83234-0

"Talk." In *The Cow-Tail Switch and Other West African Stories* by Harold Courlander and George Herzog. Holt, 1988. ISBN 0-8050-0288-X

"Three Strong Women. In *The Woman in the Moon and Other Tales of Forgotten Heroines* by James Riordan. Dial, 1985. ISBN 0-8037-0194-2

"Two of Everything." In *The Scott, Foresman Anthology of Children's Literature* by Zena Sutherland and Myra Cohn Livingston. Scott, Foresman, 1984. ISBN 0-673-15527-7. *Two of Everything,* a picture book by Lily Toy Hong, is a simpler retelling. Whitman, 1993. ISBN 0-8075-8157-7

"Uncle Bouqui Rents a Horse." In *Uncle Bouqui of Haiti* by Harold Courlander. Morrow, 1942. o.p. Also in *Storytelling: Art and Technique* 3rd ed., by Ellin Greene. Bowker, 1996. ISBN 0-8352-3458-4

"The Voyage of the Wee Red Cap." In *The Long Christmas* by Ruth Sawyer. Viking, 1941. o.p. Also in *Storytelling: Art and Technique* 3rd ed., by Ellin Greene. Bowker, 1996. ISBN 0-8352-3458-4

"What Is Trouble?" In *The Knee-High Man and Other Tales* by Julius Lester. Dial, 1985. ISBN 0-8037-4593-1

Why the Sky Is Far Away: A Folktale from Nigeria retold by Mary-Joan Gerson. Little, Brown, 1992. ISBN 0-316-30852-8

The Wise Old Woman by Yoshiko Uchida. Illustrated by Martin Springett. Simon & Schuster, 1994. ISBN 0-689-50582-5. Also see Spencer Shaw's retelling in *Storytelling: Art and Technique* 3rd ed., by Ellin Greene. Bowker, 1996. ISBN 0-8352-3458-4

"The Yellow Ribbon" by Maria Leach. In *Juba This and Juba That* 2nd ed., selected by Virginia A. Tashjian. Little, Brown, 1995. ISBN 0-316-83234-0

"The Yellow Thunder Dragon." In *Magical Tales from Many Lands* retold by Margaret Mayo. Dutton, 1993. ISBN 0-525-45017-3

"Young Kate." In *The Little Bookroom* by Eleanor Farjeon. Godine, 1984. o.p.

Read-Aloud Sampler: 50 Personal Favorites

Alderson, Brian, reteller. *The Arabian Nights: Or Tales Told by Sheherezade During a Thousand Nights and One Night.* Illustrated by Michael Foreman. Morrow, 1995. ISBN 0-688-14219-2

Andersen, Hans Christian. *The Snow Queen.* Translated by Naomi Lewis. Illustrated by Angela Barrett. Holt, 1988. ISBN 0-8050-0830-6

Bond, Michael. *A Bear Called Paddington.* Illustrated by Peggy Fortnum. Houghton, 1960. (First in this series.) ISBN 0-395-06636-0

Brown, Margaret Wise. *Sneakers: Seven Stories About a Cat.* Illustrated by Jean Charlot. HarperCollins, 1985. ISBN 0-201-00625-1

Burnett, Frances Hodgson. *A Little Princess.* Illustrated by Graham Rust. Godine, 1989. ISBN 0-87923-784-8

———. *The Secret Garden.* Illustrated by Graham Rust. Godine, 1987. ISBN 0-87923-649-3

Carroll, Lewis. *Alice's Adventures in Wonderland.* Illustrated by John Tenniel. Morrow, 1992. ISBN 0-688-11087-8

Cecil, Laura, comp. *Listen to This.* Illustrated by Emma Chichester Clark. Greenwillow, 1988. ISBN 0-688-07617-3

Chaucer, Geoffrey. *Canterbury Tales.* Selected, translated from Middle English, and adapted by Barbara Cohen. Illustrated by Trina Schart Hyman. Lothrop, 1988. ISBN 0-688-06201-6

Cooper, Susan. *The Boggart.* Simon & Schuster, 1993. ISBN 0-689-50576-0

Cushman, Karen. *Catherine, Called Birdy.* Houghton Mifflin, 1994. ISBN 0-395-68186-3

Foreman, Michael. *Michael Foreman's World of Fairy Tales.* Arcade, 1991. ISBN 1-55970-164-1

Fox, Paula. *The One-Eyed Cat.* Illustrated by Irene Trivas. Simon & Schuster, 1984. ISBN 0-02-735540-3

George, Jean C. *My Side of the Mountain.* Dutton, 1988. ISBN 0-525-44392-4

Godden, Rumer. *Four Dolls: Impunity Jane, the Fairy Doll, Holly, Candy Floss.* Illustrated by Pauline Baynes. Greenwillow, 1984. ISBN 0-688-02801-2

Hastings, Selina, reteller. *Reynard the Fox.* Illustrated by Graham Percy. Morrow, 1991. ISBN 0-688-09949-1

Hauff, Wilhelm. *Dwarf Nose.* Translated from the German by Anthea Bell. Illustrated by Lisbeth Zwerger. North-South, 1994. ISBN 1-55858-261-4

Henkes, Kevin. *Words of Stone.* Greenwillow, 1992. ISBN 0-688-11356-7

Hoban, Russell. *The Mouse and His Child.* Illustrated by Lillian Hoban. HarperCollins, 1967. ISBN 0-06-022378-2

Hodges, Margaret, adapt. *Don Quixote and Sancho Panza* by Miguel de Saavedra Cervantes. Illustrated by Stephen Marchesi. Simon & Schuster, 1992. ISBN 0-684-19235-7

———. *Gulliver in Lilliput.* Illustrated by Kimberly Bulcken Root. Holiday House, 1995. ISBN 0-8234-1147-8

———. *St. George and the Dragon.* Illustrated by Trina Schart Hyman. Little, 1984. ISBN 0-316-36789-3

Hughes, Shirley. *Stories by Firelight.* Lothrop, 1993. ISBN 0-688-04568-5

Hunter, Mollie. *The Mermaid Summer.* HarperCollins, 1988. ISBN 0-06-022628-5

Jarrell, Randall. *The Animal Family.* Illustrated by Maurice Sendak. HarperCollins, 1995. ISBN 0-06-205084-2

———. *The Bat-Poet.* Illustrated by Maurice Sendak. HarperCollins, 1995. ISBN 0-06-205088-5

Jimenez, Juan Ramon. *Platero y yo/Platero and I.* Selected, translated, and adapted from the Spanish by Myra Cohn Livingston and Joseph F. Dominguez. Illustrated by Antonio Frasconi. Houghton Mifflin, 1994. ISBN 0-685-71523-X

Kipling, Rudyard. *The Jungle Book.* Illustrated by Jerry Pinkney. Morrow, 1995. ISBN 0-688-09979-3

Konigsburg, E. L. *From the Mixed-Up Files of Mrs. Basil E. Frankweiler.* Simon & Schuster, 1970. ISBN 0-689-20586-4

LeGuin, Ursula K. *Catwings.* Illustrated by Stephen D. Schindler. Orchard, 1988. (First in this series.) ISBN 0-531-08359-4

Lewis, C. S. *The Lion, the Witch and the Wardrobe.* Illustrated by Pauline Baynes. HarperCollins, 1994. (First in this series.) ISBN 0-06-023481-4

Lowry, Lois. *The Giver.* Houghton Mifflin, 1993. ISBN 0-395-64566-2

McCaffrey, Anne. *Black Horses for the King.* Harcourt, 1996. ISBN 0-15-227322-0

MacGrory, Yvonne. *The Secret of the Ruby Ring.* Illustrated by Terry Myler. Milkweed, 1994. ISBN 0-915943-92-1

McKissack, Patricia. *The Dark-Thirty: Southern Tales of the Supernatural.* Illustrated by Brian Pinkney. Knopf, 1992. ISBN 0-679-81863-4

MacLachlan, Patricia. *Sarah, Plain and Tall.* HarperCollins, 1985. ISBN 0-06-024101-2

Mayne, William. *Hob and the Goblins.* Illustrated by Norman Messenger. Dorling Kindersley, 1994. ISBN 1-56458-713-4

Murphy, Shirley Rousseau. *The Song of the Christmas Mouse.* Illustrated by Donna Diamond. HarperCollins, 1990. ISBN 0-06-024357-0

Norton, Mary. *The Borrowers.* Illustrated by Joe Krush and Beth Krush. Harcourt, 1953. (First in this series.) ISBN 0-15-209990-5

O'Rourke, Frank. *Burton and Stanley.* Illustrated by Jonathan Allen. Godine, 1993. ISBN 0-87923-824-0

Paterson, Katherine. *Bridge to Terabithia.* Illustrated by Donna Diamond. HarperCollins, 1977. ISBN 0-690-01359-0

Pearce, Philippa. *Tom's Midnight Garden.* HarperCollins, 1992. ISBN 0-397-30477-3

Price, Rosalind, and Walter McVitty, eds. *The Viking Bedtime Treasury.* Illustrated by Ron Brooks. Viking, 1990. ISBN 0-670-83147-6

Rylant, Cynthia. *Harry and Mudge: The First Book of Their Adventures.* Illustrated by Suçie Stevenson. Simon & Schuster, 1987. (First in this series.) ISBN 0-02-778001-5

Stevenson, Robert Louis. *Treasure Island.* Illustrated by Robert Ingpen. Viking, 1992. ISBN 0-670-84685-6

Stewart, Mary. *A Walk in Wolf Wood: A Tale of Fantasy and Magic.* Illustrated by Emanuel Schongut. Morrow, 1980. ISBN 0-688-03679-1

Thomas, Gwyn, and Kevin Crossley-Holland. *Tales from the Mabinogion.* Illustrated by Margaret Jones. Gollancz, 1985. ISBN 0-575-03531-5

Thurber, James. *The Great Quillow.* Illustrated by Steven Kellogg. Harcourt, 1994. ISBN 0-15-232544-1

White, E. B. *Charlotte's Web.* Illustrated by Garth Williams. HarperCollins, 1952. ISBN 0-06-026385-7

White, Terence H. *The Sword in the Stone.* Illustrated by Dennis Nolan. Putnam, 1993. ISBN 0-399-22502-1

A Sampling of Storytelling Recordings

Unless otherwise noted, all recordings are cassettes.

Abiyoyo and Other Story Songs for Children. Smithsonian/Folkways SF 45001. Sung by Pete Seeger.

Aladdin and the Magic Lamp. Rabbit Ears Book/Cassette. Simon & Schuster ISBN 0-689-80063-0. Told by John Hurt with music by Mickey Hart of the Grateful Dead.

An Anthology of African American Poetry for Young People. Smithsonian/Folkways SF 45044. Arna Bontemps reads poems from his anthology *Golden Slippers.*

Ashley Bryan: Poems and Folktales. Audio Bookshelf ISBN 1-883332-11-7. A vibrant presentation of "The Cat's Purr" and other African folktales plus poems from Bryan's collection *Sing to the Sun.*

The Boy Who Lived with the Bears and Other Iroquois Stories. Harper Children's Audio ISBN 1-55994-541-9. Joe Bruchac, accompanying himself with drumming and chanting, relates stories from his collection. This recording is part of the outstanding Parabola Storytime Series: Traditional Tales by Traditional Storytellers.

Charlotte's Web. Bantam Books/Distributed by Recorded Books, Inc. T21611 ISBN 0-553-47048-5. E. B. White reads his book in its entirety.

Chillers. The Folktellers/Mama-T Artists MTA-2. The Folktellers tell "Mary Culhane and the Dead Man," and other chilling tales.

Classic Tales from the Picture Book Parade. Weston Woods RWW734C. Ruth Sawyer reads her *Journey Cake, Ho!*; Ian Thomson narrates "The Three Little Pigs" and "Goldilocks and the Three Bears"; Neil Innes narrates "The Elves and the Shoemaker"; and Roderick Dook narrates "The Musicians of Bremen."

Creation Stories of the Native American Tradition (Seneca-Iroquois). Sounds True Recordings. Sister José Hobday tells eight creation myths in which the "wishes of the mind" form the land and the people. Songs are interspersed among the stories.

The Dancing Granny and Other African Stories. Caedmon TC 1765. In his powerful, rhythmic style, Ashley Bryan tells "The Dancing Granny" from his book and three other trickster tales.

The Devil's Storybook. Weston Woods RWW487C. Samuel Babbitt skillfully reads stories about the devil from the collection by his wife Natalie Babbitt.

The Dragons Are Singing Tonight. Listening Library FTR168CXR. Jack Prelutsky reads and sings poems from his book.

Elsie Piddock Skips in Her Sleep: Stories and Poems by Eleanor Farjeon. A Gentle Wind GW1025. Ellin Greene reads poems by Eleanor Farjeon and tells three Farjeon tales: "Elsie Piddock Skips in Her Sleep," "Nella's Dancing Shoes," and "The Sea-Baby."

Enchantments. Stories Told by Susan Danoff. Music by Brad Hill. Includes Laurence Housman's fairy tale "Gammelyn the Dressmaker" and five folktales from five different cultures.

The Emperor's New Clothes and Other Tales. Harper Children's Audio ISBN 0-89845-863-3. Sir Michael Redgrave performs "The Tinder Box," "The Emperor's New Clothes," "The Staunch Tin Soldier," and "The Emperor's Nightingale."

An Evening at Cedar Creek. Wellspring CS 4902. Beth Horner tells "The Mousedeer and the Buffalo Chip," "Phantom Black Carriage," and five other stories. Country music performed by Win and Paul Grace.

Everywhere Everywhere Christmas Tonight. Marianne McShane. In a gentle, quiet voice Marianne McShane gives her listeners a gift of six Christmas stories, including "The Little Clockmaker" from Ruth Sawyer's *This Way to Christmas* and "The Three Magi" from *The Tiger and the Rabbit and Other Tales* by Pura Belpré.

The Flood and Other Lakota Stories. Harper Children's Audio ISBN 1-55994-677-6. Kevin Locke, a Lakota of the Standing Rock Reservation of South Dakota, incorporates the Lakota language and sounds of his flute in a compelling presentation. This recording is part of the outstanding Parabola Storytime Series: Traditional Tales by Traditional Storytellers.

Folk Tales and Legends of Eastern Europe. CMS Records CMS-X4519 Various distributors. A selection of Czech and Polish folktales, including "Clever Manka," told by Anne Pellowski. One in a series of folktales and legends from around the world.

Folk Tales from West Africa. Smithsonian/Folkways 7103. Harold Courlander reads the title story and four others from his book *The Cow-Tail Switch*.

Folk Tales from the Picture Book Parade. Weston Woods RWW717C. Includes *A Story, A Story* by Gail E. Haley, read by Dr. John J. Akar; *Suho and the White Horse* by Yuzo Otsuka and *The Great Enormous Turnip* by Alexei Tolstoy, narrated by Charles Cioffi; *Stone Soup* told by Marcia Brown; and *Arrow to the Sun* narrated by Gerald McDermott.

Folktales of Strong Women. Yellow Moon Press. Doug Lipman has spliced many variants for his retelling of these five tales: "The Chicken Woman," "The Woman Who Saved the City," "The Young Woman of Vietnam," "The One with the Star on Her Forehead," and "Godmother Death." A companion cassette is *Milk from the Bull's Horn: Tales of Nurturing Men,* six stories that come from Jewish, Persian, Irish, and Appalachian sources.

Frog and Toad Audio Collection. Harper Children's Audio ISBN 1-55994-709-8. Arnold Lobel reads his endearing stories about Frog and Toad.

The Girl Who Cried Flowers and Other Tales. Weston Woods RWW486C. Jane Yolen reads five stories from her appealing collection.

The Hairyman and Other Wild Tales. High Windy Audio HW1202. David Holt, accompanied by banjo, harmonica, fiddle, guitar, and buck dancing, entertains with "The Hairyman," "The Apple Tree," and four other tales. This is a good example of the performance type of storytelling in which different voices are used for different characters. Excellent pacing and relaxed style.

Hans Christian Andersen in Central Park. Weston Woods RWW713C. Six tales by Hans Christian Andersen: "Hans Clodhopper," "The Goblin and the Grocer," "The Ugly Duckling," "The Emperor's New Clothes," "The Nightingale," and "Dance, Dance Dolly Mine," as Diane Wolkstein tells them to audiences in Central Park. With the exception of "The Ugly Duckling," the stories do not suffer from Wolkstein's abridgements. Pleasing musical accompaniment by Shirley Keller and Wolkstein's daughter, Rachel.

Hansel and Gretel. Harper Children's Audio ISBN 1-55994-9066. Claire Bloom reads "Hansel and Gretel," "The Golden Goose," "Mrs. Owl," and "Shiver and Shake" from the collection of the Brothers Grimm.

Happily-Ever-After Love Stories, More or Less. Weston Woods RWW724C. In a strong, expressive voice, Carol Birch tells "The Porcelain Man" by Richard Kennedy, "Tayzanne," "Who Will Wash the Pot?" and Laurence Housman's "The Wooing of the Maze."

How Rabbit Tricked Otter and Other Cherokee Animal Stories. Harper Children's Audio ISBN 1-55994-542-7. Gayle Ross tells stories from her collection in a clear, calm, expressive voice. This recording is part of the outstanding Parabola Storytime Series: Traditional Tales by Traditional Storytellers.

How to Tell Corn Fairies When You See 'Em, and Other Rootabaga Stories. Caedmon TC 1159 Various distributors. Carl Sandburg reads from his collection *Rootabaga Stories.*

Hyena and the Moon: Stories to Listen to from Kenya. Libraries Unlimited CX695. Performed by Heather McNeil.

Irish Wonder Tales. Volumes One and Two. The Storyteller's School, Toronto. Told by master storyteller Alice Kane who says she has been influenced by the rhythms, the feeling, and the ancient qualities of the stories told by Padraic Colum and Ella Young. Volume One includes "The Golden Fly," "The Birth of Usheen," and "Usheen Returns to Ireland." Volume Two is a 55-minute telling of Ella Young's "The Wondersmith and His Son."

Iroquois Stories: Tales from the Longhouse, and Iroquois Women's Stories. Good Mind Records (0001). Joe Bruchac introduces and tells six teaching tales from his collection *Iroquois Stories. Heroes & Heroines; Monsters & Magic.*

Jack Tales: More Than a Beanstalk. Weston Woods RWW727C. Donald Davis, a native of western North Carolina, tells three Appalachian tales: "Jack and Old Bluebeard," "Jack Tells a Story," and "Jack and the Silver Sword."

Juggler of Notre Dame and Other Miracle Stories. Clancy Agency. In his inimitable style, Ed Stivender tells traditional folktales and stories from the Bible, including a rap song about the first Christmas.

Lakota Love Songs & Stories. Kevin Locke. Hearing Locke's voice and his flute music evokes Paul Goble's story, *The Love Flute.*

Legends of the North American Indians Vols. 1 and 2. Indian Sounds. These stories from various tribes show the Native Americans' respect for the earth, admiration for clever animals, and brave acts by humans. Told by Jackalene Crow Hiendlmayr.

Medusa and Other Good Ol' Greeks. Pandora Productions 102. "Ancient myths retold with postmodern wit." Barbara McBride-Smith tells "Medusa and Perseus," "The Trojan War: The Beginning," "Demeter," and "Baucis and Philemon" in a manner suited to young adults. To introduce children to Greek mythology, *Greek Myths* by master storyteller Jim Weiss is a more appropriate choice. Includes "King Midas and the Golden Touch," "Arachne," "Perseus and Medusa," and "Adventures of Hercules." Greathall 1124-02. ISBN 1-882513-02-9.

Nightmares Rising. Frostfire 100. Carol Birch tells "Mary Culhane and the Dead Man," "Mr. Fox," and other bloodcurdling tales.

Peach Boy. Rabbit Ears Book/Cassette Simon & Schuster ISBN 0-689-80192-0. The beloved Japanese folktale, read by Sigourney Weaver, with music by Ryuichi Sakamoto.

The People Could Fly. Knopf/Random House. Twelve tales from Virginia Hamilton's book *The People Could Fly,* narrated by Virginia Hamilton and James Earl Jones.

Perez and Martina. CMS Records CMS 505. Various distributors. Pura Belpré tells this traditional Puerto Rican folktale in English on side 1 and in Spanish on side 2.

Plum Pudding. Stories and Songs with Nancy Schimmel and the Plum City Players. Sisters' Choice Recordings. Includes "The Tailor," "The Woodcutter's Story," and a story song about Annie Oakley.

Richard Kennedy: Collected Stories. Listening Library YA 840CX.

Rootabaga Stories. Caedmon TC1089 Various distributors. Rootabaga stories told by the author, Carl Sandburg, in his slow-moving, rhythmic voice.

The Rudyard Kipling Audio Collection. Harper Children's Audio ISBN 1-55994-811-6. Boris Karloff performs all of the "Just So" stories and selections from *The Jungle Book.*

Scary Stories to Tell in the Dark: Collected from American Folklore. Harper Children's Audio. ISBN 0-89845-758-0. George S. Irving tells ghost stories from the collection by Alvin Schwartz.

Stories for the Road. The Folktellers/Mama-T Artists MTA-5C. Folktellers Connie Regan-Blake and Barbara Freeman perform a variety of stories, including "How to Eat Peanut Butter," "Jazzy Three Bears," and "The Dancing Man," by Ruth Borstein.

Stories from the Other Side. Turtle Creek Recordings TC 1003. Told by Dan Keding. Listen for the style of telling a suspense story as well as for the stories themselves.

Stories—Old as the World, Fresh as the Rain. Weston Woods RWW712C. Laura Simms, accompanied by musician Steven Gorn, tells stories from Africa and the Far East: "A Single Grain of Rice," "The Woodcutter," "Magoolie," "The Magic Crystal," "Superman," and "The Wooden Box." This vivacious storyteller is at her best when she doesn't indulge in exaggerated voice changes.

The Story of Sleeping Beauty. Harper Children's Audio. ISBN 0-89845-817-X. Performed by Claire Bloom, accompanied by the music of Tchaikovsky.

The Tale of Peter Rabbit and Other Stories. Harper Children's Audio. ISBN 0-89845-575-8. Claire Bloom reads five nursery tales by Beatrix Potter.

Tales from an Irish Hearth. The Storytellers School of Toronto. Alice Kane tells ten traditional Irish tales taken from the works of Patrick Kennedy, T. Crofton Croker, and others.

Tales from Cultures Far and Near. Greathall Productions. Storyteller Jim Weiss relates tales from a wide range of cultures, from the Lakota Sioux to Senegal, unified by inherent morals that give a clear sense of the ideals of each culture.

Tales of Womenfolk. Weston Woods RWW729C. In minstrel style, Heather Forest tells five folktales featuring resourceful heroines: "The Squire's Bride," "Janet and Tamlin," "The Hedley Kow," "Three Strong Women," and "The Lute Player."

The Tell-Tale Heart and Other Terrifying Tales. SL Productions SL105. Syd Lieberman tells six terrifying tales adapted from Poe, Bierce, Chaucer, and the first adventure of Beowulf. His adaptations are good examples of how to edit a long story for oral presentation.

Touch Magic . . . Pass It On: Jane Yolen Stories. Weston Woods RWW741C. Milbre Burch performs "The Cat Bride," "Sleeping Ugly," "Princess Heart O'Stone," "The King's Dragon," and four other stories by this popular writer.

Uncle Bouqui of Haiti. Smithsonian/Folkways. Folkways 07107. Augusta Baker tells "Uncle Bouqui and Godfather Malice," "Uncle Bouqui Rents a Horse," and "Uncle Bouqui Gets Whee-Ai" from Harold Courlander's book.

Why the Dog Chases the Cat: Great Animal Stories. High Windy ISBN 0-942303-07-5. Storyteller cousins David Holt and Bill Mooney delight listeners with amusing pourquoi stories, many adapted from *The Complete Tales of Uncle Remus.*

Why Mosquitoes Buzz in People's Ears and Other Tales. Harper Children's Audio. ISBN 0-69451-187-0. Ruby Dee and Ossie Davis perform stories from Africa.

Zlateh the Goat and Other Stories. Caedmon CPN 1842. ISBN 0-89845-975-3. Various distributors. Theodore Bikel's marvelously rich voice conveys the humor and pathos in these seven stories by Isaac Bashevis Singer.

STORYTELLERS TALK ABOUT STORYTELLING

Augusta Baker. "Storytelling." In *Prelude: Mini-Seminars on Using Books Creatively, Series 1.* Children's Book Council, 1975. Augusta Baker discusses the values of storytelling, the criteria for selection, and the qualities of a good storyteller. She offers hints on preparing and presenting stories to children and tells "Why Crow is Black and Men Find Precious Stones in the Earth" from *The Earth Is on a Fish's Back: Tales of Beginnings* by Natalia Belting. Don Reynolds, a librarian-storyteller, reads from *A Toad for Tuesday* by Russell E. Erickson, and tells "What Is Trouble?" from *The Knee-High Man and Other Tales* by Julius Lester.

————. *Augusta Baker on Storytelling. Lesson 13 in the series, "Jump Over the Moon: Sharing Literature with Young Children."* Co-produced by the South Carolina ETV Network and the University of South Carolina. South Carolina ETV, P.O. Drawer L, Columbia, SC 29250. Video Color 30 min. Augusta Baker talks about storytelling and tells "Uncle Bouqui and Godfather Ti-Malice."

Caroline Feller Bauer. *Storytelling with Caroline Feller Bauer.* H. W. Wilson. Video. Color. 30 min. A dynamic storyteller demonstrates a wide variety of ways of captivating children and turning them on to books and reading.

Jay O'Callahan. *Jay O'Callahan: A Master Class in Storytelling.* Vineyard Video Productions. 16 mm. Color. 33 min. Also available on video. O'Callahan clearly demonstrates the joy and power of storytelling in this award-winning teacher-education film.

Anne Pellowski. "Using Folklore as an Introduction to Other Cultures." In *Prelude: Mini-Seminars on Using Books Creatively, Series 2.* Children's Book Council, 1976. From her experience as director of the Information Center on Children's Cultures of the U.S. Committee for UNICEF, Anne Pellowski talks about ways in which folklore can be used to help children learn about other cultures. She describes folkloric programs, combining folktales with music, food, clothing, and/or artifacts, and tells "Eat, My Fine Coat," from

Watermelons, Walnuts and the Wisdom of Allah by Barbara Walker. On the same tape, Hewitt Pantaleoni tells "Tweriire' from *Songs and Stories from Uganda* by Moses Serwadda, translated and edited by Pantaleoni.

The Power of Stories. Weston Woods. 16mm. Color. 17 min. Also available on video. Three Australian educators discuss the values of storytelling, with shots of young children enjoying stories in a variety of settings.

Storytelling: Tales & Techniques. The Folktellers/Mama-T Artists. Video. Color. 60 min. An "entertaining workshop video" for teachers and librarians presented by the Folktellers. The video ends with the duo telling "Jazzy Three Bears." Connie Regan-Blake tells "I Know an Old Lady" in sign language on *Pennies, Pets & Peanut Butter: Stories for Children.* Video. Color. 30 min.

Audiovisual Producers/Distributors

Alcazar Records, P.O. Box 429, Waterbury, VT 05676

American Library Association Video/Library Video Network, 320 York Road, Towson, MD 21204-5179

August House, Box 3223, Little Rock, AR 72203

Beth Horner Productions, P.O. Box 540, Wilmette, IL 60091

Caedmon. See Harper Children's Audio and various record distributors.

Center for Parent Education, 81 Wyman Street, Waban, MA 02168

Clancy Agency, 5138 Whitehall Drive, Clifton Heights, PA 19018

CMS Records. Various record distributors.

Dan Keding, Turtle Creek Recordings, P.O. Box 1701, Springfield, IL 62705

Educational Activities, Inc., 1937 Grand Ave., Baldwin, NY 11510

Elephant Records, c/o Drive Entertainment, Inc., 10351 Santa Monica Blvd., Suite 404, Los Angeles, CA 90025-6937

Enchanters Press, P.O. Box 441195, West Somerville, MA 02144

The Folktellers/Mama-T Artists, P.O. Box 2898, Asheville, NC 28802

Frostfire, P.O. Box 32, Southbury, CT 06488

A Gentle Wind, P.O. Box 3103, Albany, NY 12203

Good Mind Records. The Greenfield Review Literary Center, 2 Middle Grove Road, Greenfield Center, NY 12833

Greater Vancouver Library Federation, 110-6545 Bonsor Ave., Burnaby, BC V5H 1H3, Canada

Greathall Productions, P.O. Box 813, Benica, CA 94510

Harper Children's Audio, 10 E. 53rd St., New York, NY 10022

High Windy Audio, P.O. Box 553, Fairview, NC 28730

Indian Sounds, P.O. Box 6038, Moore, OK 73153

Kevin Locke, P.O. Box 241, Mobridge, SD 57601

Kids Records, Box 670, Station A. Toronto, ON M5W 1G5, Canada

Kimbo Educational, Dept. W, P.O. Box 477, Long Branch, NJ 07740

Libraries Unlimited, P.O. Box 6633, Englewood, CO 80155-6633

Lightyear Entertainment, 350 Fifth Ave., Suite 5101, New York, NY 10118-5197

Listening Library, One Park Ave., Old Greenwich, CT 06870

Marianne McShane, 37 W. Main St., Mt. Kisco, NY 10549

Pandora Productions, Barbara McBride-Smith, Route 2, Box 132, Stillwater, OK 74075

Parabola Storytime Series. Distributed by Harper Children's Audio, 10 E. 53rd St., New York, NY 10022

Recorded Books, Inc., 270 Skipjack Rd., Prince Frederick, MD 20678

Red Rover Records, P.O. Box 124, Lake Bluff, IL 60044

The Roosevelt Middle School Tellers, Robert Rubenstein, 90 E. 49th Ave., Eugene, OR 97405

Sisters' Choice Records, 1450 Sixth St., Berkeley, CA 94710

Smithsonian/Folkways Mail Order, 414 Hungerford Dr., Suite 444, Rockville, MD 20850. (For complete catalog, write to Smithsonian/Folkways Recordings, Center for Folklife Programs & Cultural Studies, 955 L'Enfant Plaza, Suite 2600, MRC 914, Washington, DC 20560

Sounds True Recordings, 735 Walnut St., Boulder, CO 80302

The Storytellers School of Toronto, 412A College St., Toronto, ON M5T 1T3, Canada

Susan Danoff, P.O. Box 7311, Princeton, NJ 08543

Syd Lieberman, SL Productions, 2522 Ashland, Evanston, IL 60201

Troubadour Records Ltd., 6043 Yonge St., Willowdale, ON M2M 3W3, Canada

Vineyard Video Productions, Dept. JS, Elias Lane, West Tisbury, MA 02575

Wellspring Music, Route 1, Box 182, 11990 E. Baker Rd., Columbia, MD 65201

Weston Woods, Weston, CT 06883

Yellow Moon Press, P.O. Box 1316, Cambridge, MA 02238

Glossary

Ballad—A narrative song, e.g., "Tam Lin."

Circular story—A story in which the main character ends up in the same place or condition from which he started, e.g., *Once a Mouse* by Marcia Brown.

Cumulative tale—A repetitive tale that builds on the last action, characterized by minimum plot and maximum rhythm, e.g., "The Gingerbread Boy."

Droll—A humorous story about sillies or numbskulls, e.g., "When Shlemiel Went to Warsaw" by Isaac Bashevis Singer.

Epic—A cycle of tales centered around one hero, e.g., *The Green Hero: Early Adventures of Finn McCool* by Bernard Evslin.

Fable—A brief story that teaches a moral lesson, e.g., Aesop's fables. Usually the main characters are animals that speak as humans.

Fairy tale—A story involving the "little people" (fairies, elves, pixies, gnomes, dwarfs, brownies, leprechauns), e.g., "The Woman Who Flummoxed the Fairies."

Folklore—The traditional creations of the folk or common people, comprising beliefs and superstitions, customs, recipes, weather lore, proverbs, riddles, songs and dances, arts and crafts, etc.

Folktale—A narrative story that comes from the oral tradition. Equivalent to "Traditional tale."

Formula tale—A story with a predictable pattern that makes it easy to learn and to tell, e.g., "Toads and Diamonds." See *Putting the World in a Nutshell* by Sheila Dailey.

Fractured fairy tale—A traditional tale retold from a different point of view to create a parody, e.g., *The True Story of the 3 Little Pigs!* by A. Wolf as told to Jon Scieszka.

Hero tale—A tale that recounts the exploits of a human hero who embodies the ideals of a culture, e.g., *The Story of King Arthur and His Knights* by Howard Pyle.

Jump tale—A tale with an unexpected ending that startles the listener, e.g., "The Teeny Tiny Bone."

Legend—A narrative about a person, place, or event involving real or pretended belief, e.g., *The Legend of the Cranberry: A Paleo-Indian Tale* by Ellin Greene.

Literary fairy tale—A story that uses the form of a traditional folktale or fairy tale but which has an identifiable author, e.g., the stories of Eleanor Farjeon.

Märchen or wonder tale—A traditional story in which quite ordinary people have extraordinary adventures involving magical objects, transformations, talking animals, e.g., "East o' the Sun and West o' the Moon."

Motif—The smallest element that persists in a traditional tale, e.g., the favorite youngest child.

Myth—A story about the gods or culture heroes, e.g., *Theseus and the Minotaur* by Warwick Hutton. Creation myths attempt to explain natural phenomena, e.g., "Persephone," or the origins of a people.

Nursery tale—A simple folktale appropriate for telling to young children, e.g., "The Three Billy Goats Gruff."

Pourquoi story—A narrative that explains the origin of a physical or cultural phenomenon, e.g., *The Cat's Purr* by Ashley Bryan.

Realistic story—A story that is true to life. It may be a biography, historical fiction, an adventure tale, or an animal story, e.g., *Julie of the Wolves* by Jean George.

Religious tale—A story that uses elements of religious belief, e.g., "The Juggler of Notre Dame."

Romance—A medieval story in verse or prose based on chivalrous love and adventure, e.g., *Sir Gawain and the Loathly Lady* by Selina Hastings.

String story—A story using string to form figures in the story, e.g., "The Mosquito" in Anne Pellowski's *The Story Vine*.

Talking animal tale—A story that teaches a moral lesson but so subtly that we are not aware of it, e.g., "The Three Little Pigs."

Tall tale—Exaggerated story about extraordinary persons or events, e.g., *Swamp Angel* by Anne Isaacs.

Traditional tale—A story that has been handed down from one generation to another, either by writing or by word of mouth. There is no identifiable author.

Trickster tale—A traditional tale with a trickster as the main character, e.g., *The Tales of Uncle Remus: The Adventures of Brer Rabbit* by Julius Lester.

Type—A recognizable tale for which variants are known.

Variant—A different version of the same tale, e.g., "Tom Tit Tot" is the English version of the German "Rumpelstiltskin."

Wishing candle—A candle lit at the beginning of the story hour to help the children focus. At the end of the program, the children make a wish and blow out the candle. (Be sure to use a dripless candle.)

Index

Note: Authors and titles of works appear in the Appendix, and are not indexed.

Violence, 75
in folk tales, 23, 38
Visual approach to learning a story, 63–64
Visualization, 37, 42, 68, 152, 159
Vocabulary, 34, 40, 41, 76, 99
Vocabulary-controlled books, stories, 45, 59–60
Vocal production and control, 45, 151, 153
Voice, 22, 30, 45, 64, 66, 69, 82, 98, 112
"Voice" of storyteller, 66, 158
Voice exercises, 153
see also Speech exercises

Walton, Carole, 108, 110–11
Weaver, Mary C., 6
Weeks, Betty, 28
Weiss, Mitch, 159–60
Welty, Eudora, 44
Werner, Craig, 98
Westcar Papyrus, 2
Western Reserve Library School, 11
Weston Woods (co.), 98
White, Burton L., 27
White, Clarence Cameron, 26
Whiteman, Edna, 9–10
Whole-language movement, 29, 42–43
"Why" (*pourquoi*) stories, 53
Wilde, Oscar, 55
Wilner, Isabel, 150–51
Wishing candle, 15, 85, 86, 87, 127, 182

Word pictures, 67, 75
Word play, 44, 153
Words, 34, 44, 98
foreign, 77
providing atmosphere, 85–86
unfamiliar, 85, 99
using author's own, 76
Workshops, 29, 116, 169
for day-care/Head Start staff, 181
for first-time parents, 181–82
in-staff, for beginning storytellers, 178–79
one-day, 179
planning, 176–82
for teachers, 157
for young storytellers, 152, 153
World Folklore Series, 58
World-Wide Web, 6
Written language/literature
shift from oral to, 22–23, 34, 40
Wyche, Richard T., 5–6

Yoga, 70
Yolen, Jane, 53, 55
Young adults
story hour for (sample), 164
as storytellers, 138, 149–60
storytelling to, 138–48

Zhang, Meifang, 38